The Roth Family, Anthropology, and Colonial Administration

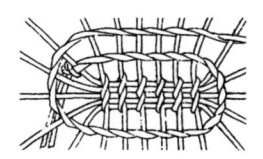

Publications of the Institute of Archaeology, University College London
Director of the Institute: Stephen Shennan
Founding Series Editor: Peter J. Ucko

The Institute of Archaeology of University College London is one of the oldest, largest and most prestigious archaeology research facilities in the world. Its extensive publications programme includes the best theory, research, pedagogy and reference materials in archaeology and cognate disciplines, through publishing exemplary work of scholars worldwide. Through its publications, the Institute brings together key areas of theoretical and substantive knowledge, improves archaeological practice and brings archaeological findings to the general public, researchers and practitioners. It also publishes staff research projects, site and survey reports, and conference proceedings. The publications programme, formerly developed in-house or in conjunction with UCL Press, is now produced in partnership with Left Coast Press, Inc. The Institute can be accessed online at http://www.ucl.ac.uk/archaeology.

ENCOUNTERS WITH ANCIENT EGYPT Subseries, Peter J. Ucko, (ed.)
Jean-Marcel Humbert and Clifford Price (eds.), Imhotep Today
David Jeffreys (ed.), Views of Ancient Egypt since Napoleon Bonaparte
Sally MacDonald and Michael Rice (eds.), Consuming Ancient Egypt
Roger Matthews and Cornelia Roemer (eds.), Ancient Perspectives on Egypt
David O'Connor and Andrew Reid (eds.), Ancient Egypt in Africa
John Tait (ed.), 'Never had the like occurred'
David O'Connor and Stephen Quirke (eds.), Mysterious Lands
Peter Ucko and Timothy Champion (eds.), The Wisdom of Egypt

CRITICAL PERSPECTIVES ON CULTURAL HERITAGE subseries, Beverley Butler (ed.)
Beverley Butler, Return to Alexandria
Ferdinand de Jong and Michael Rowlands (eds.), Reclaiming Heritage
Dean Sully (ed.), Decolonizing Conservation

OTHER TITLES

Andrew Gardner (ed.), Agency Uncovered
Okasha El-Daly, Egyptology, The Missing Millennium
Ruth Mace, Clare J. Holden, and Stephen Shennan (eds.), Evolution of Cultural Diversity
Arkadiusz Marciniak, Placing Animals in the Neolithic
Robert Layton, Stephen Shennan, and Peter Stone (eds.), A Future for Archaeology
Joost Fontein, The Silence of Great Zimbabwe
Gabriele Puschnigg, Ceramics of the Merv Oasis
James Graham-Campbell and Gareth Williams (eds.), Silver Economy in the Viking Age
Barbara Bender, Sue Hamilton, and Chris Tilley, Stone World
Andrew Gardner, An Archaeology of Identity
Sue Hamilton, Ruth Whitehouse, and Katherine I. Wright (eds.), Archaeology and Women
Gustavo Politis, Nukak
Sue Colledge and James Conolly (eds.), The Origins and Spread of Domestic Plants in Southwest Asia and Europe
Timothy Clack and Marcus Brittain (eds.), Archaeology and the Media
Janet Picton, Stephen Quirke, and Paul C. Roberts (eds.), Living Images
Tony Waldron, Paleoepidemiology
Eleni Asouti and Dorian Q. Fuller, Trees and Woodlands of South India
Russell McDougall and Iain Davidson (eds.), The Roth Family, Anthropology, and Colonial Administration
Elizabeth Pye (ed.), The Power of Touch
John Tait, Why the Egyptians Wrote Books

The Roth Family, Anthropology, and Colonial Administration

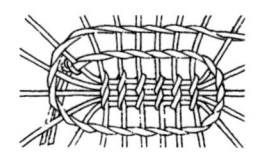

Edited by
Russell McDougall and Iain Davidson

Left Coast Press Inc.

Walnut Creek, California

Left Coast Press Inc.

LEFT COAST PRESS, INC.
1630 North Main Street, #400
Walnut Creek, CA 94596
http://www.LCoastPress.com

Copyright © 2008 by Left Coast Press, Inc.

All rights reserved. No part of this publication may be reproduced, stored in a retrieval system, or transmitted in any form or by any means, electronic, mechanical, photocopying, recording, or otherwise, without the prior permission of the publisher.

ISBN 978-1-59874-228-2 hardcover

Library of Congress Cataloging-in-Publication Data

The Roth family, anthropology, and colonial administration/edited by Russell McDougall, Iain Davidson.
   p. cm. – (Publications of the institute of archaeology,
University College London)
ISBN 978-1-59874-228-2 (hardback : alk. paper)
  1. Roth, H. Ling (Henry Ling), 1854–1925. 2. Roth, Walter E. (Walter Edmund), 1861?–1933. 3. Roth family. 4. Anthropologists–Great Britain–Biography. 5. Ethnology–Australia. 6. Ethnology–Indonesia. 7. Ethnology–South America. 8. Australia–Social life and customs. 9. Indonesia–Social life and customs. 10. South America–Social life and customs. I. McDougall, Russell. II. Davidson, Iain, 1948–
GN20.R58 2008
301.092'2–dc22
[B]   2008002749

Printed in the United States of America

⊗™ The paper used in this publication meets the minimum requirements of American National Standard for Information Sciences—Permanence of Paper for Printed Library Materials, ANSI/NISO Z39.48—1992.

08 09 10 11 12 5 4 3 2 1

Contents

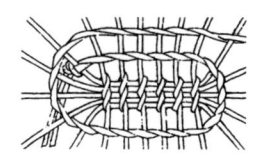

List of Illustrations   7
Acknowledgments   9
Introduction: Russell McDougall and Iain Davidson   11

Part 1: The Background and Scope of the Roth Family

Chapter 1   Making Otherness the Norm   31
Judit Brody

Chapter 2   The Family Background and Achievements of Walter Edmund Roth   41
Barrie Reynolds

Part 2: Henry Ling Roth

Chapter 3   Henry Ling Roth: *The Natives of Sarawak and British North Borneo*   59
Robert Hampson

Chapter 4   The Making of *Great Benin*: Felix Norman Roth and Henry Ling Roth   73
Russell McDougall

Chapter 5   The Primitive Body and Colonial Administration: Henry Ling Roth's Approach to Body Modification   93
Alice Gorman

Part 3: Walter E Roth and the Scientific Collection of Data about Australian Indigenous People

Chapter 6   From Oxford to the Bush: WE Roth, WB Spencer and Australian Anthropology   107
John Mulvaney

Chapter 7   Ethnological Studies and Archaeology of North West Central Queensland   121
Iain Davidson

| Chapter 8 | WE Roth and the Study of Aboriginal Languages in Queensland
Gavan Breen | 133 |

Part 4: Walter E Roth and Controversy in Australia

Chapter 9	WE Roth on Asians in Australia *Regina Ganter*	157
Chapter 10	The Legacy of a 'Lazy Character': Walter Roth's Contribution to the Ethnography Collections of the Queensland Museum *Richard Robins*	171
Chapter 11	The Life and Times of Walter Edmund Roth in North Queensland: The First Protector, the Australian Museum and Scandal *Kate Khan*	181
Chapter 12	Naked Shame: Nation, Science and Indigenous Knowledge in Walter Roth's Interventions into Frontier Sexualities *Ann McGrath*	193
Chapter 13	Walter Edmund Roth: Royal Commissioner of Western Australia, 1904 *Geoffrey Gray*	209
Chapter 14	Walter Roth and Ethno-Pornography *Helen Pringle*	221

Part 5: Walter E Roth in Guyana

| Chapter 15 | An Indigenous Compendium: Walter E Roth and the Ethnology of British Guiana
Neil L Whitehead | 235 |
| Chapter 16 | 'Protector of Indians': Assessing Walter Roth's Legacy in Policy Towards Amerindians in Guyana
Janette Bulkan and Arif Bulkan | 255 |

Part 6: The Roth Legacy

| Chapter 17 | Vincent Roth: The Man, His Life and His Work
Michael Bennett | 267 |
| Chapter 18 | George Kingsley Roth and the Fijian Way of Life
Julian Croft | 277 |

| Index | 287 |
| About the Contributors | 302 |

List of Illustrations

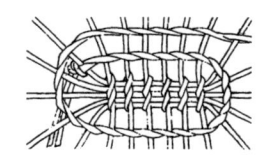

Figures

Figure 0.1	World map	12
Figure 0.2	Map of North Queensland	17
Figure 1.1	Mathias Roth (1818–91)	32
Figure 2.1	Henry Ling Roth (1855–1925)	43
Figure 2.2	Felix Norman Roth (1857–1921)	43
Figure 2.3	Reuter Emerich Roth (1858–1924)	43
Figure 2.4	Walter Edmund Roth (1861–1933)	43
Figure 2.5	Drawing by Walter Roth, showing his careful attention to detail	53
Figure 3.1	The cover of the original subscription flyer for *The Natives of Sarawak and British North Borneo*	60
Figure 3.2	Photograph of 'Sea Dyaks' from *The Natives of Sarawak and British North Borneo*	63
Figure 3.3	Photograph of Sakarang women from *The Natives of Sarawak and British North Borneo*	63
Figure 4.1	Map of Benin Province	76
Figure 4.2	View of Warri	76
Figure 4.3	Frontispiece of 'Souvenir of Warri' album	82
Figure 4.4	'A Sobo boy & Myself'	83
Figure 4.5	'Effroon, Sobo country. Ju-ju tree on the right'	84
Figure 4.6	'Coffee tree; the first one planted in Warri'	85
Figure 4.7	'Uvorami (Overami) Nabeshi, The Last King of Benin'	86
Figure 6.1	'Morphological Laboratory, Oxford, 1884'	109
Figure 7.1	Trade items documented by Walter Roth for the Selwyn Ranges	124
Figure 7.2	Men dressed for ceremony at Boulia in 1895	125

List of Illustrations

Figure 7.3	The site Roth didn't visit and Ken Isaacson at one of the painted anthropomorphs to the right of the Kurrajong tree	127
Figure 7.4	Anthropomorphic paintings on Devoncourt station	128
Figure 7.5	Map of movements from Roth (1897)	129
Figure 7.6	Map of dreaming tracks and stone arrangements in the region	130
Figure 8.1	Language map	134
Figure 8.2	Visit to Mapoon Presbyterian Mission, Western Cape York Peninsula, May 1902	138
Figure 8.3	Sign Language	147
Figure 9.1	Keppel Islanders in 1898, photographed by Walter Roth	166
Figure 9.2	A second photo that was not submitted as evidence of the present condition of the Keppel Islanders	166
Figure 11.1	Walter Roth in outback northern Queensland	182
Figure 11.2	Nautilus shell head and neck band, Bloomfield River	184
Figure 11.3	Feather headdress, Butcher's Hill	185
Figure 11.4	Crescent-shaped woven basket, Atherton	186
Figure 15.1	The Walter Roth Museum	237
Figure 15.2	Illustration of basketry drawn by Walter Roth	241
Figure 15.3	Jules Crevaux's illustration of a Makushi shaman	247
Figure 17.1	Walter Roth with Vincent Roth	268
Figure 17.2	Map of Guyana	271
Figure 18.1	George Kingsley Roth with Henry Ling Roth	278

Table

Table 7.1	Chronology of significant events in North West Central Queensland	122

Acknowledgments

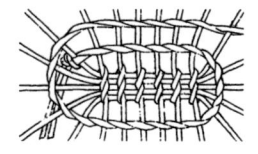

The editors would like to thank first and foremost Rosemary Williamson, without whose expert text preparation, careful research and project management assistance, this book would not have been possible. We are also grateful to the following: David Elkins for photographic expertise; Mike Roach for cartographic expertise; Ken Kippen; Joanne McMillan; Gillian Willis; Michael and Audrey Bennett; Timothy Bennett. We thank the Faculty of Arts, University of New England, for its financial support of this project; and Sharon Gallen, UNE Conference Company, for her friendly and professional handling of the Roth Family, Anthropology and Colonial Administration Conference in Coffs Harbour (Australia), 2004.

Introduction

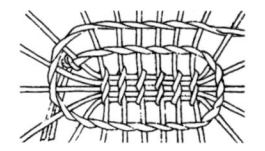

Russell McDougall and Iain Davidson

This book is a product of one of those happy pieces of serendipity that can occur in universities. Both editors had an interest in the work of members of the Roth family, Davidson as an archaeologist interested in the documentation of the material culture of 19th century Aborigines, and McDougall as a scholar of postcolonial literatures encountering the Roth name and legend through the fiction of Caribbean novelist and essayist Wilson Harris. We discovered our mutual interest through competition for the same books in the library, and, our curiosity piqued by the coincidence of interest by people of such apparently distinct disciplines, we began to talk. It soon emerged that the grand theme in studies of the Roth family was the question of the relation between a nascent anthropology and a colonial administration.

We convened a conference and might have been content with that. But it established a dialogue among scholars working on the Roths across a remarkable number of different disciplines, and we wanted not only to continue but also to provide some broader access to that dialogue. Seven descendants of Mathias Roth, the Hungarian founder of this remarkable family, also attended the conference. Some had not met or even known of each other before. All were intrigued that their family should excite scholarly interest and attract people from overseas to attend a conference in Australia. For both of us, one of the highlights was to be greeted in the foyer of the hotel adjacent to the conference venue with a cheery 'Hello, my name is Walter E Roth', a mere hundred years after Wally's grandfather of the same name was Chief Protector of Aborigines for Queensland.

Family

One of the themes of this book, then, is family. How did one family produce two great names – Henry Ling Roth (1855–1925) and Walter Edmund Roth (1861–1933) – in one discipline, anthropology, at a time when the discipline itself was so young? And how did so many others of

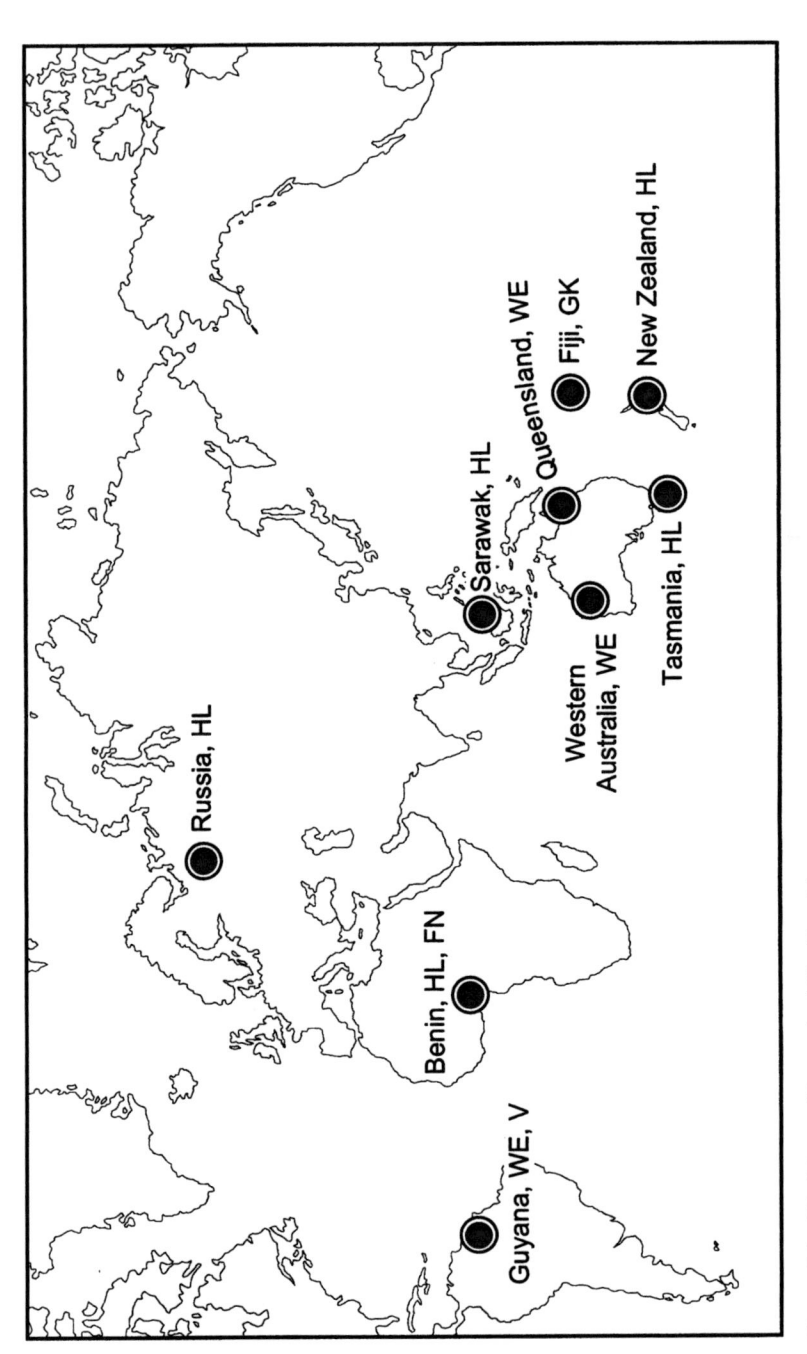

Figure 0.1 World map (Drawn by Mike Roach)

the family – Felix Norman Roth (1857–1921), Vincent Roth (1889–1967) and George Kingsley Roth (1903–60) – come to make their own contributions to the same discipline? Part of the answer is provided in the figure of Mathias Roth. Hungarian by birth, Jewish yet from a town where Jews were not allowed to live, he left his homeland after the failed Hungarian revolution of 1848. Henry, Walter and Felix were three of his seven sons and two daughters, all born in England after his marriage to a Christian woman, Anna Maria Collins. In an atmosphere of pluralistic religious pragmatism, and a household that provided the focus of a cosmopolitan society of liberal-minded people from all over Europe, the Roth family 'made otherness the norm' as Judit Brody – herself a refugee from Hungary to England after the Russian invasion of 1956 – phrases it in Chapter 1 of this volume.

Mathias was a medical doctor, a follower of the approach to healthy living of the Swedish gymnast Per Henrik Ling (from whom Henry got his second name). Among Mathias's sons, Bernard (1852–1915), Felix, Reuter (1858–1924) and Walter all qualified medically, while Alfred died before qualifying. Further details of the family are set out in Chapter 2 by Barrie Reynolds, who has been researching a biography of Walter Roth for 20 years.

Travel

Henry initially entered business as an accountant with the Austro-Hungarian Bank and then with Kann, Roth and Co in London, but in 1875 he accepted an offer to help manage a sugar plantation in British Guiana. He stayed only six months in the West Indies, as his employer failed to honour the agreement. For two years after that he managed the estates of Munro Butler-Johnstone in the Samara province of eastern Russia. Following publication of his *Notes on the Agriculture and Peasantry of Eastern Russia* in 1878, he was commissioned by English businessmen to investigate the Queensland sugar industry (HL Roth 1880). He had an uncle in Australia, his mother's brother, and he leapt at the opportunity.

Felix followed him out a few years later. He was a ship's engineer at this stage, trading for tortoiseshell and other exotic items up and down the east coast of Australia. Around the southern parts of New Guinea he traded flatiron for spearheads and knives and cartridges for old Snider rifles in return for bird of paradise skins. Sometimes too he was engaged on the 'coffin ships' (tramp steamers) and mail boats, but he preferred to avoid these if he could. In Brisbane for a while he helped a black Barbadian friend, Jack Dowridge ('The Black Diamond'), run his boxing saloon. In later life Felix was full of wild tales of pearl prospecting, shark fishing, cargo broaching, shipwrecks and native attacks in the islands. But in 1881 he married, and returned to England to study medicine.

Bernard by this time had joined his father in orthopaedic practice, specialising in the treatment of lateral curvature of the spine, although he also published on medical gymnastics and the sanitary aspects of dress (Plarr 1930:246). But Reuter had only just matriculated when Felix arrived home from the South Seas, and no doubt his brother's tales of adventure assisted his own decision to emigrate. Reuter spent most of his life in Sydney, and was one of the founders of the St John Ambulance Association in New South Wales, as well as being prominent in establishing the Royal Life-Saving Society and the Red Cross Society in Sydney ('Obituary' 1914:1083).

Henry was Honorary Secretary of the Mackay Planters' and Farmers' Association (Queensland) from 1881 to 1884. He worked in Mackay as an agent for the wealthy agricultural scientist and founder of Rothamstead Experimental Station in England, Sir JB Lawes. But after Felix's departure, he too returned to England. Next he accepted a commission to France, reporting to British interests on the dairy-farming industry, peasant proprietorship and continental systems of irrigation (see HL Roth 1882, 1885a, 1885b).

Then Walter decided to emigrate, leaving his marriage to elope with a woman who died soon after their arrival in the colony in 1887. Reynolds provides the detail of Walter's early years in Australia in Chapter 2. In 1894 Walter was appointed government surgeon attached to hospitals in far western Queensland first at Boulia then at Cloncurry and Normanton, and in 1898 he became the state's first Northern Protector of Aborigines. He served in that position until 1904, when he was made Chief Protector. In 1904 he was seconded to head the Royal Commission into the condition of Aboriginals in north-west Western Australia.

Henry married, settled in Halifax and acquired the part-time position of Curator of the Bankfield Museum in June 1890, graduating to its part-time and finally to full-time Keeper. He built the previously chaotic institution into a model teaching museum of prime importance. Felix's marriage was less happy, and he escaped it by entering the Medical Service of the Niger Coast Protectorate in West Africa, where he was stationed from 1892 to 1898. Henry writes: 'When Benin was captured the King [ie the Oba] escaped and my brother with three officers was sent after him into the bush. The hardship was so great that these three officers died within twelve months, while my brother got blackwater fever and was incapacitated whereupon the grateful Government gave him the Noble Order of the Boot' (Norman-Roth nd:3). Returning to England, Felix discovered that he had already been reported dead in the press. In fact, he died of heart failure on 11 November 1921 in Monte Carlo, aged 65.

Anthropology
Henry Ling Roth

The family's first contributions to anthropology were made by Henry Ling, who like many British ethnologists of his time saw no necessity to visit the peoples and places that he wrote about. Thus he never visited Tasmania, although the heavily revised second edition of his first book, *The Aborigines of Tasmania* (1899), remained the basic source until publication of George Augustus Robinson's journals in 1966. The first edition of Henry's book was published in 1890 in a limited edition of 200 copies. In his Preface, Edward Tylor praised Roth's picture of 'the extinct native race of Tasmania' as approaching 'absolute completeness' (HL Roth 1890a). In the recent controversy surrounding attempts to downplay the degree of settler violence against the Tasmanians, attention has turned again to Henry's work (see McDougall 2007). Henry also did not visit Sarawak or Benin, although he wrote major works about the indigenous cultures of both places. Robert Hampson considers the Sarawak material in Chapter 3, and Russell McDougall discusses the West African work in Chapter 4.

While Henry's principal contributions to early anthropology were based on careful scholarly synthesis of the observations of others – *Great Benin: Its Customs, Arts and Horrors* (1903) is partly based on first-hand accounts by his brother Felix, *The Natives of Sarawak and British North Borneo 2 Vols.* (1896) is based chiefly on the papers of Hugh Brooke Low – it cannot be said that his approach was simply derivative. Henry enunciated the principle that anthropology is 'essential to every civilised community which trades with, or is called upon to govern native communities' (quoted by Hampson in Chapter 3 of this volume). He believed that colonial administrators, in their management of indigenous peoples, needed to take account of the level of civilisation they had achieved. Body marking, in his view, was one way to determine that level. Alice Gorman discusses Henry's various studies of body marking in Chapter 5.

Henry's published output was as prodigious as it was culturally and geographically diverse. *Great Benin* was republished as recently as 1969 in the US. He extended his work on Sarawak and Borneo into a book entitled *Oriental Silverwork, Malay and Chinese... A Handbook for Connoisseurs, Collectors, Students and Silversmiths* (1910). It was revived for publication in 1966 and again in 1993, and remains 'a standard reference' for scholars and collectors of antique Malay and Peranakan silver (Fraser-Lu 1993:vii). His writings about Pacific cultures also were extensive (see McDougall & Croft 2005), although he was not able to complete before his death the major work on tattoo and the decorative arts that he planned. *The Maori Mantle* (1923) was said by Sir Peter Buck (Te Rangi Hiroa) to contain 'the most intensive work that has so far been published on any Polynesian craft' (1924:77). Perhaps the most ambitious of his many writings on weaving, spinning and handmade textiles, it was reprinted in 1979. *Studies in Primitive Looms* (1918) was reprinted in 1934, 1950 and again in 1977, and remains an important source for contemporary artisans. Henry also established the long and successful Bankfield Museum Notes series of publications, 23 numbers in all, primarily based around the museum's own ethnographic collections (now dispersed and lost forever) and financed entirely from his own pocket.

Walter Edmund Roth

But it is Henry's younger brother, Walter, who is probably the most remarkable figure in the history of anthropology. Reynolds in Chapter 2 provides the outline of his life, and John Mulvaney lays out the intellectual roots and contexts of his pioneering work in anthropology in Chapter 6. One of the motivations for this book, and the conference that preceded it, was the claim that Baldwin Spencer and Frank Gillen were the founders of fieldwork-based anthropology (Morphy 1997), systematising a discipline that had otherwise been based on unsystematic observations and anecdotes from travellers and geographers. Yet Walter's first great work, *Ethnological Studies among the North-West-Central Queensland Aborigines* (1897), preceded their first book, and it too was based on fieldwork. Mulvaney shows how enmeshed were the lives and careers of Spencer and Roth and goes some way toward providing the re-assessment of Roth that he proposed in his 1985 biography of Spencer (Mulvaney & Calaby 1985:387).

Mulvaney's chapter is the first chapter by an archaeologist. In Chapter 7 Iain Davidson, also an archaeologist, deals directly with North West Central Queensland. Davidson shows that despite the dreadful destruction of Aboriginal societies – people for whom Walter cared as a doctor, and studied as an anthropologist – there is both oral knowledge and archaeological evidence to fill the gaps in his account. In another example of survival of oral history, Larissa Behrendt's (2003) assessment of the accounts of Eliza Fraser's shipwreck and survival on Fraser Island in the 1830s and Olga Miller's (1998) oral history of the Aboriginal perspective on the same events suggests the more recent

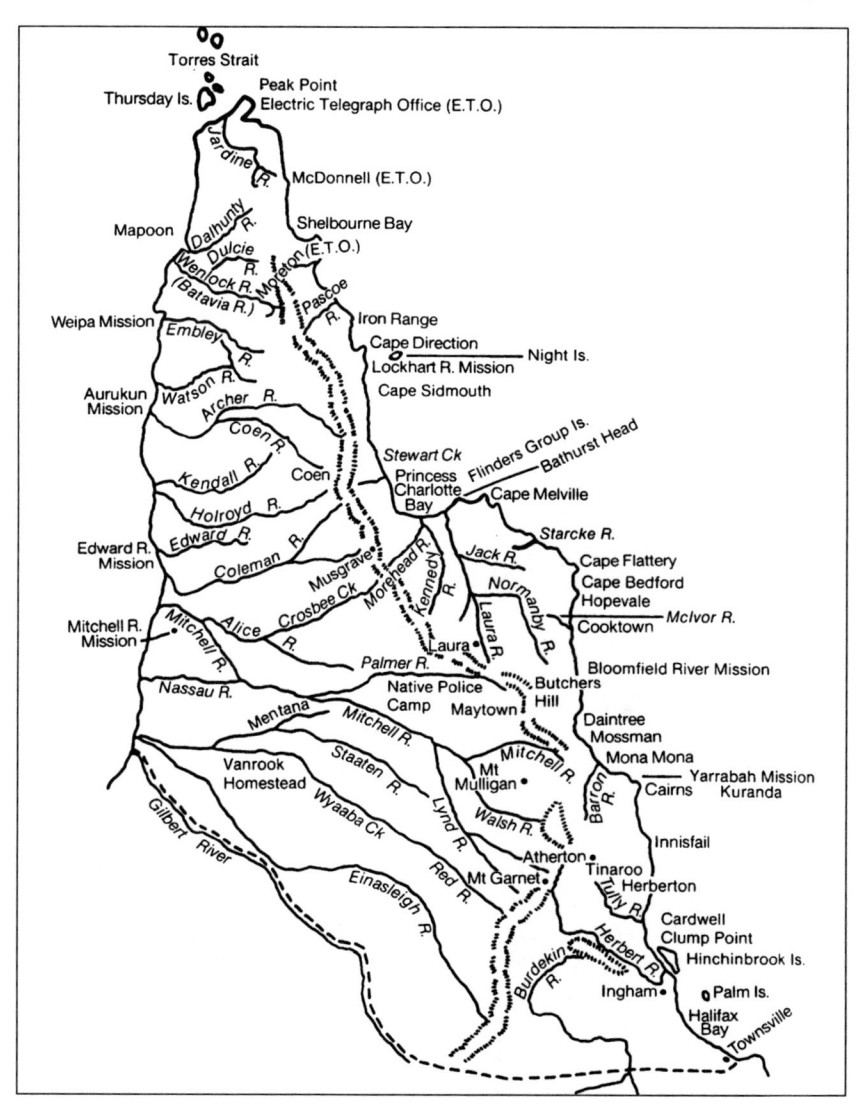

Figure 0.2 Map of North Queensland (Drawn by Kate Khan, reproduced with the permission of the Australian Museum)

evidence is the more accurate. This enables us to understand better the constraints under which Walter Roth undertook his anthropological investigations.

Whatever the constraints and however deep the destruction of people and society, those who survived still spoke the languages they had been brought up with – and some still do. Walter made every effort to record the languages of the peoples he worked with. In Chapter 8 Gavan Breen, himself an authority on a number of these same languages, synthesises and assesses all of Roth's linguistic work. This will doubtless become a standard starting point for considering North Queensland languages, and it has only been possible because, as Breen says, of Walter's ability 'to elicit vocabulary correctly from an unfamiliar language was as good as that of a competent modern linguist'.

Walter's other great contribution to Australian Aboriginal studies was through his material culture collections – often the focus of interest for archaeologists. In Chapter 10 Richard Robins considers the importance of his collections in the Queensland Museum and something of their original motivation; and in Chapter 11 Kate Khan discusses the larger collection that Walter controversially sold to the Australian Museum. Robins emphasises the importance of Walter's documentation of his collections through his publication. He also stresses that the collections had little impact in raising awareness of Aboriginal culture in Queensland. Khan considers the reasons why Walter sold the bulk of his collection to the Australian Museum – an act that formed one of the ostensible pretexts for political opposition to him in Queensland.

Colonial Administration and Controversy

From the publication of his *Ethnological Studies* in 1897 to his departure from Queensland in 1906, Walter's life was increasingly taken up with colonial administration and controversy. This history is determined to large degree by another significant 1897 publication: the *Aboriginals Protection and Restriction of the Sale of Opium Act*. In the following year Walter was appointed Protector of Aboriginals for the Northern and Central Division, which involved a move to Cooktown, in Cape York Peninsula. This was a position created and defined by the 1897 Act. Perusal of Walter's annual reports shows that he was concerned about the implementation of the Act, and he records the instances in which Aboriginal people in each town were in court for offences relating to alcohol and opium – a practice not followed by his successors. Boulia, where Walter had originally been posted as medical officer, was the centre of a region where the endemic, nicotine-based drug *pituri* was traded (Watson 1983). Here he recorded no instances of opium abuse in the courts, partly because there may have been fewer Asians selling opium, but perhaps because the indigenous trade he documented was still going on – as, indeed, knowledge of it continued into the 1970s. Because of its sections about the sale of opium, the Act affected people of Asian origin as well as Aborigines. As Regina Ganter shows in Chapter 9, interactions between Aborigines, non-Aborigines and Asians were complex in relation to both employment and intermarriage.

Walter clashed with the Southern Protector, Archibald Meston, who was one of the architects of the Act, over the removal of Aboriginal people to reserves. Walter's approach was apparently more sympathetic to their remaining on their ancestral lands. When Meston was removed from office, Walter became Chief Protector, and Meston became his enemy, campaigning publicly against him.

The opposition of Queensland's pastoralists may have been a point in favour of Walter's appointment to head Australia's first Royal Commission into the treatment of Aborigines. So might the fact that he had never been to Western Australia before. He was generally well informed, fearless and impartial. As President of the anthropological section of the Australian Association for the Advancement of Science (1902) and an honorary member of both the Berlin Anthropological Institute and the Anthropological Society of Florence, his credentials also were impeccable. Curiously, the Governor of Western Australia at the time was Sir Frederick Bedford, who had led Walter's brother Felix in the attack against Chief Nana in the Niger Coast Protectorate several years earlier.

In Chapter 13 Geoffrey Gray explores the effects of Walter's actions as Royal Commissioner, investigating the much publicised and debated condition of Aboriginals in Western Australia. The recommendations of the Roth Royal Commission were for the most part intended to bring race relations more securely 'under the rule of law', granting greater powers to the Chief Protector (in part to prevent sexual relations between black and white), but they also included some measures aimed at preserving traditional lifestyles – such as the establishment of native reserves. Predictably, the Report caused a furore when it was tabled in the Western Australian parliament, and generated great debate in the local press, and Walter again was the subject of ridicule, particularly from the pastoralists. But it was discussed much more favourably in the British House of Commons, and so could not be ignored. Roth's recommendations led directly to the many reforms of the 1905 Aborigines Act, including the abolition of neck chains for native prisoners. But the Roth Report did little substantially to alter the condition of the Aboriginal population in Western Australia. And the international attention it received proved ironically counterproductive in other areas of darkness. After hearing of the harsh treatment of Aborigines in Western Australia, King Leopold of Belgium, for example, 'refused to accept British strictures on Belgian atrocities in the Congo' (Healy 1978:209; see also *The Sadness of a Dying Race*). Gray's view is that the negative impact on Aborigines of a number of the policy outcomes of the Commission could not have been envisaged by its author, who stated unambiguously in his Report that 'the cruelties and abuses met with in the unsettled areas cannot be longer hidden or tolerated' (quoted by Gray, Chapter 13).

Back in Queensland, Walter was under fire from influential people in the white society of Cooktown, who petitioned the State Member for Cook against his reappointment as Chief Protector. This was tabled in the Legislative Assembly in November 1905. Walter answered each of the accusations, and the petition was rejected. Within a year, however, he resigned his post and left Australia forever.

Ann McGrath and Helen Pringle discuss the dirty campaign against Walter in more detail in Chapter 12 and in Chapter 14. Although, as McGrath documents, the opposition was fierce from white men outraged at being forced by the Act and the Protector to pay Aboriginal workers and to refrain from sexual relations with Aboriginal women, Walter was also accused of peddling pornography. He had used the word himself in the famous final section of his 1897 monograph, although as Pringle says, the subject matter was hardly the stuff we would call pornography today. While Walter was away conducting the Royal Commission into the condition of Aborigines in Western Australia, the argument became heated. It turned upon a photograph he had taken, apparently to prove a point made by a small line drawing in the 1897 book, which had subsequently been disputed. McDougall points out in Chapter 4, in his discussion of Felix's West African photographs, that photography had been an important ethnographic tool at least since the 1850s. Yet the history of anthropological photography is so chequered, particularly in relation to its apparent fetishising of sexual subjects, that many modern anthropologists remain uneasy about its validity. Certainly Walter was not alone in showing an anthropological interest in sexual matters. After all, Malinowski's *Sexual Life of Savages* (1932) is one of the founding texts of modern anthropology. Pringle observes that Walter was particularly interested in genital cutting. The contentious photograph, of an Aboriginal man and woman in coitus, was intended to demonstrate an unusual sex position as important evidence that the cutting of the penis did not prevent fertilisation. In Walter's view the photograph was simply the proof of a scientific argument. However, we have chosen not to reproduce the offending photograph in this book.

It is clear from Pringle's and McGrath's evidence that there was a systematic campaign against Walter, purportedly beating up a moral controversy, yet in reality responding to his attempts to curb both the economic and sexual exploitation of Aborigines. Still, by present standards, McGrath suggests, Walter's photograph places him ironically among those many other white men in colonial Queensland whom he opposed as sexual opportunists. In effect, he compromised the integrity of his own efforts to protect the Aboriginal subjects in his care, depriving them of their dignity before the camera lens.

When Downing Street requested a report on Walter's services, and upon the circumstances leading to his resignation, the Governor of Queensland, Lord Chelmsford, wrote ungenerously: 'Although Dr. Roth during the time he held the position of Chief Protector of Aborigines did valuable work there were a number of complaints with regard to the manner in which he, at times, performed his duties'.[1] So ended Walter Roth's career in Australia.

British Guiana

The official reason for Walter's resignation as Chief Protector of Aborigines in Queensland was ill health. But then why would he have applied immediately to the Imperial Government for a post in British Guiana (now Guyana)? He spent 23 years in the British Colonial Service there, first as the government medical officer, magistrate and Protector of Indians in the Pomeroon district, then as Stipendiary Magistrate of the Demerara River District. He was later Government Archivist and Curator of the Georgetown Museum. He wrote three major works, all published by the US Bureau of American Ethnology: *An Inquiry into the Animism and Folklore of the Guiana Indians* (1915), *An Introductory Study of the Arts, Crafts, and Customs of the Guiana Indians* (1924) and *Additional Studies of the Arts, Crafts, and Customs of the Guiana Indians, with Special Reference to those of Southern British Guiana* (1929). He also translated a number of the important earlier works of the region's ethnographic and travel literature from the Dutch and German sources (Van Berkel 1925; MR Schomburgk 1922–23; RH Schomburgk 1931).

Neil Whitehead gives an overview in Chapter 15 of Walter's ethnology of British Guiana. While understandable, it is a shame that his South America work is so little known in Australia, or for that matter that his Australian writings are not better known in Guyana, Venezuela and Surinam. The Walter Roth Papers in Georgetown suggest, for instance, that shortly before his departure from Australia he must have met the German anthropologist Hermann Klaatsch (1863–1916), as a number of Klaatsch's photographs are held there. Walter's Queensland fieldwork undoubtedly laid the foundation for his subsequent Amerindian researches. In British Guiana, whenever a difficulty of interpretation presented itself, Walter naturally searched his Australian experience for some clue or point of reference (see McDougall 1998, 2002). He contrasts Amerindian powers of visual mimicry – the use of visual camouflage or decoys as a hunting skill – with Queensland Aboriginals' use of smell to make an inanimate object imitate the presence of a human being (by placing a spear moistened with sweat in the path of a kangaroo, for example, to turn the animal in the direction of the hunter).

More importantly, perhaps, the comparison moves him to conclude that fraud and imposture (unlike mimicry) are a result of colonisation: they come as a result of the Indian's envy of the white man and his aping the low-caste European with whom it usually was his unfortunate lot to come into contact (WE Roth 1921:34; see also, in Roth 1903:16, his 'Suggested explanation of the "black jump-up white-fellow" idea'). He concludes:

> I find great consolation in knowing that though the principle which governed my efforts on behalf of the North Queensland aboriginals could not be carried out in its entirety, owing to the scarcity of first-class upright conscientious missionary men and women willing to sacrifice their lives for the benefit of the savage, I strained every point to secure immense Reserves where the natives are confined, where fire-arms, trade, clothes, and Europeans are not permitted, with the result that the race is allowed to work out its own destiny and suffered to live and die in peace (WE Roth 1921:34).

This hints at the degree of influence Roth's Australian experience must have had upon his framing of the Aboriginal Protection Acts in British Guiana. Remarkably, in both countries he worked towards conditions similar to those suggested by the Act in Queensland, with regulated wages, reserves and removals of children for their protection. In Chapter 16 Janette Bulkan and Arif Bulkan explore the legacy of Walter Roth's colonial administration in British Guiana, and observe its continuing influence upon legislation affecting the lives of Amerindians in modern Guyana.

AP Elkin credited Walter Roth as the founder of social anthropology in Australia, and the obituary published in the Georgetown *Daily Chronicle* dubbed him 'the father of Ethnology in British Guiana' (WIG 1933:2). He was, at the time of his death in 1933, the sole life member of the American Anthropological Association.

The Next Generation

Vincent Roth, OBE 1951

Walter had a number of children from different marriages and other relationships. Only Vincent Roth, born in Brisbane, followed in his father's footsteps. In 1907, when he arrived in British Guiana to join his father, Vincent was 18. He spent the next 30 years in the interior, working as a surveyor and magistrate, and then only departed for Barbados after the blackwater fever had nearly killed him. Folklorist, historian, legislator, naturalist and long-serving Honorary Secretary of the Royal Agriculture and Commercial Society, Vincent contributed immensely to the development of Guyana. He was also the author of many works of natural history and wildlife, including *Fish Life in British Guiana: A Popular Guide to the Colonial Fishes* (1943), *Notes and Observations on Animal Life in British Guiana, 1907–1941: A Popular Guide to Colonial Mammalia* (1943), *Path-Finding on the Mazaruni: The Journal of Six Expeditions on the Banks of the Mazaruni River in British Guiana in Search of an Alignment for a Road or Railway during the Years 1922, 1923 and 1924* (1949), *A Plea for the Better Conservation and Protection of Wild Life in British Guiana, together with a Comparative Schedule of the Wild Life Protection Laws in other English-Speaking Lands and a Proposed Wild Life Protection Ordinance* (1949) and *Tales of the Trails* (c 1960). Michael Bennett, Vincent's son-in-law and the editor of his diaries (Bennett 2003a, 2003b), provides a sketch of Vincent's life and his contribution to the cultural history of Guyana in Chapter 17.

George Kingsley Roth, OBE 1957, CMG 1954

Henry Ling Roth married Nancy Harriette Haigh at Lightcliffe in June 1893. They had two sons, Alfred Bernard (1898–1951) and George Kingsley (1903–60), named after the famed African traveller Mary Kingsley. Alfred took a degree in colour chemistry at the University of Liverpool and devoted most of his working life to managing John Bright and Co's carpet mill at Rochdale (near Halifax). George Kingsley studied initially at the University of Liverpool, but after his father's death in 1928 he applied for a position with the Colonial Office in the Far East. In 1928 he joined the colonial administration in Fiji, and except for a short stint at Zanzibar (1937) he served there more or less continuously from that time. He produced two important books: the fourth edition of *Fiji: Handbook of the Colony* (1936), which described in detail the history, economy, culture and administrative organisation of the colony; and *Fijian Way of Life* (1953), which celebrated both the traditional culture and the contemporary administrative and social structure. It is the latter that provides Julian Croft's focus in Chapter 18. George Kingsley was Secretary for Fijian Affairs from 1954 until his retirement in 1957, when he returned to England and became Honorary Keeper of the Fijian Collection at Cambridge University Museum of Archaeology and Anthropology. His brother, Alfred, willed his estate to the Museum; and the George Kingsley Roth Fund, established at Christ's College, now supports scholarship at Cambridge in East Asian, South Asian and Pacific Basin studies.

As George W Stocking (1993) pointed out over a decade ago: 'Ironically, as the link between anthropology and colonialism became more widely accepted within the discipline during the 1960s and 1970s, serious interest in examining the link diminished'. More recently the relationship between anthropology and colonial administration has become the subject of contentious discussion (eg Thomas 1994; Cheater 1986). But there has been little sustained biographical or empirical focus to the discussion. This book aims to examine the relationship between colonial administration and anthropology, across a range of colonial and cultural contexts, through consideration of the multiple contributions of the remarkable Roth family.

We emphasise Walter Roth's contribution in particular because of the importance of his empirical contributions and the depth of his involvement in colonial administration. Between 1901 and 1906, apart from his regular administrative reports to the Police Commissioner in Brisbane concerning Aboriginal welfare, Walter published 18 bulletins on northern Queensland ethnography. He laid the foundation for ethnography in northern Queensland; and in British Guiana his work was similarly foundational. Walter's ethnography of Guyana's Indians has a cross-cultural potentiality built into it that extends beyond Latin America and the Caribbean to northern Queensland. Yet he did not attempt any grand overarching theory. Rather he simply brought into juxtaposition materials not cross-referenced before so that they might resonate intellectually and excite the curiosity of those who followed – as they did, for example, the novelist Wilson Harris in Guyana.

Of the family members considered here, only Henry was not active in colonial administration. Yet his anthropological work on Benin and Sarawak relied heavily on the first-hand experience of those who were involved – his brother Felix with the Niger Coast Protectorate and Hugh Brooke Low with the Sarawak Government Service. In any case, a number of the theoretical issues suggested by Henry's anthropology also are part of the context for Walter's work, underscoring the philosophy that made his protection of Aboriginal people unpopular in Queensland and led to his departure for British Guiana.

In part at least, Henry's lack of profile in modern anthropology is a result of the ideological embedding in his work of an evolutionist 'hierarchy of races'.[2] This was the dominant paradigm of Victorian anthropology, and while it was discredited in the early 20th century by Franz Boas and others working away from alleged biological fixities and categories of 'race' and toward a more 'plastic' conception of cultural identity, it did not entirely disappear. Rather, it found its métier through Europe's need to manage its empires, in a hugely diverse range of cultural contexts where anthropology functioned in the service of colonial administration, and by the similar needs of the United

States with its 'internal colonialism' of American Indians (O'Flaherty & Shapiro 2002). Henry questioned the relativities of some of the racial types yet embraced the overall system of physical anthropology (see McDougall 2002). And his son, Kingsley, took into the field the lingering hierarchies of that earlier science as they appeared in the new salvage anthropology. Confined to armchair anthropology by health and marriage, Henry was in many ways proto-Boasian, recording in as much detail as possible the supposedly vanishing races and their cultures. There is now an intellectual suspicion of those whose emphasis was on gathering information, rather than on assisting the cultural survival of the peoples they studied. Yet the same racial typologies were at work in the cultural anthropology of empire management. In British Guiana as in Queensland, the protectionist agenda that Walter administered (and indeed helped to establish) contributed dramatically, though unintentionally, to the racialising of colonial society.

In Queensland, Walter had been pleased by the opportunity for fieldwork that colonial service gave him. So, when things went bad there, his main reason for accepting the Imperial Government's offer of a post in British Guiana was to conduct an 'ethnographical survey' of its indigenous peoples.[3] After some years, however, he began to think that the 'official life' of administration was 'scientifically wasteful', and he looked for 'some congenial billet' in the US.[4] Failing that, he hoped the Smithsonian Institute might be induced to engage him at least on some temporary 'piece of South American work' that would be of 'mutual advantage'.[5] But when the US decided to enter the war the financial commitment involved in that decision dashed all his hopes. He was caught permanently then on the horns of a dilemma: reviewers of his anthropological works regretted that he did not say how he came by his information; but if he answered their objection, he risked the authorities thinking that he neglected his official duties.[6] In the first 16 years, he took hardly a single holiday from colonial service.[7] Yet his anthropological achievements are enormous.

As modern scholarship continues to unpick and re-work the complex colonial entanglements of colonial administration and anthropology, the work of the Roth family – Henry, Felix, Vincent, George Kingsley and especially Walter – deserves a new focus.

Notes

1. [Lord Chelmsford] Letter to Lord Elgin, 9 October 1906, Queensland State Archives, Hom J20 2198.
2. The closing remarks of this Introduction draw upon and are elaborated further in McDougall & Croft 2005.

3. WE Roth to FW Hodge, 5 October 1915, Records of the Bureau of American Ethnology (BAE), Correspondence 1909–50, Rossi-Ryus, Box 90, National Anthropological Archives, Smithsonian Institution.
4. Roth to Hodge, 28 October 1919, BAE, Correspondence 1909–50, Rossi-Ryus, Box 90, National Anthropological Archives, Smithsonian Institution.
5. Hodge to Roth, 30 January 1917, BAE.
6. Roth to Hodge, 27 February 1917, BAE.
7. Roth to J Walter Fewkes, 21 May 1920, BAE.

Works Cited

Behrendt, L (2003) 'Eliza Fraser: a colonial and legal narrative', in McCalman, I and McGrath, A (eds), *Proof and Truth: The Humanist as Expert*, Canberra: The Australian Academy of the Humanities, 189–99
Bennett, Michael (ed) (2003a) *Vincent Roth. A Life in Guyana. A Young Man's Journey. Volume 1: 1889–1923*, Leeds: Peepal Tree
———. (2003b) *Vincent Roth. A Life in Guyana. The Later Years. Volume 2: 1924–1935*, Leeds: Peepal Tree
Buck, Sir Peter (Te Rangi Hiroa) (1924) 'Review of Ling Roth, *The Maori Mantle* (Halifax 1923)', *Journal of Polynesian Society*, 33, 77
Cheater, Angela P (1986) *Social Anthropology: An Alternative Introduction*, 2nd edn, Gweru, Zimbabwe: Mambo Press
Fraser-Lu, Sylvia (1993) 'Preface', in Roth, HL, *Oriental Silverwork: Malay and Chinese*, Kuala Lumpur: Oxford
Healy, JJ (1978) *Literature and the Aborigine in Australia 1770–1975*, St Lucia: University of Queensland Press
McDougall, Russell (2007) 'Henry Ling Roth and *The Aborigines of Tasmania*: investments in extinction', in McDougall, R and Hulme, P (eds), *Travel, Anthropology, Writing*, London: IB Tauris, 43–58
———. (2002) 'Walter and Henry Ling Roth: "On the signification of couvade". The place of Australia and British Guiana in the *fin de siècle* debate concerning the history of mankind', *Australian Cultural History*, 21, 61–68
———. (1998) 'Walter Roth, Wilson Harris and a post-colonial/Caribbean theory of modernism', *University of Toronto Quarterly*, 67(2), 567–91
McDougall, Russell and Croft, Julian (2005) 'Henry Ling Roth and George Kingsley Roth's Pacific Anthropology', *Journal of Pacific History*, 149–170
Malinowski, B (1932) *The Sexual Life of Savages in North-Western Melanesia: An Ethnographic Account of Courtship, Marriage, and Family Life among the Natives of the Trobriand Islands, British New Guinea*, London: Routledge and Kegan Paul
Miller, O (1998) 'K'gari: Mrs Fraser and Butchulla oral tradition', in McNiven, IJ, Russell, L and Schaffer, K (eds), *Constructions of Colonialism: Perspectives on Eliza Fraser's Shipwreck*, London: Leicester University Press, 30–36
Morphy, H (1997) 'Gillen – Man of Science', in Mulvaney, DJ, Morphy, H and Petch, A (eds), *'My dear Spencer': The Letters of F.J. Gillen to Baldwin Spencer*, Melbourne: Hyland House, 23–50
Mulvaney, DJ and Calaby, JH (1985) *'So Much That Is New': Baldwin Spencer 1860–1929*, Carlton: Melbourne University Press
Norman-Roth, F (nd) *Some Experiences of an Engineer Doctor: With an Introduction on Our Schooldays by H. Ling Roth*, reprinted from the *Halifax Courier & Guardian*, January–May 1922
'Obituary, WE Roth' (1914) *The British Medical Journal*, 6 December, 1083

O'Flaherty, Brendan and Shapiro, Jill S (2002) 'Apes, essences and races: what natural scientists believed about human variation, 1700–1900', Columbia University Department of Economics Discussion Paper Series, Discussion Paper #:0102-24.http://216.239.57.104/search?q = cache:yT7FuUERTQUJ:www.columbia.edu/cu/economics/discpapr/DP0102-24.pdf + %22hierarchy + of + races%22 + pacific + anthropology&hl = en&ie = UTF-8, accessed 28 February 2005

Plarr, VG (comp) (1930) 'Roth, Bernard Matthias Simon', in *Plarr's Lives of the Fellows of the Royal College of Surgeons*, revised by Sir D'Arcy Power with the assistance of WG Spencer *et al*, Bristol

Reports by the Under Secretary for Public Lands and Dr. Roth Re complaints against Dr. Roth, Chief Protector of Aborigines (1905) *Parliamentary Papers, Vol I*, Legislative Assembly, Queensland

Roth, George Kingsley (1953) *Fijian Way of Life*, rev 2nd edn 1973, Melbourne: Oxford University Press

———. (ed) (1936) *Fiji: Handbook of the Colony*, Suva: Government Printer

Roth, Henry Ling (1923) *The Maori Mantle*, Halifax (reprinted 1979, Victoria Farmhouse, Carlton, Bedford: Ruth Bean, with a review (1924) by Sir Peter Buck (Te Rangihiroa)

———. (1910) *Oriental Silverwork, Malay and Chinese. With over 250 original illustrations. A Handbook for Connoisseurs, Collectors, Students and Silversmiths*, London: Truslove and Hanson

———. (1899) *The Aborigines of Tasmania by H. Ling Roth; Assisted by Marion E. Butler and Jas. Backhouse Walker; With a chapter on the osteology by J.G. Garson, M.D.; Preface by Edward B. Tylor, D.C.L.*, Halifax (England): [s.n.]

———. (1890a) *The Aborigines of Tasmania. By H.L. Roth. Assisted by Marion E. Butler. With a chapter on the Osteology, by J.G. Garson... And a preface by E.B. Tylor... F. Index*, London: Kegan Paul and Co

———. (1890b) *A Guide to the Literature of Sugar: A Book of Reference for Chemists, Botanists, Librarians, Manufacturers, and Planters, with Comprehensive Subject Index*, London: Kegan Paul, Trench, Trubner & Co

———. (1885a) 'Arbère. A short contribution to the study of peasant proprietorship', *Journal of the Royal Statistical Society*, 23, 81–91

———. (1885b) *Franco-Swiss Dairy-Farming*, London: W Clowes & Sons

———. (1882) *Notes on Continental Irrigation*, London: Trübner & Co

———. (1880) *A Report on the Sugar Industry of Queensland*, Brisbane: Gordon & Gotch

———. (1878) *A Sketch of the Agriculture and Peasantry of Eastern Russia*, London: Baillière, Tindall & Cox

Roth, Vincent (c 1960) *Tales of the Trails*, Georgetown: Daily Chronicle

———. (1949a) *Path-Finding on the Mazaruni: The Journal of Six Expeditions on the Banks of the Mazaruni River in British Guiana in Search of an Alignment for a Road or Railway during the Years 1922, 1923 and 1924*, Georgetown: Printed by the Daily Chronicle, Guiana Edition, No 13

———. (1949b) *A Plea for the Better Conservation and Protection of Wild Life in British Guiana, together with a Comparative Schedule of the Wild Life Protection Laws in other English-Speaking Lands and a Proposed Wild Life Protection Ordinance*, Georgetown: Daily Chronicle

———. (comp) (1946–47) *Handbook of Natural Resources of British Guiana, Compiled under the Direction of the Interior Development Committee of British Guiana and its Chairman, Vincent Roth. With an Introduction by Sir Gordon J Lethem*, 2 vols, Georgetown: Daily Chronicle

———. (1943a) *Fish Life in British Guiana: A Popular Guide to the Colonial Fishes*, Georgetown: Daily Chronicle

———. (1943b) *Notes and Observations on Animal Life in British Guiana, 1907–1941; A Popular Guide to Colonial Mammalia*, Georgetown: Daily Chronicle

Roth, Vincent (1943c) *Notes and Observations on Fish Life in British Guiana, 1907–1943; A Popular Guide to Colonial Fishes...*, Georgetown: Daily Chronicle

Roth, Walter (1984) *The Queensland Aborigines*, with Foreword by Barry Reynolds, facsimile edn, Carlisle, WA: Hesperian Press

———. (1929) *Additional Studies of the Arts, Crafts, and Customs of the Guiana Indians, with Special Reference to those of Southern British Guiana*, Bulletin 91, Bureau of American Ethnology, Washington, DC: Smithsonian Institute

———. (1924) *An Introductory Study of the Arts, Crafts, and Customs of the Guiana Indians*, 38th Annual Report, Bureau of American Ethnology, Washington: Government Printing Office, 1–110

———. (1921) 'Some examples of Indian mimicry, fraud and imposture', *Timehri*, VII, 29–40

———. (1915) *An Inquiry into the Animism and Folklore of the Guiana Indians*, Extract from the 30th Annual Report, Bureau of American Ethnology, Washington: Government Printing Office, 103–396

———. (1905) *Report of the Royal Commission on the Condition of the Natives of Western Australia*, Perth

———. (1903) 'Superstition, Magic and Medicine', *North Queensland Ethnography Bulletin No 5*, Brisbane, Government Printer (rpt in Roth, *The Queensland Aborigines*, Vol II)

———. (1897) *Ethnological Studies among the North-West Central Queensland Aborigines*, Brisbane: Government Printer

Sadness of a Dying Race, The (nd) Aborigines' Uplift Society

Schomburgk, Moritz Richard (1922–23) *Richard Schomburgk's Travels in British Guiana during the Years 1840–1844: Translated and Edited, with Geographical and General Indices, and Route Maps, Edited and Transcribed by Walter E Roth*, 2 vols, Georgetown: Daily Chronicle

Schomburgk, Robert Hermann (1931) *Robert Hermann Schomburgk's Travels in Guiana during the Years 1835–1839... Edited by Otto A Schomburgk. With a Preface by Alexander von Humboldt together with his Essay on some Important Astronomical Positions in Guiana... Translated by Walter E Roth*, Georgetown: 'The Argosy' Co

Stocking Jr, George W (ed) (1993) *Essays on the Contextualization of Ethnographic Knowledge*, History of Anthropology series, Vol 7, Madison: University of Wisconsin Press

Thomas, Nicholas (1994) *Colonialism's Culture: Anthropology, Travel and Government*, Princeton University Press

Van Berkel, Adriaan (1925) *Adriaan Van Berkel's Travels in South America between the Berbice and Essequibo Rivers and in Surinam, 1670–1689*, Georgetown: Daily Chronicle, Reprints and Original Works Dealing with all Phases of Life in British Guiana, No 2 (originally published in Dutch in Amsterdam in 1695, translated and edited by WE Roth)

Watson, PL (1983) *This Precious Foliage*, Oceania Monographs 26, Sydney: University of Sydney

WIG (1933) 'Dr. Walter Roth dead', *Daily Chronicle*, Georgetown, British Guiana, 6 April, 1, 8

PART 1

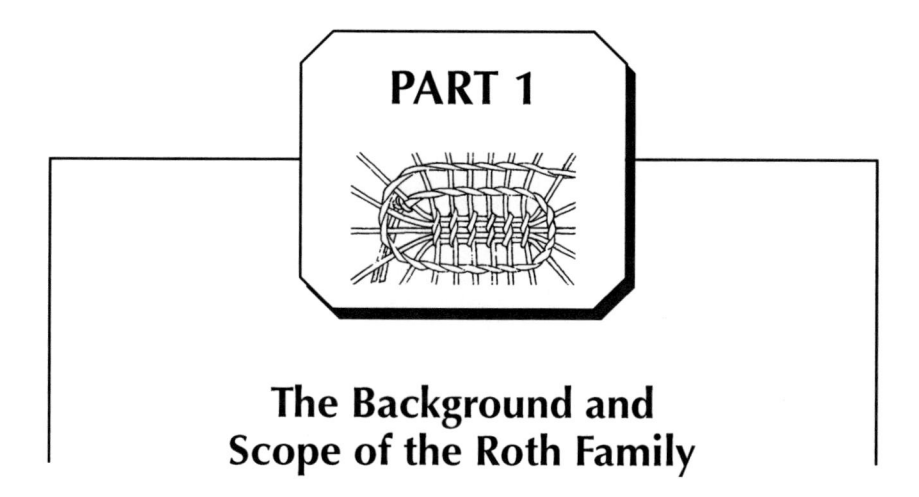

The Background and Scope of the Roth Family

CHAPTER 1

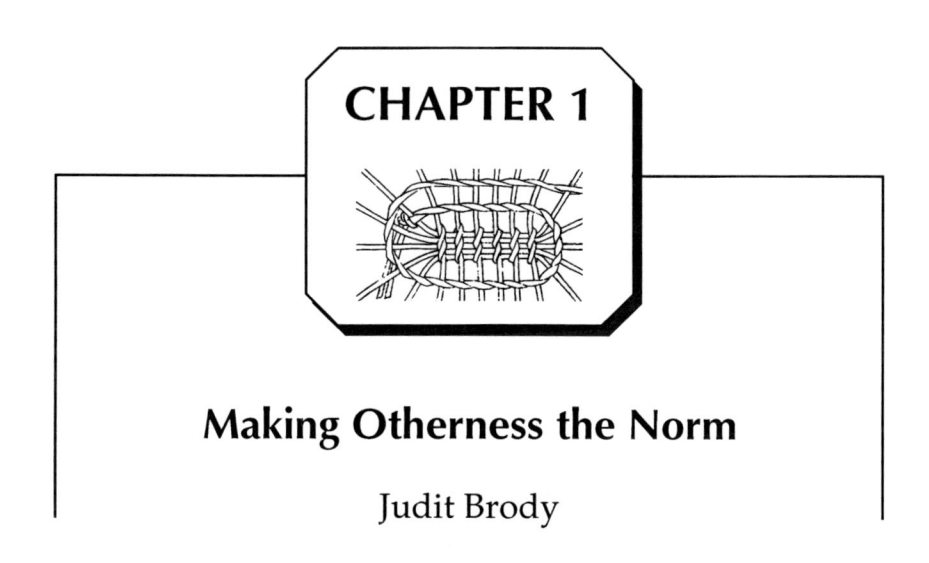

Making Otherness the Norm

Judit Brody

If any single occupational group deserves the credit – or the blame – for bringing us into the postmodern era, it is the anthropologists. They created a new profession out of otherness, and their findings made it impossible for any literate person to believe that there is only one way of seeing the world (Wagner 1995:53).

Walter Edmund Roth and Henry Ling Roth were pioneers of anthropology. They undoubtedly recognised that there are cultures authentic in their own right, which are outside their own social order and system of values. In the 19th century such a pluralistic attitude was remarkably rare. Not even in our present era is it always easy to imagine other cultures as 'natural' and equal to one's own. The following notes on the cultural *milieu* of the Roth family will show that from the start Walter Roth and his brothers could not take one single view of the world for granted. They had the advantage (some may call it a disadvantage) of having to see the world from several different standpoints, and this made them already outsiders to the world they originally inhabited. Therefore it was 'natural' for them to make a mental leap and accept the existence of many, to some degree equivalent, but different cultures. They recognised other people as strange yet understandable; not alien, only a different variant of humanity. The Roth brothers had to accept from an early age that different perspectives could be equally valid when viewing and describing the world, and this may even have given them their motive to investigate other cultures.

I envisage two main counter-arguments against my reasoning. First, that the Roth brothers' original otherness was not fundamental because

Figure 1.1 Mathias Roth (1818–91) (Reproduced with the permission of Michael Bennett)

it was all within the Western tradition. But I would say that it was real and deep enough for them to have a more open mind than that of many of their contemporaries, and that it was unsettling enough to have to reconstruct it. The second objection could be that they were unable to override completely their own set of values, and this influenced not only their ethnographic research but also their official activities. This is an entirely valid argument. The sons of Mathias Roth were children of the Enlightenment, a European phenomenon putting European values on centre stage. This had a constant effect on their mental attitudes; they could not shed their own skin completely even though that skin was, like that of a rhinoceros, full of wrinkles.

The Roth Family Background in Europe

Let us go a little deeper into the Roth family background. The main influence on the Roth boys during their formative years was their father, Mathias Roth. He was born in 1818 in what is now Slovakia, then part of Hungary, and within the Hapsburg Empire. The exact location of his birth is still a matter of debate. His parents were Jewish, and at the time of his birth Jews were not allowed to live in the so-called 'Free Royal Cities' – in fact they were not even allowed to spend one single night there. Mathias claimed that he was born in Košice, a Free Royal City, but could that be true? The city archivist, with whom I had a good-humoured argument in 1997, was convinced that this was impossible. It is indisputable that later during their childhood Mathias and his brothers did live in the town and that they were the only Jewish children there. Košice is in Slovakia, but the Roth family was not Slovak. Although the family came originally from what is now Poland, they considered themselves Hungarians for the following reasons: first, because there was no Slovak middle-class and they aspired to middle-class status; and second, since the power was in the hands of the Hungarians it was advantageous to be associated with the ruling element. On the other hand, Hungarians would never consider them as Hungarians, but simply as Jews who happened to live outside the close-knit Jewish community.

It is not easy to imagine what life was like for a Jewish youngster in rural or small-town Eastern Europe. Jews mostly lived in their own villages (*shtetls*) and were not accepted as part of the community. Right to the end of the 19th century many restrictions were placed on them, and in some areas pogroms regularly took place. In order to be more assimilated, integrated and finally accepted, many young Jewish men embraced the Enlightenment and replaced the study of religious texts with the study of the sciences, the arts and music. Mathias and his brothers followed this path, and later, in England, Mathias imparted the Enlightenment values to his sons.

From Košice, Mathias and his brothers travelled to Vienna for further studies. How could their widowed mother, who ran a kosher restaurant in town, afford to support them? The answer probably lies in charity as a major factor. In Hungary the custom was that poor Jewish students did what was called 'eating days'. In other words, they were invited to a different family each day of the week for a good meal. It is quite possible that Mathias and his brothers 'ate days' in Vienna. But money spent on their education was not wasted. Of Mathias's three brothers, David (also known as Didier and under the pseudonym Beauvais de Saint-Gratien) became a homoeopathic physician in Paris, doctor and art adviser to the Rothschild family; Felix, a stockbroker in Vienna who was awarded the knighthood of the Order of Francis Joseph; and Emerich Emanuel (Imre Mano), a well-known painter and photographer.

Mathias received his Medicinae Doctor (Doctor of Medicine) from Pavia in 1840, and by lucky coincidence this was the very year when by an extension of rights Jews at last were allowed to settle in Košice. Taking advantage of the new regulations he returned to his home town and for the next nine years he practised there as a physician. Later, in partnership with a gentile, he opened a hydropathic institution.

Mathias in England

In 1849 Mathias arrived in England as an asylum seeker. We do not know what part exactly he played in the 1848–49 Hungarian Revolution and War of Independence but we do know that – like practically all Jews in the country – he sided with the Hungarians, who were ultimately defeated, and not with the Austrians or the Slovaks. We also know that, young as he was, he was asked to be one of the signatories of the petition to the British Parliament for the emancipation of Jews.

Fleeing his native land, he agreed to the revolutionary government's request that he carry documents to England. He was apprehended and imprisoned. His brothers did everything in their power to have him freed, and 60 prominent citizens of Košice were asked to testify to his good character. All complied except one, who accused him to the authorities of republican sentiments – but that could have been just personal enmity (Roth 1888:438).[1]

Once in England, Mathias did not take any overt political stance except for inviting friends on the anniversary of the start of the revolution. Luckily so, because the situation was quite complex. The Hungarian revolution had been defeated with the help of the

Russian army, called in by the Austrian Emperor Francis Joseph. The controversial revolutionary leader Lajos (Louis) Kossuth (1802–94) escaped to Turkey, a country that was at odds with Russia at the time. Britain, especially Foreign Secretary Palmerston, was opposed to Russia gaining more power in the Middle East while preferring, for the sake of European equilibrium, that the Austrian monarchy should survive instead of being broken up into small statelets. On the other hand, when Kossuth arrived in England from his exile in Turkey, the influential Peace Society (one of its leaders was John Bright, whose daughter later married Mathias's eldest son) warned people against treating him as a romantic hero. In spite of this warning, Kossuth was enthusiastically received in England by large crowds. However, the *Times* newspaper attacked him relentlessly; this may have been the reason that he reported sick and took to his bed. It was Mathias Roth who was first asked to attend to him as a physician in spite of the fact that he did not sign the greeting the other Hungarian refugees presented to Kossuth on his arrival to practise as a homeopath.

Mathias and Medicine

Mathias possessed a valid qualification as doctor of medicine and could have joined the ranks of the regular doctors, the allopaths, but he chose to remain a homoeopath because of his conviction that homoeopathy was the scientific method of medicine. These were days when in England the profession of physicians and surgeons was still in a fluid state. Therefore it was especially important – mostly for unacknowledged financial reasons – to segregate quacks and alternative therapists from those with officially accepted qualifications. The influential journal, the *Lancet*, called homoeopathy 'globule quackery' (*Lancet* 1850:300). In 1852 the Committee of Irregular Practice of the Provincial Medical and Surgical Association (forerunner of the British Medical Association) decreed that candidates for admission to the Association must state in writing that they neither were, nor intend to become, professors or practitioners of homoeopathy. Similarly the Society of Apothecaries would refuse to certify those who held 'mischievous tendency' to homoeopathy (*London Journal of Medicine* 1852:202). Although Mathias managed to be placed on the first Medical Register in 1858, to the end of his life he remained within the small group of ostracised homoeopaths. Even so, he managed to earn a good living.

After coming to England, Mathias specialised in what we now call orthopaedics. He tried to reshape the bodies of young women who became deformed due to the wearing of corsets, stays, the backboard and countless other artificial mechanical contraptions that were originally designed to impart good posture but usually had the opposite effect. In general, Mathias was against mechanical aids. He was especially keen to promote Swedish gymnastics as developed by Per Henrik Ling (1776–1839).[2] Mathias believed that it was the best method, if not to cure then at least to stabilise, spinal deformities. His enthusiasm for Swedish gymnastics accounts for the name of his son, Henry Ling Roth. Mathias's oldest son, Bernard, who became a regular orthopaedist, also recommended giving up stays and corsets and plaster jackets. Bernard followed his father in recommending Swedish exercises to his patients, and his brothers Felix Norman and Reuter, who were physicians, did likewise.

Mathias Roth's liberal attitudes, as informed by the Enlightenment, cannot be separated from his medical entrepreneurialism. 'What can straightening people's bodies be... [other] than a metaphor for straightening the political constitutions of state?' (R Cooter 2003, pers comm). The physical medicine as pursued by Mathias could have been his way of seeking control, and of impressing the moral values of his discarded religion through his patients on wider society.

The Roth Circle in England

Henry Ling Roth says of his father: 'He was an industrious, able man, and got on, but the anti-English feelings which dominated him, and which he was never able to subdue, caused in later years a good deal of friction between himself and the members of his family, as well as of the medical profession' (Norman-Roth 1922:3). The expression 'anti-English feelings' needs some interpretation. It does not mean that Mathias disliked the English. What he did was to criticise certain English customs and point to practices in other countries that might provide positive alternatives. He had seen, and he had lived, in different circumstances; and some of these, he thought, were more desirable than those he encountered in England. He came from a multicultural environment that was mostly Hungarian, Slovak and Jewish with a German, Gypsy and Ruthenian element thrown in. As a consequence, being a Jew, a Hungarian and a homoeopath, he could not fit easily into the relatively monocultural society of Victorian England.

Soon after arriving in England Mathias married Anna Maria Collins, an English girl from a good middle-class family. They produced nine children: seven sons and two daughters. It seems that their mother had precious little influence on the children's physical and intellectual upbringing, which was firmly dictated by their father. On the other hand, although Mathias was a nonbeliever, he did make concessions for his wife's sake and occasionally sent his brood to church: whatever church happened to be in the neighbourhood.

Within a short time Mathias managed to mix with the English upper classes; yet his real friends were fellow refugees from the old country in addition to a liberal-minded, radical and socialist, international crowd. Later in life Henry Ling said that the children 'got to hate the sight of foreigners, mostly the Hungarians, who came to the house' (Norman-Roth 1922:4). Kossuth counted him as a friend, as did Francis Pulszky (1814–97), the politician and archaeologist around whom the Hungarian refugees gathered and who later, on his return to Hungary, became director of the National Museum in Budapest. The French socialist Louis Blanc (1811–82) and the radical Peter Taylor (1819–91) were Mathias's friends as well.

A younger friend, a talented linguist and pioneer anthropologist, may have been a model for Mathias's son Walter. This was Gotlieb Wilhelm Leitner (1840–99). Born in Hungary into the famous Saphir family, he was adopted by a medical missionary in Turkey. At 15 years of age he acted as interpreter to the British in Constantinople; and at 21 he was professor of Arabic at King's College in London. Leitner spent many years in India teaching, studying native languages, travelling on ethnographical expeditions, collecting artefacts, publishing journals, raising money to set up the Oriental University of the Punjab and founding schools, literary societies and public libraries.

Foreigners did not come only for tea and cakes – several resided in the Roth household. They ranged from housemaids and governesses from German-speaking countries, ensuring that the children become proficient in foreign languages, to artists supported by Mathias. Among them were the painter Wolfgang Boehm (1834–1890), brother of Queen Victoria's sculptor, Joseph Edgar Boehm and the French sculptor Adolph Megret (1829–1911).

Henry Ling said, and not with approbation, that his father 'had very peculiar notions as to education, was a great believer of the one-time famous educationist Pestalozzi, and full of the ideas of German education of the period, for German ideas dominated Hungary' (Norman-Roth 1922:3). This one sentence incorporates three points of criticism: of the methods of the educational reformer Johann Heinrich Pestalozzi (1746–1827); of German education in general; and of his father's attachment to his Hungarian roots. How much the regime in the Roth family was actually based on European educational philosophy, and how much on Mathias's own personal view, is debatable. But he certainly insisted on some strange rules. Henry Ling blamed later health problems on Mathias's insistence that the boys should run around barefoot in all weathers. Nursery rhymes and fairy stories were absolutely forbidden. Instead Mathias engaged foreign teachers to tutor his boys in mathematics, and in the physical and natural sciences. This brings to mind not only Gradgrind in *Hard Times* by Dickens but also a famous Hungarian play, *The Tragedy of Man*, first published in 1862. In this, Adam the time traveller arrives in a future where science and technology rule the world. He asks a scientist: 'Fairy tales that nurses love to tell, do they not fill the children's tender minds with fancied things?' To this the scientist answers: 'Tis true and therefore our nurses speak of truths numerical and tell the children of geometry' (Madách 1963:159).

As the boys got older, University College School, catering to nonconformists and liberals of any hue, was the natural choice for their schooling. However, two of them were sent to boarding school in Germany after an unsuccessful escapade when they tried to run away from home. Here again they were made to feel very much the outsiders. Their German peers' 'awe of authority' (Norman-Roth 1922:10) clashed with their own notion of the importance of the individual, one of the Enlightenment values instilled in them by their father. In addition, time spent with close family in Vienna and in Paris introduced them to yet another set of values.

Conclusion

Outsiders are of two kinds. There are those who are voluntarily outsiders, and there are those upon whom the state of being an outsider is thrust. I have tried to show that Walter Roth and his siblings were, by reasons of their family background, of the latter kind. Then, by exposure to and the study of different cultures, they became voluntary outsiders and through their ethnography gained a psychologically more secure position. It has been said that in the act of discovering another culture the anthropologist actually invents his own; we can see how this in a sense legitimises an outsider's own position. The Roth brothers made the otherness that was thrust on them their norm.

Notes

1. Actually what was said was *'quod is Democraticorum principiorum homo sit'*, Košice City Archives (1849) September #3157.
2. A special system of physical exercises, not gymnastics as in the contemporary use of the term.

Works Cited

Lancet (1850) 2, The globule-quackery
London Journal of Medicine (1852) 4, Society of Apothecaries' Resolution

Madách, I (1963) *The Tragedy of Man*, transl Horne, GCW, Budapest: Corvina
Norman-Roth, F (1922) *Some Experiences of an Engineer Doctor: With an Introduction on Our Schooldays by H. Ling Roth*, reprinted from the *Halifax Courier & Guardian*, January–May 1922
Roth, M (1888) 'A Farewell dinner to Dr Roth at the Criterion 20th June 1888', *Monthly Homoeopathic Review* 32, 433–44
Wagner, R (1995) 'The idea of culture', in Anderson, WT (ed), *The Truth About the Truth*, New York: Tarcher/Putnam

CHAPTER 2

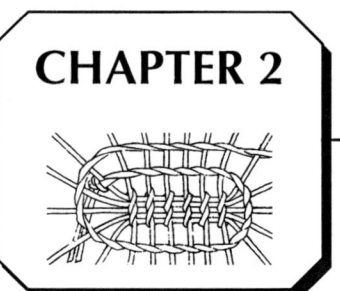

The Family Background and Achievements of Walter Edmund Roth

Barrie Reynolds

The Roth Family

The professional families of the 19th century produced a number of people who went on to make their mark in different fields and on different continents. The Roth family was one such. Today, we are particularly aware of the contributions made to anthropology by two of them, Henry Ling Roth and Walter Edmund Roth. But they, like some of their brothers and sisters, made contributions that went beyond this discipline. Family influences had an obviously strong effect on their thinking and the professions they chose, and instilled in them a driving work ethic that resulted in a high level of dedication and productivity.

The early years of anthropology provide a rich field for exploration. Most of the leading anthropologists of the late 19th and early 20th centuries had been trained in other disciplines and had a broad range of interests and experience that extended well beyond anthropology. These influenced the ways they approached their research and determined their objectives, how they organised their data and even their findings. To understand them as anthropologists, therefore, it is important that one takes into account these background influences.

To place Henry and Walter Roth in context, this chapter outlines the diversity of the contributions that members of the Roth family made across a number of fields, ranging from art to public health, and discusses the importance of the contributions made to anthropology, particularly by Walter Roth.

Mathias Roth

Henry and Walter Roth were two of the seven sons and two daughters of Mathias Roth (1818–91). Born in Hungary, Mathias was the youngest of four brothers: Felix moved to Vienna; David became a successful homoeopathic doctor in Paris and art adviser to the Rothschild family; Emerich trained as a portrait painter in Paris and Vienna and later lived in Constantinople and Egypt; Mathias studied medicine in Vienna and Pavia before returning home to practise.

Because of his involvement in the Revolution, Mathias left Hungary in 1849 to settle in London, where he married an Englishwoman, Anna Maria Collins, and established a highly successful medical practice. His homoeopathic interests led him into the field of public hygiene where he made a number of significant contributions, notably in school hygiene and the health needs of the working classes. This was, of course, at a time when Victorian England was becoming increasingly aware of the problems of disease, of the health of the poor and of the need to raise standards of sanitation.

Mathias worked hard. In addition to his clinical work, he taught hygiene and exercise regimes to groups of teachers and others. In 1857, he was a key founder of the Ladies Sanitary Association that over the next 30 years was to distribute two million pamphlets on hygiene and similar topics. He also produced many articles and books, one of which, on the *Gymnastic Exercises* of Per Ling, was to run to seven editions by 1887 (Roulet 1892; Reynolds 1990).

The Roth Children: Their Early Education

It was in this busy medical household that the Roth children grew up. Influenced by their father's example and with his encouragement, four of the sons were became doctors and were strongly attracted to public health and the value of physical exercise. Mathias had firm views on the importance of education and again applied his professional ideas of exercise to his children. Games were discouraged in preference to gymnastics. The boys went barefoot for much of the time and led rather spartan lives. Caning was frequent, a cane being kept in each room. Reading later accounts of their schooldays, one can perhaps sympathise a little with their father, working long hours and no longer young, in trying to control his boisterous sons (FN Roth 1922).

The Roth boys were educated at University College School in London and most at schools in France and Germany. The girls were educated at home. The Roths were Jewish in origin but Mathias no longer practised his religion. Under the influence of their mother, the children sometimes

The Family Background and Achievements of Walter Edmund Roth

Figure 2.1 Henry Ling Roth (1855–1925) (Reproduced with the permission of Michael Bennett)

Figure 2.2 Felix Norman Roth (1857–1921) (Reproduced with the permission of Michael Bennett)

Figure 2.3 Reuter Emerich Roth (1858–1924) (Reproduced with the permission of the late Jane Roth)

Figure 2.4 Walter Edmund Roth (1861–1933) (Reproduced with the permission of Michael Bennett)

attended church, but religion seems to have played little part in their lives. Yet Walter was later to enjoy good relations with many missionaries and church leaders. Both he and his older brother Reuter became Freemasons, Walter joining while at Oxford University.

Bernard Mathias Roth

The first child, Bernard (1853–1915), trained at University College Hospital and worked in Paris, Brussels, Vienna and Berlin before joining and later succeeding his father in his practice, where he was to remain for 27 years, becoming a prominent orthopaedic surgeon. Bernard was similarly interested in homoeopathy and in problems of public hygiene. He published various papers and books, including *The Treatment of Lateral Curvature of the Spine* (1889).

Bernard also became interested in early British coins and published on the subject. A Vice-President of the British Numismatic Society, he was elected Fellow of the Society of Antiquaries and built a large collection that, after his death, took three days to auction.

Henry Ling Roth

The second son, Henry (1855–1925), studied natural history and philosophy in Germany then visited British Guiana, now Guyana. He spent 1876 and 1877 farming in Russia and wrote the book *Agriculture and Peasantry of Eastern Russia* (1878), his first work of an anthropological nature.

From 1878, Henry was in Queensland investigating the sugar industry on behalf of a group of English businessmen. Returning to Europe in 1883, he wrote on farming practices in south-east France, where his parents would retire in 1888. Throughout the 1880s, Henry wrote various papers on sugar cane (climate, indentured labour, diseases and parasites, and the history of cane) but increasingly, his interest was shifting to anthropology.

Henry then worked for the Bankfield Museum, Halifax, part time from 1890 and full time as Keeper from 1912, and improved greatly the museum's exhibitions and educational programmes. His writing began in earnest in 1890 with *The Aborigines of Tasmania*, which became a standard work for over 50 years. In 1896, he published *The Natives of Sarawak and British North Borneo*, drawing upon the papers of Hugh Brooke Low, and, in 1903, *Great Benin*, based on the letters and diaries of his brother Felix. In 1906, his numismatic book appeared, *Yorkshire Coiners 1767–1783*, and, in 1908, *The Discovery and Settlement of Port*

Mackay, Queensland. He wrote numerous papers, mainly on crafts and material culture, in the fields of anthropology and local history.

In 1917, Henry published a series of papers describing types of archaeological and ethnographic weaving looms. These papers, reprinted in book form in 1918 under the title *Studies in Primitive Looms*, became a standard work which was still required reading in 1951 for anthropology students at Cambridge.

For much of his anthropological career, Henry's role was that of armchair ethnologist, collating data from fieldworkers, especially on material culture and technology, and re-working this information into broader comprehensible groupings. He kept in touch with his brother Walter, and drew on Walter's field knowledge, in both Australia and British Guiana, for his own museum work and papers.

Felix Norman Roth

The third son, Felix (1857–1921), chose a career in marine engineering and spent 16 years in vessels sailing between England and South Africa and in the Pacific. Much of his time was spent as Chief Engineer in vessels plying along the Queensland coast and to New Guinea, rising to Superintendent Engineer. In 1888, however, he decided to change to medicine and enrolled for seven months at the Macquarie Street Infirmary, Sydney, before returning to London to complete his training.

In 1892, Felix was appointed to the Colonial Service as a medical officer, based in southern Nigeria and, in 1894, was attached to the Benin Expedition (see Chapter 4 in this volume). Afterwards, he returned to his post as medical officer and sometimes acting vice-consul but the tropical Nigerian coastal region took a heavy toll on his health and, in 1898, he was invalided home. In 1901, he was appointed house surgeon to St Mary's Hospital.

Felix's few publications were limited to short notes on medicine, a joint ethnographic paper on southern Nigeria and his reminiscences as an 'Engineer Doctor' (FN Roth 1922).

Reuter Emerich Roth

The fourth son, Reuter (1858–1924), qualified as a doctor in 1881 and moved to Sydney to practise. Like his father, he was interested in public health and the exercise theories expounded by Per Ling, and introduced his ideas to Australia. He lectured for many years at Sydney Technical College and focused on the practical health requirements of schools, from building and school furniture design to hygiene.

Appointed medical inspector in the Department of Public Instruction, he provided advice to schools on exercise regimes for pupils.

Reuter helped establish what is now the physiotherapy department of the Royal Prince Alfred Hospital, where he served as honorary medical officer until 1918. In 1888, he formed the Ladies Sanitary Association in Sydney, as his father had done in London, and became its honorary secretary. He was involved as a founder and held key offices in a number of important organisations, notably St John's Ambulance, Red Cross and the Royal Life Saving Association.

As a schoolboy, Reuter developed an interest in the army, joining the City of London Rifle Brigade Cadet Corps and, in 1874, the Artists' Rifles. In 1890, he was appointed captain-surgeon to the New South Wales Public Schools Cadet Force.

Reuter served with distinction in the Boer War, being mentioned in dispatches and awarded the Distinguished Service Order. On his return to Australia he was appointed principal medical officer of Commonwealth forces in New South Wales. During the First World War he served with equal distinction in Gallipoli, Egypt and France, being promoted to colonel and Deputy Director of Medical Services in 1916. Wounded later that year he was invalided home to an administrative appointment. Reuter retired in 1921 with the rank of honorary brigadier-general, and died in Noumea while on a diplomatic mission.

During his military career, Reuter was described as 'energetic, efficient and respected for his ability to delegate and consult' (Walker 1988:462–63). He was twice mentioned in dispatches and made a Companion of the Order of St Michael and St George in 1917. He had earlier been appointed a Knight of Grace in the Order of St John of Jerusalem for his work with the Ambulance Brigade.

Reuter made valuable organisational contributions to Australian public health and medicine. His few writings were confined to these interests. He was close to his brother Walter, and gave him significant support during his years in Australia.

Other Daughters and Younger Sons

The fifth son, Walter Edmund, is discussed separately later in this chapter. Of the two youngest brothers, Richard Cuvier (1863–1937) spent much of his adult life in a medical institution. Alfred Lawrence (1866–87) enlisted in 1887 in the Canadian North-West Mounted Police, giving his background as 'medical student'. Appointed a hospital steward, he died of typhoid fever at Regina in December. Had he survived, he too, no doubt, would have become a doctor.

Of the two daughters of Mathias, Julia Anna (1854–1935?) remained as her mother's companion until her death in 1907. Her sister, Edith May (1868–1959), became an accomplished portrait painter, exhibiting her work frequently at the Royal Academy from 1897 to 1925. Anthropologists know her best, however, for her illustrations of the 1890 first edition of Henry's *Aborigines of Tasmania*.

Walter Edmund Roth

Walter (1861–1933) studied natural sciences at University College, being awarded a Silver Medal in Zoology and Comparative Anatomy, then at Oxford University in preparation for a medical career. At Oxford, he became aware of anthropology at the Pitt Rivers Museum, before returning to London, in 1884, to begin medical training at St Thomas's Hospital.

In 1886, Walter also enrolled as a law student but, late in 1887, suspended his studies in both law and medicine and moved to Australia. For the next few years, he taught at Brisbane and Sydney grammar schools and was the Foundation Director of the South Australian School of Mines in Adelaide. Early in 1891, however, Walter resumed his medical training at St Thomas's, returning to Sydney in mid-1892 to be a locum for his brother Reuter, and then, throughout 1893, in a medical partnership in Young, New South Wales.

Even before he qualified, Walter was writing on public health. In 1884, he published in the *British Medical Journal* on the school hygiene exhibits at the International Health Exhibition in London, in which his father's displays figured prominently. In 1886, he published *The Elements of School Hygiene*, drawing heavily, no doubt, on his father's work. The bibliography alone ran to some 700 references. This was favourably reviewed in the *British Medical Journal*.

Theatre

Walter then focused on public theatres, publishing two papers, 'Fires in theatres' (1887) and 'Hygiene of the theatre' (1888), with the whimsical subtitle of 'Histrionic hygiene', and, in early 1888, a book, *Theatre Hygiene* (1888a), dedicated to his brother Alfred, which sought to set standards of construction, fire safety and hygiene. He lectured at the Sydney Technical College and gave a paper at the foundation meeting, in 1888, of the Australasian Association for the Advancement of Science, which promptly set up a committee, including Walter, 'to consider certain points in the Construction and Hygienic Requirements of Places of Amusement in Sydney' (*Report of the AAAS* 1889:xxxiii). Walter's interest in theatres led to his being appointed honorary surgeon to the

Imperial Opera House and Her Majesty's Theatre, Sydney. However, his links with the theatre declined as his interests shifted elsewhere and his work on theatre hygiene gained little Australian recognition.

Numismatics

Soon after his arrival in Sydney in 1887, Walter's interests took a turn that marked his first real involvement with material culture. He built a large collection of Australian coins, tokens and medals, which, in 1893, he sold to David Scott Mitchell. When Mitchell's historical collections later passed to the State Library to form the Mitchell Library, the numismatic collection was included.

Walter wrote a catalogue of tokens (1893?) and, jointly with Arthur Basset Hull, began a history of early Australian coinage (1899). These unpublished manuscripts formed the major resource for the handbook *Australasian Tokens and Coins*, by Arthur Andrews, published by the Mitchell Library in 1921. Later writers (for example, Myatt & Hanley 1982) also drew on these texts and on Walter's 1895 series of popular articles in the *Queenslander* on 'A numismatic history of Australia'.

Although by 1900 Walter's interests had shifted elsewhere, his contributions to Australian numismatics proved significant. It is unlikely that there would have been a numismatic collection in the Mitchell Library if David Scott Mitchell had not acquired the Roth collection. There would then have been no 1921 catalogue. Furthermore, Andrews relied heavily on Walter's, and to a lesser extent, Hull's writings. His handbook, and the history of Australian numismatics, would have been far poorer without these mainly unpublished sources (Reynolds 2003, 2004).

Medicine

This early phase in Walter's career ended in 1893. He had been very active in Young, serving as locum to his senior partner and medical officer to the hospital and giving classes in first aid and home nursing for the St John's Ambulance Association, which made him an honorary life member early in the year. It would seem, however, that a country town offered too little for the energetic and ambitious Walter.

In November, he suddenly left Young, despite the high local regard in which he was held, to sail as a ship's doctor to China and Japan and offered his services to the latter in the Sino-Japanese War that had erupted. This offer was refused, and by March 1894, he was back in Brisbane, where he published his impressions of life and culture in these two countries.

The second phase in Walter's career was his work in Queensland. In April 1894, he was appointed surgeon to the hospital at Boulia and subsequently at Cloncurry and Normanton. The demands of his professional work in Boulia were very light, leaving him free to devote time to the study of local Aboriginal language and culture. He continued this study at the other centres. His training in biology and medicine, and the powers of observation and clear description that these had encouraged, proved invaluable. The result was his 1897 book, *Ethnological Studies among the North-West-Central Queensland Aborigines*.

Northern Protector of Aboriginals, Queensland

In 1897, the Queensland Government created the *Aboriginals Protection and Restriction of the Sale of Opium Act*, and Walter was appointed Protector of Aboriginals for the Northern and Central Divisions of the State and based in Cooktown. In addition to applying the Act, he was also to provide medical services and submit scientific reports on the Aborigines. Archibald Meston was appointed Southern Protector, to be based in Brisbane. The two Protectors answered to the Home Secretary, initially through William Parry-Okeden as overall Queensland Protector, a post he held in addition to his substantive responsibility as Police Commissioner. Parry-Okeden had met Walter in Cloncurry and had been instrumental in his appointment as Protector. Magistrates and police were appointed as local protectors answerable to the two new Protectors.

The Act was not well received by employers and others who saw it as an impediment to their dealings with Aborigines. As is all too common, their complaints often took the form of personal attacks on the Protector. Since the Act had been created to curb the illicit sale of grog and opium, the exploitation of Aborigines in employment and their sexual abuse, the potential for conflict was there from the outset. At this period, the Far North was not the peaceful region it is today. Gold miners, pearl-fishing crews and station owners were often harsh in their dealings with Aborigines. Aboriginal employees were often cheated out of their wages on stations and vessels. Someone strong was needed to apply the new Act, and Walter Roth appears to have been an appropriate choice.

Venereal disease and the trade in opium and grog were widespread and were closely associated with the prostitution of Aboriginal women to Chinese and Europeans. The protection of neglected children, especially those of only part-Aboriginal parentage, was again the responsibility of the Protectors.

Walter Roth's Approach to his Work. Walter embarked on his new role with energy and enthusiasm. He travelled widely throughout the region, spending up to eight months in the field annually, and dealt with the substantial volume of work generated by the new legislation. He also sent to Brisbane a steady stream of scientific reports on the

Aboriginal communities he visited. In 1900, he was given a vessel, the *Melbidir*, to help him patrol more effectively the pearl-fishing industry and to assist in his touring work.

Walter found the mission stations keen to assist, especially with the protection of children in need of care. His work included inspecting their activities and assisting them in practical matters, such as the freighting of much-needed rations and equipment via the *Melbidir*. He was also very much involved in the creation of reserves around Aboriginal communities to safeguard important subsistence resources against destruction by pastoralists, timber-getters and commercial fishermen.

With the encouragement of the Minister, Justin Foxton, Walter began to collate his scientific reports for publication as Bulletins. The first eight were submitted to Parliament and were published between 1901 and 1906. The remaining 10 were published by the Australian Museum between 1907 and 1910. The 18 Bulletins did not appear in book form, however, until 1984 (MacIntyre 1984).

Chief Protector, Queensland; WA Royal Commissioner

In March 1904, Walter was appointed Chief Protector of Aboriginals based in Brisbane. Meston had ceased to be Southern Protector the previous December and Walter was now Protector for each district, in addition to his overall responsibilities as Chief. This was a period of financial stringency, and in 1903, Parliament had cut civil service salaries by 15%. Walter, with his enlarged workload, was financially no better off.

In August 1904, Walter was appointed to investigate, as sole Royal Commissioner, the treatment of Aborigines in Western Australia. His report (1905) to the Western Australian government generated much public debate and, as in Queensland, Walter was criticised by some for his findings and even for his motives. Although a new Protection Act resulted in late 1905, Walter was disappointed by the small amount of land allocated to reserves.

The Final Years in Queensland

By 1905, Walter was losing heart in Queensland. The financial constraints and his heavy workload must have taken their toll. He had also been under constant attack for some years from what he saw as hostile vested interests in the north, aired through Parliament. Though exonerated by a departmental enquiry, which cast serious doubts on the credibility of the complainants, he must have been under considerable pressure (Scott 1905).

Foxton and Parry-Okeden, with whom he worked very amicably, had both gone: Foxton to the Federal Parliament in 1903 and Parry-Okeden into retirement in 1905. Significantly, Walter tendered his resignation two days after Parry-Okeden's retirement. In his letter he noted that he had served for a continuous seven and a half years without leave. Although, in response to an appeal from the Council of Churches, he withdrew his resignation, he had clearly lost his enthusiasm for his work and felt discouraged by the attitude of his political masters.

In 1906, Walter was again attacked in Parliament and must have noted with concern the obvious lack of support from his own minister. In March, he wrote, 'vested interests are becoming too strong for me, & I am beginning to feel disheartened' (Mitchell Library ML MSS 1131). In June, he resigned and left Queensland and subsequently Australia.

Walter brought to the position of Protector, skills, energy and a humanitarian approach that were largely unmatched by his successors. He was given a very difficult job of applying a new Protection Act, with little guidance and limited resources and expected to undertake medical and scientific duties in addition. Despite all the difficulties, he established a workable system and helped greatly to reduce the worst excesses of exploitation. Naturally, he made mistakes, but often those for which he was criticised were not of his making.

British Guiana

The year 1907 marked the start of the third phase in Walter's career, his work in British Guiana. Until his retirement in 1928, he served as a medical magistrate, district commissioner and protector of indigenous Indians. In 1910, he helped draft the Aboriginal Protection *Ordinance*. He also continued his anthropological fieldwork, visualising initially 'an ethnographic survey of the native tribes of British Guiana, somewhat along the lines I had already followed in … North Queensland' (WE Roth 1915:107). He wrote papers for anthropological journals overseas as well as for local consumption. The Smithsonian Institution published three of his monographs in 1915, 1924 and 1929.

In 1928, Walter was appointed Curator of the Georgetown Museum, a post his son Vincent later held. He was also Government Archivist. During this period, he translated many works by early explorers of the country, as he had done prior to 1928. Some were published, but at his death in 1933, he left 21 manuscripts.

Walter Roth, Anthropologist

In his anthropology career, Walter achieved the unusual distinction of international recognition in two separate fields, Australian Aboriginal studies and American Indian studies. The honours he received in recognition of his work included the award of the Clarke Medal in 1909 by the Royal Society of New South Wales, election to the anthropological societies of Berlin and Florence and corresponding member of the Royal Anthropological Institute in 1904, and honorary fellow of the latter in 1931 and sole life member of the American Anthropological Association in 1932.

His contributions to anthropology. Walter's research ranged from archaeology and linguistics to medical anthropology, but perhaps his strongest interest was in material culture and technology. He was a careful and painstaking fieldworker. His collecting, in Queensland alone, of some 600 plant specimens for herbarium identification is an indication of this. His drawings are simple but clear and his observations succinctly expressed. His work was strong on the technology of manufacture and usage of artefacts and on typology. It was less effective in his coverage of symbolic and social aspects of material culture.

As Protector in Queensland, Walter's publications were in the form of bulletins, each on a separate topic and collating data from his scientific reports. This approach was shaped not only by his interest in ethnographic surveys but also perhaps by the demands of his administrative responsibilities, which precluded his focusing all his attention on one area in order to produce a field monograph.

Even so, as a comparison with other Australian writers of the time shows, his work was outstanding. He also published promptly. Haddon's volume on Torres Strait material culture (1912) for example was more detailed, but it did not appear until 14 years after his return from the field.

Walter's work, both in Queensland and in Guyana, became the basic accounts on which subsequent anthropologists have relied, for his observations were sound. It is significant that, in tropical Queensland, material culture field studies, with few exceptions, did not begin again for some 60 years. Walter's work also included the amassing of comprehensive artefact collections. These he always placed in museums; they did not pass into private hands. His Australian material is mainly in the Queensland and Australian Museums. His Guyanan collections are in the British Museum, the Ethnographic Museum in Goteborg and the Smithsonian Institution in Washington. Unfortunately, the main collection in the museum in Guyana is no longer intact.

Conclusion

Walter's research reflected his upbringing. He worked hard and for long hours. His observation of detail (see for example Figure 2.5) and his clear reporting were what one would expect of a medical man

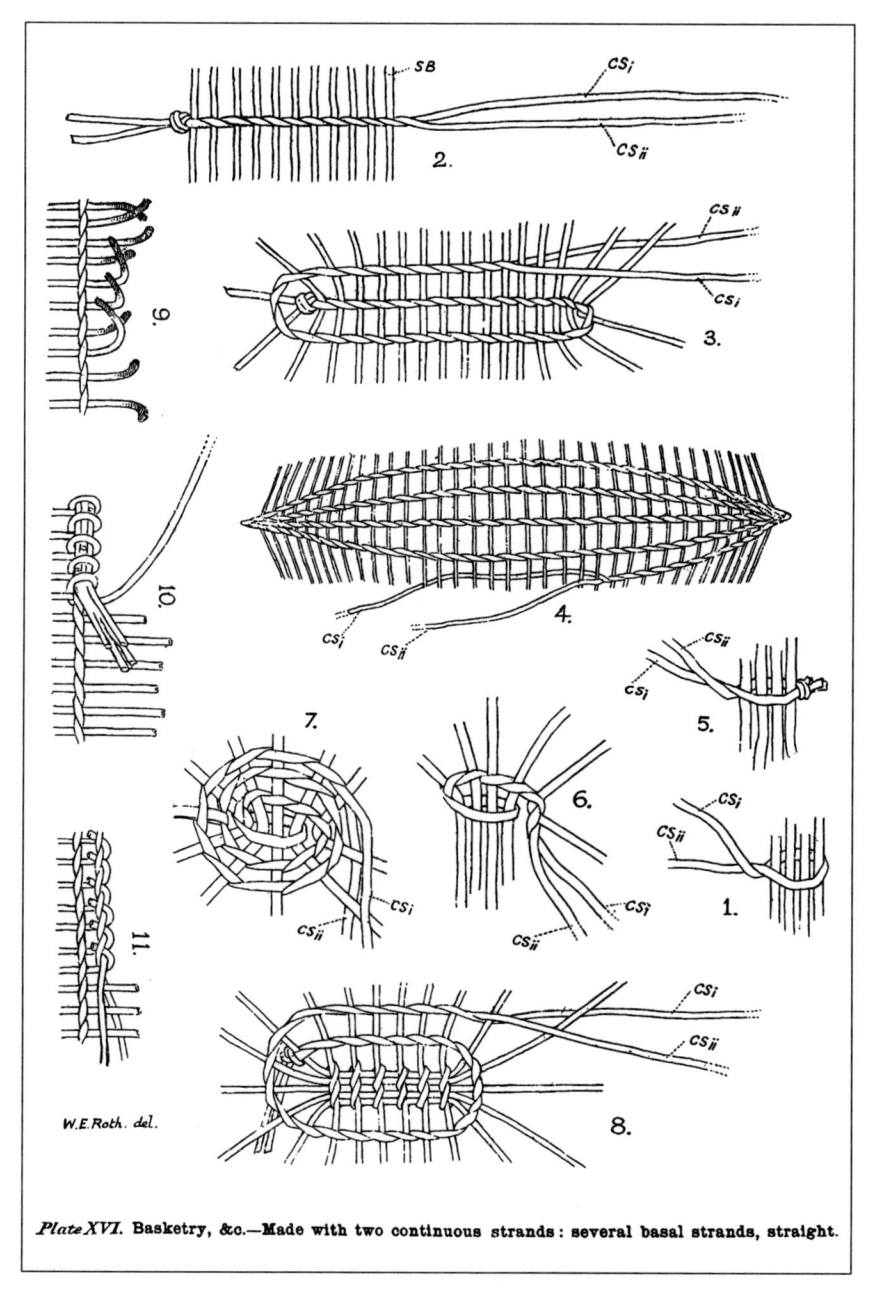

The Family Background and Achievements of Walter Edmund Roth | 53

Plate XVI. Basketry, &c.—Made with two continuous strands: several basal strands, straight.

Figure 2.5 Showing Walter's careful attention to detail. This is one of 19 plates he drew to illustrate his Bulletin (WE Roth 1901)

and a scientist. His interest in material culture, which began with his numismatic work, continued throughout his anthropology career. While he was not averse to receiving information from other observers, which he was careful to acknowledge, he was primarily a field observer himself. Theorising about anthropology did not seem to interest him; he preferred to observe and record.

Walter enjoyed teaching, both in schools and through the ambulance courses he gave in Young and again in North Queensland, as a surgeon and later Protector. It seems a pity that he did not move into a university where he could have passed on his anthropological knowledge. University life would also have had a stimulating effect on his thinking and his approach to his work. But this opportunity appears never to have been available to him.

Unlike his brother Henry, Walter was dedicated to fieldwork. His contributions to anthropology were significant, both in published data and in the building of collections, yet in Australia these were based on but a few years' research. A comparison of his Australian publications with the much more mature books he wrote in Guyana leads one to wonder what would have been his contribution to Australian anthropology had he stayed in this country. As it was, he documented the material cultures of his period and provided the baseline artefact collections now in our museums. Without his contributions, our knowledge of Queensland Aboriginal material cultures in the late 19th century would be sparse indeed.

Acknowledgments

This work was in part supported by an Australian Research Council Grant.

Works Cited

Andrews, Arthur (1921) *Australasian Tokens and Coins: A Handbook*, Sydney: Mitchell Library

Griffin, Helga M (1988) 'Roth, Henry Ling (1855–1925)', in *Australian Dictionary of Biography*, Vol 11, Melbourne: Melbourne University Press, 461–62

Haddon, AC (1912) *Reports of the Cambridge Anthropological Expedition to Torres Straits. Vol. IV Arts and Crafts*, Cambridge: Cambridge University Press

MacIntyre, KF (ed) (1984) *The Queensland Aborigines*, 3 vols (Facsimile edition of Walter E Roth's book and Bulletins), Perth: Hesperian Press

Myatt, Bill and Hanley, Tom (1982) *Australian Coins, Notes and Medals*, Melbourne: Castle Books

Report of the Australasian Association for the Advancement of Science (1889), Vol 1, Sydney: Australasian Association for the Advancement of Science

Reynolds, Barrie (2004) 'Walter Roth and the missing manuscript', *Journal of the Numismatic Association of Australia* 15, 52–63

———. (2003) 'The numismatic collection and papers of Dr. Walter Roth', unpublished report, Mitchell Library, Sydney, MLMSS 7378

Reynolds, Barrie (1990) 'Mathias Roth', Townsville: unpublished memoir
———. (1988) 'Roth, Walter Edmund (1861–1933)', in *Australian Dictionary of Biography*, Vol 11, Melbourne: Melbourne University Press, 463–64
Roth, Bernard (1889) *The Treatment of Lateral Curvature of the Spine with Appendix on the Treatment of Flat Foot*, no publication details
Roth, F Norman (1922) (Ed by Roth, H Ling) 'Some experiences of an engineer doctor', 'With an introduction on our schooldays' by HLR, Halifax: privately reprinted from the *Halifax Courier & Guardian*
Roth, Henry Ling (1918) *Studies in Primitive Looms*, Halifax: F King & Sons
———. (1908) *The Discovery and Settlement of Port Mackay, Queensland*, Halifax: F King & Sons
———. (1906) *The Yorkshire Coiners 1767–1783*, Halifax: F King & Sons
———. (1903) *Great Benin: Its Customs, Art and Horrors*, Halifax: F King & Sons
———. (1896) *The Natives of Sarawak and British North Borneo*, London: Truslove & Hanson
———. (1890) *The Aborigines of Tasmania*, London: Kegan Paul, Trench, Trubner & Co
———. (1878) *A Sketch of the Agriculture and Peasantry of Eastern Russia*, London: Baillière, Tindall, & Cox
Roth, Mathias (1887) *Gymnastic Exercises Without Apparatus, According to Ling's System*, 7th edn, London: AN Myers
Roth, Walter E (1929) *Additional Studies of the Arts, Crafts, and Customs of the Guiana Indians with Special Reference to those of Southern British Guiana*, Bulletin 91, Bureau of American Ethnology, Washington: Smithsonian Institution
———. (1924) *An Introductory Study of the Arts, Crafts, and Customs of the Guiana Indians*, 38th Annual Report, Bureau of American Ethnology, Washington: Government Printing Office, 23–745
———. (1915) *An Inquiry into the Animism and Folk-Lore of the Guiana Indians*, 0th Annual Report, Bureau of American Ethnology, Washington: Government Printing Office, 103–396
———. (1905) *Royal Commission on the Condition of the Natives: Report*, Perth: Government Printer
———. (1901) 'String, and other forms of strand: basketry-, woven bag-, and net-work', *North Queensland Ethnography Bulletin No 1*, Brisbane: Government Printer (This is the first of 18 *Bulletins* published between 1901 and 1910.)
———. (1897) *Ethnological Studies among the North-West-Central Queensland Aborigines*, Brisbane: Government Printer
———. (1895) 'A numismatic history of Australia', 11 chapters, Brisbane: *The Queenslander*
———. (1894) 'The land of chrysanthemums', 8 parts, Brisbane: *The Queenslander*
———. (1893?) 'Catalogue of Australian tokens', unpublished text, Mitchell Library, Sydney, ML.B226
———. (1889) 'Theatre hygiene', *Proceedings of the Australasian Association for the Advancement of Science*, Vol I, 514–25
———. (1888a) *Theatre Hygiene*, London: Baillière, Tindall, and Cox
———. (1888b) 'Some suggestions and materials for a study of the hygiene of the theatre', *The Sanitary Record*, IX, 99–103
———. (1887) 'Fires in theatres', *The Sanitary Record* VIII, 527–30
———. (1886) *The Elements of School Hygiene*, London: Baillière, Tindall, and Cox
Roth, WE and Hull, AF Basset (1899) 'Early Australian coinage and catalogue of Australian coins and tokens', Sydney: Dixson Library, DL.ADD.39B
Roulet, Gustave (1892) *Docteur Mathias Roth, M.D.*, Geneva: Haussmann & Lips
Scott, WJ (1905) *Report by the Under Secretary for Public Lands and Dr. Roth re Complaints Against Dr. Roth, Chief Protector of Aboriginals*, Brisbane: Government Printer
Walker, DR (1988) 'Roth, Reuter Emerich (1858–1925)', in *Australian Dictionary of Biography*, Vol 11, Melbourne: Melbourne University Press, 462–63

PART 2

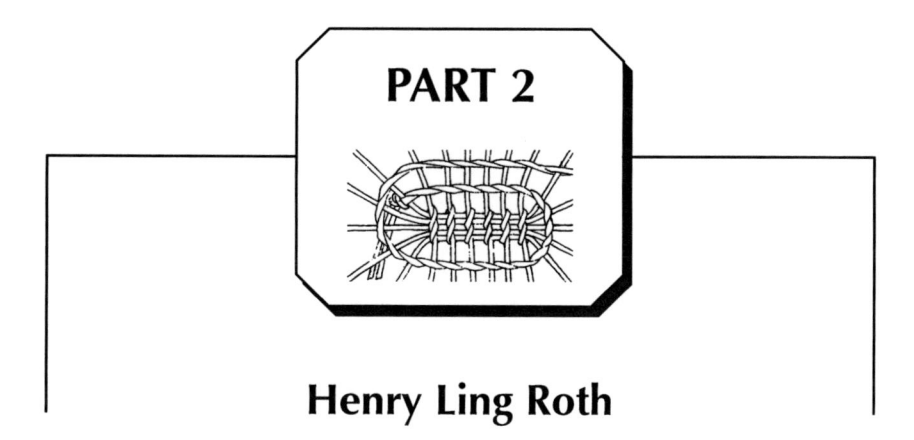

Henry Ling Roth

CHAPTER 3

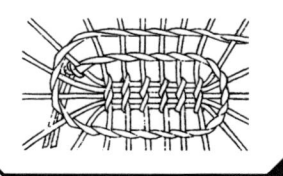

Henry Ling Roth: *The Natives of Sarawak and British North Borneo*

Robert Hampson

Origins

When Hugh Brooke Low died in 1887 at the early age of 38, he left behind, among his effects, a parcel of papers, written in pencil, eaten by insects and damaged by damp. This 'fragmentary and half-obliterated' manuscript, whose writing was so fine that it had to be read with a magnifying glass, was given to Henry Ling Roth by the celebrated anthropologist EB Tylor (Tylor 1892:134). Roth worked up 'a fair portion' of this manuscript and published the transcription as two articles in the *Journal of the Anthropological Institute* (Roth 1892, 1893).[1] The manuscript also became the basis of Roth's *The Natives of Sarawak and British North Borneo* (1896a).

Low was born in Labuan on 12 May 1849. He was the son of Hugh Low, then Colonial Secretary to the newly appointed Governor of Labuan, Sir James Brooke. Hugh Low, a botanist, had gone out to Sarawak in 1845 to collect plants for his father's nursery in London and had stayed on. His wife, Catherine, was the daughter of William Napier, the Lieutenant Governor of Labuan. Hugh Brooke Low was clearly born into the colonial official class. In 1869, however, he failed the examination for the Indian Civil Service. He joined the Sarawak Government Service instead, and was appointed by the new Raja of Sarawak, Sir Charles Brooke, to a station on the Rejang River, where he spent the next 18 years of his comparatively short life.[2] Here he studied the Dyak and Kayan peoples, made a collection of local artefacts and

Figure 3.1 The cover of the original subscription flyer for *The Natives of Sarawak and British North Borneo*

worked on his manuscript. When Roth transcribed this manuscript, he was already the author of *A Sketch of the Agriculture and Peasantry of Eastern Russia* (1878) and *The Aborigines of Tasmania* (1890).

The Natives of Sarawak and British North Borneo thus has a dual origin, but it can also be seen to have a double textual origin in another sense. To begin with, it can be related to the textual tradition established by William Marsden's *The History of Sumatra* (1783) and Stamford Raffles's *The History of Java* (1817). *The History of Sumatra* begins with brief chapters on the geography, climate, geographical features, flora and fauna of Sumatra before turning to the human inhabitants and civil society of the island. Raffles, who took Marsden's work as his model, similarly begins with a mapping of Java and an account of its seasons, flora and fauna, before turning to its population; their agriculture, manufacture and handicrafts; their 'intellectual and moral character'; their institutions and government; and their 'usages and customs' (Raffles 1817:244). Marsden's work was explicitly and self-consciously connected to a European Enlightenment 'world of science' (Marsden 1783:I, 373) and is marked by a scientific concern for evidence. Marsden had spent nine years in Sumatra (1770–79), but he wrote his *History* in London as part of Sir Joseph Banks's scientific circle. Raffles spent five years in Java (1811–16), but took advantage of his position as Lieutenant Governor to reactivate a network of scholarly societies in Batavia and to organise a systematic survey of the island. *The Natives of Sarawak and British North Borneo*, by comparison, is based on a manuscript begun by Low in isolation from learned circles and then augmented and completed by Roth 'in [his] evening leisure' at Bankfield Museum in Halifax, far away from centres of scientific research (Roth 1896a:xlii). The second textual origin derives from the book's reliance on existing reports and documents. Although Hugh Brooke Low had ample opportunity to study the local Dyak and Kayan peoples from his station on the Rejang River, and also had experience of other parts of the territory under the control of the Raja of Sarawak, he was obliged to draw heavily on 'travellers' statements' (Roth 1896a:xli) and on missionary publications (especially those of the Reverend W Crossland) for information about Sarawak and North Borneo, as Roth notes in his Introduction. Roth, in turn, when he took over the task of turning the manuscript into a book, could not draw on first-hand experience of Sarawak and British North Borneo but augmented the text through library research. He is, accordingly, not so much the author of the work as, in his own words, 'the compiler' (Roth 1896a:xxi) of information from a range of sources.

In compiling the book, Roth could draw on the model he had followed in *The Aborigines of Tasmania*, and would follow again in *Great Benin: Its Customs, Art and Horrors* (1903). In his Preface to *The Aborigines of*

Tasmania, Tylor praised Roth for his 'long and conscientious labour', bringing together, with 'an approach to absolute completeness', information 'scattered through voyages, histories, colonial documents, and other sources from which first-hand information, however fragmentary, could be obtained' (Roth 1899:v, vii). He followed the same method with the new work and used similar categories to organise his material.

Difficulties

The Natives of Sarawak and British North Borneo begins with an account of the geographical distribution of the different peoples of the region – Land Dyaks, Sea Dyaks, Milanaus, Kayans, Muruts, Ukits, Bisayans and so on – derived initially from the work of FRO Maxwell, formerly Chief Resident. This chapter is characterised by a taxonomic drive to distinguish and categorise the different peoples on the basis of culture and ethnicity that is constantly being thwarted. One of the difficulties Roth faces in trying to map the distribution of peoples is suggested by the foundation myth of the Sennah people, which is a story of successive migrations and settlements. In his Introduction, Roth noted another difficulty: 'occasionally, … where different tribes are in close neighbourship, travellers in their narratives run on without stating to which tribes their remarks apply' (Roth 1896a:xii). Another, more basic difficulty is suggested by Maxwell: 'I have only seen one Ukit and he was a chief, a well-built man about 5 feet 8 inches high, slim, and with a rather refined face and a rather more prominent nose than the Dyak, Malay, or Kayan; but this characteristic may have been peculiar to the man' (Roth 1896a:19). Maxwell raises the question of the representative nature of the sample experienced by the European observer, and whether qualities are specific to individuals or, indeed, characteristic of a group.

The photographs that accompany the text concretise this issue and pass it on to the reader. The group of 'Sea Dyaks' (Figure 3.2) (Roth 1896a:13), arranged like a public school sports-team photograph, challenges the reader to determine what is representative and what is individual – as well as what is characteristically Dyak; what is in response to being posed and photographed by a European colonial official, and what is the result of the necessarily long exposure time. The photograph of a group of Sakarang women (Figure 3.3) contains another challenge to Roth's effort. The caption states: 'The one in the centre is wearing a silver coronet designed by Mr F. R. O. Maxwell. The women are fond of change, and once a deputation waited upon him to invent a new head gear, and for a time his design was very fashionable and spread up and down the river' (Roth 1896a:4). What looks like

BATANG LUPAR (?) SEA DYAKS. (Sir Hugh Low Coll.)

Figure 3.2 Photograph of 'Sea Dyaks' from *The Natives of Sarawak and British North Borneo*

SAKARANG WOMEN.
The one in the centre is wearing a silver coronet designed by Mr. F. R. O. Maxwell. The women are fond of change, and once a deputation waited upon him to ask him to invent a new head gear, and for a time his design was very fashionable and spread up and down the river. (Sir Hugh Low Coll.)

Figure 3.3 Photograph of Sakarang women from *The Natives of Sarawak and British North Borneo*

authentic local costume in an ethnographic photograph turns out to be designed by the British Resident. Culture is not static, but assimilative and open to dialogue with other cultures – including (as 20th century anthropology came to realise) those which seek to record it.

Other difficulties are suggested by the contradictory accounts of the Punans. According to JAI Hose, they are nomadic hunter-gatherers who 'build no houses' and live in trees, but according to Spenser St John, they run up 'temporary huts' (Roth 1896a:16); they are the most primitive 'and furthest removed from civilisation' (Roth 1896a:17), but also, 'having intermarried with the Dyaks, they have gained an idea of property and supply their new acquirements [sic] by working jungle produce with assiduity' (Roth 1896a:16). The taxonomy assumes essential differences, but the 'first-hand' accounts bring in an historical dimension which includes the specific time and place of the European's observation, as well as contact (and even intermarriage) with other peoples on the part of the observed. From the various accounts Roth includes, it is quite evident that intermarriage between the different groups – and intermarriage with Malays and Chinese – is very common. The gauge of 'civilisation' is also problematic. For the European sources, it is clearly building houses or having 'an idea of property', but for the local informants the distinctive sign is 'to eat rice and use a blanket' (Roth 1896a:16). Roth, in a discreet footnote, also reveals another difficulty faced by the armchair anthropologist trying to reconcile different accounts: 'There is every probability that the Punans, Pakatans, and Ukits are all one and the same people' (Roth 1896a:19). Nevertheless, despite all these uncertainties and undecidables, the chapter ends with a detailed list of tribes in Borneo, differentiating 20 major groupings.

Anthropological Content

The second chapter then offers a short essay on the 'misuse of the word "Dyak"'. It begins with Mundy's record of James Brooke's view that 'though all the wild people of Borneo are by Europeans called Dyaks, the name properly is only applicable to one particular class inhabiting parts of the north western coast and the mountains of the interior' (Roth 1896a:39). This is challenged by Charles Brooke's later observation that 'the generic term *Dyak* … simply means *inland*' (Roth 1896a:39) and more radically by the suggestion that 'dayah' in the Sarawak dialect simply means 'man'.[3] The term 'Dyak' seems to have been in use in Batavia and the Dutch East Indies by 1780, but the distinction between Land Dyaks and Sea Dyaks was first made by James Brooke.[4] Despite this discussion of the problematic nature of the term, however, Roth uses it freely in the rest of the book.

The next two chapters are devoted to the 'physique' of the various peoples and what is described as 'character notes and sketches'. The former includes observations such as Mr Grant's praise of Land Dyaks ('a step as sure as that of a Highland pony' [Roth 1896a:45]) or Lieutenant Marryat's differently appreciative view of Land Dyak women: 'They have good eyes, good teeth, and good hair; – more than good: I may say splendid; – and they have good manners, and know how to make use of their eyes' (Roth 1896a:46). It concludes with tables of measurements of height and varieties of skin colour. As the title suggests, the latter chapter, 'Character notes and sketches', is an assemblage of anecdotes from various sources designed to illustrate the 'character' of various peoples. It concludes with a final section on 'Amoking', which begins with Charles Brooke's observation ('I have never yet known a case of a Dyak amoking') and then follows it with a couple of cases of Dyak amok. As we have seen with the attempt to offer a taxonomy of the different peoples of the region, one of the problems with armchair anthropology is the difficulty of reconciling or even negotiating between contradictory accounts. Roth's solution in this volume is, as in this instance, simply to provide the contradictory accounts and to display the contesting interpretations.

Subsequent chapters address themselves to more recognisably anthropological concerns: beliefs and superstitions surrounding pregnancy and childbirth (Chapter V); customs and practices relating to courtship and marriage (Chapter VI), including tables of 'prohibited degrees' (Roth 1896a:122); customs and beliefs relating to 'The disposal of the dead' (Chapter VII); religious beliefs (Chapter VIII); and feasts, festivals and dancing (Chapter IX). Again, Roth makes explicit his necessary reliance on existing textual sources. Chapter VIII, for example, begins by reproducing the Reverend William Chalmers's paper on Land Dyak religion, followed by the Venerable Archdeacon J Perham's account of Sea Dyak gods. There is an obvious danger of bias, given these missionary sources. Chalmers, for example, starts his paper with the observation 'Were I asked what is the religion of the Land Dyaks, I should say none worthy of the name', before offering a detailed account of four major spirits, numerous minor spirits and a complex taxonomy of ghosts – those who died natural deaths, those who died accidentally, women who died in childbirth, men who were killed in war and lost their heads. Perham's account of the Sea Dyaks not only distinguishes between spirits who appear in dreams and spirits who appear in animal form, but also offers a detailed account of sacrifices, burial rites and omens – and the mythology that explains the reading of sacred birds as omens. These two accounts produce quite different impressions of Land Dyak and Sea Dyak religions, but whether that difference is substantive or produced by the different approaches of Chalmers and Perham is impossible to determine. This raises an issue about observation and interpretation with which Roth does not engage.

Later chapters deal with medicine men and women (X); pathology (XI); legends (XII); daily life (XIII); agriculture, land tenure and domestic animals (XIV); and hunting and fishing (XV). The second volume is more diverse with chapters on 'habitations' (XVI); weaving, dying and dress making (XVII); the intriguingly titled 'fashionable deformities' (XVIII); tattooing (XIX); wars and weapons (XX); headhunting (XXI); blowpipes and poisons (XXII); slaves, captives and human sacrifice (XXIII); government, trade, mensuration and natural productions (XXIV); boating, swimming and riding (XXV); music (XXVI); and language, names and colours (XXVII). The chapter on pathology provides a survey of common diseases (fevers, cholera, smallpox) and various treatments (including bleeding, cupping and cauterising). However, the splitting of 'pathology' from the account of medicine men and women represents a very obvious European imposition of categories. As Roth observes, 'in the minds of the natives there is no real distinction between the magic of their doctors and true medical knowledge' (Roth 1896a:289). The various rituals described in the chapter on medicine men and women are as much part of the treatment of disease as processes such as bleeding, cupping and cauterising, which were also part of contemporary European medicine. As Archdeacon Perham puts it, with some lack of self-reflection: 'Where all rational conception of the causes of disease and of medicine is entirely absent, magical ceremonies, incantations, pretensions to supernatural powers in the cure of the sick have the whole field before them' (Roth 1896a:271).

Chapter X begins with various accounts of 'the Dyak theory of sickness'. In the Reverend Chalmers's account, this theory has three components: 'either that it is caused by the presence of evil spirits in the patient's body, or that he has been struck by one of them or that one of them has … enticed his soul out of his body' (Roth 1896a:260). Mr Grant offers a simpler formulation: 'The doctrine of sickness held by all the Dyaks is that it is caused by the absence of "principle of life", *Semangat*, which has been abstracted from the body of the patient by an inimical *antu*. The Land Dyaks seem to think that a man has but one *Semungat* [sic]' (Roth 1896a:264). This bears comparison with James Brooke's suggestion that Sea Dyaks regard 'a sick person as being possessed with an evil spirit' (Roth 1896a:266), but clashes somewhat with Brooke Low's account: 'The Dyaks believe that every individual has seven souls (*samangat*), and that when a person is sick one or more of these are in captivity, and must be reclaimed to effect a cure' (Roth 1896a:267). Apart from the obvious contradiction about the number of souls (which might be a variation between Land Dyak and Sea Dyak belief), there is also evident, in these different accounts, greater and lesser degrees of cultural translation: Chalmers Christianises his account by the use of the terms 'evil spirits' and 'soul'; Grant maintains the difference of Dyak belief by using Dyak terms. There is an obvious danger in translating *samangat* as 'soul' in that it might suggest a complete correspondence between the two concepts. In the earlier chapter on religion, however, one of Roth's sources notes that, among Land Dyaks at least, 'many of them, at the present time, have no idea of the immortality of the soul' (Roth 1896a:217), while another observes the belief that 'the spirit is supposed to leave the body during dreams' (Roth 1896a:232).

The chapter carefully distinguishes the different roles of medicine men and medicine women. The Land Dyaks have (male) *daya beruri*, who deal with human sickness, and (female) *barich*, who are responsible for the health of the paddy. According to Brooke Low, the Sea Dyaks have (male) *manang laki*, (female) *manang indu* and *manang bali*. Brooke Low provides a detailed account of the role of the *manang bali*. The *manang bali* is a medicine man who wears female clothes, but also, 'before he can be permitted to assume female attire he is sexually disabled' (HL Roth 1896a:270). Subsequently, the *manang bali*'s 'chief aim in life is to copy female manners and habits' (Roth 1896a:270), and this includes sleeping with men and having a husband. Perham offers a different account. After noting that both men and women may become *manangs*, he observes: 'In former times, I believe, all *manangs* on their initiation assumed female attire for the rest of their lives; but it is rarely adopted now … and I have only met with one such' (HL Roth 1896a:282). Perham offers a theory that attempts to explain the single *manang bali* he encountered as a survival of an earlier custom. Perhaps his native informants were less forthcoming than those of Brooke Low. It is also interesting that the book text is less explicit than that published in the *Journal of the Anthropological Institute*. That text explains that the 'organ of penetration (*membrum virile*) is disabled' (Roth 1892:115). Similarly, where the chapter on 'fashionable deformities' deals with such things as teeth-filing and depilation, Brooke Low's text published in the journal included a detailed account of Dyak sexual aids: the *palang* and the *palang unus*. The former, which Brooke Low describes as 'the spritsail yard in the penis' is a bone or metal Prince Albert; the latter is a palm-fibre collar worn round the neck of the glans.

Strengths and Weaknesses

In his Preface to *The Natives of Sarawak and British North Borneo*, Andrew Lang observes: 'The writers quoted by Mr Ling Roth were not, or not usually, anthropologists who knew what to look for. And the worst of it is, that inquirers who know what to look for, are only too likely to find it, whether it is there or not' (Roth 1896a:ix). This pithy expression of what Lang terms 'the dilemma of anthropological evidence' – the untrained informant does not know what to look for or what questions to ask, whilst the trained observer is capable of merely 'reading his knowledge into the actual facts' (Roth 1896a:ix) – plays onto debates opened up 30 years earlier. In his essay for the volume celebrating Tylor's 75th birthday, *Anthropological Essays Presented to EB Tylor*, Lang notes that 'a fresh *scientific* interest in matters anthropological was "in the air"' in the 1860s when Tylor began his career (Lang 1907:1). Tylor's work had, indeed, been instrumental in developing this 'scientific' approach. His monograph, *Researches into the Early History of Mankind and the Development of Civilization* (1865) led to his major work on *Primitive Culture* (1871), which asserted from the outset 'the science of culture': 'the history of mankind is part and parcel of the history of nature, ... our thoughts, wills, and actions accord with laws as definite as those which govern the motion of waves, the combination of acids and bases, and the growth of plants and animals' (Tylor 1871:I, 2). For Tylor, culture is a 'complex whole' (Tylor 1871:1), and, despite the 'enormous complexity of evidence' and the 'imperfection of methods of observation' (Tylor 1871:3), the anthropologist should aim to show connections and 'elicit general principles of human action' (Tylor 1871:4). Tylor's basic model is explicitly Linnaean: 'the bow and arrow is a species, the habit of flattening children's skulls is a species. ... The geographical distribution of these things, and their transmission from region to region, have to be studied as the naturalist studies the geography of his botanical and zoological species' (Tylor 1871:7). Tylor's engagement with contemporary anthropology went beyond his own researches. Lang observes that Tylor 'has sent his pupils into many strange lands; they have been the field naturalists of human nature' (Lang 1907:1). More than that, Tylor, with his 'Notes and Queries on Anthropology' had also prepared 'catechisms for field anthropologists' (Lang 1907:3). In Lang's words, the problem was: 'Many intelligent European and American observers, among savages, are interested in, and desire to record, what they see and hear, but are not acquainted with what is already known to specialists, and are painfully vague in their terminology' (Lang 1907:3). In compiling *The Natives of Sarawak and British North Borneo*, Roth confronted (and made manifest) precisely this problem: a plethora of reports and documents by untrained observers, keen to record, but untrained and 'vague in their terminology'.

In his Preface, Lang notes that, 'as in his valuable work on the extinct Tasmanians', Roth has 'collected from every side what is essential to a knowledge of the habits, and history, and ethnology of the people of British Borneo' (Roth 1896a:viii). This is both the strength and the weakness of the book. Roth's Introduction subtly qualifies Lang's statement by observing that 'little is said on the great ethnological questions of origin, totems, and relationships' (Roth 1896a:xlii). In other words, Roth is aware that *The Natives of Sarawak and British North Borneo* does not address itself to current debates in ethnology. Instead, as he recognises, the book is an assemblage of data, a compilation of various accounts. To some extent, it positions itself as an example of salvage anthropology. Roth affirms that 'the natives are *not* inferior to Europeans, but different' (Roth 1896a:xix), but, at the same time he asks, 'Can they be raised to the condition of Europeans?' At other times, his inquiry (perhaps influenced by his work on Tasmania) operates within the conceptual framework of possible extinction, as he explicitly speculates which of the local peoples he is at such pains to taxonomise will survive.[5]

Roth's assemblage of data, then, is slightly at odds with the anthropology introduced by Tylor. Where Tylor treats culture as a 'complex whole', Roth is really working with an earlier agglomerative model. In his Introduction to Basil Hall Chamberlain's *Aino Folk Tales* (1888), for example, Tylor had first presented the task of anthropology in terms of the need to settle the Aino's 'physical connection with other Asiatic tribes' (Chamberlain 1888:v). Roth's attempt to provide a taxonomy of the different peoples of Sarawak and British North Borneo is clearly in line with this. However, when Tylor then turns to the Aino folktales, his concern is with 'the many touches of Aino ideas, morals, and customs, which their stories disclose' (Chamberlain 1888:vi). This repeats the concern with culture as 'knowledge, belief, art, morals, law, custom' which he had articulated at the start of *Primitive Culture* – and which Roth's various categories recognise. However, Roth makes no effort to make connections between informations or to judge between his informants. Roth, like Brooke Low, offers a descriptive anthropology, whereas Tylor emphasises an analytic purpose behind the accumulation of data. Indeed, when Tylor explains the 'complex network of civilisation' (Tylor 1871:16) by reference to the history of clothes and the development of language (Tylor 1871:17), he approaches a 20th century view of culture as a complex structure of significations, an intuition far beyond Roth's compilation.

Conclusion

The Natives of Sarawak and British North Borneo thus both contributes to and unconsciously enacts a critique of ethnography as 'a rising curve of cumulative findings'; it also suggests how the simple accumulation of ethnographic 'facts' can be seen as a kind of imperialist loot (Geertz 1973:25). In the 20th century, Clifford Geertz argued that the 'claim to attention' of the ethnographic account is not this capturing of 'primitive facts in faraway places', but rather the attempt to 'clarify what goes on in such places' and 'to bring us in touch with the lives of strangers' (Geertz 1973:16). Roth's ethnography seems to have a simpler, more instrumental purpose. In one of his appendices to *Great Benin*, he asserts that anthropology 'is essential to every civilised community which trades with, or is called upon to govern native communities' (Roth 1968:xix). He explains: 'a thorough knowledge of the native races ... can teach what methods of government and what forms of taxation are most suited to particular tribes, or to the stage of civilisation in which we find them' (Roth 1968:xix). This takes us back to the motives of Marsden and Raffles. It is very far from Tylor's scientific concern with laws and the 'general principles of human action'.

Notes

1. 'Negritoes in Borneo' (1896b), which was also included in the book, was Roth's own work.
2. Sir James Brooke, who became Raja of Sarawak in 1840, died in 1868 and was succeeded by his nephew, Charles. Sarawak became a British protectorate in 1888, and Charles was officially recognised as Raja by King Edward in 1904.
3. In the same way, '*aino*' in Aino simply means 'man'.
4. Radermacher uses the term 'Dajak' in 1780, whereas Valentijn (1726) and Buffon (1749) speak of 'Borneers' and 'inhabitants of Borneo', respectively (Roth 1896a:41). See Radermacher (1780).
5. He comments on the Land Dyaks: 'we may not be far wrong in holding the opinion that many generations of them cannot survive' (Roth 1896a:xx).

Works Cited

Chamberlain, Basil Hall (1888) *Aino Folk Tales*, London: The Folk-Lore Society
Geertz, Clifford (1973) *The Interpretation of Cultures*, New York: Basic Books
Lang, Andrew (1907) *Anthropological Essays Presented to EB Tylor*, Oxford: Clarendon Press
Marsden, William (1783) *The History of Sumatra*, reprint of 3rd edn, 1966, Kuala Lumpur: Oxford University Press
Radermacher, JCM (1780) *Beschrijving van het eiland Borneo*, Bataviaasch Genoots. d. Kunst on wetens
Raffles, Thomas Stamford (1817) *The History of Java*, reprinted 1965, Kuala Lumpur: Oxford University Press
Roth, Henry Ling (1903) *Great Benin: Its Customs, Art and Horrors*, Halifax: F King
———. (1899) *The Aborigines of Tasmania*, 2nd edn, Halifax
———. (1896a) *The Natives of Sarawak and British North Borneo*, 2 vols, London: Truslove & Hanson
———. (1896b) 'Negritoes in Borneo', *Journal of the Anthropological Institute* XXV, 262–71

Roth, Henry Ling (1893) *Journal of the Anthropological Institute* XXII, 22–64
———. (1892) 'The Natives of Borneo', *Journal of the Anthropological Institute* XXI, 110–37
———. (1890) *The Aborigines of Tasmania*, London: Kegan Paul, Trench, Trubner & Co
———. (1878) *A Sketch of the Agriculture and Peasantry of Eastern Russia*, London: Baillière, Tindall & Cox
Tylor, EB (1892) *Journal of the Anthropological Institute* XXI, 134
———. (1871) *Primitive Culture*, 2 vols, London: John Murray
———. (1865) *Researches into the Early History of Mankind and the Development of Civilization*, London: John Murray

CHAPTER 4

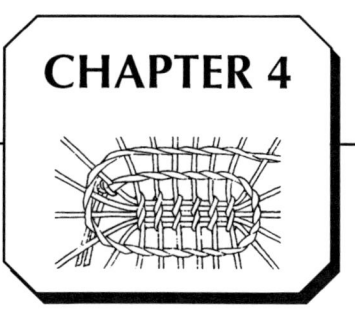

The Making of *Great Benin*: Felix Norman Roth and Henry Ling Roth[1]

Russell McDougall

The 1897 punitive expedition against Benin City was arguably one of the key events in the history of the British Empire and certainly pivotal in West African history. Ola Rotimi's tragic drama depicting the episode, *Ovonramwen Nogbaisi* (1974), is one of the best-known plays within Nigeria; there is also the pageant, *Oba Ovonramwen* (1996), Emwinma Ogieriakhi's dramatisation of the fall of Benin. The story has been told variously by European as well as Nigerian historians (Egharevba 1960; Ryder 1969; Home 1982). This chapter, however, is concerned with the contribution to the historical and ethnographic record by Henry Ling Roth (1855–1925) and his brother Felix Norman Roth (1857–1921). They had a major influence upon late Victorian and early Edwardian British and European understandings of the history and culture of the Niger River peoples, the effect of which is subtly continuing. Felix worked with the Medical Service of the Niger Coast Protectorate, and took part in the sacking of Benin, while Henry was what we would now consider a 'salvage anthropologist', curator of the Bankfield Museum in Halifax (Yorkshire), and author (six years after the sacking) of an apparently exhaustive study of the traditional culture of Benin, which he wrongly believed to have been totally extinguished by the British invasion (HL Roth 1903[1968]).

Felix Norman and Henry Ling Roth provide a window onto a period that not only, as Basil Davidson says, prophesied the triumph of imperialism in Africa (1978:30), but that also, not coincidentally, saw the emergence in Britain of African Studies. As JD Fage points out, there was 'no concept of African Studies as a discrete activity' in Britain prior to the founding of the African Society in 1900 (1995:369). Most of the Society's early members, like the Roths, were amateurs whose careers had in one way or another brought them into contact with Africa. Less than 10% of those listed as members in 1906 feature subsequently in the *Dictionary of National Biography* (Fage 1995:371). Neither Henry nor Felix are among them, which indicates a serious oversight in Benin studies.[2]

The Consequences of Invasion

In Nigeria today violence is increasing across a number of separate ethnic and religious conflicts. Wole Soyinka describes it as a nation 'on the brink of a massive violent implosion'. The wave of mass killings that occurred in May 2004, he warns, is a likely precursor to the 'balkanization' of Nigeria, Africa's most populous nation and major oil exporter (quoted in Ashby 2004). One of the most serious conflicts is between the Itsekiri, Urhobo and Izhon peoples, who occupy the delta area of the Niger River (see, for instance, Imobighe, Bassey & Asuni 2002). The modern dimension of this particular dispute concerns government favour and oil revenue, for this impoverished area contains the bulk of Nigeria's oil reserves. Nigeria now produces about 2.5 million barrels of oil a day, more than half of which goes to the United States. But the delta cultures of the Niger enjoy little economic benefit in return, and they are locked in a struggle for control of what essentially is the shared economic lifeblood of the nation – crude oil. Armed gunmen cruise the winding creeks of the densely forested delta in a flotilla of speedboats (see, for instance, 'Self-styled rebel' 2004), much as they did in their war canoes in the mid-to-late 19th century. As Soyinka says, everyone in Nigeria now is making contingency plans for its dissolution (cited in Ashby 2004).

The roots of this dispute, like so many, go back to a time before the formation of Nigeria (see Ikime 1969). The consequences of Britain's 1897 invasion of Benin were profound. It destroyed the power of one of the few remaining chiefdoms capable of resistance and prepared the way for the colony and Protectorate of Southern Nigeria that was founded two years later. The punitive expedition involved nothing less than the 'invasion and destruction of the state' of Benin, now known as the Edo nation. It was followed by 'the show trial of its king, the execution of its leading chiefs, the torching of the royal palace, and the burning of innumerable [surrounding] villages' (Gott 1997). The army sacked the city, and 'the official booty of the expedition' was put up for sale in London, as the Foreign Office put it, 'to defray the cost of the pensions for the killed and the wounded' (Fagg 1981:21). Of course, there was also a great deal of 'unofficial loot', not reported to the Admiralty (Eyo nd). Many artefacts – the now-famed Benin bronzes, ivories, woodcarvings and ironwork – were shared among the officers, as was 'the custom of war in the nineteenth century' (Fagg 1981:21). Some remained in private hands, but most were sold at auction and so found their way into British and European museums (see Duerden 2000). Thus the looting of Benin had a profoundly positive effect on Western art and museum development. While it is now customary for art historians to locate the European 'discovery' of African art with the masks favoured by Fauvism and Cubism, in fact Benin's bronzes entered the European canon of beauty almost a decade earlier, soon after the British sacking. Finally, as Sven Lindqvist says, while we cannot be certain of any direct influence upon Conrad's *Heart of Darkness*,[3] the first British readers to encounter that novel's European anti-hero revelling in the 'unspeakable rites' of the Dark Continent undoubtedly saw in their mind's eye the sensationalised images of London's illustrated press coverage of the Benin incident from just two years earlier: the mass media imagery of skulls littered on the ground, and men and women hanging in crucifixion trees, their bellies ripped open and their insides hanging down (Lindqvist 1996:61).

Felix Roth at Warri

The Oil Rivers Protectorate had been administered by the British Foreign Office since 1885, but was expanded and renamed the Niger Coast Protectorate in 1893. Felix Roth spent six years in the Protectorate, from 1892 to 1898, stationed at Warri trading station (now Warri Township), which is where the Vice-Consulate for the Warri district was located.

Warri lay some 40 miles up the Forcados River. It was an important trans-shipping point for ocean-going vessels, which received their cargoes of palm oil, but also of rubber, cacao, peanuts, hides and skins from the river boats there. But it was Benin, the neighbouring district to Warri, which the British saw as having the greatest potential for trade.

Felix was one of 13 qualified medical men in the Protectorate, under the Principal Medical Officer, Dr Robert Allman. Officially, his task was to look after the health of the European and native populations in his district, but there were only 16 Europeans in Warri. In any case, the Commissioner and Consul-General, Major Claude M Macdonald, had told him explicitly that his task was 'to open up trade' (*BPP* 1895a; Norman-Roth nd:20) – that is, to assist in clearing the way for the trade monopoly of the Royal Niger Company.

76 | Chapter 4

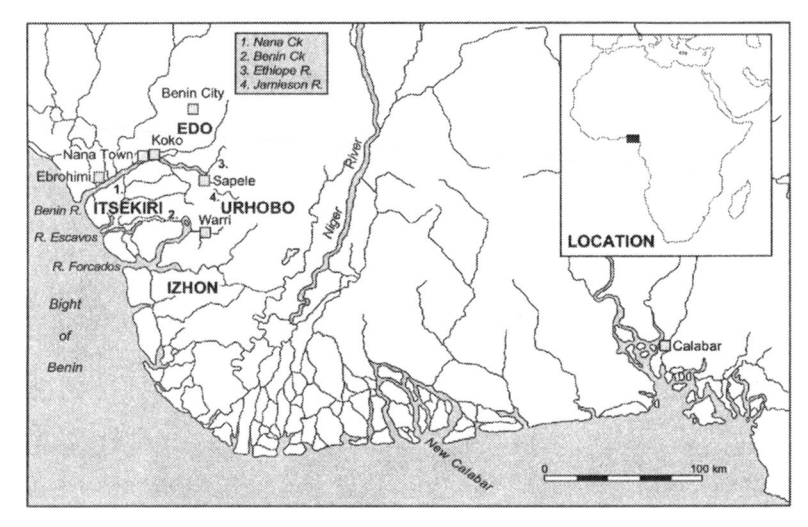

Figure 4.1 Map of Benin Province (with inset of map of Nigeria) (Drawn by Mike Roach)

View of Warri.

Figure 4.2 View of Warri (Reproduced with the permission of the Horniman Museum)

Chief Nana of Brohimi

The first obstacle was the powerful Itsekiri chief, Nana Olomu of Brohimi. Nana had a stranglehold on trade for 120 miles around Warri, from the Niger's mouth some 50 miles up the Jamieson and Ethiope

Rivers to the point where they join and form the Benin River at Sapele.[4] He led a force of some 3,000 to 4,000 men and innumerable canoes, some capable of holding 40 or 50 paddlers and mounted with rifles (Norman-Roth nd:20). His personal arsenal consisted of '106 cannon, 14 tons of gunpowder, 445 blunderbusses adapted for use on [the] war canoes, and a machine-gun' (Crowder 1962:200). Defying British demands that the rivers should be free to traders, Nana stopped trade at the Sapele market and placed a bar across the creek that led to his headquarters. The British, sowing the seeds of ethnic discontent, had previously empowered Nana as a District Governor. But now he had to be eliminated (see *BPP* 1895b:1–46).

The Izhon (Idzo, Ijo, Ijaw) chief, Erigbe, was a staunch supporter of Nana (see Anene 1966:158). Early in August 1894 Felix took part in the expedition that burned Erigbe's village, Efferonu, to the ground. A short time later Felix took charge of Hausa reinforcements for the offensive led by Lieutenant-Commander Heugh that torched the village of Otegheles, also said to be under Nana's control (*BPP* 1895b:4, 11, 27). 'It is impossible to form any idea of the number of natives killed', Heugh reported, for he had cleared the bush with rockets and machine gun as he proceeded up Brohemie Creek (*BPP* 1895b:11).

Nana responded to the shelling of his headquarters at Brohemie Town with a great deal more force and military strategy than the British had reckoned with, and two cruisers had to be dispatched to rescue the gunboat responsible for the shelling. On 25 September the British launched a full-scale offensive on Brohemie Town. The town was captured and destroyed. Nana escaped, but gave himself up to authorities in Lagos, where he was tried and deported to permanent exile on the Gold Coast.

This narrative, which appears as a footnote to the invasion of Benin in a number of the European histories of Nigeria, derives from the official records of the Colonial Office. By contrast, Felix Roth's brief and fragmentary published memoir says little about the assault on Nana, only that the Acting Consul-General, Sir Ralph Moor, sent him up the river to tend to the wounded; and it says nothing of the torching of Efferonu, or the shelling of Otegheles, in both of which he was actively involved. In fact, Felix was acting Vice-Consul at Warri at the time of the Nana offensive, which meant that, as well as being the district's Medical Officer, he was also its Shipping Master, Postmaster and Treasurer, and he had charge of Customs, Police and Soldiery. He was with the attacking column led by Rear-Admiral Fred Bedford on the day of the deciding battle,[5] and he was mentioned in dispatches. Ten years later, as Governor of Western Australia, Bedford appointed Felix's brother Walter to conduct a Royal Commission into the conditions of Aborigines (see Chapter 13).

By the time Felix published his serialised memoir in the *Halifax Courier and Guardian* (Norman-Roth nd), some 28 years after the event, the Nana episode was completely forgotten in Britain, eclipsed by the much more sensational 1897 punitive expedition against Benin City. The attitude to empire had changed too. For 18 of the 27 years between 1874 and 1902 the Conservatives held government in Britain, seeking to extend or consolidate the Empire. A wave of sentiment surrounded the Empire. Yet even as its extension and economic exploitation continued, a new idea had been developing, of duty and service to humanity. By 1906, when Britain elected a Liberal government on the anti-imperialist policy of home social welfare, the decline of imperialism as material self-aggrandisement was well under way. By 1922, when Felix published his memoir, it had become politic to underplay empire heroism. Thus his narrative contains little of the self-dramatising 'opera bravura' that Dorothy Hammond and Alta Jablow found in the mid-Victorian travel narratives of East Africa, for instance (Hammond & Jablow 1970:10; see also Brantlinger 1988; Franey 2003), and instead it bears the blandly modest title 'Some experiences of an engineer doctor'. It prefers to focus on its author's earliest days at Warri, when few white men had even heard of Benin City, let alone visited it, and the atrocities were only hearsay.[6] Felix presents the Nana episode as a brief exploit, seen as through the eyes of a boy, yet unopened to Africa's realities, before the whole adventure turned sour.

Felix Roth and the River Pirate

Raymond Blathwayt, who visited Warri when Felix was Acting Vice-Consul, eulogised him as 'a statesman, a builder of Empire… idolized by the simple and childlike natives… a great Fetish doctor' (1917:318). Paradoxically, and unintentionally, Blathwayt also gives us a keen sense of the omissions of Felix's own memoir.

One day, Blathwayt says, a captive is brought in from the jungle, who was 'responsible for many murders and for the loss of much valuable merchandise from the interior'. Felix invites his visitor to witness the trial,[7] at which the prisoner is promptly sentenced to death, taken out into the courtyard and chained to a pillar to await execution the next morning. On the verandah a couple of planters join Felix and his visitors for dinner, including Consul-General Ralph Moor, drinking wine and poking fun at the poor wretch below (Blathwayt 1917:323).

The next morning Felix orders that the prisoner's eyes be bandaged. 'I no fear. I want to die like a black man', the man protests.

The orderly responds, 'White man has bandage when he shot'.

Felix steps forward and draws 'a glaring white circle' with a stick of chalk upon the prisoner's naked breast, 'right round his heart'; and the Yoruba firing squad bursts into laughter. Felix signals, the orderly gives the command and the Yorubas fire.

'Throw his body into the bush!' Felix orders.

'Oh, but why not give him [a] decent burial?' asks Blathwayt.

'To teach these people a lesson', replies Felix. 'They will see his dead body treated like carrion and it will never be forgotten' (Blathwayt 1917:325).

Warri was at this time apparently multi-ethnic, but is subject to conflicting claims of ownership by different cultural groups (see Edevbie 2000). Felix intended a lesson to them all. Almost certainly the executed prisoner was the Idzon chief Erigbe, Nana's lieutenant from Efferonu, whom Lieutenant-Commander Heugh describes in a dispatch as 'nothing more than a river pirate' (*BPP* 1895b:6). Blathwayt does not identify the prisoner by name, but describes him with the same words, as 'a famous river pirate' (Blathwayt 1917:323).

The Battle for Benin City

In November 1896, at the beginning of the palm-oil season, the Oba of Benin, finding that the price of guns and powder and gin had escalated beyond what he was prepared to pay, closed all markets to outside trade. The Protectorate's export figures for the year were already unpromising. The Consul-General, Ralph Moor, was on leave in Britain in January 1897 when his rather raw colleague, Acting Vice-Consul JR Phillips, decided to pay the Oba a visit. The Oba sent repeated messages not to advance upon the city, for his people were in the midst of religious observances for the Igue festival. It is a time of sacred importance, when the Oba must fast in seclusion and not be seen by visitors (Iyi-eweka nd). When Phillips ignored the warning, the Edo attacked and killed him and all but two of his party.

Three separate columns mounted the British retaliation. Felix was advance surgeon to the main column (HL Roth 1903:175).[8] His account of the experience appeared in print later that year. Obviously, unlike the later memoir, this extract from his diary was written close to the heat of the moment.[9] The advance guard is in the jungle for several days preparing for battle, and Felix has time to record the attractions of the landscape. He enters the 'hostile blacks' into the catalogue of irritations that disturb his meditations in the 'quiet places' (FN Roth 1898:vi) of the jungle, along with the ants and other insects (pp iii–iv). The style, unlike that of the official reports, has more in common with descriptive travel writing. The point of view is that of an interloper. There is no transitional or in-between stage where he questions his own values, no dismantling of social convention. Instead, Felix presents the 'unquestioning extrovert face of Imperialism', little concerned with the complexities and ambiguities of his journey into the unknown (see Carroll 1992).

But he also gives perhaps the frankest picture of the battle that is available. Ologbo, 12 February: 'We shelled the village, and cleared it of the natives. As the launch and surf-boats grounded, we jumped into the water... at once placed our Maxims and guns in position, firing so as to clear the bush where the natives might be hiding' (FN Roth 1898:v). Cross-Road Camp, 15 February: 'Luckily', Felix records, 'no white men were wounded; we all got off scot-free' (p vi). The reason was that those native troops, earlier feminised in Felix's diary for their annoying chatter (p iii), formed a protective buffer zone around the British soldiers. 'Our black troops', he writes, 'with the scouts in front and a few Maxims, do all the fighting' (p vii). This is an important detail, omitted from official reports and not much quoted in British histories, but central to indigenous accounts.

On 19 February, when the battle was won and he had tended to all the wounded, Felix paused to recall the previous day's approach to Benin City:

> It is a charnel house. All about the houses and streets are dead natives, some crucified and sacrificed on trees, others on stage erections, some on the ground, some in pits.... We passed several human sacrifices, live women-slaves gagged and pegged on their backs to the ground, the abdominal wall being cut in the form of a cross, and the uninjured gut hanging out... (p ix).

Soon Benin became known as the City of Blood, and narratives such as this unwittingly assisted Britain to install the fiction that the aim of its war on Benin had nothing to do with trade. Rather, it was to vanquish barbarism.

Felix concludes the published extract from his diary with a word of praise for his 18-year-old assistant from Accra, Charles Nartey, who has carried his bag of bandages and tourniquets unflinchingly through battle. 'Although he was simply my own boy, Consul-General Sir Ralph Moor ordered me to put his name down for a medal and clasp, for behaving so well' (p xii). Here again the diary differs from the memoir, where his account of Benin, although considerably muted, concludes with the hunting down of the Oba, his ridiculous trial at Old Calabar and Felix taking charge of the escort for his favourite wife. 'I tried to amuse her', he says, 'and show her all over the Consulate, and also let her see how the white man lived' (Norman-Roth nd:26).

The Souvenir: History, Ethnography, Photography

I want to turn my attention now to another aspect of the historical narrative, a small home-made photograph album with a Halifax bindery sticker on its back and the title 'Souvenir of Warri', which I found three years ago in the Horniman Museum on the outskirts of London. The Horniman purchased this manuscript photograph album for two shillings in 1949. It contains 28 plates, all photographs by Felix Roth, and with his captions, copied in his brother Henry's hand. So far as I can determine, these have not been published before.[10]

The title page, inscribed in Henry's hand, reads:

Souvenir of Warri
>In the Bight of Benin
>Where for one who comes out
>There are nine who stay in.

>F. NORMAN-ROTH, M.R.C.S.,
>One who came out

>From his affectionate brother
>H. Ling Roth,
>who did not go in

Africa is not named, but is a translation of that place braved by Felix which might also be the underworld, the unknown, the realm of the dead and departed. Felix enters that darkness, but rather than succumbing to it, he returns so that Henry can play Marlow. Henry mythologises Felix but preserves for himself the role of mediator, presenting Africa to England. It is a very interesting comment on British armchair anthropology in its relation to colonial administration in the field, with Henry and Felix together providing a kind of psycho-dynamic portrait of the mythic late-Victorian man of empire.

In his diary of the invasion of Benin, in the calm before battle, Felix found time for ominous humour: 'Chumpy has a seven-year-old nigger servant, who has been taught, whenever he brings a drink to anybody, to say the following: – "God bless the Queen, and I hope we beat hell out of the King of Benin". He says this while saluting, with a most serious face' (FN Roth 1898:iv). But the focus of the frontispiece to the souvenir album (Figure 4.3) is less on the boy with the rifle than on the striking artefact at the centre. It is impossible not to read this image elegiacally, for the sacking of Benin caused a hiatus in artistic production that lasted decades. Although manufacturing began to pick up again in

Figure 4.3 Frontispiece of 'Souvenir of Warri' album (Reproduced with the permission of the Horniman Museum)

the 1920s, the aesthetic and creative functionality of indigenous artistic tradition had been destroyed all but permanently (Dark 1982:xii). The souvenir image here offers visual confirmation of the self-presentation of Felix's war diary, the imperial adventurer, entering 'forbidden and dangerous places' and 'returning with his treasure' (Carroll 1992:161) to the civilised world with his power completely preserved. It is a very posed photograph, and Felix has his hand resting possessively on the sculpture. With his dog at his feet and his hand on the trophy, he appears closely allied to the image of the great white hunter.

In terms of visual composition, Figure 4.4 is very similar, and offers useful comparison. Where before the hand rested proudly on the trophy artefact, here it rests in fatherly fashion on a young boy's shoulder. Felix wears a solar topee, which presents him looking more formal than the Panama hat did, and the boy has an umbrella. What makes the previous photograph more historical perhaps, and this one ethnographic, is the caption underneath it. In fact, Figure 4.3 is the only image in the entire album that Henry allows to stand without a caption, and he places that photograph at the beginning as a kind of visual epigraph to the entire album, so that it gives the code for deciphering all the other images that follow. The caption for Figure 4.4 – in Henry's hand but Felix's

"A Sobo boy & Myself. The boy is aged about 12 years but is not a characteristic Sobo."

Figure 4.4 'A Sobo boy & Myself' (Reproduced with the permission of the Horniman Museum)

words – states that the boy is 'not a characteristic Sobo'. Henry wanted reliable descriptions of the people and their culture. He suggested that Felix take notes in the field, and also that he take photographs.

Photography had been an important ethnographic tool at least since the 1850s, as Lacan observes in his comments on the Paris Exhibition; and probably Henry had heard Everard Im Thurn's 1893 lecture on the anthropological uses of photography at the Anthropological Institute (Falconer 1984:16). There are very few photographic collections from the Niger River region in the 1890s. By far the most extensive is Reginald Granville's collection in the Pitt Rivers Museum. The photographs in it were taken with a camera that Henry supplied (HL Roth 1903:vi). Possibly he did the same for Felix. In any case, Felix must have had some instruction as to what photographs Henry wanted, and that is why he felt the need to warn on this occasion that the boy was allegedly uncharacteristic of his kind.

What is a characteristic Sobo, we may wonder? Felix provided Henry with a number of ethnographic portraits – of Edo, Itsikeri and Urhobo men and women. We may assume, I think, when a caption says nothing of the subject's trueness to type it is because Felix believed that he or she was indeed representative. The British difficulty with names during the

84 | Chapter 4

1890s and early 1900s is in part responsible for the continuing friction between the diverse cultural groups. There are in fact no such people as the Sobo. The Urhobo Progress Union successfully prevailed upon the colonial government in 1938 to change the corrupted name 'Sobo' (referring to a colonial type that the administration regarded as inferior, easily cowed and controlled) to its original 'Urhobo'.[11]

Henry was in close contact with EB Tylor, who had developed a theory of animism to account for fetishism. But Henry was not entirely convinced by this attempt to place ju-ju lower down the evolutionary scale of religious development. He asked his friend Mary Kingsley her views on ju-ju fetishism: did it constitute a distinct religion or not? Her answer was forthright. 'I think that if it were left alone to go on – if it were in the heads of a more mystically minded set than our Africans [–] it would end in Brahmanism'.[12] Though she was criticised for her view in some quarters, she believed that a sharp distinction needed to be maintained between witchcraft and religion.[13] It is probable that Henry particularly wanted photographs of ju-ju ceremony. This one (Figure 4.5) was taken at Efferonu, which Felix later helped burn to the ground.

Henry quotes his brother frequently in the chapter on the 'Fetish and kindred observances' of the Edo in his book *Great Benin: Its Customs, Art and Horrors* (HL Roth 1903:48–84). The discussion is heavily illustrated,

Effroon, Sobo country. Juju tree on the right. These photos are the only ones taken before we were turned out.

Figure 4.5 'Effroon, Sobo country. Ju-ju tree on the right' (Reproduced with the permission of the Horniman Museum)

but not by Felix's photographs – probably these were taken before the ritual began, and with himself usually front and centre. Instead, Henry chooses more sensational images of ritual objects, more suggestive of witchcraft than religion, to continue with Kingsley's distinction – Allman's photographs of the crucifixion trees (p 51), Granville's photo of a Ju-ju altar laden with the skulls of slaves (p 64) and Cyril Punch's 1891 photograph of a sacrifice to make the rain cease (p 52).

At the mouth of the Niger, at Old Calabar, the British had established botanical gardens. They cut down the adjoining bush and established a coffee plantation, 22 acres fenced with wire, with 2,100 coffee trees raised from seed. The local indigenous population supplied the labour under a West Indian overseer. By July 1895 the plants were 27 months old and stood generally around six feet (*BPP* 1893b:20, 21; *BPP* 1895a:1).

What is remarkable about Figure 4.6 is in part the caption, which ignores the human and focuses only on the botanical image. It frames the image deliberately to eschew the ethnographic in favour of the historical. The commodification of the 'native' subject in this photograph functions as a visual gauge of the healthy growth and height of the colonial import, the coffee plant.

The Consul-General believed that the Protectorate's future likely lay in coffee and cocoa. The British provided coffee plants to local chiefs on the condition that they clear the ground for sowing, and with the

Figure 4.6 'Coffee tree; the first one planted in Warri' (Reproduced with the permission of the Horniman Museum)

promise of an honorarium based on the number of healthy trees in the plantation at the end of each year. In November 1894 the administration placed an order in Liberia for seeds that they hoped would make 100,000 plants ready for distribution by the next season. Felix's photograph (Figure 4.6), then, is a form of advertising for a plantation economy, a boast and a prophecy (for indeed, coffee *is* now the second- or third-highest-earning Nigerian export). The irony is that, at the time it was taken, Henry was agitating in England for a museological rationale that would place ethnographic display beyond the novelty of the exotic and on an equal footing with botanical and zoological display (*BPP* 1893b:20–21; *BPP* 1895a:1–4; HL Roth 1911:286–90).

Many of these photographs, regardless of their original intention, are both historical and ethnographic, and this double function makes the framing of their subjects complex and often contradictory. The same might be said for Henry's African anthropology. Poised between a Victorian and a modern sense of culture, it has as much in common with Kingsley's *Travels in West Africa* (1897) as Conrad's *Heart of Darkness*.

Figure 4.7 'Uvorami (Overami) Nabeshi, The Last King of Benin' (Reproduced from HL Roth, *Great Benin: Its Customs, Art and Horrors*, 1903)

Great Benin

We realise from the first page of *Great Benin*, where the photograph of the exiled Oba appears incorrectly captioned 'The Last King of Benin', that its attempt to provide a complete and comprehensive overview of Benin culture is based on the author's firm belief that the punitive expedition had permanently destroyed that culture. There is no doubt that Henry considered Benin 'savage', and he could not forget the mass media horror images that had followed the punitive expedition, or his brother's tales of 'witchcraft' and blood. 'If ever a city deserved its fate', Henry writes, 'that city was Benin' (HL Roth 1903:5). Yet Felix's photographs, and the treasures that he and other members of the punitive expedition brought back to Britain, also made it impossible for Henry to subscribe to the dominant anthropological theory of the Edo as a degenerate race (see Coombes 1994:13ff).

In fact, Henry openly questioned the influential Hamitic Hypothesis (based on the 'Biblical account of the dispersal of Noah's sons after the flood')[14] that Africa's history could only have been made by foreigners, choosing to end his pioneering study of Benin culture, after surveying all of the evidence and weighing all of the opinion, with the 'only one conclusion' that was possible: the Benin bronzes were 'a form of real native art' (HL Roth 1903:234).[15] There is no irony in his title, *Great Benin*. Yet he could not entirely resist the evolutionist paradigm. While he questioned the relativities of some of the racial types, he did not question the overall system of Victorian anthropology, the evolutionist concept of a 'hierarchy of races'. As Annie Coombes points out, the three most influential proponents of the 'degenerationist thesis' about Africa were Alfred Cort Haddon, Charles Hercules Read and Henry Balfour. Haddon was a close friend, and Henry relied upon both Balfour at the Pitt Rivers Museum and Read at the British Museum for access to their Benin collections.[16] Unlike Kingsley and Conrad, Henry wrote about places that he had never been. He relied upon minute observation of the artefacts of material culture held in the collections of his beloved Bankfield Museum and in other British museums and private collections. For access to these he depended upon a network of curators and other anthropologists, facilitated by his membership of the various professional associations. As Frank Willett, then Professor of African Art and Archaeology at Northwestern University (Evanston, Illinois), wrote in his review of the 1968 US reprint: '*Great Benin* is a remarkably comprehensive survey of the history and culture of Benin as it could be discovered in the years immediately following the punitive expedition', without of course ever going there (Willett nd). Yet it was stimulated by an experience of travel, albeit by Henry's brother Felix as his proxy, and it relied heavily upon Felix's collaborative testimony.

Salvage Anthropology

The brothers' working relationship raises interesting questions about the connection between British armchair anthropology at the turn of the century and the growing importance of fieldwork as the discipline became professionalised. Felix travelled, Henry stayed home, yet Felix extended Henry's power of observation into the untravelled distance, into the cultural field of his anthropological subject. Thus, at the heart of Henry's African ethnography is a paradox of positioning, which is the paradox of travel and armchair anthropology, dwelling and displacement. It meant that England was not for Henry the first condition of his cultural analysis, as it was for many other major anthropologists of his day – Tylor, Balfour, Haddon, Read, for example. Henry's own situation, or location, inevitably applied limits and pressures to his ethnography. These were both institutional and more broadly cultural. Correspondingly, Felix's position in colonial administration in the Niger Coast Protectorate modified and to a degree relativised the pressures and limits set by 'England'. England and Africa were part of a continuous topography. Perhaps this is one reason that Henry's work is less well known today than, say, Haddon's or Balfour's, because his audience, relatively speaking, was less stable.

Yet Henry's work is less contaminated by ideology than that of most of his contemporaries. Perhaps the more difficult problem for his reputation since World War II has been his focus on material culture, for after that time anthropology largely lost interest in material culture studies. The study of material culture became more the province of Marxist-type analysis of objects as commodities, or semiotic analysis of objects as symbols. More recently, however, the ethnographic approach has been regaining momentum, regarding objects again principally as artefacts. James Clifford's work has connected ethnography to social history and literary forms of narrative (Clifford & Marcus 1986). And his later work on the 'post-colonial crisis of ethnographic authority' has been influential in theorising how 'a Western will to power' has shaped knowledges of non-Western peoples (Clifford 1988). But whatever its sins, salvage anthropology provided an archive which many colonised peoples would draw upon later to assist in reclaiming their heritage, reinterpreting previously collected objects and images as part of a modern process of identity formation.[17]

Notes

1. This is a revised and condensed version of a plenary paper given at the 'Sharing Places' EACLALS Conference, Malta, March 2005.
2. Coombes is a notable exception, referring to Henry Ling Roth at some length, as 'an individual who figured prominently in the history of interpretation of Benin culture'

(1994:44). Henry's *Great Benin* (1903) is also listed in Charles Gore's 'Bibliography of published research on Benin City', http://www.cgore.dircon.co.uk/a1a.htm., accessed March 2005.
3. *Heart of Darkness* was solicited by William Blackwood on 30 December 1898 and appeared as a serial in three parts in *Blackwood's Edinburgh Magazine* the following year.
4. Salubi (1960:15): 'SAPELE which is today one of the most important industrial port towns in the Western Region of Nigeria was a small village belonging to the people of Okpe in Urhobo country. Sapele, Sapoli, and Sapeli, are the European rendering of the Okpe name of the village which is *Urhiapele* or *Urhuapele*. The hinterland Urhobo call it *Isapele* and the Itsekiri people generally call it *Usapele*, both obviously after the European rendering. *Urhiapele* or *Urhuapele* is a combination of two Urhobo words – *Urhie* or *Urho* and *Apele*. *Urhie* or *Urho* means a river or a stream, and Apele is a name of a Ju-ju of the Okpe owners of the village. *Urhiapele* or *Urhuapele* therefore means the 'River or the stream of Apele'".
5. Sir Frederick George Denham Bedford (1838–1913) is remembered mainly for organising the Nile flotilla that relieved Khartoum (1884–85), for his command of the Cape Station (1892–95) and for his governorship of Western Australia (1903–9). However, his Niger River exploits did not end with victory over Nana at Brohemie. Exactly one year later he laid siege to Brass, chief city of the Izhon people of Nembe, again razing the enemy's city to the ground. It is estimated that 'more than 2000 people, mostly women and children, perished in that attack' (cf Monbiot 2001:14).
6. Sir C MacDonald to the Earl of Roseberg, 12 January 1893: 'I am of the opinion that there are very great possibilities for this district [Benin] ... the great stumbling-block to any immediate advance being, the fetish "reign of terror" which exists throughout the Kingdom of Benin, and which will require severe measures in the not very distant future before it can be stopped' (*BPP* 1893a:3).
7. The Consular Court at Warri was in the lower part of the Vice-Consul's residence.
8. Notice of Felix Roth's services to the expedition is also given in *BPP* (1898:7).
9. Felix's is not the only first-hand account. Captain Reginald Hugh Spencer Bacon (later Sir Admiral Bacon), the expedition's Intelligence Officer, published *Benin: City of Blood* in the same year, and his *A Naval Scrap-Book, First Part, 1877–1900* also contains an account of the campaign. Captain A Boisragon, one of the two survivors of the ill-fated Phillips outing, wrote *The Benin Massacre* (1898). The principal medical officer with the punitive expedition, Dr R Allman, published 'With the punitive expedition in Benin City' (1897). And the unpublished diary of Reginald K Granville, Deputy Sub-Commissioner at Warri, is held in the Pitt Rivers Museum, Oxford. So is GL Egerton's unpublished diary.
10. 'Souvenir of Warri', Horniman Museum, L9517.
11. Similarly, although Felix and Henry refer to the 'Bini', and many modern scholars use the terms 'Edo' and 'Bini' interchangeably, properly speaking the people of Benin are the Edo. Felix and Henry also refer to the 'Jekri'. Other commentators of the period refer variously to 'Jakri' and 'Jekeri', but these also have reverted officially to their correct name, which is 'Itsekiri'. Finally, Henry and Felix refer to the 'Ijo', variously known in the colonial period as 'Ijo', 'Ijaw' and 'Ezon'. The preferred name now is 'Izon' (Ekeh 2004).
12. Mary Kingsely to Henry Ling Roth, 10 March 1898, Mary Kingsley Papers, British Empire and Commonwealth Museum, Bristol.
13. Victorian views of Indian religion varied, but Brahmanism was often seen as the essence of Hinduism. 'Brahmanism' here probably equates roughly with superstition and caste. Kingsley's is the negative aspect of Monier-Williams's view, who,

opposing Max Müller's presentation of Hinduism as an ossified religion, praised its flexibility and adaptability: 'it holds out the right hand of brotherhood to nature-worshippers, demon-worshippers, animal-worshippers, tree-worshippers, fetish-worshippers. It does not scruple to permit the most grotesque forms of idolatry, and the most degrading varieties of superstition. And it is to this latter fact that yet another remarkable peculiarity of Hinduism is mainly due – namely, that in no other system in the world is the chasm more vast which separates the religion of the higher, cultured, and thoughtful classes from that of the lower, uncultured, and unthinking masses' (Monier-Williams 1891:11).
14. Sanders (1969) gives a succinct account of the Hamitic thesis, according to which 'everything of value in Africa had been introduced by the Hamites, supposedly a branch of the Caucasian race'.
15. Coombes (1994:46) points out that Pitt Rivers privately agreed with Henry.
16. Sir Charles Hercules Read was Keeper of the Department of British and Medieval Antiquities and Ethnography at the British Museum from 1896 to 1921. Professor Henry Balfour was Curator of the Pitt Rivers Museum from 1891 until his death in 1939. Between them they dominated the Anthropological Institute of Great Britain and Ireland from 1899 to 1904, taking turns at its presidency. With OM Dalton, Read authored *Antiquities from the City of Benin and from Other Parts of Africa in the British Museum* (1899).
17. The point was made by Elizabeth Dell, in a paper given at the ASEASUK Conference at Brighton (2000) on the photographs of the Kachin people of Burma taken by Colonel James Green in the 1920s and '30s. Reported by Nick Ford, 'Art, culture and the media of Southeast Asia', *IIAS Newsletter Online*, No 24, http://www.iias.nl/iiasn/24/asianart/24ART2.html, accessed 28 February 2005.

Works Cited

Allman, R (1897) 'With the punitive expedition in Benin City', *The Lancet* 2, 43–44
Anene, JC (1966) *Southern Nigeria in Transition, 1885–1906. Theory and Practice in a Colonial Protectorate*, Cambridge: Cambridge University Press
Ashby, Tom (2004) 'Nigeria on brink of violent implosion', *The Namibian*, 12 July 2004, http://www.namibian.com.na/2004/July/world/0452620618.html, accessed March 2005
Bacon, Reginald Hugh Spencer (1925) *A Naval Scrap-Book. First Part, 1877–1900*, London: Hutchinson & Co
———. (1898) *Benin: The City of Blood*, London: Edward Arnold
Blathwayt, Raymond (1917) *Through Life and Round the World, Being the Story of My Life*, London: Allen and Unwin
Boisragon, Captain A (1898) *The Benin Massacre*, London: Methuen
Brantlinger, Patrick (1988) *Rule of Darkness: British Literature and Imperialism, 1830–1914*, Ithaca: Cornell University Press
British Parliamentary Papers (BPP) (1898) 'Annual report on the Niger Coast Protectorate for the year 1896–97', London: Harrison and Sons
———. (1895a) 'Report on the administration of the Niger Coast Protectorate 1894–95 [In continuation of "Africa No. 1 (1895)"]', London: Harrison and Sons
———. (1895b) 'Report on the administration of the Niger Coast Protectorate, August 1891 to August 1894', London: Harrison and Sons
———. (1893a) 'Affairs of the West Coast of Africa', London: Harrison and Sons
———. (1893b) 'Administration of the Niger Coast Protectorate, August 1891 to August 1894', London: Harrison and Sons

Carroll, David (1992) 'African landscape and imperial vertigo', in Gatrell, Simon (ed), *The Ends of the Earth, Vol. 4. 1876–1918*, Atlantic Highlands, NJ: Ashfield Press, 157–72

Clifford, James (1988) *The Predicament of Culture: Twentieth-Century Ethnography, Literature and Art*, Cambridge, Mass: Harvard University Press

Clifford, James and Marcus, George (eds) (1986) *Writing Culture: The Poetics and Politics of Ethnography*, Berkeley: University of California Press

Coombes, Annie E (1994) *Reinventing Africa: Museums, Material Culture and Popular Imagination in Late Victorian and Edwardian England*, New Haven: Yale University Press

Crowder, Michael (1962) *The Story of Nigeria*, rev edn 1966, London: Faber & Faber

Dalton, OM and Read, Sir Charles Hercules (1899) *Antiquities from the City of Benin and from Other Parts of Africa in the British Museum*, London

Dark, Philip (1982) *An Illustrated Catalog of Benin Art*, Boston: GK Hall

Davidson, Basil (1978) *Africa in Modern History. The Search for a New Society* Harmondsworth: Penguin

Duerden, Denis (2000) 'The "discovery" of the African mask', *Research in African Literatures* 31(4), 29–47

Edevbie, Onoawarie (2000) 'Who owns Warri? The politics of ethnic rivalry in the western Niger-Delta region of Nigeria', Urhoobo Historical Society, Niagara Falls, Ont., Canada. First Annual Conference (November 2000), http://www.urhobo.kinsfolk.com/Conferences/FirstAnnualConference/ConferenceMatters/MillenniumSession/WhoOwnsWarri.html, accessed March 2005

Egharevba, JU (1960) *A Short History of Benin*, 3rd edn, Ibadan: Ibadan University Press

Ekeh, Peter (2004) 'The mischief of history: Bala Usman's unmaking of Nigerian history', http://www.ngex.com/personalities/voices/pekeh043001.htm, accessed 18 January 2004

Eyo, Ekpo (nd) 'Benin: the sack that was', http://www.edo-nation.net/eyo.htm, accessed March 2005

Fage, JD (1995) 'When the African Society was founded, who were the Africanists?' *African Affairs* 94, 376, 369–81

Fagg, William (1981) 'Benin: the sack that never was', in Kaplan, Flora and Shea, MA (eds), *Images of Power: Art of the Royal Court of Benin*, New York: Museum Studies Program New York University, 20–21

Falconer, John (1984) 'Ethnographical photography in India 1850–1900', *Photographic Collector* 5(1), 16–46

Franey, Laura (2003) *Victorian Travel Writing and Imperial Violence: British Writing of Africa 1855–1902*, London: Palgrave Macmillan

Gott, Richard (1997) 'The Looting of Benin', *The Independent*, 22 February, ARM (Africa Reparations Movement) Press cutting: http://www.arm.arc.co.uk/lootingBenin.html, accessed March 2005

Hammond, Dorothy and Jablow, Alta (1970) *The Africa that Never Was: Four Centuries of British Writing about Africa*, New York: Twayne

Home, Robert (1982) *City of Blood Revisited: A New Look at the Benin Expedition of 1897*, London: Collings

Ikime, Obaro (1969) *Niger Delta Rivalry: Itsekiri-Urhobo Relations and the European Presence 1884–1936*, New York: Humanities Press

Imobighe, TA, Bassey, CO and Asuni, JB (2002) *Conflict and Instability in the Niger Delta: The Warri Case*, Abuja: Academic Associates Peaceworks

Iyi-eweka, Ademola (nd) 'Igue Festival', http://www.edo-nation.net/igue.htm, accessed March 2005

Lindqvist, Sven (1996) *Exterminate All the Brutes*, London: Granta

Monbiot, George (2001) 'Introduction' to Okonta, Ike and Douglas, Oronto, *Where Vultures Feast: Shell, Human Rights, and Oil in the Niger Delta*, San Francisco: Sierra Club Books

Monier-Williams, Sir Monier (1891) *Brahmanism and Hinduism: or, Religious Thought and Life in India, as Based on the Veda and Other Sacred Books of the Hindus*, 4th edn, London: Murray

Norman-Roth, F (nd) *Some Experiences of an Engineer Doctor: With an Introduction on Our Schooldays by H. Ling Roth*, reprinted from the *Halifax Courier & Guardian*, January–May 1922

Ogieriakhi, Emwinma (1966) *Oba Ovonramwen* and *Oba Ewuakpe*, London: University of London Press

Roth, Felix Norman (1898) 'Diary of a Surgeon with the Benin Punitive Expedition', *Journal of Manchester Geographical Society*, rpt as Appendix II in Henry Ling Roth (1903), ii–xii

Roth, Henry Ling (1911) 'On the use and display of anthropological collections in museums', *The Museums Journal* 10, 286–90

———. 1903[1968] *Great Benin: Its Customs, Art and Horrors*, reprint London, 1968, Halifax: F King & Sons

Rotimi, Ola (1974) *Ovonramwen Nogbaisi: An Historical Tragedy in English*, Benin City and Ibadan: Ethiope

Ryder, AFC (1969) *Benin and the Europeans 1485–1897*, London: Longmans

Salubi, Adogbeji (1960) 'The origins of Sapele township', *Journal of the Historical Society of Nigeria* 2(1), 115–35

Sanders, ER (1969) 'The Hamitic hypothesis: its origin and function in time perspective', *Journal of African History*, 521–32

'Self-styled rebel seeks independence for oil-producing Niger delta', IRINnews.org (2004) http://www.irinnews.org/report.asp?ReportID=42230&SelectRegion=West_Africa, July 2004, accessed March 2005

Willett, Frank (nd) Typescript of 'Review for the *Journal of Asian and African Studies*. Roth, H.L., *Great Benin*', HL Roth Papers, copy in the author's possession.

CHAPTER 5

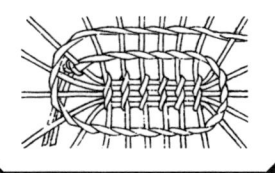

The Primitive Body and Colonial Administration: Henry Ling Roth's Approach to Body Modification

Alice Gorman

As a collector, curator and ethnographer, Henry Ling Roth (1855–1925) had wide-ranging interests, writing about insects, agriculture, the sugar industry, trade, textiles, archaeology and indigenous people in Australia, Africa, the Caribbean and South East Asia. He was one of many in the nascent discipline of anthropology intrigued by the body modifications encountered among 'primitive races' in the era of Britain's most aggressive colonial expansion. In his major works on Tasmania (1890, 1899), Sarawak and North Borneo (1896), and Benin (1903), Ling Roth collated sources to give comprehensive accounts of body practices in these regions. He collected the material culture of body modification for the Bankfield Museum, where he was Curator, and some of his artefacts were later acquired by the Horniman Museum. In particular, he became interested in the tattoo traditions of the Pacific Roth (1900a, 1901, 1905, 1906, nd [1923]).

Ling Roth contributed to the debate on some of the most pressing anthropological questions of the era: the cultural and genetic relationship between the Tasmanian Aborigines, the Melanesian Papuans and the pygmy Negrito people of the Andaman Islands. By arguing that scarification was a primitive version of the art of tattoo, Ling Roth supported an evolutionary hypothesis concerning this relationship. Precursors of modern anthropology like Ling Roth used body modification to construct a notion of the primitive that suited the agendas of colonial administrations in Australia and the Andaman Islands. Despite this, Ling Roth's views were complex and reflected the instabilities of colonial anthropology.

The Most Primitive Races on Earth

In the 1700s, the colonial move into South East Asia brought an extraordinary fact, long known by the Chinese and Arab travellers of the first millennium, to European attention. Inhabiting the Andaman Islands and isolated pockets of the Philippines, the Malay Peninsula and Thailand were a pygmy people with coal-black skin and frizzy hair. They were called Negritos or 'little Negroes' by the Spanish, who presumed them to be the descendants of a shipwrecked slave vessel from Africa.

From the start, the Negritos, particularly the Andamanese, were perceived to have physical and cultural affinities with the Tasmanian Aborigines (Hambly 1931:8; Garson 1899; Lane Fox 1878; Bonwick 1870; Huxley 1870:404). The Andamanese and the Tasmanians were seen as exceptionally 'backward' on account of their lack of arithmetic, inability to make fire and poverty of stone tools. Indeed both populations were held to be barely capable of producing stone tools, thus failing to meet the first criterion of 'savagery' (Gorman 2000:156; Hambly 1931:91; Roth 1899:v, vii; Powell 1888). There was also a question about their relationship with the Papuans: physical similarities between the Tasmanians and Melanesians had been noted by Cook in 1777 (Ryan 1981:51); and in some parts of Papua-New Guinea, short stature had been observed (eg Bonwick 1870:222; WWT 1932). Compared with that of Polynesians, the material culture of the darker-skinned and frizzy-haired Melanesians in the New Hebrides, New Caledonia and Fiji was seen as rudimentary (Thomas 1994:101). Moreover, the Andamanese, Tasmanians and Papuans all practised the body modification known as scarification or cicatrisation, in which the skin was cut to form a pattern of scars.

Were these races separate species, or did they have a common physical and cultural origin? Were the Tasmanians the 'missing link' in the evolutionary chain (Ryan 1981:2) or the Andamanese the most 'pure' race on Earth (Gorman 2000:156)? These thorny problems were a litmus test for conflicting theories of cultural and physical diversity in the British Empire: polygeny and monogeny, evolution and diffusion.

Quantifying the Primitive Body

From the 18th to the 20th centuries, it was believed that human physical, moral, intellectual and social development could be determined by and perceived in the body. Measurements of the body became an integral part of defining race. In the field, colonial administrators, like MV Portman in the Andaman Islands, took photographs, examined hair type, measured proportions and drew outlines of hands to quantify the primitive body (Portman & Molesworth 1893–94).

Other 'characteristics' of race were also assessed and compared: resistance to thirst, stamina, physical strength, intellect, temperament, emotional responses and responses to pain. Moral and emotional states were seen as immutable characteristics expressed through the body (eg Bonwick 1870:131; Thomas 1994:84–85). One form of this expression was body modification.

At the extremities of empire, travellers were astonished to witness extensive, lengthy, dangerous and extremely painful body modification regimes based on tattoo and scarification. In tattoo, the skin is pierced to introduce pigment and form a coloured pattern. Scarification, or cicatrisation, is a technique of cutting the skin to make a decorative raised scar pattern. Scar formation can be enhanced by recutting or rubbing with an irritant. The Tasmanians, Ling Roth recorded, rubbed charcoal into the cuts to stimulate the growth of scar tissue (1899:125).

Because it often seemed that these 'savage' people bore the pain of body modification with far less fuss than a 'civilised' European, it was presumed that they felt less pain – in effect, that their nervous systems were less developed. Later research showed that pain, and the ability to bear it, were aspects that gave the modifications their high social value (eg Bohannan 1956:121). Craniometrical evidence was used to support this presumption. The interior of crania supposedly showed that Tasmanian brains had fewer convolutions, demonstrating a nervous system different from that of Europeans (Bonwick 1870:130). In this way body modifications could be construed as direct evidence of a primitive physiological body. They were both a racial characteristic and an indication of place in the hierarchy of savagery to civilisation.

Polygenists regarded these traits as fundamental, indicating the existence of distinct races with separate origins. Races were adapted to the environment in which they arose: the possibility of migration did not exist. In this way scarification was considered a defining 'characteristic' of Papuan race rather than a practice with a historical genesis (Bonwick 1870:125; Maury quoted in Bonwick 1870:223). Monogenists, influenced by Darwin, considered human variation to be the result of environmental conditions modifying an original species (Quatrefages de Bréau 1877:21). As the original species dispersed, they carried with them common ancestral traits, and these similarities could be used to understand the evolutionary relationship between races. Thus, polygenists and monogenists held opposing views on the methods and rationale of anthropology as a science (Quatrefages de Bréau 1877:213).

Descent, Migration and the Lost Continent

To account for the perceived similarities between the Tasmanians, Andaman Islanders and Papuans, WH Flower, a monogenist, argued that the Negritos were a primitive human type from which African negroes and Melanesians were descended (1880, 1884).[1] It was well known that Tasmanians and Andamanese were not proficient in manufacturing sea-craft or navigation; Quatrefages de Bréau (1895) therefore proposed that Negrito people had drifted on currents to disperse over a vast domain from New Guinea to the Persian Gulf, and from the Malay Archipelago to Japan. On the polygenist side, Nott argued that neither the Tasmanians, the Australians nor the Andamanese exhibited any tendency towards migration; and moreover they were separated by vast ocean areas and living in very different climates. These facts pointed towards an autochthonous origin (Bonwick 1870:213).

Others favoured a far more romantic hypothesis to account for the wide geographical separation of the Negritos: the lost continent of Lemuria (Bonwick 1870:261; Falkinder 1931:69). This neat explanation also accounted both for the distribution of flora and fauna and the presence of Papuan Moriori people in New Zealand (Bonwick 1870:255–57):

> Some straggled towards what is now the north-western part of Australia, and so spread over the equatorial region. Another branch by slow movement followed, perhaps, the latitude of Van Diemen's land, left deposits of life in the forests by the way, and pressed onward to New Zealand, to the Chatham Isles, and to more distant points which have since been swallowed up by the swelling ocean (Bonwick 1870:265).

According to this theory, as the continent became submerged, the Negrito groups were isolated at the edges in the pattern observed at the time of European colonisation (Falkinder 1931:69).

In 1894, the distribution of Negrito people in South East Asia was discussed at a meeting of the British Association for the Advancement of Science. At this time Ling Roth was working on *The Natives of Sarawak and British North Borneo* (1896). Against some opposition, he argued that there was insufficient evidence to determine if a Negrito population survived in Borneo (Roth 1896:293). He suggested that skulls of Negrito appearance found in Borneo, illustrated in Quatrefages de Bréau and Hamy's famous *Crania Ethnica* (1882), were more likely to be those of Andaman Islanders, who had been widely traded as slaves in the region (Roth 1896:298). On the other hand, the evidence he had mustered in two editions of *The Aborigines of Tasmania* (Roth 1899:Chapter XIV) had led him to conclude that the Tasmanians were a remnant Negrito people:

> It would appear therefore that, from comparisons made between Tasmanians and Negritos, we find close relationship, as regards the osteology, the hair, and the language, and we are, perhaps, not far wrong in concluding that this Nigritic stock once peopled the whole of the Australian continent and Tasmania, until annihilated and partly assimilated by the invaders now known as Australians (Roth 1899:227).

It was in this context that Ling Roth took a closer look at how tattoo and scarification mapped on to the geographical distribution of races in the Pacific.

Techniques and Design in Modifying the Skin

'Scarification' and 'tattoo' were interchangeable terms in early ethnography. In collecting information on body practices in Tasmania, Roth realised that the term 'tattoo' was inadequate to describe what was in fact scarification (Roth 1899:126). He proposed a classification of skin-marking methods to avoid the confusion so evident in the accounts of travellers and ethnographers (Roth 1900b:118):

1. TATTOO: Tattooing by pricking, leaving the skin smooth after healing (Pacific Islands)
2. MOKO: Tattoo combined with chiselling to leave furrows in the skin (New Zealand)
3. CICATRIX: Scarification by carving using a knife or chisel (West Africa)
4. KELOID: Scarification, by irritating and re-opening the wound to form a raised scar (Tasmania, Australia, Melanesia, Central Africa)

This classification expressed both texture, moving from the raised keloid scars so grotesque to the European observer to the smooth-coloured skin resulting from tattoo, and colour, from darkest skin to lightest skin. Keloid scarring was associated with people considered the most primitive: the dark-skinned hunter-gatherers of Tasmania and Australia, as well as dark-skinned Melanesians. The lighter-skinned Polynesians exhibited a higher level of civilisation in their body decoration. Ling Roth directly equated the technique of body modification with technological level: for example, 'the Tasmanian, with his rude stone implement still in the Palaeolithic stage, could not produce what the Samoan could with his finished pricking tool' (Roth 1900b:117). Implicit in the classification was an evolutionary development from the most primitive form of body modification to the most sophisticated. In the path from savagery to civilisation, scarification was a 'primitive' form of tattooing (Portman 1899 Vol 1:237).

The place of Maori *moko*, which combines the pigmentation of tattoo with the textural features of scarification, was initially unclear. In *moko*, lines are cut into the face to a depth of 4 mm by an adze and a mallet, and black pigment or red ochre is rubbed into the cuts, producing a raised and coloured pattern (Hambly 1925:39, 262). At first Roth speculated that *moko* had evolved from the more widespread Polynesian tattoo (Roth 1900b:118). By the following year, when he wrote a comprehensive article about Maori tattoo and *moko*, Ling Roth was wondering if it might not be the other way around. Some travellers to New Zealand had commented on the *tangi*, a mourning scarification made by women. '[H]as the *tangi* been at the bottom of the whole system of Maori tattoo and moko?' he asked (Roth 1901:34).

Scarification was a racial characteristic of Negroes, Negritos and Papuans, not of Polynesians. But there were some reports of a pre-Maori Papuan population in New Zealand, known as the *Moriori*. Crozet had seen 'true negroes with woolly heads, and shorter' in 1771 (1891:28). Neither Cook nor Joseph Banks mentioned the presence of Papuans in New Zealand. But Ling Roth found a comment by Banks that 'A few [natives] had on their faces or arms regular scars, as if made with a sharp instrument, such as I have seen on the faces of negroes' (quoted in Roth 1901:51). In Roth's classification of skin-marking techniques, and also in the opinion of the polygenist school, scarification was a characteristic of the Papuan race (Bonwick 1870:215).

In classifying the designs of Maori *moko* and tattoo, Ling Roth noted that the dominant spiral motifs were unlike designs elsewhere in Polynesia (Roth 1901:59). However, the Papuan branch of the Melanesians 'revelled' in spirals, suggesting either that there had been considerable contact or that the design elements derived from the Papuan population in New Zealand (Roth 1901:60). In his careful way, he suggested that 'there was no reason why the almost infinite variety of spirals and scrolls as depicted in Maori art could not have had an independent origin' (Roth 1901:61), but that the hypothesis could be put to the test by correlating designs with geographic locations, to see if differences appeared in places where a Melanesian presence was recorded. In the end, he inclined to the view that the spiral had become such a distinctive element of Maori art through Papuan influence. Although he was concerned by conflicting reports, Ling Roth interpreted the evidence to indicate that (1) there was a pre-Maori Papuan population in New Zealand, and (2) Maori tattoo and *moko* had evolved from the earlier and more primitive form of scarification practiced by the Papuans. This argument resolved the ambiguous form of *moko* yet preserved the evolutionary hierarchy of body modification in which Negrito people were both an older and more primitive race. It also supported the case for migration as presented by Flower and Quatrefages de Bréau. Ling Roth interpreted the distribution of body modification types in the Pacific within an evolutionary, monogenist framework.

Administering the Primitive Body

EB Tylor always hoped that anthropology would develop 'from a derided byway to truth to a time when its help and decisions are sought for by governments' (quoted in Penniman 1935:189). Ling Roth's views sometimes differed from those of his mentor, but in this case he was of the same mind. He argued that anthropology was an essential tool in the government of the empire:

> Politically, it is of the first importance that our governing officials should have a thorough knowledge of the native races subject to them – and this is the knowledge that anthropology can give them – for such knowledge can teach what methods of government and what forms of taxation are most suited to the particular tribes, or to the stage of civilisation in which we find them (Roth 1903 Appendix IV:xix).

Much depended on the 'stage of civilisation', as the method of colonial rule was frequently tailored to an assessment of evolutionary development. Social and economic inequalities between indigenous people and their colonial rulers could be justified by reference to their position in the evolutionary hierarchy (Heinz 1998:427). Body modification was one of a suite of 'racial' characteristics that could be used by colonial administrators to assign a people to their proper place on that scale. For example, in Fiji, people in the western interior, perceived as Melanesian because of their physical appearance, were administered differently from other Fijians on the basis that they were more primitive (Thomas 1994:109). This was far from a simple equation, however; as Thomas points out, there was a 'multiplicity of colonizing projects and potential subversions of them' (Thomas 1994:195).

Both the Tasmanians and the Andamanese were initially seen by early travellers and ethnographers as 'noble savages', living in a state of nature (Gorman 2000:156; Travers 1968:13; Ryan 1981:3–4). Attitudes towards them shifted as colonial intentions towards their land changed. It was not until the 1830s, when pastoral settlers had taken up all available grazing land, that the Tasmanians became irredeemably problematic (Travers 1968:13; Ryan 1981:3–4). Anthropometric measurements of the size of the foot and the proportions of the arms and legs were used to equate the Tasmanians with the orang-utan and the mandrill

(Bonwick 1870:122). By 1890, when Ling Roth published the first edition of *The Aborigines of Tasmania*, Europeans considered that the Tasmanians had been 'extinct' for 15 years. The classification of the Tasmanians as the most primitive type of humanity led to the conviction that this was a natural outcome (Ryan 1981:1–3). Colonial policies of genocide were in fact irrelevant in the face of natural selection: the doom of the Tasmanians was immanent in their primitive bodies.

In the 1870s, pacification of the fiercely resistant Andaman Islanders became a priority for the protection of British shipping and for the convict-run agriculture and logging industries (Portman 1899). The 'pure savages' were transformed into near-animals by 1890, when Conan Doyle employed an Andaman Islander as a character in the Sherlock Holmes story 'The sign of four': 'Never have I seen features so deeply marked with all bestiality and cruelty. His small eyes glowed and burned with a sombre light, and his thick lips were writhed back from his teeth, which grinned and chattered at us with half-animal fury' (Conan Doyle 1952:235).

In both Tasmania and the Andaman Islands, the administrative solution was removal to reserves, missions and homes located on the least economically valuable land, where the Andamanese and Tasmanians could continue to enjoy such benefits of civilisation as agriculture and European houses. Today, India is intent on 'civilising' the surviving Jarawa and Jangil people in the Andaman Islands, in order to acquire their land for resettlement.

Conclusions

The process of recording and documenting the bodies of Negrito people in Tasmania, the Andaman Islands and the Pacific served to emphasise their difference from the civilised Europeans. Scarification was one of the features, along with skin colour, short stature and hair type, that marked their bodies as primitive. As the form of body modification at the base of the hierarchy of skin-piercing techniques classified by Ling Roth, scarification could indicate a primitive nervous system, a body not yet fully evolved.

Conjecture about the poly- or monogenesis of human races had direct outcomes for the administration of 'primitive' people. In North America, for example, a polygenist argument was used by some to justify slavery (Quatrefages de Bréau 1877:22). A leaning towards monogeny in British anthropology, influenced by Huxley, Tylor and Quatrefages de Bréau, allowed colonised people to be assessed as to their level of evolution, and recognition of land tenure was tied to this (Powell 1888). Moral obligations towards the subject people were also defined on the basis of evolutionary level. Anthropologists were both complicit in and critical of this process (James 1973). Despite his monogenist allegiance, Ling Roth acknowledged the causal role of European policies in the 'sad and untimely destruction' of the Tasmanians (Roth 1899:228).

Although Ling Roth favoured evolution and monogeny to account for human diversity, he was far from a vulgar unilinear evolutionist. He believed a single explanation for the widespread practice of body modification was too simple: 'Whatever may have been the original ideas or chance circumstances which may have brought it into existence, ultimately its objective became manifold' (Roth 1900b:116). He cited the widely differing motivations for body modification seen in different parts of the world, such as social obligation, personal prowess, high birth, arriving at marriageable age, protection from evil spirits and tribal affiliation (Roth 1900b:116–17). In this he prefigured the functionalist and structuralist anthropologists who saw body modification as an element of a cultural whole. Alfred Gell acknowledges his debt to Ling Roth and other early anthropologists, who 'are far less appreciated than they should be as creative anthropologists rather than as dull but useful data providers' (Gell 1993:v).

Monogenist theories about a Negrito migration to Tasmania continue to have an impact in archaeology, anthropology and colonialist administration in Australia. They informed Birdsell's trihybrid theory of the population of Australia and Tasmania, in which the Negrito Barrineans were ousted from the mainland by the Murrayians, who in their turn gave way to the Carpentarians (Birdsell 1967; Tindale & Birdsell 1941).[2] More recently, Windschuttle and Gillin (2002) cited Ling Roth's *The Aborigines of Tasmania* in support of their argument that the Negrito occupation of Australia has been concealed by an academic cabal for political reasons. By this argument, contemporary Aboriginal people have a weaker claim to rights as traditional owners because they are not the original inhabitants of the continent. Understanding the context in which Ling Roth undertook his research on body modification is startlingly relevant for a nation still grappling with the structures of an earlier century.

Notes

1. Recent research using Mitochondrial DNA (mtDNA) and other genetic markers suggests that the Andamanese are more closely related to the original out-of-Africa population of anatomically modern humans than they are to other South East Asian populations (eg Thangaraj *et al* 2005; Macaulay *et al* 2005).
2. Morphometric analyses by Abbie (1963, 1966) and Larnach and Macintosh (1966) demonstrated that differences between Tasmanians and mainland Aboriginal people stem from genetic isolation over 12,000 years, and this has been supported by recent mtDNA evidence.

Works Cited

Abbie, AA (1966) 'Physical characteristics', in Cotton, BC (ed), *Aboriginal man in south and central Australia Part I*, Adelaide: Government Printer, 9–15
———. (1963) 'Physical characteristics of Australian aborigines', in Shiels, Helen (ed), *Australian Aboriginal Studies*, Melbourne: Oxford University Press, 89–107
Birdsell, JB (1967) 'Preliminary data on the trihybrid theory of the Australian Aborigines', *Archaeology and Physical Anthropology in Oceania* 2, 100–55
Bohannan, Paul (1956) 'Beauty and scarification amongst the Tiv', *Man* 56, 117–21
Bonwick, James (1870) *Daily Life and Origin of the Tasmanians*, London: Sampson Low, Son and Marston, reprint 1967 by Johnson Reprint Corporation, London and New York
Conan Doyle, A (1952) 'The sign of four', in *The Complete Sherlock Holmes. Long Stories*, London: John Murray, 143–271
Crozet, Julien Marie (1891) *Crozet's Voyage to Tasmania, New Zealand, the Ladrone Islands, and the Philippines, in the Years 1771–1772/Translated by H. Ling Roth; With a Preface and a Brief Reference to the Literature of New Zealand by Jas. R. Boosé*, London: Truslove & Shirley
Falkinder, JS (1931) 'The extinct Tasmanians. Part III', *Mankind* 1(3), 67–71
Flower, WH (1884) 'Additional observations on the osteology of the natives of the Andaman Islands', *Journal of the Anthropological Institute of Britain and Ireland* 14, 115–20
———. (1880) 'On the osteology and affinities of the natives of the Andaman Islands. 24 June', *Journal of the Anthropological Institute of Britain and Ireland* 9, 108–35
Garson, JG (1899) 'Osteology', in Roth, HL, *The Aborigines of Tasmania*, Halifax: F King and Sons, Chapter XIII
Gell, Alfred (1993) *Wrapping in Images: Tattooing in Polynesia*, Oxford: Clarendon Press
Gorman, AC (2000) 'The archaeology of body modification. The identification of symbolic behaviour through use-wear and residues on flaked stone tools', unpublished PhD thesis, University of New England
Gupta, Bandana (1976) *The Andamans, Land of the Primitives*, Calcutta: Jijnasa
Hambly, Wilfrid D (1931) 'Types of "Tronattas" or stone implements used by the Aborigines of Tasmania', *American Anthropologist* 33(1), 88–91
———. (1925) *The History of Tattooing and its Significance, With Some Account of Other Forms of Corporal Markings*, London: HF and G Witherby
Heinz, Andreas (1998) 'Colonial perspectives in the construction of the psychotic patient as primitive man', *Critique of Anthropology* 18(4), 421–44
Huxley, TH (1870) 'On the geographical distribution of the chief modifications of mankind', *Journal of the Ethnological Society of London* 2, 404–12
James, Wendy (1973) 'The anthropologist as reluctant imperialist', in Asad, Talal (ed), *Anthropology and the Colonial Encounter*, London: Ithaca Press, 41–69
Lane Fox, Major-General A (aka Pitt Rivers) (1878) 'Observations on Mr Man's collection of Andamanese and Nicobarese objects', *Journal of the Anthropological Institute of Britain and Ireland* VII, 434–69
Larnach, SL and Macintosh, NWG (1966) 'The craniology of the Aborigines of coastal New South Wales', *Oceania Monograph* No 13
Macaulay, V, Hill, C, Achilli, A, Rengo, C, Clarke, D, Meehan, W, Blackburn, J, Semino, O, Scozzari, R, Cruciani, F, Taha, A, Shaari, N, Kassim, R, Joseph M, Patimah Ismail, P, Zainuddin, Z, Goodwin, W, Bulbeck, D, Bandelt, H-J, Oppenheimer, S, Torroni, A and Richards, M (2005) 'Single, Rapid Coastal Settlement of Asia Revealed by Analysis of Complete Mitochondrial Genomes', *Science* 308(5724):1034–36
Penniman, TK (1935) *A Hundred Years of Anthropology*, London: Duckworth
Portman, MV (1899) *A History of Our Relations with the Andamanese. Compiled From Histories and Travels, and From the Records of the Government of India*, 2 vols, Calcutta: Office of the Superintendent of Government Printing

Portman, MV and Molesworth, W (1893–94) *Andaman Islanders*, 15 vols, Calcutta
Powell, JW (1888) 'From barbarism to civilisation', *The American Anthropologist*, 1(1), 97–123
Quatrefages de Bréau, Jean Louis Armand de (1895) *The Pygmies*, transl Frederick Starr, London and New York: Macmillan
———. (1877) *L'espèce humaine*, 3rd edn, Paris: Librairie Germer Baillière et Cie
Quatrefages de Bréau, Jean Louis Armand de and Hamy, EJ (1882) *Crania Ethnica: Les cranes des races humaines, décrits et figurés d'après les collections du Muséum d'Histoire Naturelle de Paris, de la Société d'Anthropologie de Paris et les principales collections de la France et de l'étranger*, Paris: JB Baillière et fils
Roth, Henry Ling (nd [1923]) *Some Tatu Notes from the Pacific*, Halifax
———. (1906) 'Tonga Islanders' skin marking', *Man* 6, 6–9
———. (1905) 'Tatu in the Society Islands', *Journal of the Anthropological Institute of Great Britain and Ireland* 35, 283–94
———. (1903) *Great Benin: Its Customs, Art and Horrors*, repr 1968, London: Routledge and Kegan Paul
———. (1901) 'Maori tatu and moko', *Journal of the Royal Anthropological Institute of Great Britain and Ireland* 31, 29–64
———. (1900a) 'Artificial skin marking in the Sandwich Islands', *Internationale Archiv für Ethnographie* 13, 198–201
———. (1900b) 'On permanent artificial skin marks: a definition of terms', *Journal of the Royal Anthropological Institute of Great Britain and Ireland* 30, 116–18
———. (1899) *The Aborigines of Tasmania*, assisted by Marion E Butler and Jas. Backhouse Walker, with a chapter on the osteology, by JG Garson, Preface by Edward B Tylor, 2nd edn, revised and enlarged with map, Halifax: F King and Sons. Facsimile of second edition printed [1968] by Fullers Bookshop, Hobart. First edition 1890
———. (1896) *The Natives of Sarawak and British North Borneo*, 2 vols, London: Truslove & Hanson
Ryan, Lyndall (1981) *The Aboriginal Tasmanians*, St Lucia: University of Queensland Press
Thangaraj, K, Chaubey, G, Kivisild, T, Reddy, AG, Singh, VK, Rasalkar, AA, and Singh, L (2005) 'Reconstructing the Origin of Andaman Islanders', *Science* 308(5724):996
Thomas, Nicholas (1994) *Colonialism's Culture: Anthropology, Travel and Government*, Melbourne: Melbourne University Press
Tindale, NB and Birdsell, JB (1941) 'Results of the Harvard-Adelaide Universities Anthropological Expedition, 1938-1939. Tasmanoid tribes in North Queensland', *Records of the South Australian Museum* 7, 1–9
Travers, Robert (1968) *The Tasmanians. The Story of a Doomed Race*, Melbourne: Cassell Australia
Windschuttle, Keith and Gillin, Tim (2002) 'The extinction of the Australian pygmies', *Quadrant* 46(6), 7–18
WWT (1932) 'South Pacific races', *Mankind* 1(4), 85

PART 3

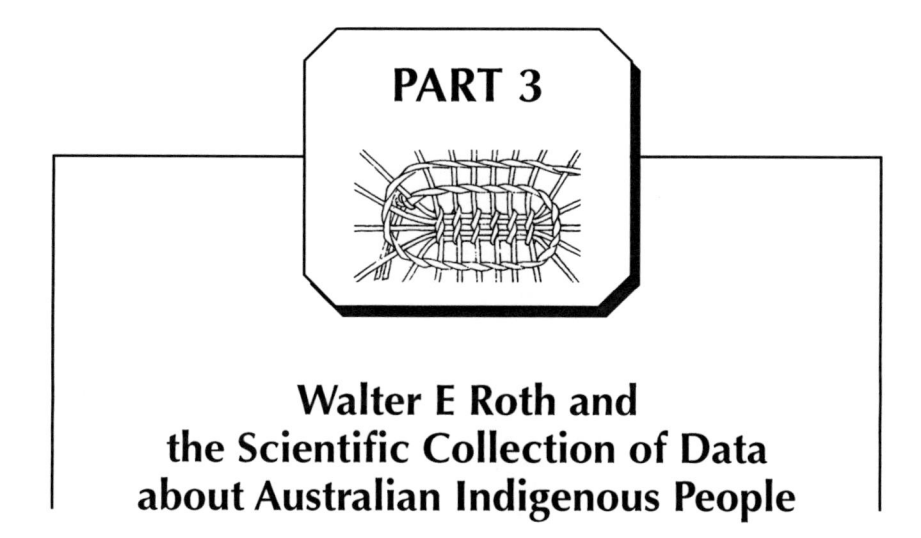

Walter E Roth and the Scientific Collection of Data about Australian Indigenous People

CHAPTER 6

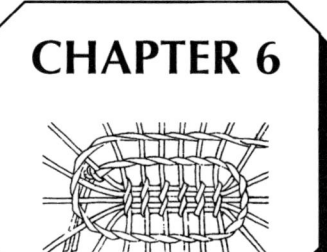

From Oxford to the Bush: WE Roth, WB Spencer and Australian Anthropology

John Mulvaney

When writing Baldwin Spencer's biography in 1978, I commented that Walter Roth's 'stature is overdue for reassessment' (Mulvaney & Calaby 1985:387), a belated need met by this volume and by the conference that preceded it. This paper makes personal amends by examining the evidence for the interaction between Spencer and Roth. Although I had noted Spencer's private misgivings concerning Roth's work, I failed to emphasise the extent to which he encouraged Roth during the period from 1897 to 1903.

Education in England

Spencer's and Roth's careers followed a remarkably parallel trajectory from 1881, when they both entered Oxford University to take the newly established Darwinian biology course in the University Museum. As Spencer was born in 1860 and Roth in 1861, both men were somewhat older and more acquainted with science than most undergraduates.[1]

Following education at University College School, London, Roth spent an academic year at University College, where he achieved a silver medal in comparative anatomy and biology (Reynolds 1988:463–64). This presumably explains his entry to Magdalen College, Oxford, as Demy Scholar.

Spencer received a sound education at Old Trafford School, Manchester, followed by a year at art school. During the 1879–80 academic year he enrolled at Owens College (soon renamed Manchester University). He was fortunate in the quality of his teachers for his intended medical career, four of whom were Fellows of the Royal Society. He was inspired by the newly appointed Zoology professor, Arthur Milnes Marshall, at 27, a champion of evolutionary biology.

Marshall emphasised practical descriptive laboratory research, thereby influencing the careers of several important scientists and changing Spencer's orientation from medicine to biology. It is relevant that when, at 26 years old, Spencer occupied Melbourne's Biology chair, he emulated Marshall's example of inspirational laboratory training and meticulous descriptive research. Also relevant to Spencer's intellectual formation was that he learned geology from Boyd Dawkins, whose interests embraced Palaeolithic society. During Spencer's first year Dawkins published *Early Man in Britain*, preceded in 1874 by his celebrated *Cave Hunting*.

Because Owens College was not authorised to award degrees, at the end of the first year Spencer sat the London University medical examination. He was awarded First Class Honours, resulting in a scholarship to Exeter College, Oxford. He prudently deferred his entry, remaining at Owens for another year. Remarkably for an undergraduate, during that time he published a research paper on the cranial nerves of the dogfish, jointly with his mentor Marshall.

From the commencement of Oxford's 1881–82 academic year, Roth, Spencer and possibly 11 other students enrolled in biology. Just before their final examination in 1884 a class photograph was taken.[2] It reveals images of 10 students and three teachers, a staff-student ratio the stuff of dreams today.

Their most influential teacher was Henry Nottridge Moseley (1844–91), professor of Human and Comparative Anatomy. As a naturalist on the *Challenger* expedition of 1872–76, he had visited Australia. Like Marshall he was a first-generation evolutionary biologist. During his global tour, he became interested in material culture, amassing a large ethnographic collection. His enthusiasm evidently influenced students, especially his outdoor boomerang and spear-throwing demonstrations. Spencer, whose rooms in Exeter College were adjacent to Moseley's, later commented that Moseley 'really knows considerably more concerning anthropology than even Tylor' (Mulvaney & Calaby 1985:45).

Testimony to Moseley's influence are the subsequent careers of at least six of the students. Apart from Roth's and Spencer's activities in Australia, WL Sclater went to British Guinea on an anthropological expedition, later becoming Director of the South African Museum, Capetown. Henry Balfour was Pitt Rivers Museum curator between 1891 and 1939. SJ Hickson did biological and ethnographic fieldwork in

E. D. Y. Pode   H. Balfour   G. H. Fowler
          W. L. Sclater   F. E. Lewin

Rev. H. Johnson   S. J. Hickson   W. E. Roth   H. Y. Oldham
                        Prof. H. N. Moseley   P. N. Waggett
   William Hine   W. B. Spencer   G. C. Bourne   Dr. H. W. Acland   J. G. Ogle
                        MORPHOLOGICAL LABORATORY, OXFORD, 1884

Figure 6.1 Morphological Laboratory, Oxford, 1884 (Reproduced with the permission of Pitt Rivers Museum, University of Oxford)

Celebes (Sulawesi), while Gilbert Bourne researched on the coral atoll of Diego Garcia. These last two scholars subsequently held chairs of Zoology at Manchester and Oxford, respectively (Mulvaney & Calaby 1985:68).

Spencer threw himself into Oxford's intellectual life, becoming founding secretary of an active student science society, attending Ruskin's lectures on art and Edward Tylor's on anthropology. He graduated with First Class Honours. He assisted Tylor and Moseley in transferring the Pitt Rivers ethnographic collection from Bethnal Green, London, to its ugly new Oxford home. He soon was appointed to a Fellowship at Lincoln College. Spencer's meteoric rise culminated late in 1886 with his appointment to Melbourne's foundation Chair of Biology. Amongst the selection committee were TH Huxley and MB Foster, a prominent Cambridge scientist whom, three years earlier, Spencer had arranged to address the Oxford student science society.

Roth and Spencer in Australia

Roth graduated at the same time as Spencer, in 1884. Yet, on his own admission, his Oxford years lacked Spencer's promise. In 1903, when Roth was Queensland's Northern Protector of Aboriginals at Cooktown, he received a letter from Spencer which evidently referred nostalgically to their Oxford period. 'Yes', Roth replied. 'I often think of the dear old times at Oxford, and how I wasted my opportunities. But I think I've now made up for all deficiencies and errors of early youth! – at least I've worked hard since, and certainly tried to make up for lost time'.[3]

Spencer's experience of Roth at Oxford led him to doubt his classmate's ability to apply himself when research opportunities arose. Having met Roth again in 1902, Spencer told Balfour:

> Roth is the same as of old and I shall be very much surprised if he does anything except publish a series of bulletins dealing with games... and dialects and at the same time hold a very comfortable billet. He has chances such as no one else in Australia has with a perfectly free hand and also a boat at his disposal and stores to distribute amongst the natives by means of which he could if judiciously used do no end of ethnographic work.[4]

So thought the envious and busy Professor Spencer, who met Roth on his voyage to Melbourne with Frank Gillen following their dusty year of anthropological travel, when they were marooned at Borroloola.

Spencer and Roth had pursued parallel careers. Spencer arrived in Australia early in 1887, only a few months before Roth. Roth subsequently returned to London University to complete his medical qualifications before again voyaging to Australia in 1892. As we have seen earlier in this volume, Roth began his anthropological career when appointed surgeon to hospitals in north-western Queensland. In 1894, Spencer's participation in the Horn scientific expedition to Central Australia launched his anthropological vocation, although at this period they had no contact with each other.

Spencer and Ethnological Studies

Roth compiled the fruits of his ethnological gleanings in Queensland in his *Ethnological Studies among the North-West-Central Queensland Aborigines*, whose preface is dated September 1897, a period during which Spencer and Gillen were feverishly preparing their *Native Tribes of Central Australia*. It is doubtful whether even this electronic age could surpass the speed with which Roth's book was published and peer reviewed. Spencer's appreciative 3,000-word review appeared in the *Australasian* on 18 December 1897. His praiseworthy comments should be evaluated within the situation where Roth had scooped Spencer and Gillen, who apparently were unaware that his research was in progress and might have felt some hostility, resulting in disparaging remarks. This was not so.

I infer this from two letters which Spencer sent to Balfour, curator at the Pitt Rivers Museum. On 20 September 1897 he wrote: 'I hear that a "Dr Roth" has been working amongst Queensland natives... and that he has a work of "very great value" concerning their customs in press. I fancy it is the celebrated Roth of our times' (Marett & Penniman 1932:136). By 2 December 1897 Spencer had received his review copy. '[O]ur old friend Roth has been at work amongst the natives of Queensland', he told Balfour: '[His] book... contains some valuable material. He has evidently worked in complete ignorance of what has been done by others which in certain respects makes his work all the more valuable'. James Frazer received similar tidings from Spencer, written on 6 December 1897.[5]

Spencer's review opened in comparable vein (Spencer 1897). Because Roth worked in isolation, he noted, his book possessed greater virtues: particularly 'with regard to certain disputed questions [it] is of all the more value'. Before discussing Spencer's review, it is appropriate to examine this strange claim, virtually that a little ignorance is a good scientific thing.

It reflected Spencer's view of the factual basis of systematic ethnographic research. He explained this to Frazer, the *Golden Bough* pundit, in July 1897 during his first contact with Frazer, before he knew about Roth's project.[6] Explaining his partnership with Gillen, he informed Frazer that he supported Gillen with 'endless questions and things to find out, and by mutual agreement he reads no one else's work so as to keep him unprejudiced in the way of theories'. In other words Spencer believed that 'facts' existed independently without reference to any preconceptions or hypotheses.

This also conformed with Frazer's firm conviction, as for example, when a year later he praised the *Native Tribes* manuscript for having 'rigidly excluded comparisons and speculation' (Marett & Penniman 1932:24). It was within this perversely constraining context that Spencer praised Roth's 'objectivity', yet he also reprimanded him for not discussing totems (a contradiction discussed below).

Spencer's charitable review betrayed no hint of irritation that Roth's unheralded book had publication priority over *Native Tribes*. He acknowledged the care and time-consuming nature of Roth's fieldwork, 'the most detailed of any yet published... consequently of peculiar value'. He particularly praised Roth's documentation of sign language, which was illustrated 'by the facile pen of the author' (1897:1354).

That this was sincere praise is confirmed by Spencer's words to Balfour, that this 'most valuable chapter [was]... the best yet published'. 'I do not think', Spencer continued, 'that any one worker has... got anything like the results which Roth has except the man with whom I am working – Gillen who has got still deeper'.[7] Indeed, Spencer noted several comparisons with and anticipations of their own research. He praised Roth's data on *pituri* trade and ceremonial exchange routes, including the travels of the 'Molonga corroboree' (which Spencer and Gillen were to document in 1901).

In this intellectual context I wondered whether it was Roth who provided the clue for Spencer's advice to trace 'the wanderings of the various totems', which so enthused Gillen as a 'happy inspiration'. But Gillen received that message well before June 1897, when he announced successful outcomes from that approach (Mulvaney, Morphy & Petch 1997:166). Both Roth and Spencer merit credit for their close observation of Aboriginal societies, independently discerning their cultural dimensions, despite only dim comprehension.

Spencer's generous assessment of Roth's book concluded with the tribute that it 'adds materially to our knowledge of Australian anthropology, and which will be of permanent value'. He was more correct and appreciative than AP Elkin's terse appraisal – 'a book for specialists' (Elkin 1975:20).

Spencer on Ethno-Pornography

Not that Roth escaped Spencer's criticism. Surprisingly, in view of his comments in correspondence, he wished for more information in the concluding chapter on 'certain rights of initiation'. Roth titled this illustrated chapter 'Ethno-pornography', discussing subincision and a variety of sexual themes. Roth warned readers that it was placed last 'in the hope that those who do not wish to peruse its pages need not unwittingly find themselves doing so' (Roth 1897:v–vi). HM Green wryly observed that this precaution 'suggests that Dr Roth was amazingly ignorant of human nature' (Green 1962:822).

That chapter certainly offended Spencer's late-Victorian sensibilities. 'He has invented the term ethno-pornographical which is most objectionable', he complained to Balfour.[8] 'Pornographical implies something almost deliberately "dirty" and as it is merely a matter of scientific inquiry I am very sorry that he has used this term'. 'The one great drawback of Roth's work', Spencer continued, 'is that he has looked at their customs from what we might call a "dirty" point of view and the expressions he uses such as "bucks" and "gentry" make you feel wild to think that he should spoil such a valuable piece of work in this way. It is execrably written, but despite all this it is the most valuable piece of work done for many years... I never thought Roth would have stuck to a thing in this way'.

When Spencer chided Roth for his terminology, Roth was unrepentant. 'Bye the bye. Pornography is no invention of mine – you an Oxford man too! Look up any dictionary... and you will find it to express "obscenity in general"'.[9]

Because the chapter is celebrated amongst anthropological cognoscenti, Roth's further explanation merits inclusion here:

> Furthermore the government originally intended omitting the last chapter with accompanying plate, and publishing it separately for special distribution to certain people only; mainly for the purpose of drawing public attention to the present condition of certain of the aborigines in view of the legislation proposed to be enforced. The ordinary reading public had in a sense to be protected by being told that such and such a chapter was obscene, and that they could please themselves if they chose to read it. And after all, scientific and interesting as these particulars may be to men like us, they are certainly not so to the general lay reader. Personally I admire and respect the aborigines – so long as they are not corrupted by opium, alcohol and syphilis.[10]

Modern critics who abhor the 'stolen generation' being removed from their families need to acknowledge that 'experts' such as Roth, as voiced here, held sincere humanitarian motivation for their misguided authoritarian policies.

Totemism (or What Passes for It?)

Contemporary anthropological debate raged around totemism, a North Amerindian term. Aboriginal religion is not simply 'totemism' but a great variety of totems. Today totemism is recognised to embrace many conceptual categories. It involves beliefs and practices in which there exist individual or group relations between other groups, natural species or natural phenomena, such as lightning, diseases and even emotional states. Clan totems symbolise relationships of clan members to each other, to ancestors or to special places. Neither Roth nor Spencer appreciated this complex spiritual world. Spencer and Gillen were soon to supply invaluable data in *Native Tribes* (1899), particularly evidence sought by James Frazer, totemism's guru and patron to these partners. Spencer worried that Roth failed to discover totemism in Queensland, because he envisaged its universal occurrence as basic to Australian group relations. He went so far as to infer from internal clues in Roth's book that totems existed in his area on the model of the Arrernte people.

Spencer wrote to Balfour in some exasperation:

> For the various forms of relationship he has invented a series of names which I think inadvisable as they will tend to complicate matters without any compensating advantage. The tribal name he calls a Patronym, the mother's tribal division a Gamonym and the mother's child's name... a Paedomatronym and the terms of relationship are either Heteronyms or Genaeonyms.[11]

While it was correct that Roth's outlandish classification terminology complicated the already esoteric scheme of Europe's armchair scholars, Spencer's vexation possibly lay in the precedence which such terms held over the forthcoming nomenclature in *Native Tribes*. It is relevant that Roth was aware of scientific precedence. In his detailed response to Spencer's review, written in January 1898, Roth agreed that his term 'Patronym' was unsuitable, yet added, 'I don't like your expression totem-names'. 'But after all', he concluded, 'what does it matter, so long as our readers can understand what we mean? On the other hand if one of us employs a term such as Climanym [Roth 1897:65, 169]... it would be inadvisable I think for you to alter or re-name it, especially in view of the fact that I am first in the field to have recorded it'. He added optimistically, 'At any rate I know that you will give me credit for anything I may have done in the way of priority'.[12]

In fairness to Roth in what must have been an embarrassing situation, it is obvious that his research was undertaken under remote frontier conditions, possibly even unpremeditated before he realised his unprecedented observational opportunities as an itinerant outback doctor. He was unread in Australian anthropological literature, which Spencer's review hinted at and which Roth was happy to admit. 'You were quite right in your surmises', he told Spencer, adding that since his book's publication he had read Howitt and Fison.[13]

Roth made no secret of such limitations, in fact the reverse. Robert Etheridge prepared the bibliography for inclusion in the *Ethnological Studies* memoir, stating that 'while away in the North working at his mss, Dr Roth was unaware of the existence of the following literature' (Roth 1897:vii–x).

Roth responded immediately to Spencer's 'kindly criticism' in the *Australasian*, explaining that he avoided the word 'totem' because he believed that its formal application was to North American Indians, and that its meaning was inapplicable in Queensland. He outlined his reasoning in two letters,[14] basically that in his State 'the social grouping has been devised by a process of natural selection to regulate the proper distribution… of food'.[15]

Roth's evolutionary interpretation had been presented openly a month before Spencer's review. In a lecture to the Royal Society of Queensland during November 1897, he concluded: 'I am strongly of opinion that the whole class system has been devised, by a process of natural selection, to regulate the proper distribution of the total quality of food available' (Roth 1898:48).

Spencer's pressure proved too great, as Roth reluctantly gave way. Immediately following Roth's explanation, Spencer told Balfour: Roth 'tells me that as [totems] didn't fit in with those among N. Am. indians [sic] he came to the conclusion that they were not totems in the strict sense of the word'.[16] By October 1898 Roth evidently accepted the wisdom of Spencer's terms of social relationship: 'Class, Sub-class, Status term, Relationship term, Totem name, Term of address, etc. they are simple, definitive and do not arrogate too much'.[17]

As previously mentioned, Roth and Spencer finally met in Brisbane in March 1902, when Spencer and Gillen returned by sea from Borroloola. Totemism was pursued by Spencer, who informed Balfour that Roth 'now says he was mistaken' that totemism was absent amongst his tribes.[18] But Roth refused to publish a recantation. He may have surrendered, but following their meeting he had the last qualifying word. 'So far as I am personally concerned, I doubt if we shall ever arrive at the true origin of totemism, *or rather what passes for it out here in Australia*' [my emphasis].[19]

Later Interactions

Spencer's sense of superiority, that only he had access to 'wild savages', led him to deprecate the findings of his old friend AW Howitt (Mulvaney & Calaby 1985:393). Similarly he erroneously assumed that some of Roth's faults were explicable because his informants were mission and station people. 'He comes very little into contact with the wild savage', he informed Balfour. 'His Boulia and Normanton blacks are all civilised and clothed and, as he himself describes, adjourn for tea!'[20] Spencer obviously overlooked the reality that he and Gillen worked along the Overland Telegraph line which traversed Aboriginal lands 30 years before their fieldwork amongst what he termed 'howling savages'. In all cases, simply because informants were clothed and spoke English, this did not mean that their traditional knowledge was 'contaminated' (Mulvaney & Calaby 1985:212, 214).

Across the next few years Roth and Spencer accepted each other, or agreed to differ amicably. As Roth observed in 1902, 'for the sake of old friendship's sake, I know you won't hesitate to talk as straight to me as

I have to you! Besides if we can't have disputes or any little differences of opinion, what's the good of being pals'.[21]

Whether Spencer thought of himself as Roth's pal is doubtful, but he did acknowledge and assist him in various ways. He commended Roth's work in *Native Tribes*, stating in the preface that because *Ethnological Studies* was published 'when our manuscript was written... we have added references to it chiefly in the form of footnotes'. These amounted to 10 footnotes and three text inclusions, which incorporated reference to the importance of Roth's account of 'barter' and 'expressing our high appreciation of the worker' (Spencer & Gillen 1899:vii, 575).

They sometimes exchanged social news, both admitting that Australian conditions suited them. '[L]ike yourself', Roth agreed, 'Australian life has a great charm for me. I love the freedom of existence, the hospitality... the climate, and I'm extremely fond of my work'.[22] In 1899 Roth suggested that Spencer visit Queensland during the next year, when 'we could work the Queensland and Northern territory border together'.[23] Spencer's partnership with Gillen took priority.

With the approach of the 1900 congress of the Australasian Association for the Advancement of Science (AAAS), Roth requested that Spencer arrange for an official invitation be sent to him, in order that the State government might permit his attendance. The ruse failed to obtain his release.[24] He was more successful in 1902, however, when he attended the Hobart congress. Given Spencer's close association with the AAAS council, it is probable that he recommended Roth's appointment as president of the Anthropology section (Gillen presided at the 1900 congress). Roth (1903a) delivered his presidential address on the 'Games, sports and amusements of the Northern Queensland Aboriginals'. This deadpan factual narrative contained neither theory, totemism nor personal thanks to patrons and sponsors.

To judge from the names of the attendees included in the congress report, Roth's brother Reuter attended, as did Spencer. Also present were Howitt and Lorimer Fison, together with RH Mathews. This raises curiosity. Was Mathews present when Roth, Howitt and Fison presented papers? What about etiquette at social gatherings, because numbers were small? Spencer's and Howitt's detestation of Mathews are well known. Spencer told Roth that Mathews was 'a perfect fraud', that 'Howitt and myself have agreed to ignore him and I am glad to see that you do the same'.[25] Roth responded with accusations of 'dirty work' and plagiarism by Mathews.[26] It was hardly a congenial band of ethnographers assembled at Hobart!

When Roth (1903b) compiled his *Bulletin* 5, on superstition, magic and medicine, he sought Spencer's advice, followed by proofs with an urgent request for criticism.[27] These tasks completed, Roth thanked Spencer for 'the hints and references which in almost every case I have followed'. He acknowledged Spencer's 'kindly assistance, advice and encouragement' in the Preface. In his turn, Spencer told Roth that the bulletin was 'first rate, and most valuable' (Marett & Penniman 1932:152).

One subject in this bulletin interested Spencer so much that he wrote to James Frazer,[28] informing him of the welcome news that Roth:

> has now got clear evidence of the belief in children not being the result of sexual intercourse but due to the fact that spirits enter woman. He told me that he had some evidence of this before we published [*Native Tribes*] but did not like to publish it – was afraid to. He has also given up his old ideas as to the non-existence of totemism amongst his people.

This heartening news was repeated in the Preface to Spencer and Gillen's *The Northern Tribes of Central Australia* (1904), to bolster the case for similar beliefs in Central Australia. Despite Spencer's satisfaction, this was not the final solution to the debate. It remained a vexed issue in anthropological discourse through the 20th century. Les Hiatt (1996:120–41) lucidly surveyed the issues under the evocative heading 'conception and misconception'. Neither Spencer nor Roth comprehended the essential spirituality and symbolism of the Aboriginal world-view. Anthropologists today approach 'truth' as culturally conditioned and relative to indigenous social and ideological contexts. A century ago both men were scientists situated in the Western intellectual tradition, fixed in an evolutionary mindset.

A further parallel was that both Roth and Spencer served as Aboriginal Protectors and independent advisors to government on Aboriginal administrative policy. Their evident humanitarian concerns conflicted with a harsh authoritarianism originating in their sure conviction of racial and cultural superiority. Bleak and misguided Darwinians they may seem today, but critics should remember that both men were exceptional for their sympathies during an age of social ignorance and racist dogma. They suffered unpopularity as Protectors for attempting to understand and mediate in Aboriginal affairs.

Conclusion

Ten years before Spencer was sent to Darwin to formulate a Commonwealth blueprint for Aboriginal welfare, Protector Roth set out for Spencer his own guiding principles for Queensland's Aboriginal population:[29]

> I look upon [mission] stations rather as workhouses, no work no food! – and am always impressing upon the superintendents the danger of over-educating the blacks under their charge. I am basing and organising all my work up here on the belief that

(a) in the struggle for existence, the black cannot compete with the white
(b) it is not desirable that he should mix with the white
(c) with advancing civilisation, the black will die out
(d) while he lives, the black should be protected from the abuses to which he is subjected by the white.

Regrettably these were shibboleths with which Spencer agreed, and such principles evidently dominated welfare policies for decades to come. Roth neither possessed the private means nor social status of Spencer, but across 12 years in Queensland he achieved invaluable field data under difficult conditions while employed by an uncaring government. He placed modern Aboriginal people and anthropologists in his debt. In the same letter to Spencer he reflected in true Australian colloquial manner,[30] 'Yes, I have been retrenched 15% off my screw. I could make more in private practice, but I love my scientific work too much to chuck it now'.

Notes

1. The letters from Roth to Spencer are archived at the Pitt Rivers Museum, Oxford, in the extensive Spencer Collection. All references to correspondence in this paper are to this collection. I am indebted to Alison Petch for sending me copies of the letters. Information concerning Spencer's career in Manchester and Oxford is discussed in detail in Mulvaney and Calaby 1985.
2. Roth to Spencer, 8 February 1903, p 4, states that the photograph was taken before they sat their final examination.
3. Roth to Spencer, 8 February 1903, p 4.
4. Spencer to Balfour, 28 August 1902.
5. Spencer to Balfour, 20 September, 2 December 1897; Spencer to James Frazer, 6 December 1897.
6. Spencer to Frazer, 12 July 1897. Reprinted in Marett and Penniman 1932, p 10.
7. Spencer to Balfour, 2 December 1897.
8. Spencer to Balfour, 2 December 1897. Most of this letter is in Marett and Penniman 1932, pp 136–38, but this and other personal comments were omitted.
9. Roth to Spencer, 19 January 1898, pp 16–17.
10. Ibid.
11. Spencer to Balfour, 2 December 1897.
12. Roth to Spencer, 19 January 1898, pp 10–11, 18.
13. Roth to Spencer, 19 January 1898, p 20, 22 December 1897, p 3.
14. Roth to Spencer, 22 December 1897, p 1, 19 January 1898, pp 1–9.
15. Ibid., 22 December 1897, p 3, 19 January 1898, p 7.
16. Roth to Spencer, 28 January 1898. (This letter is a continuation to the letter, then unposted, written on 2 December 1897.)
17. Roth to Spencer, 8 October 1898, p 8.
18. Spencer to Balfour, 28 August 1902.
19. Roth to Spencer, 6 October 1902, pp 2–3.
20. Spencer to Balfour, 28 August 1902.
21. Roth to Spencer, 6 October 1902, p 6.

22. Roth to Spencer, 8 October 1898, p 2.
23. Roth to Spencer, 12 November 1899, p 2.
24. Roth to Spencer, 8 October 1898, p 9, 28 March 1899, 12 November 1899, p 2.
25. Spencer to Roth, 30 January 1903. (This comment was omitted from Marett and Penniman 1932, p 154).
26. Roth to Spencer, 8 February 1903, p 2.
27. Roth to Spencer, 6 October 1902 p 2, 3 January, 8 February 1903.
28. Spencer to Frazer, 7 June 1903. An edited version is in Marett and Penniman 1903, pp 78–81.
29. Roth to Spencer, 6 October 1902, pp 3–4.
30. Roth to Spencer, 6 October 1902, p 5.

Works Cited

Dawkins, W Boyd (1880) *Early Man in Britain and His Place in the Tertiary Period*, London: Macmillan
———. (1874) *Cave Hunting*, London: Macmillan
Elkin, AP (1975) 'RH Mathews', *Oceania* 46, 1–24
Green, HM (1962) *A History of Australian Literature*, Sydney: Angus and Robertson
Hiatt, LR (1996) *Arguments about Aborigines*, Cambridge: Cambridge University Press
Marett, RR and Penniman, TK (1932) *Spencer's Scientific Correspondence*, Oxford: Clarendon Press
Mulvaney, DJ and Calaby, JH (1985) *'So Much That Is New': Baldwin Spencer 1860–1929*, Carlton: Melbourne University Press
Mulvaney, J, Morphy, H and Petch, A (1997) *My Dear Spencer. The Letters of F.J. Gillen to Baldwin Spencer*, Melbourne: Hyland Press
Reynolds, B (1988) 'Roth, Walter Edmund (1861–1933)', in *Australian Dictionary of Biography*, Vol 11, Melbourne: Melbourne University Press, 463–64
Roth, WE (1903a) 'Games, sports and amusements of the Northern Queensland Aboriginals', *Report of the Australasian Association Advancement of Science* 9, 484–520
———. (1903b) 'Superstition, magic and medicine', *North Queensland Ethnography, Bulletin No 5*, Brisbane: Government Printer
———. (1898) 'Notes on social and individual nomenclature among certain North Queensland Aboriginals', *Proceedings of the Royal Society of Queensland* 13, 39–50
———. (1897) *Ethnological Studies among the North-West-Central Queensland Aborigines*, Brisbane: Government Printer
Spencer, B (1897) 'The Queensland Aborigines', *The Australasian*, 18 December 1897, 1354
Spencer, B and Gillen, FJ (1899) *The Native Tribes of Central Australia*, London: Macmillan

CHAPTER 7

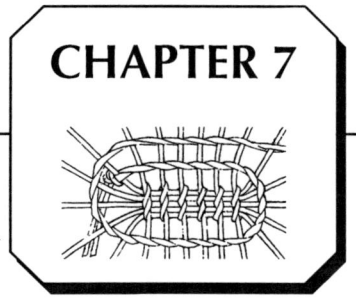

Ethnological Studies and Archaeology of North West Central Queensland

Iain Davidson

Introduction

Walter Roth was appointed in 1894 as the doctor in the hospitals in Boulia and Cloncurry and immediately engaged in studying the behaviour and habits of the Aboriginal people who lived there. This is the country of Kalkadoon, Yellunga (the modern descendants call themselves Yulluna: Tom Sullivan, pers comm), Undekerebina and Pitta-Pitta people and others. Roth's work resulted in the publication, within three years, of one of the great works of anthropology: *Ethnological Studies among the North-West-Central Queensland Aborigines* (WE Roth 1897).

Roth's work began only 34 years after Burke and Wills struggled through the same country. It was less than 20 years since the beginning of the killings which led to the destruction of much of the way of life of the Aboriginal peoples of the region, a process which was complete, according to some (Fysh 1933; Mulvaney 1989), 11 years before Walter arrived (Table 7.1). Roth's 1897 volume deals with this destructive interaction succinctly but unequivocally:

> Owing to the opening up of the country with the advent of the Europeans, some of these tribal camps have been shifted of late years from their original quarters or else amalgamated with others, while in a few cases, what with privation, disease, alcohol, and lead, the whole community has been annihilated (Roth 1897:§45, p 41).

In spite of this, Roth's work recorded details of the material culture, the languages, the kinship and the interactions of the different people

Table 7.1 Chronology of significant events in North West Central Queensland

	Indigenous history	Non-indigenous history
1860s		1861 Burke and Wills
		1867 Henry finds copper at Cloncurry
1870s	1878 Kennedy and Eglinton begin fight against Indigenous people	1876 Cloncurry laid out
		1878 Death of Molvo at Wonomo waterhole
1880s	1884 Urquhart on Calton Hills; Battle Mountain etc	1880 Argylla copper mine
		1882 Mt Oxide mine
		1883 Death of Beresford
1890s	1897 *Aboriginals Protection and Restriction of the Sale of Opium Act* ('The Act')	1894 WER appointed to Boulia
	1898 WER Northern Protector	1897 *Ethnological studies*
1900s	1901 Amendments to Act	1901–1906 *Bulletins*
	1904–1905 WER WA Royal Commission	1907–1910 *Records*
	1904–1906 WER Chief Protector	1907 WER in British Guinea

of the region with an attention and accessibility unusual for any study in Australia, certainly unusual for any study of the end of the 19th century.

In this paper, I discuss four things:

- Walter Roth's pioneering descriptions of the life of the various tribes in North West Central Queensland
- Current evidence from archaeological research in the same region
- Gaps in Roth's record, most notably in the rock art
- Cooperation with family members of those who must have known Roth during his time in Boulia

I will treat each of these in turn, and ask the question: what does this tell us of the conditions of the indigenous people in the region at the time Roth reported, and of the status of the knowledge he recorded?

Roth's Pioneering Descriptions of the Life of the Various Tribes in North West Central Queensland

Anthropology in the 1890s was a discipline very different from the one it would become in the 20th century. Under the influence of founding fathers such as Edward Tylor (1881) and Lewis Henry Morgan (1877), much of the effort of the early anthropologists went into collecting informal accounts of primitive people and translating them into more formal statements that might elucidate earlier forms of society, and ultimately be used in arguments about social evolution. Some of this work consisted of collecting together all of the accounts of a society and interpreting them – something at which Walter's brother Henry Ling Roth excelled.

Others were in the field too, of whom AC Haddon in the Torres Strait and Baldwin Spencer and Frank Gillen in Central Australia stand out, while JG Frazer was sitting in his study at Cambridge receiving the more and less credible accounts from all over the world for his huge and quirky *The Golden Bough* (Frazer 1890), including letters from Spencer (Marett & Penniman 1932).

Mulvaney, Morphy and Petch edited the letters written by Gillen to Spencer (Mulvaney *et al* 1997). Howard Morphy's (1997) introduction to the volume demonstrated in detail how Gillen's fieldwork proceeded in theoretical discussion with Spencer and produced a field-based specialist anthropology that was much less inclined to see global evolutionist explanations of the particularities of Arrernte life. Morphy commented that this led to 'the development of a recognisably modern anthropology' (Morphy 1997), suggesting that Roth's work (and Haddon's too) had a less 'modern feel' (p 41) than the work of Spencer and Gillen (1899). His argument is about the importance of fieldwork in anthropology, in contrast to the 'expert at home' (Urry cited by Morphy), of which Henry Ling Roth might be an outstanding example.

There is, I believe, remarkably little documentation of Walter's data collection methods, but they clearly stand in contrast with Henry's work on Tasmanians, for Henry never set foot in Tasmania. Walter's work is transitional work – a remarkable compilation of data from the field – even if it did not involve fieldwork as detailed as that of Gillen and Spencer, and was not embedded in the theoretical issues of the day. Some of the imperfections of Walter Roth's work, which Gillen so enjoyed pointing out, may have been a result of the ravages suffered by Aborigines of Queensland from 'privation, disease, alcohol, and lead', and also of acculturation. Gillen unwittingly drew attention to the acculturation in referring to the *Molonga* or *Mudlungga* ceremony – a ceremony Roth described in detail (see below) which Gillen had also observed in Central Australia. In Queensland women would stop the ceremony to prepare tea (WE Roth 1897:123; Mulvaney, Morphy & Petch 1997:231). We might also point to the report of the use of a jam tin in the process of forming the headdress for the ceremony (WE Roth 1897:124). The acculturation is further emphasised in Gillen's discussion of his desire to put Roth right by spending some time with the Pitta-Pitta (whom he calls Pitti-Pitti): 'I hear that the blacks in that Country speak English like Whitemen and I feel confident I could unearth and clear up their system in a fortnight' (WE Roth 1897:231). John Mulvaney documents elsewhere in this volume (see Chapter 6) the debate between Roth and Spencer about the theoretical interpretation of the Queensland data.

One of the ways in which Roth's work differs from that of Spencer and Gillen is in his documentation of some aspects of the material culture. Roth's work is of importance to archaeologists because it documents the massive movement of materials around, into and out of the region between Boulia and Cloncurry – here illustrated by *pituri* (a plant, *Duboisia hopwoodii*, which was consumed as a drug, the active constituents of which are nicotine and nor-nicotine [Watson 1983]), axes, an ochre quarry and a stone knife (Figure 7.1).

The extent of trade is well synthesised by Mulvaney's paper 'The chain of connection' (Mulvaney 1976), and much of the material trade is summed up by his expression of the long-distance interconnections:

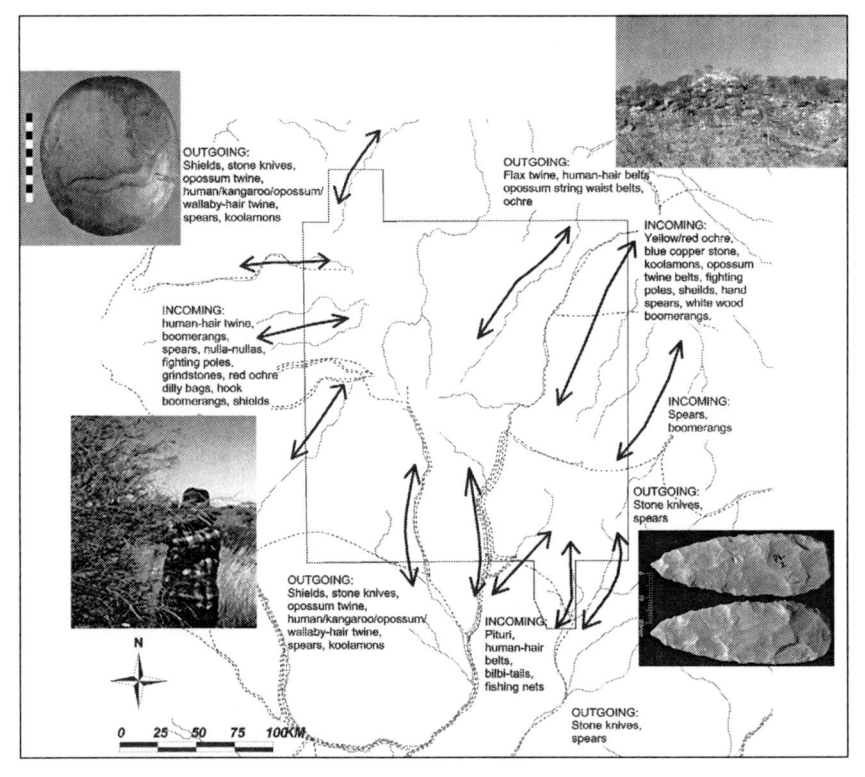

Figure 7.1 Trade items documented by Walter Roth for the Selwyn Ranges. Photographs show an axe from the quarries near Mount Isa found in an archaeological site 150 km to the south-east (photo Mark Moore); Nick Cook and Noeleen Curran at an ochre quarry in the Selwyn Ranges; a bifacial point from the edge of the Simpson; and Annie Hanson and Jim Dwyer with *pituri* on Glenormiston station (Photos by Iain Davidson unless otherwise stated. Base map by Malcolm Ridges.)

'In theory it was possible for a man who had bought *pituri* from the Mulligan River and ochre from Parachilna to own a Cloncurry axe, a Boulia boomerang and wear shell pendants from Carpentaria and Kimberley' (Mulvaney 1976:80). The range of traded items was much more extensive, including pearl shell from the Gulf of Carpentaria, spinifex (*Triodia*) resin for hafting tools, softwood shields, boomerangs, woven bags, animal skins, feathers, fibre cords, string made from human hair and ceremonies.

Roth (1897:118) documented the movement of the *Molonga* ceremony, also known as *Mudlungga*, from the upper reaches of the Georgina River before 1893 to Boulia in 1895. Mulvaney (1976) added evidence that the ceremony also reached east of Lake Eyre and in Alice Springs in 1901, west of Lake Eyre in 1902 and on the Nullarbor Plain by 1918. In Boulia, Kalkadoon men were photographed[1] painted and dressed for the ceremony in 1895, and another photograph shows men painted for the ceremony (with different motifs, but similar headdress) at Killalpaninna, east of Lake Eyre, in 1906 (Gregory 1906; Hercus 1980). This is the ceremony Gillen observed in Central Australia, where it was known as *Chitching-alla* (Mulvaney *et al* 1997), and which he said came from

Figure 7.2 Men dressed for ceremony at Boulia in 1895 (Reproduced with the permission of the Oxley Library)

the saltwater country to the north east of Alice Springs – presumably triangulating to a single source on the Gulf of Carpentaria.

Current Evidence from Archaeological Research in the Same Region

My research has been about the archaeology of a relatively small part of the region that Roth worked in, documenting hundreds of archaeological sites in the area, recently synthesised by Malcolm Ridges (2003) and my team (Davidson *et al* 2005). One of the points of interest is the documentation of the trade in ground-edged hatchet heads. Archaeological evidence shows that the hatchets were traded from quarries in North West Central Queensland and reached as far as Cape York in the north and Adelaide in the south.

There are many quarries in the region of many different raw materials, and sites with axes such as those traded from around Mount Isa (see Figure 7.1). Our evidence of the axes suggests that they were used as they passed through the trading system and that these high-quality goods for trade were used in a world where there was also small-scale production from local sources. The existence of local manufacture of axes suggests that they were traded in and through that country for reasons that were not simply economic or utilitarian – as documented for recent interactions in northern Australia (Paton 1994). The Mount Isa trade axes were used even though there were axes available made from local stone (Davidson *et al* 2005).

Similarly, Roth talked about the use and trade in ochres (eg 1897:111) used for colouring objects and painting bodies. The objects included circlets (p 110), bull-roarers (p 129), toy clay balls for the spin-ball game (p 130), message sticks (p 136), fluted boomerangs (p 145), shields (p 149) and amulets (p 163). The body was painted for ceremony (p 114; see Figure 7.2), as a cure for sickness (p 162), as a sign of mourning (p 164) and as a sign of initiation (p 175). Elsewhere he wrote about the practice of roasting yellow ochres to make them red (WE Roth 1904:14–15) – a practice attested in the archaeological record through our excavation of an ochre roasting pit at Cuckadoo 1, dated to 4,300 years ago (Davidson *et al* 1993).

The trade in ochre certainly involved the introduction of ochre from far away, but our work shows that it was also obtained locally (Ridges *et al* 2000; Davidson *et al* 2005). As with the axes, the trade in ochre seems to have involved motives other than simple utility, since it was traded into areas where ochre could be obtained. The documentation of trade by Roth, combined with the results of archaeological research, enables us to go beyond what could be seen in 1897 to understand the complexity of Aboriginal life in North West Central Queensland.

Gaps in Roth's Record, Most Notably in the Rock Art

Although Roth describes body ornamentation, by paint and by scarring, in some detail, there is a curious lack of information about what he calls 'Mural Painting, Art, and Draughtsmanship' (1897). 'The only two localities where examples of mural painting have been met with, to my knowledge, in these North-West-Central Districts are on Ooorindimindi Station, and at a small water-hole on the old Normanton road, about six miles from Cloncurry'. In addition, he reports that Coghlan had told him of rock engravings on Glenormiston which Roth had not seen.

In truth, there is a remarkable body of art in the Selwyn Range, most notably some distinctive anthropomorphic paintings analysed by June Ross (1997). These have some features that appear similar to the form of the body painting in the Roth photographs included here (see Figures 7.2 and 7.3).

We know that by the time Roth was in Boulia and Cloncurry, Alexander Kennedy, the man who led the destruction of the tribes of North West Central Queensland, was in possession of Devoncourt (Fysh 1933).

Figure 7.3 The site Roth didn't visit on Oorindimindi Station and Ken Isaacson at one of the painted anthropomorphs to the right of the Kurrajong tree

Figure 7.4 Anthropomorphic paintings on Devoncourt station

I presume that he, and any Aboriginal people living on the property, would have known the painting in a rock shelter on the property.

But I think I am right in saying that Roth does not mention Kennedy. Is it possible that he never visited Devoncourt? He does not mention the property when enumerating the tribes of the district, and refers to the Yellunga[2] as 'fast disappearing' and goes on to say, 'I have never succeeded in obtaining a reliable ... Yellunga vocabulary' (WE Roth 1897:41–42), though he does mention Devoncourt when describing trading routes (pp 134–35).

Cooperation with Family Members of Those who Must have Known Roth in Boulia

Roth certainly had some knowledge of movements around this central part of the region, but it is less certain that he moved around it himself, or recorded the whole range of knowledge available among the people who had survived the initial destruction of their society. He reports, for example, on the movement of spears and coolamons (wooden bowls) through the central part of the region (Figure 7.5).

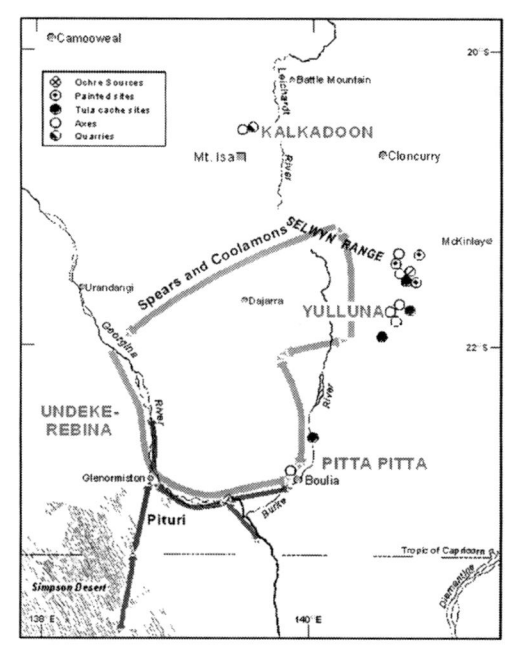

Ethnological Studies and Archaeology of North West Central Queensland | 129

Figure 7.5 Map of movements from Roth (1897) (Drawn by Mike Roach)

Our archaeological work in North West Central Queensland has been assisted by working with members of the Yulluna and Kalkadoon people, notably Tom Sullivan. Tom's father, Willie, bore the last name of Ernest Eglinton (Blake 1979), the man who led the police avenging the death of Molvo, the first non-Aboriginal person to die in the frontier conflict (Fysh 1933:93–98). But he did not pass the name Eglinton on to his family; rather they took the name of the Mount Merlin station manager, Daniel O'Sullivan. From his Yulluna family Tom learned many of the traditions and songlines for the region. He learned of the movements of Ancestors. Figure 7.6 maps the movements of the Yellowbelly Dreaming and the Rainbow Serpent from two important water sources in the region. Roth enumerated several stories of the Pitta-Pitta but was uncertain of their status: were they told for entertainment or as supernatural explanations? The story of the Two Fishermen (WE Roth 1902:9) certainly mentioned places, but eight other stories (WE Roth 1903:11–14) had no geographic reference.

Tom Sullivan also learned of the importance of the stone arrangements which were centres for ceremony in the region. In particular, as a boy, he probably went to the Colinaringo stone arrangement (Figure 7.6) while a ceremony was taking place there. Just as important for our story,

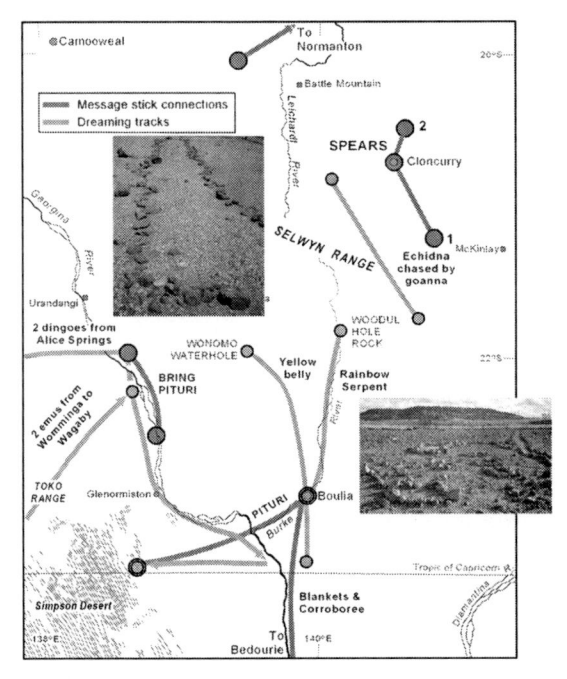

Figure 7.6 Map of Dreaming tracks from evidence given to Iain Davidson by Annie Hansen and Tom Sullivan (Drawn by Mike Roach) and stone arrangements in the region

he knows the Double Crossing stone arrangement which lies beside the only road direct from Boulia to Cloncurry. I think I am right in saying that stone arrangements are not mentioned by Roth. It seems likely, then, that Roth did not travel from Boulia to Cloncurry along this road.

Conclusion

The ethnography and ethnohistorical accounts are never complete records of the lives of societies, any more than historical documents are. Each is biased by the recorders' particular opportunities and interests. The dispute between Roth on one side and Spencer and Gillen on the other can be seen as a dispute about the nature of the emerging discipline of anthropology, but it may also be symptomatic of the circumstances in which Roth recorded the details of the lives of people only 10 years after the most destructive battle in the history of the region.

Roth was able to record that there was an extensive trade in many classes of material, and he was also able to record and collect some of the items of material culture which do not survive in the archaeological record, but which were such an important part of people's lives. In addition, he was able to observe some aspects of methods of production of goods. But there are things we do not know. Roth did not record how the archaeological record is formed from the various activities he described; he almost completely missed the abundant rock art of the region; he makes very little mention of religion and mythology and apparently did not encounter the Dreaming stories of the Yulluna, which were passed down to people living at the beginning of the 21st century. Roth drew his informants from a society fragmented by a brutal contact history. Perhaps this fragmentation is to blame for the omission. But perhaps too Roth's account was limited by the dominance of the region by Alexander Kennedy, the destructive pastoralist responsible for much of the brutality.

Notes

1. Roth does not actually claim to be the photographer, but published the photograph without other attribution in WE Roth 1910. It is reproduced here from that publication.
2. The Yellunga, now known as Yulluna, would have had traditional country on or around Devoncourt.

Works Cited

Blake, BJ (1979) *A Kalkatungu grammar*, Canberra: Australian National University

Davidson, I, Cook, NDJ, Fischer, M, Ridges, M, Ross, J and Sutton, SA (2005) 'Archaeology in another country: exchange and symbols in North West Central Queensland', in Macfaralane, I, Mountain, M-J and Paton, R (eds), *Many exchanges: archaeology, history, community and the work of Isabel McBryde*, Aboriginal History Inc., 101–28

Davidson, I, Sutton, SA and Gale, SJ (1993) 'The human occupation of Cuckadoo I Rockshelter, Northwest Central Queensland', in Smith, MA, Fankhauser, B and Spriggs, M (eds), *Sahul in Review: Pleistocene Archaeology in Australia, New Guinea and Island Melanesia*, Canberra: Australian National University, 164–72

Frazer, JG (1890) *The Golden Bough*, London: Macmillan

Fysh, H (1933) *Taming the North*, Sydney: Angus and Robertson

Gregory, JW (1906) *The Dead Heart of Australia*, London: John Murray

Hercus, LA (1980) '"How we danced the *Mudlunga*": memories of 1901 and 1902', *Aboriginal History* 4, 4–32

Marett, RR and Penniman, TK (1932) *Spencer's Scientific Correspondence*, Oxford: Clarendon Press

Morgan, LH (1877) *Ancient Society*, New York: Henry Holt & Co

Morphy, H (1997) 'Gillen – Man of Science', in Mulvaney, DJ, Morphy, H and Petch, A (eds), *'My Dear Spencer': The Letters of F.J. Gillen to Baldwin Spencer* Melbourne: Hyland House, 23–50

Mulvaney, DJ (1976) '"The chain of connection": the material evidence', in Peterson, N (ed), *Tribes and Boundaries in Australia*, Canberra: Australian Institute of Aboriginal Studies, 72–94

Mulvaney, DJ (1989) *Encounters in Place. Outsiders and Aboriginal Australians 1606–1985*, St Lucia: University of Queensland Press

Mulvaney, DJ, Morphy, H and Petch, A (eds) (1997) *'My Dear Spencer': The Letters of F.J. Gillen to Baldwin Spencer*, Melbourne: Hyland House

Paton, R (1994) Speaking through stones: a study from northern Australia. *World Archaeology* 26:172–184

Ridges, M, Davidson, I and Tucker, D (2000) 'The organic environment of paintings on rock', in Ward, GK and Tuniz, C (eds), *Advances in Dating Australian Rock-Markings. Papers from the First Australian Rock-Picture Dating Workshop*, Melbourne: Australian Rock Art Association, 61–70

Ridges, M (2003) Numerous indications. The archaeology of regional hunter-gatherer behaviour in northwest central Queensland, Australia. Unpublished PhD, University of New England

Ross, J (1997) 'Painted relationships: an archaeological analysis of a distinctive anthropomorphic rock art motif in northwest central Queensland', BA Honours thesis, University of New England, Armidale, NSW

Roth, HL (1890) *The Aborigines of Tasmania*, Halifax (England): F. King and Sons

Roth, WE (1910) 'Decoration, deformation, and clothing', *North Queensland Ethnography. Bulletin No 15, Records of the Australian Museum* 8, 20–54, Plates viii–x, Figs 14–30H

———. (1904) 'Domestic implements, arts and manufactures', *North Queensland Ethnography Bulletin No 7*, Brisbane: Home Secretary's Department

———. (1903) 'Superstition, magic and medicine', *North Queensland Ethnography Bulletin No 5*, Brisbane: Home Secretary's Department

———. (1902) 'Games, sports and amusements', *North Queensland Ethnography Bulletin No 4*, Brisbane: Home Secretary's Department

———. (1897) *Ethnological Studies among the North-West-Central Queensland Aborigines*, Brisbane: Government Printer

Spencer, B and Gillen, FJ (1899) *Native Tribes of Central Australia*, London: Macmillan

Tylor, EB (1881) *Anthropology*, London: Watts and Company

Watson, PL (1983) *This precious foliage*, Sydney: Oceania Monographs, University of Sydney

CHAPTER 8

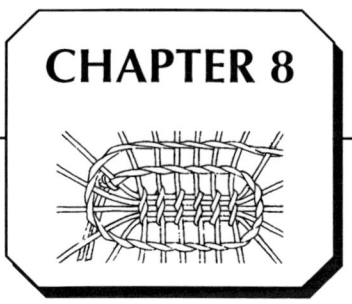

WE Roth and the Study of Aboriginal Languages in Queensland

Gavan Breen

A Revised Linguistic Survey of Australia (Oates & Oates 1970) gives the name 'Roth' in connection with 37 languages/dialects (and misses a few more). In some cases Walter Roth simply mentioned the language name, but he collected wordlists (mostly of 150 to 200 words) for about 20 different languages (and for two or more dialects of some of these). He is our only source of linguistic information in two languages, and virtually the only source in another; he provides the only data on dialects of several languages of which other dialects are known more or less well; he provides a significant portion of the scant available information in several others and very useful data on some others. He also gives information, no longer available elsewhere, on hand signs in a number of areas.

Walter E Roth was born in London but educated in France and Germany as well as England.[1] He spoke English, French, German and perhaps Hungarian (his father's language) and seems to have been familiar with Old English too. He would have studied Latin and perhaps Greek at school. Language teaching methods at that time would have had a strong emphasis on grammar. He would have analysed Australian languages along Western European grammatical lines.

Roth appreciated the necessity for language knowledge as a basis for understanding the culture of a people. He says (1897a:v):

> At Boulia, ... almost my whole time was devoted to a careful study of the local (Pitta-Pitta) language: only when this was sufficiently mastered did I find it possible to understand the complex system of social and

134 | Chapter 8

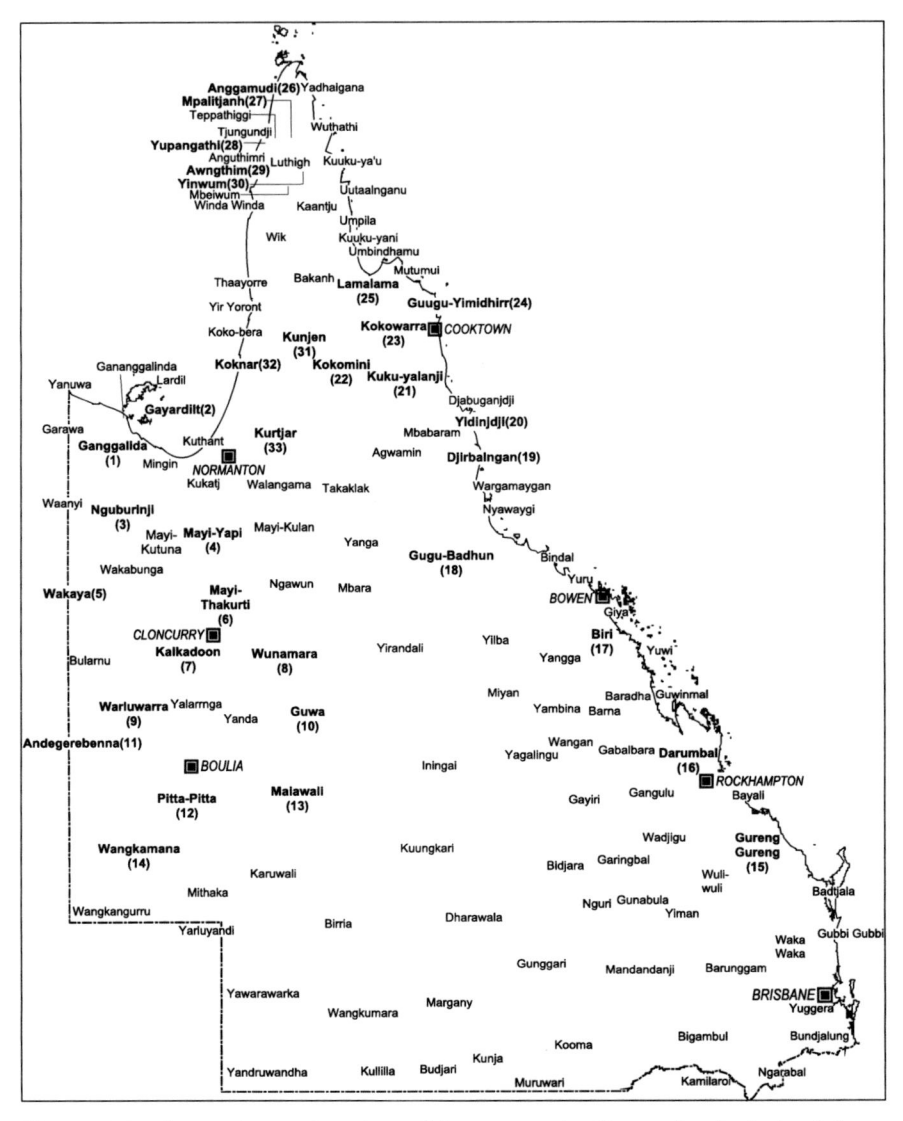

Figure 8.1 Approximate location of languages in Queensland, derived from Horton (1994) and drawn by Mike Roach. Names printed in bold face are for languages studied by Roth

individual nomenclature in vogue, and ultimately to gain such amount of confidence and trust among the natives as enabled me to obtain information concerning ... beliefs and ... rites which otherwise would in all probability have been withheld. To any future observers of, and writers on, the Queensland aboriginal, I would most strongly recommend this method of making themselves familiar with the particular language of the district before proceeding to make any further inquiries.

Major Studies

Pitta-Pitta

Roth's first venture into serious linguistics was his grammar of Pitta-Pitta (1897a). I quote part of the introductory chapter in Blake and Breen's (1971) grammar, based on work with the last few speakers:

> One of the handful of nineteenth century publications which attempt to give a description of the grammar of an Australian language is WE Roth's book, published in 1897. The first two chapters deal with the language of the Boulia district (which Roth defines fairly closely; ...), and later chapters, dealing with social structure, material culture, and other aspects of the life and belief of the Aborigines of this district, also contain some linguistic information, chiefly vocabulary.
>
> Roth's grammar begins with an explanation of his spelling system; he took great care with this aspect of the work, dividing words clearly into syllables, using diacritics[2] to specify the sounds more accurately and marking the stress. Unfortunately, however, his ability as a phonetician was not on a par with his ability as a grammarian, and, in some ways, his spelling is hardly superior to that of the graziers and government officials who provided the other early published word-lists. His analysis of the morphology is good, however, and only on a few points can the present authors dispute his conclusions. However, a number of grammatical forms which Roth did not find can now be described. On the other hand, some of Roth's statements cannot be confirmed because of the lack of knowledge of present-day informants.
>
> Chapter I concludes with a vocabulary containing over five hundred Pitta-Pitta words. Most of these have now been recorded on tape, so that Roth's spelling can be corrected, but some are unknown to the present-day informants, and it appears that Roth has included a number of words from related dialects and even from other languages. ... In general, however, our fieldwork has confirmed the correctness of Roth's vocabulary (Blake & Breen 1971:2–3).

Capell, in his entry for Bidabida (Pitta-Pitta), says, 'Roth's spelling is very unsatisfactory though the rest of the account is good' (1963:G3). Blake says: 'The grammar is fairly accurate but all the phonemic distinctions that Europeans find difficult are missed' (1979b:186).

Pitta-Pitta, like many Australian languages, distinguishes in its grammar between *agent* (subject of a transitive verb) and *subject* (intransitive); unlike many of these it also distinguishes subject from *object*. It is almost unique in that this three-way distinction does not apply in the future tense, in which the agent and subject are treated alike, with suffix *-ngu* (on a noun), while the object takes suffix *-ku*. This contrasts with suffixes *-lu* (agent) and *-nha* (object), and suffixless subject in other tenses. Certain aspects of this future tense situation, of great linguistic interest, had been forgotten by the last speakers, although Blake and

Breen's main informant remembered them when asked about Roth's material.

As indicated earlier, other features noted by Roth could not be checked; the speakers we worked with had presumably never learnt them or had forgotten them. And many items, especially of vocabulary, were remembered only when Roth's items were used as a reminder. (See Blake 1979b for an updated grammar of this language.)

Guugu-Yimidhirr

Guugu-Yimidhirr was the first Australian language to be recorded by outsiders;[3] wordlists were collected by (or on behalf of) Lieutenant James Cook and Sir Joseph Banks while Cook's barque, the *Endeavour*, was undergoing repairs near what is now Cooktown in 1770. More than a hundred years later serious study of the language was begun by Lutheran missionaries Flierl, Poland and especially Schwarz at Hopevale Mission. This culminated in Roth's grammar (1901a) – 'The structure of the Koko Yimidir language' – and a dictionary of 30-odd pages (1901b). The assistance of Schwarz and Poland is acknowledged on the title page of the grammar. In the words of linguist John Haviland, who studied Guugu-Yimidhirr in the 1970s:

> All of this work suffered from a basic misunderstanding of the sound system of the language (missing laminal sounds, for example, and not distinguishing long from short vowels) and from a heavy reliance on grammatical categories derived from the study of European languages and decidedly inappropriate for an analysis of Guugu Yimidhirr (1979:35).

It is not clear how much of the work was actually Roth's. Probably the fieldwork was done by the missionaries and Roth got the form of words from them, perhaps transcribing them into the spelling system he used (which was not the one that he used for Pitta-Pitta, but a 'continental' system that was recommended by the Royal Geographical Society in London[4] for geographical names) but not otherwise changing them. Roth likely turned their early unpublished efforts at a grammar, augmented perhaps by study of their raw data and his own (Roth 1898k), into his grammar, which followed the pattern of his earlier grammar of Pitta-Pitta.

A post-graduate student, Jan de Zwaan, worked on this language in the 1960s (Zwaan 1969a), 'without significantly improving on Roth' (Haviland 1979:35). John Haviland published a grammar – not long but a good basic grammar, and substantially better than the earlier ones – in 1979.

Roth (1901a:6) took a 'great interest' in Cook's wordlist (as edited and published by Hawkesworth) and found the words nearly all 'recognizable'. De Zwaan (1969a), on the other hand, claimed that the language had undergone phonological changes since 1770 and had lost or introduced words in 9 cases out of 48. Breen (1970) authored a highly critical reply, based on a study of photocopies of Cook's original manuscript journal. This was backed up by Haviland, who said:

> I suggest on the basis of my own recent fieldwork that of the three lists – Cook's (and Banks') of 1770, Roth's of 1901, and de Zwaan's from 1967 – the earliest is arguably the best, i.e. the most accurate in terms of modern spoken Gu:gu Yimidir! (1974:216).[5]

Roth also published 'Progressive Koko-yimider [sic] exercises' as part of *North Queensland Ethnography Bulletin No 11* (1908); these comprise a total of 400 phrases or sentences, in groups of 10, with English translations. They range from simple phrases up to sentences of two clauses (often quite unnatural). All those sentences in which the subject should have ergative marking (to show that a noun is agent of a transitive verb) lack it;[6] this type of construction does not occur in European languages (with a few little-known exceptions) and none of the students of Guugu-Yimidhirr (and hardly any students of other Australian languages) at that time caught on to it.

Nggerikudi

The third major language description in which Roth was involved is that of Nggerikudi (Hey 1903), a language of the northern part of Cape York Peninsula; it was written by Nicholas Hey, a Moravian missionary, and revised and edited by Roth (who also carried out his own research in the area). The name Nggerikudi or Nggéri-kudi is based, according to Roth, on the word *nggeri* 'sandbank'; the *-kudi* is the ending *-kwithi* occurring in several other dialect names, possibly equivalent to *-ngith* and *-ngithigh* in some other names, and perhaps meaning something like 'people of the country characterised by X (sandbank, mangrove, bush, etc.)'. It was the name of the people; and Yopo-timi (perhaps Yupu-thimri, meaning 'I-having', the language having *yupu* as the word for 'I') was the language name (but see Cape York Wordlists below). Hey says in his preface that:

> It should be stated that I have drawn up the following pages, section by section, on the lines followed by Dr Roth, the Northern Protector of Aboriginals, in his Bulletin No. 2 (North Queensland Ethnography), 'The Structure of the Koko-Yimidir Language'.

138 | Chapter 8

Figure 8.2 Visit to Mapoon Presbyterian Mission, Western Cape York Peninsula, May 1902. Top, left to right: Bishop Gilbert White (Bishop of Carpentaria), Rev Nicholas Hey (mission superintendent), unknown mission community member, Mrs Mary Ann (Minnie) Hey, Fred Hey (2), Ina Hey (5), Janie Hey (8), Rev JB Russell (Presbyterian Church of Queensland), Mrs Edith Roth, probably CFV Jackson (geologist), Dr WE Roth

This work is more difficult to assess. The spelling certainly leaves a lot to be desired, but it must be said that this is phonetically a very difficult language, one of the most complex in Australia; in any case, the spelling is Hey's, even if transliterated into the system Roth used, and is different from the spelling in Roth's only wordlist of this language. It is classified (by Hey initially, confirmed by Hale 1964) as one of a large number of dialects of a language spoken on and near the west coast of the peninsula north from about Weipa. Short grammars of two of the other dialects have been published: Linngithigh by Hale (1966) and Mpakwithi by Crowley (1981). None of them is spoken now, and Hale's and Crowley's grammars were based on work with last speakers with limited knowledge. Hale has also published (1997) a short dictionary.

Western Wordlists

Turning now to Roth's collected vocabularies, we begin again in far west Queensland. Roth (1897a:Chapter 2) gives comparative wordlists, of about 100 words, for a number of languages: Ulaolinya (now spelt Yurlayurlanya), Wonkajera (Wangka-Yujurru), Karanya, Pitta-Pitta and Miorli (Mayawarli) from the Boulia district (which he defines), and Walookera (Warlukarra, better known as Warluwarra), Yaroinga (Ayerrereng), Undekerebina (Antekerrepenh), Goa (Guwa), Woonamurra (Wunumara), Mitakoodi (Mayi-Thakurti) and Kalkadoon (Kalkutungu) from other districts. Of the first group, Yurlayurlanya and Karanya are otherwise quite unknown, and there is also not much other information on Mayawarli; Roth's lists show that the first is a dialect of the same language as Wangka-Yujurru (fairly well attested, and closely related to Pitta-Pitta; see Blake & Breen 1971), and the other two are dialects of the same language as Pitta-Pitta. Of the second group, Warluwarra (Breen forthcoming b) and Antekerrepenh (Breen, mostly unpublished) are fairly well studied, and Ayerrereng is very closely related to the latter. Hale worked briefly but very productively on Ayerrereng, but under the name 'Antikiripini (Georgina River variety)' (Hale 1960a), and Roth's wordlist helps us to identify it. Kalkutungu has been studied in depth by Blake (eg 1979a). Guwa had disappeared by the time that modern linguists came to the area. Roth's is one of several old lists in the language; there is also one in Tindale (1938–39) (see Blake & Breen 1990 for details).

Finally, Roth's Woonamurra and Mitakoodi wordlists can be considered along with some kinship terms he records in Miubbi (Mayi-Yapi). These are all closely related dialects and the materials on them are scanty; an incomplete grammar of one dialect was written on the basis of recordings of a partial speaker, while there are only brief notes and some vocabulary for the others (see Breen 1981). Roth's wordlists make a significant contribution to the vocabulary.

There are also unpublished wordlists compiled by Roth in two other western Queensland languages. One is Workai-a (Wakaya) (Roth 1900c), which, like a couple of the other languages in which he collected, is more a Northern Territory than a Queensland language; in fact, although he gave their 'chief camp' as Camooweal, their territory probably did not reach into Queensland at all. This wordlist has been superseded by later linguistic work (see Breen forthcoming a). Another is Obarindi (Nguburindi) (Roth 1897b); there is no other information on this apart from Roth's list, which shows that it is a dialect of the same language as the much better-known Yukulta and Kayardilt (see Keen 1983; Evans 1992, 1995).

Eastern Wordlists

The south-easternmost language in which Roth collected was Koreng-Koreng (1898a); the location he gives is Miriam Vale, which, according to Tindale (1940:158) is Goeng country, with Koreng-Koreng (his Korenggoreng) further inland (p 163). Capell (1963) and Oates and Oates (1970) follow Tindale. Brasch (1975) wrote a BA Honours thesis on this language; she also regarded it as an inland language. However, the map in the *Encyclopaedia of Aboriginal Australia* shows it (spelt 'Gureng Gureng') as extending to the coast and including land that Tindale attributed to Goeng and also Tulua (which he thought 'may be a part of the Goeng') (Tindale 1940:172). This note is absent from the entry in Tindale (1974:186). Information from a Gureng Gureng academic, Michael Williams (pers comm) casts some light on the confusion. Gureng Gureng is one of the Australian languages which is named from its word for 'no', which is *gureng* (see Tindale 1974:41–42 for other examples of this practice). Gureng on its own is sometimes used, perhaps only by people who do not know its meaning, as a name for the people. Holmer (1983) has notes on a dialect Goeng-Goeng (spelt 'Guweng-Guweng' by Dixon 2002), and this corresponds to Tindale's Goeng. Jolly (1994, quoted by Gorman *et al* 2002) regards Tindale's Korenggoreng, Goeng, Tulua and Taribelang as related, and as perhaps part of a larger entity (commonly called 'Gureng Gureng'). It is necessary to regard Roth's statement that the chief camp of his Koreng-Koreng was Miriam Vale with some caution, as there seems to be a tendency for him to sometimes give as a 'chief camp' a place where people camp, outside their own country, because of European activity or settlement there; note the reference above to Camooweal, and below to Mentana Yard. On balance, though, it appears that Roth was probably right in this case.

A little further north, a wordlist in Dappil, from Gladstone, is perhaps the only record of this language. Further north again, Roth's lists in Kuinmabara, Karunbara, Rakiwara, Tarumbal and Wapabara (1897c–g) form a substantial part of the lexical data available for the Dharumbal language – the whole of it for some dialects. Terrill has recently (2002) published what was intended to be all that could be learnt of this language (although she has missed some aspects of the grammar which can be recovered from the wordlists). A scan of Terrill's vocabulary shows that Roth was learning to hear the initial velar nasal (*ng*) by this time, but still often missed it.[7] Unfortunately, however, Terrill has omitted the diacritics from the vowels in her spelling of words from Roth's lists, describing them as 'unexplained' (Terrill 2002:fn 1, p 51). Roth's system of diacritics on the vowels in these lists is clearly the same as that he describes in his Pitta-Pitta grammar, and they are important in deciphering his spelling; for example ĭ represents the vowel in 'bit', while ī represents the vowel in 'bite'.

To the west of Dharumbal is Yettimaralla, and again Roth's list (1898m) of 75 words is all that is available. The wordlist relates it to the large Mari language group which covered much of inland Queensland

(Terrill 2002:15) as one of a group of dialects the best known of which is Biri (described by Beale 1974 and Terrill 1998). Terrill (2002:13) also mentions a Tarrumburra list by Roth but does not note (in either work) his Bauwiwara list (Roth 1898m) which RMW Dixon (pers comm) identifies as Biri. Roth (1910c:90) does mention a group he calls Tarrambarra (on his map, 'Tarramburra') but does not give a wordlist for it. This is presumably Tindale's (1974:171) Taruin-bura, a 'horde' of the Yettimaralla.

Cape York Wordlists

The remainder of the languages in which Roth collected material can be described as Cape York Peninsula languages and the first we come to, approaching from the southeast, is Dyirbal (1898c–g). This has been thoroughly studied by Dixon (1972) and others, and I quote what he has to say (pp 366–67) about Roth's work on the language:

> After his appointment as Northern Protector of Aborigines, based at Cooktown, Roth made several studies of sections of the six tribes speaking Dyirbal. In 1898 he wrote ethnological notes on three tribes encountered in the Atherton area – Chirpal-ji((Dyirbaldyi), Ngachan-ji((Ngadyandyi) and Ngikoongo-i(.... He recorded about two hundred words in each dialect – these were transcribed laboriously (with much use of diacritics) but on the whole accurately. He appears to have rewritten the three lists about 1900, simplifying and improving the transcription – thus diacritics are omitted, -oo- changed to -u-, and so on. Roth also secured a wordlist from a different group of Dyirbaldyi, at Herberton, in October 1900.
>
> Roth's most important work in the Dyirbal area was the preparation, in September 1900, of a 104-page 'Scientific Report on the Natives of the Lower Tully River'; a 22-page appendix was added in December of that year, following a further visit to the Tully. Roth includes a great deal of important information on the Malanbara tribe's organisation, habits, songs, food etc.; a considerable number of Gulngay words and phrases are included, on the whole fairly accurately transcribed. This study, and the Atherton vocabularies and notes, remain unpublished [Roth 1900a], but some important extracts did appear in various of the North Queensland Ethnography bulletins [Roth 1901–10].

Roth's better transcription at this time is probably due partly to improvement with time and experience, but perhaps also more to the fact that the interdental and retroflex sounds which occur in many other languages (and are difficult for English speakers) are absent from this language. And despite the volume of Dixon's work on this language, Roth's data on Gulngay are a significant part of our knowledge of that dialect.

Ngaygungu (Roth's Ngikoongo-ï / Ngai-kungon-ji,)(1898h) was spoken west of Dyirbal and Roth's wordlist is virtually the only source (the other being seven words collected by Tindale). It was not closely related to either Dyirbal or Yidiny.

Yidiny, north of Dyirbal, is another language that has been very thoroughly studied by Dixon. But Roth recorded vocabulary in Gunggay (1898b, 1898i), which is important because this dialect was extinct by the time of Dixon's study. There is a small quantity of other material on it, including a list collected by Tindale. Another list, supposedly in Yidiny, collected by Roth is actually Ngadyan, a Dyirbal dialect (Roth 1898j; Dixon 1977:509–11).

Further north, in the Mossman-Daintree-Helenvale area, Gugu-Yalanji is still spoken. Roth's material (1898l, 1898o, nd) in this language is insignificant in view of the substantial work done on it by Summer Institute of Linguistics linguists (William and Lynette Oates, Hank and Ruth Hershberger) and a PhD thesis leading to the published grammar by Australian National University student Elisabeth Patz (see especially Hershberger *et al* 1982 and Patz 1999). Guugu-Yimidhirr, a little further north, I dealt with earlier.

My assessment of Roth's wordlists, and their value, for the remaining languages is based largely on Sommer (1976), although I refer also to more recent research by others, especially Bruce Rigsby and Barry Alpher. Sommer, who describes Roth as 'a pioneering humanitarian', examined the wordlists appended to three of Roth's reports to the Commissioner of Police, Brisbane. Our knowledge of most of the languages on which Roth worked in this part of Queensland is sadly deficient. All of the languages are phonetically difficult. Sommer says, too, that 'only three [reports] are currently available, although more were certainly composed' (1976:127).

I will deal with the three in chronological order (which matches the direction in which I have been moving geographically). The first report is the Princess Charlotte Bay one, which has two wordlists. The first of these is of Koko-Wara, spoken on the Normanby River; a more detailed location of their country, given in another version of the list (uncatalogued ms 216, State Library of New South Wales) is:

> Chief camp in close vicinity to Balser's Knob. They follow the Normanby and Deighton Rivers as far as the Laura, travel up Station and Sandy Creeks to the Morehead, and westward they wander over to Jeannette's Tableland.

Koko-Wara (or Kuku Warra) means 'bad language'. Rigsby (nd) says that 'Kuku Warra and Kuku Mini are outsiders' names for other people's languages. One person's or group's Kuku Warra might be another's Kuku Mini'.[8] (See below for Kuku Mini, which means 'good language'.) Such names are clearly of little or no value in identifying languages. Rigsby (forthcoming) points out that *warra* has a range of meanings and that in this context it is better translated as 'strange, not intelligible'.[9] He also quotes Thomson in referring to the equivalence of the name Kuku Warra to the better-known name Wik Way (used in a similar way[10] on the west coast of Cape York).

Roth's report includes some additional vocabulary. There is nothing else known. Sommer finds this language to be similar to material recorded by himself and others in what he calls Bariman-gudinhma; the initial *ba* is the word for 'person' which is often prefixed to tribal/language/clan names in Cape York Peninsula languages, and it is called Rimanggudinhma in Godman (1993). Sommer's conclusion is that Roth's Koko-Wara is most likely the easternmost variety of a group of dialects of which Rimanggudinhma is one of the most westerly members. Dixon (in unpublished material, referred to by Godman) comes to a similar conclusion. However, Godman disputes this (as does Rigsby 2004, pers comm), saying that, despite vocabulary resemblances to Rimanggudinhma, this Koko-Wara seems from grammatical evidence (which is given more weight than lexical evidence) to be more closely related to Guugu-Yimidhirr, to its east.

Roth's location of this language is accepted by Sommer (although he points out a geographical error – Jeannette's Tableland is north, not west, of Balser's Knob), from which it follows that the assignment of much of this territory to Lamalama by Laycock (1969) (following West, unpublished) is incorrect, as is that of Hale and Tindale (1933–34). (This would be so whether Sommer or Godman are correct or not.) Sommer's opinion was supported by the opinions of contemporary informants in the area, and indeed by Roth's (correct) location of the next language to be discussed. Rigsby's and Sutton's later work in the area confirms this; see, for example, the introduction to Rigsby's (nd a) unpublished sketch of Kuku Thaypan.

The second wordlist with this report is called Rarmul (Morehead River and Saltwater Creek; Rarmul is said to be the name of the country through which the Morehead flows). It is also called Koko-Rarmul; this would be the name of the language, as opposed to the people. Sommer identifies this language with Kuku Thaypan, possibly a separate dialect, and Rigsby (nd a) confirms that it is actually the closely related dialect whose speakers called it Awu Alwang (or 'Goose Language'). Rigsby (1992 and others) has published on Kuku Thaypan (or Agu Alaya, as it is called in the language) and other languages of the Princess Charlotte Bay area; see also Jolly (1989) on Aghu-Tharrnggala, another language related to Kuku Thaypan.

The second report considered by Sommer is that on the Koko-minni (Roth 1899), but has appended wordlists of four languages. The first is of the 'Koko-minni Chief Camp: head of Annie Creek and King River'. Sommer calls Koko-Mini (literally 'speech-good' or 'speech-intelligible') a 'loose... confederation' of dialects (or even separate languages) (1976:133). There is some information on some other members of the group but none of it is substantial. Roth's wordlist is perhaps identifiable with one recorded by Sommer under the name Ikaranggal (but Rigsby thinks not [pers comm, 4 January 2004]) or with one recorded by West (c 1965) (and Sommer has collected a little) called Ogh-Alungul. Roth gives additional detail on the territory, which leads Rigsby (pers comm) to equate his Koko-Minni with Palmer's (1884) Akoonkoon (or Akoonkool) and Koogobatha, although (as Rigsby also points out) Palmer seems to have regarded these as two different languages.

The second wordlist with this report is of Koko-Olkulo. This is recognised by Sommer as the northern dialect of a language on which he has done fairly substantial work (1969, 1972, etc). More recently Hamilton (1997) has prepared a multimedia dictionary. Roth states that its 'chief camp' is 'head of Alice Creek (of the Morehead River)' (see Sommer 1976:134), which Sommer finds incomprehensible as the Alice and Morehead Rivers flow in opposite directions and never join (although they do rise in the same area). Rigsby (pers comm, 8 March 2004) has examined both Roth's original list, evidently made up during elicitation, and a later copy, cleaned up and reordered. Regarding the name and, especially, the country, there is, between the two versions, a confusing set of notes and annotations and crossings-out. Rigsby concludes that Roth did indeed locate the chief camp at the head of the Alice River.

The third wordlist is Kundara, the chief camp for which is named as Mentana. This is a language recorded by some modern linguists, first Keen and later Sommer, Breen and Sutton, under the name Kuk-Narr (spelt Gog-Nar in Breen 1976) and by Sommer as Kok-Nhang. The two dialects had about 95% vocabulary in common. Sommer refers to a recent dispute on the traditional ownership of Mentana Yard, and there seems to be some doubt as to whether Kuk-Narr country did extend so far east. Sutton added Roth's words to Keen's wordlist and found the correspondence (making allowances for Roth's spelling) remarkable; Roth's ability to elicit vocabulary correctly from an unfamiliar language was as good as that of a competent modern linguist.

The fourth wordlist included with this report is not by Roth but by Stuart-Russell (1899). Sommer identifies the language as Gurdjar.

The third report – the first discussed by Sommer – is the Pennefather-Batavia-Embley report. This contains four wordlists, which Sommer identifies with the help of Kenneth Hale's published and unpublished material (Hale 1964, 1960b) on the northern Paman languages. The first is headed 'Ng-gérikudi blacks at the mouth of the Pennefather (Coen R) and adjacent north and south coast. From Jimmy D (a Pennefather R native), Mapoon, 1 Oct. 1899'. This is identified by Hale as Yupngayth,[11] a dialect of a language that Hale calls Awngthim, and is very close to other dialects recorded by him: Mamngayth, Nrwa'angayth and (especially) Thyaenhngayth. It is, of course, also the dialect described in Hey's grammar; the name given there, Yopo-timi, has the same first constituent but a different second one. Sommer points out some items that do not correspond to words in any of Hale's lists or in Hey's vocabulary.

The second wordlist is headed 'Moreton District (mixing with the Bertiehaugh blacks – about 100 of them all told) Moreton ETO Oct. 1899'. Sommer shows that this is what Hale recorded as Yinwum, or a close dialect of it. Only three words are different. Hale and Roth are the only sources of data on this language.

The third wordlist is headed 'Bertiehaugh District (mixing with the Moreton blacks – about 100 of them all told) Moreton ETO October 1899'. Sommer identifies this as most probably corresponding to Hale's Mpalitjanh, although there are discrepancies which lead to some doubt that it was the same dialect. There is no other information.

The fourth wordlist is of the language of the 'Ducie Blacks' (not Dulcie, as in Sommer's paper). This, too, was collected at the Moreton ETO in October 1899. Sommer finds that this is clearly Uradhi, as recorded by Hale. Crowley (1983) provides a grammar of this language, based on work with speakers of three dialects, not including Uradhi proper.

Other Vocabulary

No survey of Roth's contribution to the study of Queensland languages would be complete without reference to the many items of vocabulary that can be found in his primarily anthropological works or in the primarily anthropological parts of his more general works. Breen (1981), for example, lists *'Ethnological Studies'* and nine *North Queensland Ethnography Bulletins* as sources for vocabulary for the Mayi languages. Such vocabulary includes section (and, for further west, subsection) terms,[12] kinship terms, terms relating to ceremony and terms relating to material culture and economy (including a substantial number of plant names). There are also, of course, language, tribal, clan and local group names. Sutton, who assesses some of these, remarks that:

> WE Roth, who was a brilliant field-worker in his time (see for example his analysis of naming practices in Australia [1910c:81–83]), worked

briefly in the Princess Charlotte Bay area in 1898, making some notes on the peoples whose country included Bathurst Head, the Flinders Island Group, Cape Melville and Barrow Point. Roth was usually careful to state the sources of his information, and did not attempt to go beyond immediate data to extravagant claims about social organization. One must point out that many such claims are implicit in some of the discussions of Australian languages that have been indulged in up to the present... (1979:92).

Sign Language

In much of his work Roth was a pioneer, and he has suffered the fate of pioneers: his work has largely been superseded. However, we come now to a branch of linguistics in which Walter Roth not only was a pioneer, but a brilliant one, whose work has *not* been and will not be superseded. This is the study of sign languages, which are studied by linguists in essentially the same way, and with much the same terminology, as are spoken languages (see for example Kendon 1988).

Roth notes that his signs are better called ideagrams rather than constituents of a sign language, 'each sign conjuring up an idea, modified more or less by the context of the mute conversation' (1897a:71). However, West (1963:163) says that 'Aboriginal sign language is one of only two indisputable systems of natural manual sign language extant in the world today'. (This number would certainly have to be revised substantially upward today.) Howitt (1890) was probably the first to notice that sign languages differed markedly from one area to another.

Roth's North West Central Queensland material comprises sketches, with accompanying descriptions, of 198 signs used in one or more of 10 of the language communities of the area, representing seven distinct spoken languages. These he groups into 15 categories – six categories of fauna, plus also flora, inanimate nature, human beings, material culture, one labelled 'Simple Acts, States and Conditions' and four other minor categories. The 198 signs represent, between them, some 106 different concepts (although counting by another person or on another day might yield a slightly different figure). The quality of the illustrations and descriptions of the signs is excellent. The descriptions include information on what aspect of the concept the sign illustrates – for an animal, for example, the shape of its body or face or footprint, the way it feeds, and so on.

Meggitt (1954) studied this material and divided Roth's 10 'tribes' into three well-defined groups. These were Mayi-Thakurti and Kalkutungu, on the north of the main group, Wunumara and Guwa on the east, and the remainder. Meggitt found the differences between the three groups to be statistically significant.

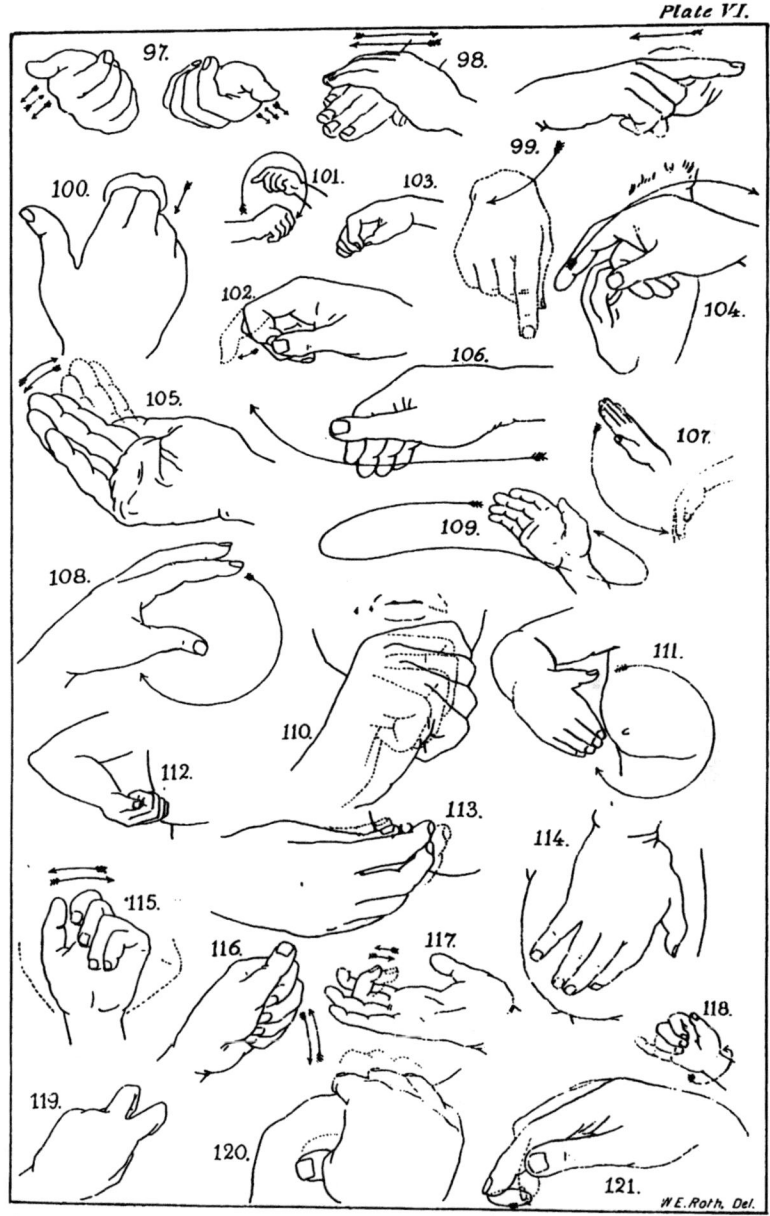

WE Roth and the Study of Aboriginal Languages in Queensland | 147

Sign-Language (Cont⁴) Figs. 97-104, Plants. Figs. 105-109, other Objects of Nature. Figs. 110-121, Individuals, Family Relatives Etc.

Figure 8.3 Sign Language

Meggitt concluded that similarity of sign language is a function of the geographical distance between tribes. Given the greater knowledge we have now of the relationships between the spoken languages of the area, it can be observed (as it was by Meggitt, but with less precision) that similarity of sign language is not correlated with similarity of spoken language. Mayi-Thakurti and Wunumara are classified as dialects of a single language, and are quite distantly related to Kalkutungu and Guwa. Of the main group, most are closely related, but Antekerrepenh and Warluwarra are not at all closely related to each other, or to any of the others. It seems that people change their sign language to conform to that of what Roth would have called their messmates, much more quickly than they change their spoken language.

Roth also collected about 110 signs on Cape York; these are described in the 'gesture language' part of 'Signals on the road; gesture language' in Roth (1908). They represent about 84 concepts. A large number of them are attested for just one source. Fourteen are the same as corresponding signs in North West Central Queensland.

The signs are no longer known in the areas where Roth worked.

I will leave the last word to RMW Dixon, who hints at the climate in which Roth had to work and which led to his departure from Australia:

> It is ... worth noting that, in the fifty years after Roth, there was – in the whole of Queensland – just one piece of professional or semi-professional linguistic research undertaken: that of McConnel [1945 etc] (1972:367).

In fact there were three – since Dixon wrote, the excellent work of Gerhard Laves has come to light and Donald Thomson's linguistic work has been assessed (Rigsby forthcoming) – but otherwise the remark is still appropriate.

Acknowledgments

I am grateful to Michael Williams, Alice Gorman, RMW Dixon, Gedda Aklif and Barrie Reynolds for relevant information, to an anonymous referee for useful comments and suggestions, and especially to Bruce Rigsby and Barry Alpher for substantial information and comments. Also to the Institute for Aboriginal Development for financial assistance for my attendance at the Roth Family Conference.

Notes

1. Information in this paragraph from Barrie Reynolds, pers comm.
2. Diacritics are signs, such as accents, added to a letter.
3. A referee notes that William Dampier recorded a word on the Dampier Land coast in 1688, probably in Bardi. People used a cry which he wrote as 'gurry gurry' (Dampier

1998 [1697]:220). The word 'gurry' is tentatively identified as *ngaarri*, 'spirit of the dead' in Bardi (Gedda Aklif, pers comm).
4. I am indebted to the Society for sending me information on this spelling system.
5. This spelling of the language name is quite consistent with the modern spelling, Guugu-Yimidhirr. The colon after the u indicates that the vowel is long, symbolised now by doubling it; the underlining of the d shows that it is dental, symbolised now by the following h; and the r is the phonetic symbol for the sound written now as rr; the sound now written r would have had a subscript dot in this system.
6. And Haviland (1979:35) observes that this is true also of other material translated into the language by Schwarz.
7. He had earlier, in his Pitta-Pitta grammar, admitted to having great difficulty with this sound, and generally omitting it. When he did write it, it was as n.
8. Rigsby (nd b) gives some examples; in one he refers to a dispute between Roth and James Earl, a pastoralist, about whether the people of the Deighton River area were Kuku Warra or Kuku Mini, and notes that both were correct, but they were referring to the perspectives of different neighbouring peoples.
9. It may seem strange that a term like Kuku Mini, coming from a language (perhaps Kuku Yalanji) which has not undergone large-scale sound changes in the fairly recent past, should be used to designate a language which has undergone such changes and so would not be at all intelligible to speakers of the 'unchanged' languages. However, multilingualism was the norm in the area, and I am assured (Alpher, pers comm) that this term, along with a number of others, is used in the 'changed' languages, so that *kuku* (for example) would be used at times instead of the changed form – *ogo* or *aghu* or *uw* or whatever – for the particular language.
10. But without the same changeability of reference, as Barry Alpher (pers comm) pointed out.
11. Crowley (1981) says that this is a Linngithigh name for the people; the version he heard from his Mpakwithi consultant is Yupungathi, and the name for the language Yuputhimri. Compare Roth's Yopotimi.
12. In a couple of cases the information Roth was given on these terms was quite wrong, with confusion involving kinship terms and other related words.

Works Cited

There are many other items which would be included in a full bibliography of Roth's work on Queensland languages. I have omitted from the reference list items which I have not cited. These include republished work, a handful of vocabularies, rewritings (sometimes with respellings) of wordlists I have cited and an unknown number of other reports that contain some language material.

Beale, Tony (1974) 'A grammar of the Biri language of north Queensland', ms, Australian National University
Blake, Barry J (1979a) *A Kalkatungu Grammar*, Canberra: Pacific Linguistics
———. (1979b) 'Pitta-Pitta', in Dixon, RMW and Blake, BJ (eds), *Handbook of Australian Languages, Volume 1*, Canberra: ANU Press, 182–242
Blake, Barry J and Breen, Gavan (1990) 'Guwa', in Breen, JG, *Salvage Studies of Western Queensland Aboriginal Languages*, Canberra: Pacific Linguistics, 108–44
———. (1971) *The Pitta-Pitta Dialects*, Linguistic Communications 4, Melbourne: Monash University
Brasch, Sarah L (1975) 'Gureng-Gureng: a language of the upper Burnett River, south-east Queensland', BA (Hons) sub-thesis, Australian National University
Breen, Gavan (forthcoming a) Wakaya Grammar and Dictionary
———. (forthcoming b) Warluwarra Grammar and Dictionary

Breen, Gavan (1981) *The Mayi Languages of the Queensland Gulf Country*, Canberra: Australian Institute of Aboriginal Studies
———. (1976) 'An introduction to Gog-Nar', in Sutton, Peter (ed), *Languages of Cape York*, Canberra: AIAS, 243–59
———. (1970) 'A re-examination of Cook's Gogo-Yimidjir word list', *Oceania* 41(1), 28–38
Capell, A (1963) *Linguistic Survey of Australia*, Sydney: Australian Institute of Aboriginal Studies
Cook, James (1773) *Lieutenant Cook's Diary*, ed Hawkesworth, John, London: W Strahan and T Cadell
———. (1770) 'Journal of proceedings of HM Bark Endeavour', 1768–71, ms, Mitchell Library, Sydney
Crowley, Terry M (1983) 'Uradhi', in Dixon, RMW and Blake, BJ (eds), *Handbook of Australian Languages, Volume 3*, Canberra: ANU Press, 306–428
———. (1981) 'The Mpakwithi dialect of Anguthimri', in Dixon, RMW and Blake, BJ (eds), *Handbook of Australian Languages, Volume 2*, Canberra: ANU Press, 146–94
Dampier, William (1998 [1697]) *A new voyage round the world: the journal of an English buccaneer*, London: Hummingbird Press
Dixon, RMW (2002) *Australian Languages: Their Nature and Development*, Cambridge Language Surveys, Cambridge: University Press
———. (1977) *A Grammar of Yidiɲ*, Cambridge Studies in Linguistics 19, London: Cambridge University Press
———. (1972) *The Dyirbal Language of North Queensland*, Cambridge: University Press
Evans, Nicholas (1995) *A Grammar of Kayardilt, with Historical-Comparative Notes on Tangkic*, Mouton Grammar Library 15, Berlin: Walter de Gruyter
———. (1992) *Kayardilt Dictionary and Thesaurus*, Parkville: Department of Linguistics and Language Studies, University of Melbourne
Godman, I (1993) 'A sketch grammar of Rimanggudinhma, a language of the Princess Charlotte Bay region of Cape York Peninsula', BA (Hons) sub-thesis, University of Queensland
Gorman, AC and Traditional Owners of the Gooreng Gooreng, Bailai and Gurang (2002) 'The history and culture of the Boyne Valley', Part III of 'Cultural heritage of the Boyne Valley: Awoonga Dam raising and infrastructure project, Calliope Shire, Central Queensland: survey, excavation, analysis and management', a report prepared for the Awoonga Alliance and the Gladstone Area Water Board
Hale, Herbert M and Tindale, Norman B (1933–34) 'Aborigines of Princess Charlotte Bay, North Queensland', *Records of the South Australian Museum* 5(1), 63–116; 5(2), 117–72
Hale, Kenneth L (1997) 'A Linngithigh vocabulary', in Tryon, D and Walsh, M (eds), *Boundary Rider: Essays in Honour of Geoffrey O'Grady*, Canberra: Pacific Linguistics, 209–46
———. (1966) 'Linngithigh', in O'Grady, GN, Voegelin, CF and FM (eds), *Languages of the World: Indo-Pacific Fascicle Six*, *Anthropological Linguistics* 8(2), 176–97
———. (1964) 'Classification of northern Paman languages, Cape York Peninsula, Australia: a research report', *Oceanic Linguistics* 3(2), 248–65
———. (1960a) 'Antikiripini (Georgina R variety)', ms and tapes, AIATSIS MS 868, tape nos A4596–7
———. (1960b) [Northern Pama field notes] [Aurukun, Weipa], AIATSIS MS 882
Hamilton, Philip (1997) *Oykangand and Olkola Dictionary*, www.geocities.com/Athens/2970/index.html
Haviland, John B (1979) 'Guugu Yimidhirr', in Dixon, RMW and Blake, BJ (eds), *Handbook of Australian Languages, Volume 1*, Canberra: ANU Press, 27–180
———. (1974) 'A last look at Cook's Guugu Yimidhirr word list', *Oceania* 44(3), 216–32
Hershberger, HD and R, Bloomfield, T, Friday, R, Roberts, B, Sykes, H, Sykes, D and Walker, J (1982) *Kuku Yalanji Dictionary*, Work Papers of SIL-AAB B7, Darwin: Summer Institute of Linguistics

Hey, Rev J Nicholas (1903) 'Elementary grammar of the Nggerikudi language' [revised and edited by WE Roth], *North Queensland Ethnography Bulletin No 6*, Brisbane: Government Printer

Holmer, Nils M (1983) *Linguistic Survey of South-Eastern Queensland*, Canberra: Pacific Linguistics D54

Horton, DR Editor (1994) *Encyclopaedia of Aboriginal Australia*. Canberra: Aboriginal Studies Press

Howitt, AW (1890) 'Notes on the use of gesture language in Australian tribes', *Journal of the Australian Association for the Advancement of Science* 2, 637–46

Jolly, Lesley (1994) 'Gureng Gureng: a language program feasibility study', Brisbane: Aboriginal and Torres Strait Islander Studies Unit, University of Queensland

———. (1989) 'Aghu Tharrnggala: a language of the Princess Charlotte Bay region of Cape York Peninsula', BA (Hons) thesis, University of Queensland

Keen, Sandra L (1983), 'Yukulta', in Dixon, RMW and Blake, BJ (eds), *Handbook of Australian Languages, Volume 3*, Canberra: ANU Press, 190–304

Kendon, A (1988) *Sign languages of Aboriginal Australia*, Cambridge: Cambridge University Press

Laycock, Donald C (1969) 'Three Lamalamic languages of north Queensland', *Papers in Australian Linguistics* 4 (PL A-17), Canberra: Pacific Linguistics, 71–97

McConnel, Ursula H (1945) 'Wikmungkan phonetics', *Oceania* 15(4), 353–75

Meggitt, Mervyn (1954) 'Sign language among the Walbiri of Central Australia', *Oceania* 25, 2–16

Oates, William J and Lynette F (1970) *A Revised Linguistic Survey of Australia*, Australian Aboriginal Studies 33, Linguistic Series 12, Canberra: Australian Institute of Aboriginal Studies

Patz, Elisabeth (1999) *A Grammar of the Kuku Yalanji Language of North Queensland* (PL 527), Canberra: Pacific Linguistics

Palmer, E (1884) 'Notes on some Australian tribes', *Journal of the Royal Anthropological Institute of Great Britain and Ireland* 13, 276–347

Rigsby, Bruce (forthcoming) 'The languages of Eastern Cape York Peninsula and linguistic anthropology', in Rigsby, Bruce and Peterson, Nicolas (eds), *Donald Thomson, the Man and the Scholar*, Canberra: The Academy of the Social Sciences in Australia

———. (1992) 'The languages of the Princess Charlotte Bay region', in Dutton, T, Ross, M and Tryon, D (eds), *The Language Game: Papers in Memory of Donald C Laycock*, Canberra: Pacific Linguistics, 353–60

———. (nd a) 'Kuku Thaypan', ms in the possession of Bruce Rigsby

———. (nd b) 'The Languages of the Quinkan and Neighbouring Region', ms in the possession of Bruce Rigsby

Roth, Walter E (1910a) 'Decoration, deformation, and clothing', *North Queensland Ethnography Bulletin No 15, Records of the Australian Museum* 8(1), 20–54

———. (1910b) 'Huts and shelters', *North Queensland Ethnography Bulletin No 16, Records of the Australian Museum* 8(1), 55–66

———. (1910c) 'Social and individual nomenclature', *North Queensland Ethnography, Bulletin No 18, Records of the Australian Museum* 8(1), 79–108

———. (1909) 'Fighting weapons', *North Queensland Ethnography, Bulletin No 13, Records of the Australian Museum* 7(4), 189–211

———. (1908) Miscellaneous Papers, 1. 'Tabu and other forms of restriction', 2. 'Counting and enumeration', 3. 'Signals on the road; gesture language', 4. 'Progressive Koko-yimider exercises', *North Queensland Ethnography Bulletin No 11, Records of the Australian Museum* 7(2), 74–107

———. (1907) 'Burial ceremonies and disposal of the dead', *North Queensland Ethnography Bulletin No 9, Records of the Australian Museum* 6(5), 365–403

———. (1904) 'Domestic implements, arts and manufactures', *North Queensland Ethnography Bulletin No 7*, Brisbane: Government Printer

Roth, Walter E (1903) 'Superstition, magic and medicine', *North Queensland Ethnography Bulletin No 5*, Brisbane: Government Printer

——. (1902) 'Games, sports and amusements', *North Queensland Ethnography Bulletin No 4*, Brisbane: Government Printer

——. (1901a) 'The Structure of the Koko Yimidir Language' [with the assistance of Revs GH Schwarz and W Poland], *North Queensland Ethnography Bulletin No 2*, Brisbane: Government Printer

——. (1901b) 'Dictionary of Koko Yimidir', Hope Vale, typescript

——. (1901c) 'Food: its search, capture and preservation', *North Queensland Ethnography Bulletin No 3*, Brisbane: Government Printer

——. (1900a) 'On the natives of the (lower) Tully River; and appendix', Cooktown, Qld: Queensland Home Secretary's Department, Office of the Northern Protector of Aboriginals

——. (1900b) 'Report [to the Under-Secretary, Home Dept., Brisbane], on the Aboriginals of the Pennefather (Coen) River district and other coastal tribes occupying the country between the Batavia and Embley Rivers', Cooktown, Qld

——. (1900c) 'Workai-a (Camooweal)' [Wakaya wordlist] [and] 'Yaro-inga (Headingly)' [Ayerrereng wordlist], in uncatalogued mss 216, State Library of New South Wales, Sydney

——. (1899) [Report to the Commissioner of Police, Brisbane], 'An Account of the Koko-minni Aboriginals, occupying the country drained by the middle Palmer River', Cooktown, Qld

——. (1898a) 'Koreng-Koreng (Miriam Vale)', in uncatalogued mss 216, State Library of New South Wales, Sydney

——. (1898b) 'Kungandji (east of Cape Grafton)', in uncatalogued mss 216, State Library of New South Wales, Sydney

——. (1898c) 'Chirpal-ji (Scrubby Creek)', in uncatalogued mss 216, State Library of New South Wales, Sydney

——. (1898d) 'Ngachan-ji (Upper Barron)', in uncatalogued mss 216, State Library of New South Wales, Sydney

——. (1898e) 'Chirpol (Herberton)', in uncatalogued mss 216, State Library of New South Wales, Sydney

——. (1898f) 'Walmal and Mallanpara (Tully)', in uncatalogued mss 216, State Library of New South Wales, Sydney

——. (1898g) 'Ngachan (Barron River)', in uncatalogued mss 216, State Library of New South Wales, Sydney

——. (1898h) 'Ngai-kungon-ji (Atherton)', in uncatalogued mss 216, State Library of New South Wales, Sydney

——. (1898i) 'Kung-gan-ji, occupying the tract of country to the east of the Murray Prior Range, Cape Grafton, etc, see letter book p305. Speak Kung-gai', in uncatalogued mss 216, State Library of New South Wales, Sydney

——. (1898j) 'Yi-din-ji – occupy the valley of the Musgrave River, along the coast line, Murray Prior Range to Cairns, see letter book p305; speak Yi-di', in uncatalogued mss 216, State Library of New South Wales, Sydney

——. (1898k) 'Kokoyimidir (Mount Cook)', in uncatalogued mss 216, State Library of New South Wales, Sydney

——. (1898l) 'Koko Yel-lan-ji (Boggy Creek)', in uncatalogued mss 216, State Library of New South Wales, Sydney

——. (1898m) 'The Aborigines of the Rockhampton and surrounding coast districts', Cooktown, Qld: Queensland Home Secretary's Department, Office of the Northern Protector of Aboriginals

——. (1898n) 'Report [to the Commissioner of Police, Brisbane] on the Aboriginals occupying the hinter-land of Princess Charlotte Bay, together with a preface containing suggestions for their better protection and improvement', Cooktown, Qld

Roth, Walter E (1898o) 'Report on Visit to Butchers Hill & Boggy Cr[eek]. Abo'l Res[erve]', Report to the Commissioner of Police, Brisbane, Cooktown, 6 June 1898
———. (1897a) *Ethnological Studies among the North-West-Central Queensland Aborigines*, Brisbane: Government Printer
———. (1897b) 'Obarindi (Nicholson River)' [Nguburindi wordlist], in uncatalogued mss 216, State Library of New South Wales, Sydney
———. (1897c) 'Ku-in-ma-ba-ra (Torilla)', in uncatalogued mss 216, State Library of New South Wales, Sydney
———. (1897d) 'Ka-rún-ba-ra (Rosewood)', in uncatalogued mss 216, State Library of New South Wales, Sydney
———. (1897e) 'Ra-kí-wa-ra (Yeppoon)', in uncatalogued mss 216, State Library of New South Wales, Sydney
———. (1897f) 'Ta-rum-bal (Rockhampton)', in uncatalogued mss 216, State Library of New South Wales, Sydney
———. (1897g) 'Wa-pá-ba-ra (Keppel Island)', in uncatalogued mss 216, State Library of New South Wales, Sydney
———. (nd) 'Group relations on the Annan River', Cooktown, item XM297 in the Howitt Collection, Museum Victoria, Melbourne
Sommer, Bruce A (1976) 'WE Roth's Peninsula vocabularies', in Sutton, Peter (ed), *Languages of Cape York*, Canberra: AIAS, 127–38
———. (1972) *Kunjen Syntax: a Generative View*, Australian Aboriginal Studies 45, Linguistic Series 19, Canberra: Australian Institute of Aboriginal Studies
———. (1969) *Kunjen Phonology: Synchronic and Diachronic* (PL B11), Canberra: Pacific Linguistics
Stuart-Russell, H (1899) 'List of Aboriginal words, Gilbert River District. Spoken by tribes south of the Mitchell, and including, with various changes, to beyond Croyden, and west to the Leichhardt or thereabouts', in Roth (1899)
Sutton, Peter (1979) 'Australian language names', in Wurm, SA (ed), *Australian Linguistic Studies* (PL C54), Canberra: Pacific Linguistics, 87–105
Terrill, Angela (2002) *Dharumbal: The Language of Rockhampton, Australia* (PL 525), Canberra: Pacific Linguistics
———. (1998) *Biri*, Languages of the World / Materials 258, Munich: Lincom Europa
Tindale, Norman B (1974) *Aboriginal Tribes of Australia: Their Terrain, Environmental Controls, Distribution, Limits and Proper Names*, Berkeley: University of California Press/Canberra: Australian National University Press
———. (1940) 'Distribution of Australian Aboriginal tribes: a field survey', *Transactions of the Royal Society of SA* 64, 130–241
———. (1938–39) 'Parallel vocabularies', collected on Harvard-Adelaide Universities anthropological expedition, ms, South Australian Museum
West, La Mont (c 1965) [tape recordings in Ogo Angkula and Ogo Alungul], OT 9412, Archives of Traditional Music, Indiana University, in the possession of Bruce Rigsby
———. (1963) 'Aboriginal sign language: a statement', in Sheils, Helen (ed), *Australian Aboriginal Studies: A Symposium of Papers Presented at the 1961 Research Conference*, Melbourne: Oxford University Press for the Australian Institute of Aboriginal Studies 160– [title page has WEH Stanner, Convenor and Chairman of the conference named above Sheils]
Zwaan, Jan Daniel de (1969a) *A Preliminary Analysis of Gogo-Yimidjir: a Study of the Structure of the Primary Dialect of the Aboriginal Language Spoken at the Hopevale Mission in Northern Queensland*, Australian Aboriginal Studies 19, Linguistic Series 5, Canberra: Australian Institute of Aboriginal Studies
———. (1969b) 'Two studies in Gogo-Yimidjir: I: diachronic comparison; the back vowel shift; II: phonological differentiation between men's and women's speech', Oceania 39(3), 198–217

PART 4

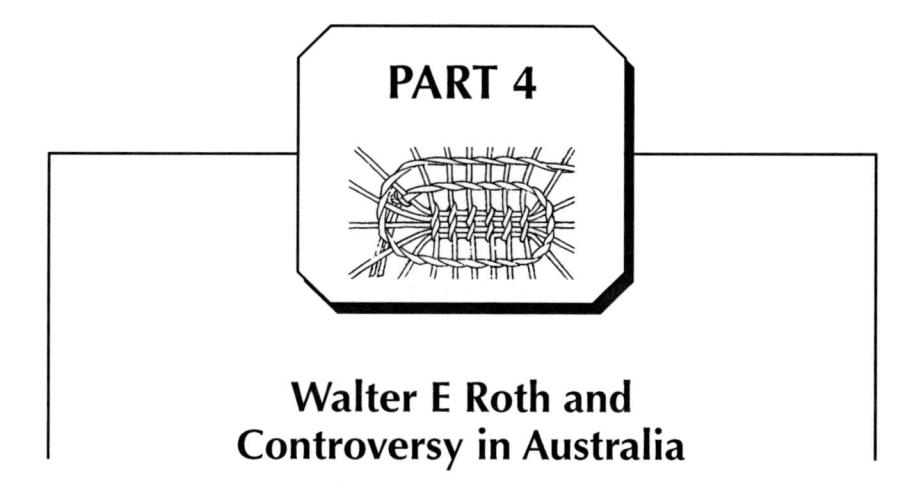

Walter E Roth and Controversy in Australia

CHAPTER 9

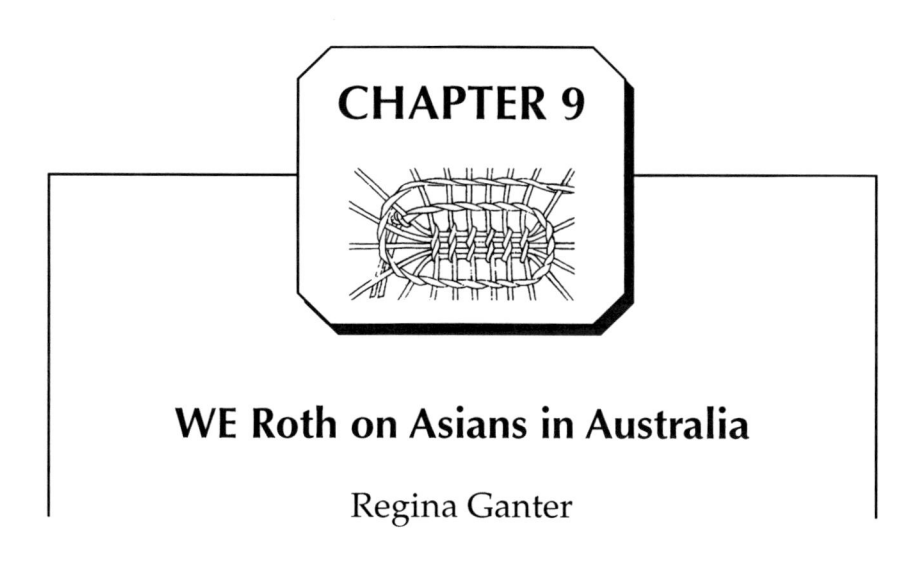

WE Roth on Asians in Australia

Regina Ganter

The question of Aboriginal welfare in Queensland, in which Walter Roth became the central figure in the late 1890s, was embedded in much wider debates about national futures, where the question of race was absolutely central. Race was the proper focus of national debate and industrial reform and the source of deep-seated anxieties. The presence of Asians and Pacific Islanders became implicated in most public debates, from temperance to cooperative village settlements, and of course also in the question of the management of Aborigines. In 1901 Roth instigated a bill which resulted in banning Chinese from employing Aboriginal labour. However, a close reading of the passage of that bill reveals that this had not been his intention. Pursuing a *realpolitik* beyond trendy rhetorical flourish, Roth attempted to interpolate himself between the self-interested representations of northern farmers, who gave damning evidence against Chinese employers of Aborigines, and the rabid sinophobia of Queensland parliamentarians.

The *Fin De Siècle* Centrality of Race

Roth came to prominence in the administration of Queensland Aborigines in 1897 with the *Aboriginals Protection and Restriction of the Sale of Opium Act*. This Act was gradually widened to become a one-stop shop of Aboriginal administration in the state, covering health, welfare, education, family, employment and training in a comprehensive administrative package, whereas previous legislative intervention had been piecemeal and targeted. The 1865 *Industrial Reform Schools*

Act already permitted the removal of the children of any Aboriginal or part-Aboriginal woman to industrial schools; and Aboriginal reserves had already been gazetted since George Bridgman's experiment, using Aboriginal 'sheltered labour' on sugar plantations in Mackay in the early 1870s. The sale and distribution of opium to Aborigines had been outlawed with the 1891 *Sale and Use of Poisons Act*. The 1897 Act created the nucleus of a bureaucracy dedicated to the administration of Queensland Aborigines, with a Chief Protector acting through the agency of local police officers and other public officers appointed as local protectors of Aborigines.

This bureaucracy displaced the Native Police, which had been the main policy instrument in Aboriginal affairs in Queensland. The new colony of Queensland inherited the Native Police at its separation from New South Wales in 1859, and there had been a series of public inquiries arising from police brutality. But it was not until the last few years of the century that the Queensland government viewed Aboriginal affairs as a serious enough issue to warrant some sweeping reform.

At this time the Australian colonies were in Federation mood, ready to shape the competing colonies into a collective future embracing a national destiny in which questions of race were absolutely predominant. Eugenic thought had lent a veneer of science and reason to xenophobic concerns, and visions of a new nation were centrally underpinned by the idea of a White Australia. Two of Queensland's major industries were put on notice to clean up their act: the sugar industry and the pearl-shell fishery, which were to be conducted by white labour only, although the pearlers eventually succeeded in being exempted from the White Australia policy (Ganter 1994). The seedling white community in the antipodes had to be protected and fostered.

Reform Agendas

Enter Archibald Meston – journalist, parliamentarian, pamphleteer, publicist, opinion-maker. Meston was appointed as 'special commissioner' of police to embark on a fact-finding tour of North Queensland and submit a report that would pave the way for change. He already knew what was required before he conducted his tour of investigation for he had submitted a 35-page report on Queensland Aborigines and a 'proposed system for their improvement and preservation' in 1895 (Meston 1895). That report envisaged a system of reservations for Aborigines. His 1896 report to the Queensland parliament argued convincingly that something must be done, and that segregation was a cheap and affordable option. The Native Police was the major expenditure on Aboriginal affairs in Queensland, and Meston recommended that the Native Police be abolished. The greatest source of abuse of Aborigines was in their employment relations. Meston recommended that a system of protective surveillance of all Aboriginal employment be implemented, premised on segregation, and that the employment of Aborigines in the marine industries be prohibited. Pearling and trepanging were the mainstay of employment of Aboriginal labour in North Queensland, and Meston's sweeping report raised the ire of the pearling interests, and of course of the police. Although Meston is generally considered the architect of the 1897 Act, his most emphatic recommendations were not, in fact, implemented. But he did initiate the reform process. William Parry-Okeden, the Queensland Police Commissioner, promptly followed up the report with a tour of inspection. His own report toned down Meston's radical proposals to a level where they could be implemented: the police would not withdraw from Aboriginal affairs but would act as protectors of Aborigines; the employment of Aborigines in the marine industries would be regulated but not prohibited; Aborigines would not be subject to wholesale segregation, but protectors would have powers to remove them to segregated reserves.

Meston had expected that he would be in charge of the new Aboriginal policy in Queensland, but in fact Parry-Okeden was installed as Chief Protector, overseeing Meston as 'southern protector', while Walter Roth was recruited from medical service in Boulia, Cloncurry and Normanton as 'Northern Protector'. The northern protectorate was the much more interesting task, since white settlement had not reached there before the 1860s, and much of this area was still a zone of first contact. Meston was eased out of the service at the end of 1903, while Roth stayed for seven years during a period that set the course for future policy. After Roth, Queensland's Aboriginal protection bureaucracy from 1913 to 1986 would be characterised by the dominant leadership of only three career bureaucrats: John Bleakley, serving 29 years (1913–42); Cornelius O'Leary, serving 41 years, of which he spent 20 (1943–63) in the Department of Native Affairs (DNA); and Patrick Killoran, serving 49 years in the Queensland public service, 22 of them in the DNA (1964–86).

There was not what might be called a dominant official sentiment about Aboriginal policy, or a politically correct position, in the 1890s. Opinion ranged from the need to 'smooth the dying pillow' to insistence on cultural preservation, from repugnance to philanthropy, from insistence on segregation to avowal that useful employment offered the only hope for long-term integration and survival. Such irreconcilable views were enshrined in the 1897 reform package, which encompassed humanitarian, xenophobic and labour regulation aspects, and left much room for discretionary judgment to the protectors of Aborigines – and therefore for dispute (Ganter & Kidd 1993). But missionaries, administrators, employers, ethnographers and philanthropists did agree implicitly that nomadism was not a sustainable lifestyle, and that Aborigines must be induced to settle down, and that opium was an enemy of Aboriginal peoples.

A concern over opium was reflected in the title of the 1897 Act, and 7 of its 33 sections dealt exclusively with restrictions of the opium trade itself, without any reference whatsoever to Aboriginal people. This was the first Act in any Australian colony to prohibit opium, which was, after all, an attractive revenue earner for colonial governments (Manderson 1993). Now only doctors, chemists and wholesale druggists were permitted to deal in opium, and unless they lived in a major city they could only stock a maximum of 900 grams. The act was a direct strike at the Chinese in Queensland, who were deemed to be the main suppliers of charcoal (inferior) opium to Aborigines. Desmond Manderson observes that 'opium smuggling began in earnest' (1993:36) after the introduction of the 1897 Act in Queensland, and Cathie May notes a dramatic increase in opium-related convictions of Chinese in Queensland, convictions that had nothing to do with Aboriginal people in most cases (1984).

Aboriginal Protection/Asian Exclusion

In a climate of racial anxieties it was not unusual to use Aboriginal policy against Asians in Australia. It could be deployed both to deprive Asians of access to cheap Aboriginal labour and to restrict interactions between Aborigines and Asians. Western Australia, with a high proportion of Asian residents in its northern townships, had 'town reserves' where Aborigines could not enter, as well as Aboriginal reserves where Asians could not enter. In Queensland, too, it became policy under the 1897 Act to deny Chinese people permits to employ Aboriginal labour (until 1902, when this became law rather than policy). In the pearling industry Asian and European employers competed for Aboriginal labour, with whites everywhere arguing that they were missing out. A Queensland pearler's complaint that 'when a Japanese is recruiting boys in the north, a European has little or no show of getting any boys' was mirrored in the Northern Territory observation that 'At one time the Europeans used to find blacks useful, but now they cannot get them away from the Chinese camps' (*SAPP* 1895:3021; Mackay 1908:236 [petition]).

The Chinese in particular had met with organised popular resistance from their white competitors on the goldfields since the 1850s. Each colony in turn passed its anti-Chinese acts as new migrants flooded in, following gold discoveries, and many of the most symbolic moments in Australian history have an undercurrent of racial anxiety. Even the 1854 Eureka Stockade inquiry discovered much fear of Chinese competition and resulted in anti-Chinese legislation in Victoria in 1855 (Curthoys 2001). Moreover, union and government efforts to fashion a national policy out of disparate colonies galvanised over the Chinese question with the 1888 Intercolonial Conference on the Chinese question. Similarly, the Queensland Shearers' Strike started in 1889 at Jondaryan Station, precisely because this station had a high proportion of Chinese and South Pacific labour undercutting union rates: 'blacklisting' wool produced by non-union labour had a racial connotation next to its class war meaning (Walker 1988). By the 1890s race was not just one of the issues the Australian governments had to also deal with. It was a central and pervasive concern.

In the far north, sparsely settled by whites and with large Asian populations contributing a lion's share of the business communities, anti-Asian sentiments were far less pronounced because Asians there did not compete with white union labour. White business communities in the north were more interested in securing white entrepreneurial dominance while still retaining access to cheap Asian labour. But a gold rush usually gave rise to anti-Chinese agitation, because miners carried their racialised experience of competition with them as they moved from California to Australia, and from one Australian goldfield to the next (May 1984). A local branch of the Anti-Chinese League had been formed at the Atherton Tablelands near Cairns in 1886, and was revived in 1892 with renewed agitation to exclude Chinese from the diggings. It was soon joined by the Barron Valley Farmers Association (later the Atherton Farmers and Progress Association), which became the mouthpiece of anti-Chinese sentiments on the Atherton Tablelands.

It was this group that made representations to the protection bureaucracy to achieve an exclusion of Chinese, Pacific Islanders and 'other Asians' from permission to employ Aboriginal labour under the new labour regulations. They insisted that these were 'the only people who supply opium' to Aborigines and that as a result it had become difficult for white employers to secure Aboriginal labour. One Mr Putt raised Roth's ire when he insinuated that the new Aboriginal policy was unnecessary and unwelcome, and was making things far too difficult for whites: 'I have shot 13 or 14 niggers in this District and this is all the government has done for me: I can't get a b.... Nigger when I want one. They all go to the Chinaman' (Roth report, 20 September 1898, quoted in Ganter 1998:15).[1] Roth made sure to cite this outburst in a report to parliament to demonstrate the unadulterated self-interest that underpinned complaints against Chinese. Mr Putt was referring exactly to the kind of abusive behaviour that Roth intended to eradicate.

Asian-Aboriginal Families: The 1901 Amendment Bill

As Northern Protector Roth was responsible for the area from the northernmost limit of Queensland to the Tropic of Capricorn (near Rockhampton), including the entire maritime industry and most sugar cane areas, both of which relied largely on Asian and Pacific Island labour. While the Southern Protector, Meston, was concerned with 'smoothing the dying pillow' and was confidently predicting that Aborigines would be extinct by the 1950s, Roth noted with concern an 'increase in half-caste' populations in his protectorate. By January 1901 he urged the Home Department that 'some check' needed to be placed on Aboriginal miscegenation, especially, he specified in parentheses, 'in the case of Asiatics and Kanakas' (Roth report, January 1902, quoted in Ganter 1998:14). He was proposing an amendment bill to the 1897 Act to widen the powers of protectors so that they could regulate mixed marriages and reduce miscegenation. Roth understood clearly and very early on that, in order to administer Aboriginal populations under separate laws, these had to be identifiably Aboriginal, and not mixed race.

During its passage through parliament from July to October 1901, Roth continued to feed information to the Home Secretary to support the bill. He had instigated a survey of mixed marriages in his protectorate and now tabled the results to demonstrate 'the evils to which the promiscuous marriage of Aboriginal women with coloured aliens may lead' (Roth progress report, October 1901, quoted in Ganter 1998:15). His zeal to contain miscegenation with 'coloured' people permitted some significant slippages of meaning: some of the coloured partners of Aboriginal women he referred to were naturalised, rather than 'alien'; and 'promiscuous marriage' was really just a way of referring to 'mixed marriage'. Roth was unhappy about the 'frequency of marriages … between Kanakas and Aboriginal women', and wanted all ministers of religion instructed not to sanction unions between Aboriginal women and coloured aliens without obtaining his advice. The Registrar General considered this proposal 'unworkable' (since there was no legislation to support it). But a carefully phrased circular memorandum was sent to all ministers and marrying justices, urging them to 'use every endeavour to prevent the marriage ceremony becoming the harbour of refuge for those men who under the 1897 Act are deemed unfit to employ natives' (4 March 1901 and 26 September

1901, quoted in Ganter 1998:15). The men thus alluded to were Chinese and 'other Asian' men.

The slippage in Roth's discourse here is that all relationships between Aborigines and coloured persons were promiscuous even if they were legally sanctioned: cross-racial affection was thus pathologised, particularly cross-racial affection involving Aboriginal and coloured people. This specific racial intention was also conveyed to parliament when some members expressed reservations about the wide powers the amendment bill bestowed on protectors, which they feared might disempower whites in their interactions with Aborigines. The Home Secretary, invoking well-worn stereotypes, explained:

> The reason why legislation is asked for is that an Asiatic, who is known to have been convicted of offences against the Act – for supplying blacks with opium for instance – upon a prosecution being attempted against him for a breach of the Act with regard to harbouring a gin and her family, perhaps a portion of that family being his own children, does this: he goes through a form of marriage with that gin, and defies the law. There are many such instances. He is a nomad, and that marriage bond is no more to him than a snap of the finger.

He was able to reassure the honourable members that:

> The permission [to marry] referred to in the Bill would never be refused in the case of any man who desired to marry an aboriginal or half-caste woman, provided he was a respectable man and was not suspected of supplying opium to aboriginals (31 July 1901, quoted in Ganter 1998:16).

In other words, whites were unlikely to become subject to the provisions of this bill. Eventually, of course, white marriage aspirants also ran aground on the provisions of the bill, even without being suspected of supplying opium or alcohol.

Having been convinced that a distinction would be clearly drawn between themselves and coloured men, the parliament now embraced the idea of greater powers for protectors of Aborigines, and proposed even to bar all Asians from employing Aboriginal labour. Asians were always already suspected of supplying opium to Aborigines, so that they could not be respectable employers. This was not a new idea. Indeed it had led to the failure of a similar bill in 1899 attempting to prevent Asians from employing Aborigines, to which the Japanese government had lodged a formal protest on the grounds that it was discriminatory, with the result that Royal Assent had been withheld. The Queensland parliamentarians now warmed to the idea of reinstating such a clause, to bar if possible all Asians, and perhaps also Melanesians and Polynesians (and ideally also Africans), from employing Aborigines. The 1901 debate demonstrates how an earlier anti-Chinese mood had by the turn of the century broadened into an anti-coloured, pro-white sentiment.

The Home Secretary and Roth strenuously resisted this new turn in the debate, fearing that it would jeopardise the whole amendment bill. There was much reference to Chinese and their semantic link with opium, which was after all a major policy concern of the 1897 Act, so that Roth followed up with a special report on the question of Chinese employers. Referring to statements made to him in the Atherton Tablelands, he countered that:

> The Chinese offer better wages, and, what is more, pay the aboriginals their wages when due; they also house and feed them well ... I cannot instruct the local Protector to prevent Chinese employing them (quoted in Ganter 1998:16).

Roth did not mean to champion Chinese as employers of Aborigines. He merely found it inadvisable to insert an anti-Asian clause in his bill; and he made it clear that much of the evidence against the Chinese was tendered in sheer self-interest. When he was called before the Legislative Council in October 1901, he averred:

> Personally I am adverse to the Chinaman employing them unless they are reputable, but in some places my hands are forced to allow the aboriginals to be employed by Chinamen (3 September 1901, quoted in Ganter 1998:16).

The Legislative Council determined that it was politically safe to exclude Chinese from employing Aborigines, because 'China was on her knees' and would not lodge a protest. When the amendment bill was passed, Section 5 clause 2 stated: 'A permit to employ an aboriginal or half-caste shall not be granted to any alien of the Chinese race'. Roth emphasised that this clause had been inserted against his advice (Givens & Roth, parliamentary debate on 3 September 1901, quoted in Ganter 1998:16).

Roth really had no purchase in an economic agenda that arose from competition between white and coloured employers of Aboriginal labour. His concern was with the maintenance of racial boundaries. His observation during his first year of office, that the administration of 'half-castes' was a major preoccupation in the north, became a self-fulfilling prophecy for Aboriginal administration in Queensland: once the 1901 bill became law, the bureaucracy received a barrage of requests for permission to marry and became the moral arbiter of desirable marriages. When Roth was vested with powers to authorise mixed marriages in June 1902, he adopted the policy to disallow marriages between Aboriginal women and coloured men.

In 1905 he again took a strong stance with reference to Asian activities in Australia, as member of a federal commission of inquiry into Customs which resulted in the first federal prohibition of opium importation. Roth had mounted a strong case that its detrimental effects on Aboriginal people far outweighed the revenue earned from its importation.

Roth and Meston

Roth was now sole Chief Protector. After 1904 the office was reorganised and Meston was eased out. Incensed, Meston protested:

> All the practical work has been done by me. [Roth] does nothing but write reports and advertise himself to make the Minister believe he is a marvellous man. When out of the service I shall let much daylight in on him and his work, and his own character (Meston, 4 December 1903, quoted in Ganter & Kidd 1993:548).

This he did. Their relationship had been uneasy from the start. Their first drawn-out contestation was over the fate of the Keppel Islanders located at the boundary of their protectorates (Ganter 1985). Meston wanted to remove the Islanders to several different reserves because they were exposed to miscegenation with whites, while Roth felt they should best be left on their island. Roth was far less enthusiastic about removals than Meston.[2] He argued that these people were not affected by fringe-dwelling, they did not use opium and only one of them, the eldest male, smoked tobacco. To demonstrate their pristine condition, he tendered a photograph of Keppel Islanders, all 'full-blooded adults', grouped by a bark humpy with traditional implements. This was taken in 1898. But he had also taken another photo which tells a different story of the Islanders (Mike Rowlands 1985, pers comm). It shows the mixed-descent children, dressed in contemporary clothing, and it suggests that the bark humpy that frames them was most likely built at Roth's request to complete the *mise en scène* while he was spending a week with his wife at the Keppel Island homestead that employed them all.

To the photograph showing the Keppel Islanders 'in pristine condition', Meston countered:

> If Dr Roth dealt less in these nude photographs of Aboriginal women he would be held in more esteem by the blacks, as both men and women resent it in a very decided manner (Meston to Home Office, 26 August 1902, quoted in Ganter & Kidd 1993:546).

Figure 9.1 Keppel Islanders in 1898, photographed by Walter Roth. This photograph is a re-enactment of 'tribal life', and only fully Aboriginal Keppel Islanders are included. Roth used this photograph in a dispute with Archibald Meston to demonstrate the 'good condition' of the Keppel Islanders. (Queensland State Library, neg no. 8972) (Courtesy John Oxley Library)

Figure 9.2 A second photo, taken by Roth at the same time, that was not submitted as evidence of the present condition of the Keppel Islanders. The same gunyah with a prominent entrance beam is shown, the grinding stone has been moved closer, and this photograph shows dressed children of mixed descent. (Queensland State Library, neg no. 8974) (Courtesy John Oxley Library)

Meston here inaugurated a debate that would seriously tarnish Roth's reputation. Popularly known as the 'Sacred Ibis' (a pun on an early piece of his scholarship) (Jonathan Richards 2005, pers comm), Meston was known for fighting words and had a talent for using the press as a public arena. He continued to publish commentaries anonymously, often using the pen name 'Ramrod', and he contributed to the public debate over Roth's credibility, discussed elsewhere in this volume, that led to his resignation. This campaign was instigated by petitions from the northern pearling and trepang interests whose continued access to cheap Aboriginal labour was threatened by interventions from the Chief Protector. During the Keppel Island dispute, Meston indicated that white residents of the northern protectorate, unhappy with Roth's decisions, had appealed to him; and it seems likely that Meston cultivated contact with Roth opponents. A *Sunday Truth* article professing inside knowledge of the bureaucracy sounds decidedly like Meston:

> It is not known how Roth suddenly became an expert on Aborigines ... where Meston communicated with the Home Secretary, Roth was responsible to Mr Parry-Okeden, the Commissioner of Police, to whom he was much indebted for his appointment (*Sunday Truth*, 15 April 1906, quoted in Ganter & Kidd 1993:549).

Among the letters of accusation submitted from North Queensland against Roth in 1906 was one from Meston. He remained convinced that he had been unfairly manoeuvred out of the Protector's office. He actually reapplied for the job when Richard Howard left late in 1913, to the consternation of the Home Secretary, who swiftly determined that despite his unquestioned knowledge about Aboriginal affairs in Queensland Meston was the 'least suited' of all the candidates. He had shown himself to be 'a most difficult officer to control. He knew no rule or regulation and was not expeditious in the conduct of business' (Ganter & Kidd 1993:547, note 51).

Conclusion

Roth left a lasting imprint on Aboriginal affairs in Queensland. The 1901 amendment bill was his own initiative – Meston complained that he had not been consulted (Meston, examination by the Legislative Council, 8 October 1901, cited in Ganter 1998). The 1897 Act, as amended in 1902, became the foundation of Aboriginal administration until the 1930s. In 1934 the definition of 'half-caste' was widened to include the now large mixed-descent coloured population, and the prevention of Asian-Aboriginal contact was again at the core of reform. As an ethnographer Roth was interested in the recording and preservation of culture and in shielding Aborigines from contaminating influences, both cultural and genetic. He therefore took a strong stance on the question of opium and on the formation of families between Aboriginal and coloured people (though he was less concerned about miscegenation with whites). It was this interest in racial purity that led him to submit his carefully choreographed photograph of the Keppel Islanders to the Home Secretary. Meston's enmity no doubt fuelled the campaign against Roth with 'inside information'. It was precisely Roth's ethnographic interest, which makes him such an interesting figure today for Australian researchers, that aroused suspicion and public resistance and finally undid him.

Roth paid a disproportionately large amount of attention to the phenomenon of racial admixture, particularly with regard to Asians and other non-white residents. To account for his concern with eugenic management, he had an ethnographic interest in tribal customs and 'pure-bloodedness', and his administrative role also required that the Aboriginal population that was to be governed by separate laws must have definable boundaries. But the eugenic agenda was to become greatly intensified between the wars by his successor, JW Bleakley.

Notes

1. It has only recently come to my notice that this statement was not made directly to Roth, as his 1898 report suggests, but to Sub-Inspector Cooper (Copland 2005, draft version, Ch 2).
2. Mark Copland (2005) found that Roth signed for 47 removals per year on average (1898–1905), while Meston averaged 90. Howard averaged 90 per year, Bleakley 257, O'Leary 146 and Killoran 33.

Works Cited

Copland, Mark (2005) 'Calculating Lives – the numbers and narratives of forced removals in Queensland 1859–1972', PhD thesis, Griffith University

Curthoys, Ann (2001) 'Men of all nations, except Chinamen', in McCalman, Iain *et al*, *Gold: Forgotten Histories and Lost Objects of Australia*, New York: Cambridge University Press, 103–23

Ganter, Regina (1998) 'Living an Immoral Life – "Coloured" women and the paternalistic State', *Hecate* 24(1), 13–40

———. (1994) *The Pearl-Shellers of Torres Strait*, Melbourne: Melbourne University Press

———. (1985) 'The history and development of the Keppel Islands', Honours thesis, Humanities, Griffith University

Ganter, Regina and Kidd, Ros (1993) 'The powers of Protectors: Conflicts surrounding Queensland's 1897 Aboriginal legislation', *Australian Historical Studies* 25(101), 536–45

Mackay, J (Chair) (1908) 'Report of the Royal Commission appointed to enquire into the working of the Pearl-shell and Beche-de-Mer Industries', *QVP* Vol 2, 1–284

Manderson, Desmond (1993) *From Mr Sin to Mr Big*, London: Oxford University Press
May, Cathie (1984) *Topsawyers: the Chinese in Cairns 1870 to 1920*, Townsville: James Cook University
Meston, Archibald (1895) *Queensland Aboriginals: Proposed System for their Improvement and Preservation*, Brisbane: Government Printer
South Australian Parliamentary Debates (SAPP) (1895) Adelaide: Government Printer
Walker, Jan (1988) *Jondaryan Station – The Relationship Between Pastoral Capital and Pastoral Labour 1840–1890*, St Lucia: University of Queensland Press

CHAPTER 10

The Legacy of a 'Lazy Character': Walter Roth's Contribution to the Ethnography Collections of the Queensland Museum

Richard Robins

Museums of general science have a simple mission – to collect, to preserve and to educate. It is a role they have been undertaking in Australia for well over 100 years; and it is reflected in museum collections containing specimens of historical importance, many rare and unique, in quality research and, most familiarly, museum display. In 1910, Robert Etheridge Jr, the curator of the Australian Museum, was prompted to remind the Queensland Government of the role of museums when he reported to it on the conditions of the Queensland Museum. After pointing out deficiencies in the building, display, labels, specimens, registration, storage and staffing (Mather 1986:53), he concluded his report by citing Dr G Brown Goode's 'The Principles of Museum Administration' (1895) from which he extracted the following:

1. A museum is an institution for the preservation of those objects which best illustrate the phenomena of nature and the works of man, and the utilization of these for the increase of knowledge and for the culture and enlightenment of the people.
2. The Public Museum is a necessity in every highly civilized community.
3. The community should provide adequate means for the support of the museum.
4. A museum cannot be established or credibility maintained without adequate provision in five directions.
    (a) A stable organisation and adequate means of support

(b) A definite plan, wisely framed in accordance with the opportunities of the institution and the needs of the community for whose benefit it is to be maintained
(c) Material to work upon – good collections or facilities for creating them
(d) Men to do the work – a staff of competent curators
(e) A place to work in – a suitable building
(f) Appliances to work with – proper accessories, installation materials, tools and mechanical assistance
5. A finished museum is a dead museum, and a dead museum is a useless museum.

Anthropology collections constituted a significant part of the purview of colonial museums of general science. Every Australian state museum at the turn of the 20th century maintained an ethnological collection. Today, these collections are more than just passive registers of passing events. They are the evidence resulting from dynamic social processes that illustrate and inform on the nature of relationships in time and space between *us* (the collecting society) and *them* (the collected society). The manufacture of an artefact is the product of a set of economic, technological and social relationships (often unknown) amongst indigenous people. A new set of relationships is generated in the interaction between the acquirer (generally non-indigenous) and the indigenous owner; another set is generated between the donor and the staff of the museum to which the object is donated. Once inside the museum the object becomes the focus for a new set of relationships among the public, staff and researchers. Not only are museum visitors drawn from all walks of life, but donors and correspondents are equally diverse. Unlike in most government departments, a diverse and intimate bond is often developed between the clients of a museum and the institution and its staff. A museum collection therefore reflects complex social interactions between governments, non-government organisations (churches, industry groups, universities etc), professional groups (museum directors, ethnographers, anthropologists and archaeologists), the general public and indigenous people. In these cases the actions of indigenous people appear passive, largely due to lack of documentation, and a tendency to talk *about* them, not *to* them or *with* them.

The Queensland Aboriginal collections of Walter E Roth are a good illustration of this complexity. While Roth's relationship with the Queensland Museum directly related to ethnography and Aboriginal people, it also raises intriguing questions about the role of museums in society now as then. More than a century after he created his collection of Queensland Aboriginal artefacts, two questions can be asked: Did the collection of artefacts by Roth increase knowledge and contribute to the culture and enlightenment of the Queensland people? Did they in any way affect the conditions of Aboriginal people? Implicitly these questions address the issue of the success of the Queensland Museum.

Walter Roth and the Queensland Museum

Roth's relationship with the Museum was a long but desultory one. It is recorded in a series of letters and notes to various Directors, and by a series of donations of artefacts as well as the sale of photographs. The first indication of the relationship comes from archival correspondence written when Roth was teaching at Brisbane Grammar School.[1] He sent his wife with a note to the Director, CW De Vis, to borrow biological teaching specimens for a lecture. The first (and only) letter of substance was written in 1895, when Roth was the Surgeon at Boulia and corresponded again with De Vis. He wrote:

> For the last six months I have been continuously and assiduously collecting notes on the ethnology of the blacks in these districts, and in the course of my investigations (which have taken me as far up the Georgina as Roxburgh – my trip to the Toko Ranges and Mulligan having been hitherto prevented by floods) have acquired numerous references etc to the fauna of this locality ...
> ... When I now show you the nature of the information which I have gathered, I think, without conceit, you won't give me a character for being lazy! However I will leave you to judge.
> I have collected (and corroborated with every precision possible out here)
>
> (1) six vocabularies of dialects.
> (2) a sign-language understood among the different tribes who otherwise would be rendered unintelligible the one to the other. I have about 120 of such signs – all illustrated.
> (3) Several corroborres, with full details, such as the particular ornamentations, all painted in the proper colours, the translations (where Known) and "stage-directions" etc.
> (4) The search for food – methods of entrapping the different animals, birds & fish, preparation of vegetable foods – cooking utensils etc.
> (5) Domestic (Camp) Life: The various games and amusements, sickness and methods of Healing, Medicine, & treatment. Burial rites etc. Rain-making etc.
> (6) Fighting implements – the meaning of the ornamentations on their boomerangs etc. (which I think is recorded for the first time). The various trade routes along which they barter these weapons, and what they get in exchange etc. Methods of Fighting. Their ideas of punishment in the camp.
> (7) Sexual Relations – and sexual mutilations.
> (8) Personal ornaments and ornamental mutilations.
>
> I believe that the most interesting are the sign-language, and the interpretation of the ornamentations – or perhaps you could inform me

whether any one has been before me in this field. You can, I well believe, understand my not having written to Messrs Meston et id genus omne, on these matters!

Believe me
Always very sincerely yours,
W.E. Roth.[2]

His final communication with the Museum came 44 years later, in December 1932, when he negotiated the sale of 167 annotated lantern slides (many with the Qld Government stamp on them) to the Museum for five pounds:

Dear Dr Longman,

Just in time! I received the fiver (and many thanks) – yesterday morning – it enabled me to drink not only to your own good health, but that of many dear old Queensland friends!
 I am so glad to know that those slides will eventually be cared for and appreciated – being close on 72 I realise that I cannot last so very much longer and am accordingly getting rid of all my scientific books, apparatus, MSS. etc., before starting on my last journey west.
 Never mind the Government stamp being on any of them. I think that they are the ones mounted by good old Mobsby.
 Kindest remembrance to Holland when next you see him, and the best of New Years greetings.

Sincerely yours,
(Sgd) Walter E. Roth

I sympathise with you over the financial conditions – any way they could (not) be worse than they are here! Its those d— Yankees again![3]

The letter is annotated: 'Mr Cleary This remarkable letter from Dr Roth is sent in lieu of a receipt. (Sgd) H.A.L. 23/2/33'. A further annotation in Longman's handwriting states: 'Dr Roth died April 6th, 1933'.

In the intervening period, he wrote two notes and 10 short letters. Most are unremarkable, although in one to Director Hamlyn-Harris he observes: 'As for arsenic only experience the poor devils had of it was when mixed purposely with station flour'.[4]

Roth also made three donations between 1900 and 1903 totalling approximately 230 artefacts from across Queensland, predominantly northern Queensland. The first, D (Donation) 10422 in 1900, is recorded in the Donation Register as 'Spears, Woomeras, and dillybags' from 'various localities' in 'Nth Qld'. The second, D11827 in March 1903, is recorded as 33 ethnographic items from 'various localities' in 'Nth Qld'. There is a handwritten list of this donation in the archives which groups the items into categories and provides Roth's register number (often applied with red paint) and a locality for each. The third, D12083 in December 1903, comprises 180 'Ethnographic items' from 'various localities' in 'Nth Qld'.[5]

There is no indication in the Museum records of the circumstance of collection, the maker's name, sex, language group or social affiliations. There is no indication in the Museum records of how Roth collected material or which items he photographed or otherwise illustrated in his published papers. Linking the artefacts collected with his published reports is at times problematic.

Roth's Collection in Context

Although Roth's collection appears to be modest in size, it was by the standards of the time a significant collection for the Queensland Museum. Other collectors/donors to the Museum at the turn of the 20th century included the Government Meteorologist Clement Wragge (the most extensive collector of this period), the missionary Nicholas Hey, property manager J Coghlan and of course Archibald Meston.

These other donors of the period made larger collections. Clement Wragge sold 576 artefacts to the Museum in 1900, as well as substantial collections of Queensland Aboriginal material to the Victorian, South Australian and overseas museums. J Coghlan made a significant and well-documented collection from Glenormiston in western Queensland that is larger than any other for that area. It also has better accompanying information.

Meston's collections provide an interesting comparison with Roth's. Both Roth and Meston were influential in the administration of Aboriginal people throughout Queensland. Both had made a significant impact on public opinion and Government policy. Both were, in a sense, amateur ethnographers.

Meston, like Roth, also had a long association with the Museum. Between 1883 and 1907 he made 15 separate donations (most of multiple items), sold more than 250 artefacts in three separate sales (1897, 1904 and 1907), and participated in two exchanges (E194 in 1898, and E214 in 1901). His approach to ethnographic recording is reflected in a 1896 letter to the Director:

> Dear De Vis,
>
> This may or may not be well known bird. shot him on head of Ducie River. had a great time. Interviewed 17 wild tribes. Have some grand weapons for you. Spears woomeras dilly bags necklaces et al. We will have a long jam when I return.
>
> Best wishes
> Sincerely yours
> Archibald Meston.[6]

On the basis of his transactions with the Museum, Meston appears to have been the more dynamic collector. Meston collected more objects, but not significantly more. In terms of geographical distribution and type of object, both collections contain rare and common items. Meston's collection has a higher percentage of imprecise locations, but both contain items with localities that are as generalised as 'Rockhampton to Tweed River', or 'Wenlock, Pennefather and Embley Rivers'. Like Roth, Meston does not provide basic information about the artefact makers, such as their names, ages or language groups.

In itself, then, there is nothing particularly remarkable about the Roth collection at the Queensland Museum. It is neither bigger nor better documented than other collections of the time. But, of course, it cannot be separated from its collection context – from the copious documentation that exists in Roth's published ethnographies and government reports, and the extensive Roth collection held by the Australian Museum. This is not the case for the collections of Meston, Wragge and other collectors of the period.

In his reports Roth's interactions with Aboriginal people are noted in detail, revealing both his concern and consideration for Aboriginal people and his capacity as an ethnographer. For example, in his 1901 report on a trip to the Wellesley Islands he describes the circumstances of meeting a Kaiadilt woman:

> Proceeding on our journey, we hit a billabong and, following it up, suddenly came upon a middle-aged woman carrying a boy pickaback on her shoulders. The subject of abject terror, she talked, yelled, and gesticulated, every now and again pointing in a direction where we subsequently found the preceding nights camp, with the words 'para-huli', rapidly repeated, the aspirate (unusual in the north Queensland vocabularies known to me) being distinctly articulated. Of course we could not make ourselves understood, but to allay her fears we gave her my handkerchief, and the child an empty match-box: unfortunately I had nothing else with me at the time except a pipe and some matches, which I did not like to strike in her presence in case of frightening her (Roth 1901:4).

In this report his collection methods for some items are also described:

> In exchange for the articles taken away for subsequent and more accurate description, I left several handkerchiefs and about two lbs weight of beads: tobacco is unknown in these parts (Roth 1901:4).

Roth's contribution will only be properly understood when all the material relating to his work in Queensland is considered. Sadly, this has yet to be achieved. Seventy-five years after he donated them, many items were still not entered in the registers of the Queensland Museum. Even now, the collection is still not fully catalogued; and the detailed collection circumstances found in his reports have not been married with the collection. Nevertheless, fragmented though our conception of it is, the contribution of Roth to knowledge about Aboriginal life and society far outweighs that of Meston and his ilk. It is the most significant body of anthropological work on Queensland Aborigines undertaken for that period.

Discussion

The Roth collection raises the question of the success of museums generally (and the Queensland Museum particularly) in increasing knowledge and enlightening society through its collections of artefacts. In the short term, and in the particular instance of the Queensland Museum, the answer is: not very successful at all. The statement by Frederic Morrison published in the *The Aldine History of Queensland*, a popular book published in 1888 can be used as a benchmark. In it he says of Queensland Aborigines:

> … we believe we but express the sentiment of nearly everyone who has been brought into contact with them, that they are, above all races of savages yet discovered, the lowest in the scale of humanity. They build no houses, perform no labour except such little as is required by the absolute necessity of hunger. They respect no moral code save that of brute force. Their condition at the time of discovery by Captain Cook, and for many years after, as low as the beasts of the field.

If Roth's work had made a significant impact on the people of Queensland one could expect evidence of some change of attitude subsequently at least in the scientific community, and particularly among those in the Queensland Museum. Yet in a public lecture in 1925, the then Director of the Queensland Museum, Hebert Longman, is reported as stating: 'The Aborigines had remarkably thick skulls, and their brains were less developed in the frontal and parietal regions than those of Europeans. In some respects the aborigines were more nearly allied to the extinct Neanderthal, than to modern Europeans' (Anon 1925), and that: 'In their primitive condition… the aboriginals were Stone Age men, but we must remember that some three hundred generations ago, our ancestors used stone axes, arrow-heads, knives and hammers. The Australian aborigines were devoid of art except for rough carvings on wood, stencils on walls and roofs of caves, and crude decorative material' (Anon 1925).

Roth's work had obviously failed to make an impression on this Museum Director at least. His desire to fulfill the wish expressed by Parry-Okeden that 'Queensland will be proud of her Aborigines' (Roth 1897:iv) remained, and perhaps still remains, unrealised. Apart from a short period under the Directorship of Hamlyn-Harris between 1911 and 1918, when important and well-documented collections were made and interesting research undertaken and published, the history of the Queensland Museum until recently has been largely one of indifference to indigenous culture. Perhaps Roth anticipated this when he sold the bulk of his ethnographic collection to the Australian Museum in Sydney and arranged for his outstanding research to be published by that same institution.

The reason Roth sold the largest part of his collection to the Australian Museum, instead of donating it to the Queensland Museum, is a matter of conjecture now as then. The issue has a complex history and includes a number of factors. Roth had been collecting for some time before he was appointed Protector and commissioned to collect for the Queensland Government. Even when employed by the government he, like Meston, Wragge and numerous other government employees, continued to maintain personal collections. In 1897 he wrote from Rockhampton to the 'Curator' of the Queensland Museum stating: 'A complete aboriginal skeleton has come into my possession: I shall be glad to offer it to the Museum in exchange for some aboriginal things of which I am in want to complete my own collection'.[7] Roth possibly felt that the donations he made to the Queensland Museum discharged his duty to the State, and that the remainder of artefacts were his to dispose of as he liked.

At the time of Roth's departure from Queensland, the Queensland Museum was in a parlous state. De Vis retired in 1905, and no Director was appointed until 1910 (Mather 1986:53). The budget was slashed during hard economic times at the turn of the 20th century and was not restored for a decade. Staff numbers were greatly reduced and those remaining were incapable of managing and displaying any new collection, let alone supervising the production of scientific reports. Mather asserts that the years 1905–06 were the nadir of the Queensland Museum (1986:53). The Australian Museum in this period was much better placed to undertake the publication of Roth's work and to look after the collection. Through his brother Reuter he had a strong connection with the Australian Museum. Further, the purchase took place within one year of the establishment of the Department of Ethnology at the Australian Museum by Robert Etheridge Jr. Such a department would not be created at the Queensland Museum for another 60 years.

Roth was also in dispute with the Queensland Government for reasons explored elsewhere in this volume. He was not disposed well to its interests, nor the government to his. The rancour lasted. Years after the controversy, after Roth had done much good work in British Guiana, Charles Headly at the Australian Museum wrote to Hebert Longman, the new Director of the Queensland Museum, observing that: 'Dr Roth would I think accept a salaried position in a Museum, when he retires from the Imperial Service on a pension. But I suppose that the Government would be prejudiced against engaging him'.[8]

The Queensland Government did not have an outstanding record for 'being proud of her Aborigines', and this was reflected in the lack of interest it displayed in documenting their culture, including the collection and documentation of material culture. Henrietta Fourmile has estimated that 65% of artefacts made by Queensland Aborigines held in Australian collections are held outside Queensland in other State museums (Fourmile 1990:59). Important collections, including those by Donald Thomson, Norman Tindale and Ursula McConnel, are held in museums in other states.

One hundred years on, the work of Walter Roth is making a significant contribution to both Indigenous and non-Indigenous understandings of Aboriginal culture, its complexity and dynamism, in a number of ways – not least through Native Title claims, where his work is used extensively. His research and artefact collections are now increasing knowledge and enlightening people. Few today would judge him to be a 'lazy character'.[9]

However, important as it is to document the past, Roth's example also illustrates that provided the task is set about with intellectual rigour and energy, the primary and most enduring obligation of public museums must be to document and explain *contemporary* society through their collection of objects. After all, '*A finished museum is a dead museum, and a dead museum is a useless museum*' (Brown Goode 1895). As in Roth's case, the intellectual paradigm that informs the collection may change over time, yet the legacy remains, knowledge continues to be created and a sound basis for public enlightenment established.

Acknowledgments

I would like to thank Kathy Buckley, Meg Lloyd, David Parkhill, Carolyn Martin and Michael Quinnell at the Queensland Museum for their assistance in accessing museum records.

Notes

1. Note by Roth in the Queensland Museum Inwards Correspondence Archive, March 1888.
2. Letter of 11 February 1895, Queensland Museum Inwards Correspondence Archive 1895/4635.
3. Letter of 26 December 1932, Queensland Museum Inwards Correspondence Archive 33/65.
4. Letter of 6 August 1915, Queensland Museum Inwards Correspondence Archive 15/1043.
5. Letter of 19 March 1903, Queensland Museum Inwards Correspondence Archive 1903/6803.
6. Letter of March 1896, Queensland Museum Inwards Correspondence Archive.
7. Letter of 4 October 1897, Queensland Museum Inwards Correspondence Archive 1897/7688.
8. Letter of 21 July 1919, Queensland Museum Inwards Correspondence Archive.
9. Letter of 11 February 1895, Queensland Museum Inwards Correspondence Archive 1895/4635.

Works Cited

Anonymous (1925) 'The Aborigines – an informative lecture', *Brisbane Courier*, 16 July 1925

Brown Goode, George (1895) 'The principles of museum administration', *Proceedings of the Sixth Annual Meeting of the Museums Association* (Newcastle), 69–147

Fourmile, H (1990) 'Possession is nine-tenths of the law: and don't Aboriginal people know it!', *COMA* 23, 57–67

Mather, P (1986) 'A time for a museum: the history of the Queensland Museum 1862–1986', *Memoirs of the Queensland Museum*, Vol 24

Morrison, Frederic W (1888) *The Aldine History of Queensland*, Sydney: Aldine

Roth, WE (1901) 'Report on a visit to some of the Wellesley Islands', 6 July 1901, Queensland Museum Anthropology archives

———. (1897) *Ethnological Studies among the North-West-Central Queensland Aborigines*, Brisbane: Government Printer

CHAPTER 11

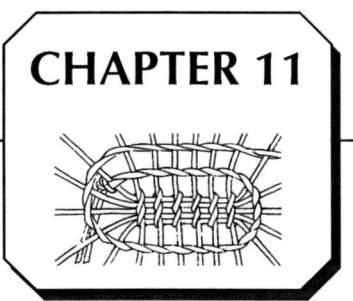

The Life and Times of Walter Edmund Roth in North Queensland: The First Protector, the Australian Museum and Scandal

Kate Khan

Who was Walter Edmund Roth? How did he come to gather together one of the most extensive collections of Aboriginal material culture from a single region of Australia, namely north Queensland, while also being the subject of a Parliamentary inquiry into his activities and his connections with the Australian Museum? And end his days in Guyana, South America?

In 1897 the Colonial Secretary of Queensland introduced the *Aboriginals Protection and Restriction of the Sale of Opium Act*. It was passed unanimously by the State Government as a response to frontier brutality against Aboriginal people. The Act henceforth restricted and controlled every aspect of the lives of all Aboriginal people in Queensland, whether they needed protection or not. It was paternalistic in the extreme. The Act made all Aboriginal and Torres Strait Islanders virtually wards of the State. This was the situation when Roth took up the position of Northern Protector of Aborigines for North Queensland.

Roth was an extraordinary man. From 1884 when he graduated from Oxford with a BA Hons in Biology, he had been a Science teacher in Brisbane and Sydney; had been Director of the Government School of Mines in South Australia; had returned to London and completed a medical degree at St Thomas's; and had married Ada Toulmin, then left her for Eva Grant, with whom he had a son, Vincent. He was appointed Medical Officer to Cloncurry, Boulia and Normanton hospitals in the

Figure 11.1 Walter Edmund Roth in outback northern Queensland (Australian Museum Photograph Archives, V.02541) (Reproduced with the permission of the Australian Museum)

Gulf country of North Queensland in 1894. During this time he wrote his first major work on Aboriginal life: *Ethnological Studies among the North-West-Central Queensland Aborigines* (1897). The following year, 1898, the Police Commissioner appointed Roth as the first Northern Protector of Aboriginals at a salary of 542 pounds per annum.

Roth wrote to one of his contemporaries at Oxford, the anthropologist Baldwin Spencer, on 19 January 1898, in which he told him of his appointment:

> I am indeed a lucky fellow: the Protectorate of the whole Northern and Central Districts in my hands. The main, and the only drawback is that, travelling about so much and over so large an area, I shall be prevented learning any language thoroughly – the real keynote of the situation – though, I shall only be accompanied by blacks as much as possible.[1]

On 4 January 1898 Roth had received a letter from the Police Commissioner in Brisbane, outlining his duties, and observing his 'enthusiastic interest in the welfare of the blacks':

> your appointment is even more due to the fact that you are a Surgeon and Doctor of Medicine ... it would be a blessing if a doctor were

appointed ... whose time would be devoted to work among the aborigines ... Directly you have proper and sufficient equipment you should proceed to Cooktown, make all possible inquiry concerning local aboriginals, numbers, disease, present condition, measurements, photographs etc ... making from time to time such local collection of ethnological and anthropological interest as possible ... [2]

As well as recording Aboriginal culture and caring for their medical well-being, a great part of his responsibilities was to prevent the exploitation of Aboriginal people. This involved protection against abuses of employment on station properties and at sea (where Aboriginal men working on coastal vessels were not articled, and often cheated of their pay), restrictions on mixed marriages and the protection of children. He also was involved in curtailing the illegal sale of opium to Aboriginal people.

The First Year: 1898

In his first year, 1898, Roth wrote enthusiastically about travelling by packhorse over the vast territory that was his domain. It covered the whole of Cape York Peninsula and included the Channel country to the west and Rockhampton in the south. Precisely where is sketchy, although hints of localities can be gleaned from collection dates for some objects, and from his frequent letters and reports.

In February and March he collected 79 objects from people living around the Bloomfield River about 80 km south of Cooktown. He was interested in every aspect of their manufacture and wrote extensive notes and prepared detailed sketches, while also gathering specimens of raw materials for identification by Aboriginal informants as well as botanists.

In March and May he seems to have been at Cape Bedford, where Hope Vale Mission had been established since 1886, as indicated by two letters written by a young Aboriginal woman, Magdalen Mulun. The first, written to the Police Commissioner in March 1898, states: 'Our friend Dr Roth has now come to pay us a visit. He is learning our language. By him I am sending you this (mark etc.ie.) letter. We will soon send by boat a button-orchid with tea-tree (attached) ...' (Roth 1901: Bulletin 2, p 33). The second letter, dated 2 April 1898, was written to Roth:

> We were pleased you came to stay with us, and treated us in a friendly way. You also had a smile for us, and called us quickly to have a talk with you. You are indeed a friend. We therefore in return cannot (may not) forget you, but bear you in mind. We say you are our friend, and do not know another white-man like you. You spent three nights with

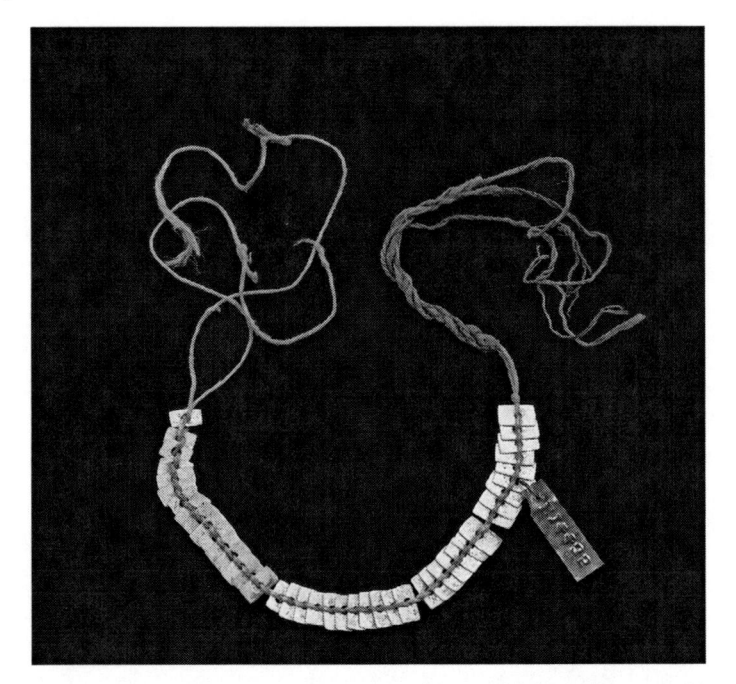

Figure 11.2 Nautilus shell head and neck band, Bloomfield River. 74 cm long. 43 rectangular pieces of shell each about 1 cm long. (Australian Museum, Sydney, E.14435. Photographer John Day) (Reproduced with the permission of the Australian Museum)

us and shewed us games. So in return we shewed you (how to play) 'cat's cradle' with the hands. You will of course come again by-and-by (won't you?) By that time you will perhaps understand our language (Roth 1901: Bulletin 2, p 32).

Roth collected 51 objects at Cape Bedford, giving them both the Aboriginal and scientific names of raw materials used in their manufacture as well as illustrating the processes involved.

Roth also visited Normanton on the Gulf coast and the Torres Straits, where he met the Cambridge anthropologist AC Haddon. He relayed this encounter to Baldwin Spencer: 'I told them how delighted I was to hear of their expedition, as they might find traces of many ethnological collecting links between New Guinea and Malaya on the one hand, and Cape York, with North Queensland, on the other'.[3] Roth was interested in what he perceived as New Guinea influences in Cape York cultures, citing outrigger canoes, bark blankets and masks; and he actively pursued these possibilities.

He must have also spent the latter part of May and early June at Butcher's Hill Station and Boggy Creek Reserve, and in the surrounding countryside south west of Cooktown. He wrote on 6 June that the previous day he had returned to Cooktown from Boggy Creek Reserve, where there had been insufficient food for the 60 Aboriginal people in residence. Roth collected 25 objects from Indigenous people living around Butcher's Hill.

In his first year he also collected 23 objects made in Cooktown – including woven baskets, shell chest ornaments, bamboo tobacco pipes, adhesives, spears and two stone axe heads.

In July Roth was in Rockhampton, where he had collected the year before being appointed Protector. His initial contact was an old man, an ex-tracker called Yorkie, whom he had known for some years. But he travelled widely, visiting Aboriginal families at Mount Morgan, Yamba, Gladstone and Miriam Vale. In October Roth was on Keppel Islands reporting on conditions there. He wrote to Spencer on 8 October 1898 of a planned overland trip to Cape York with the Commissioner,

Figure 11.3 Feather headdress, Butcher's Hill. 35.5 cm diameter. (Australian Museum, Sydney, E.14405. Photographer John Day) (Reproduced with the permission of the Australian Museum)

the same month that he submitted his *Report on Some Ethnological Notes on the Atherton Blacks*. Roth had made a sizeable collection of material from Atherton on a former visit.

Ever on the move, in November Roth spent one week inland from Princess Charlotte Bay at Musgrave Native Police Camp, surveying possible improvements to the lives of the local Indigenous people. Musgrave had become a government food relief centre. He was accompanied by Sergeant Whiteford and trackers. Although Roth was mainly carrying out protection work, he collected five objects at Musgrave: three plaited pandanus-leaf necklaces, one skirt and one healing or medicine string.

He arrived back in Cooktown on 2 December, and the next day was at Princess Charlotte Bay, on the east coast of Cape York Peninsula. Here he was an observer in an initiation ceremony. He also collected 30 objects from the local people, with detailed information on Aboriginal names for objects, the raw materials used and other documentation.

Figure 11.4 Crescent-shaped woven basket, Atherton. 23.6 cm high, mouth 15 x 13 cm, long handle 37 cm, inner handle 9 cm long. (Australian Museum, Sydney, E.14910. Photographer John Day) (Reproduced with the permission of the Australian Museum)

There are 312 objects in the Australian Museum Roth Collection dated 1898. These objects, gathered with the help of Aboriginal people, local police and station owners include model canoes as well as Roth's own photographs and sketches. In his first year Roth seems to have been everywhere in Queensland. He covered the whole of Cape York Peninsula, the Gulf region, inland and the offshore islands. Relations with Aboriginal people must have been good to enable him to collect as much information on so many aspects of their life. More objects were collected that year than in subsequent years, as administrative duties kept him tied down more than he desired.

This collection is perhaps the best remembered part of Roth's legacy, along with his 18 *Bulletins* on North Queensland ethnography. The first eight *Bulletins* were published by the Queensland Government between 1901 and 1906 (Roth 1901, 1902, 1903, 1904, 1905). The Australian Museum published the remaining 10 between 1907 and 1910 (Roth 1907, 1908, 1909, 1910). In his preface to *Bulletin 1* Roth (1901) wrote:

> By the issue of two or three such Bulletins annually, I trust that within the next eight to ten years the ethnography and anthropology of the north Queensland aboriginal will be a little better understood by the general public ...

Roth and the Australian Museum

In the *Report of the Northern Protector of Aboriginals for 1899*, Roth wrote:

> My anthropological and ethnological collections – the result of eight year's labour – comprising upwards of 800 articles, are now to be considered the property of the nation (1900:12).

Yet, five years later, on 5 June 1904, Roth wrote to Robert Etheridge Jr (then Curator of the Australian Museum) from Brisbane to arrange a day in Sydney to discuss the collection. Some months later, the Trustees of the Australian Museum received a letter from Roth in Brisbane:

> I am about to offer my collection of ethnographical objects for sale. It principally consists of materials connected with the life history of the North Queensland native, has taken upwards of 11 years to gather together, and numbers approximately over 2000 individual specimens ...
> I have reason to believe that this is the most complete collection of Queensland Aboriginal articles hitherto made. [He was correct.]
> The price I require for the complete collection is 450 pounds.[4]

The Australian Museum purchased the collection, including photographs, on 25 February 1905 (see Khan 2004, 2003, 1996, 1993).

WW Thorpe, who took charge of the Australian Museum collection on its arrival, in three months registered 2,000 ethnological objects and 240 negatives. About 150 Tasmanian stone implements were unregistered, but retained – an aggregate total of 2,390 items. Yet this collection was only part of Roth's entire collection. Some 300 objects went to the Queensland Museum, and 100 to the British Museum. An analysis of the Roth Collection held at the Australian Museum will be dealt with in a forthcoming publication.

The Roth Scandal and the Australian Museum

The consequences of the sale of his North Queensland collection to the Australian Museum was only one of Roth's problems. In 1905, while he was Royal Commissioner looking into the conditions of Aboriginal people in Western Australia, a public meeting was held in Cooktown to protest against his reappointment as Protector of Aboriginals in Queensland. Questions were asked in Parliament, and fraudulent letters were tabled, accusing Roth of the most heinous crimes. In debates in the Queensland Parliament in 1905, the Member for Clermont said:

> He had frequently defended Dr Roth, but very serious charges had been made against him, and in his own interest inquiry should be made. Another charge was that while in the custody of Government property, certain ethnological specimens, he had sold a portion of them, and pocketed the proceeds. That matter had been the subject of a question put to the Secretary for Public Lands, who had refused to write to Dr Roth and get information on the matter. There were so many charges flying about against the protector that he should at all events have the opportunity of defending himself. When giving evidence before the Legislative Council, in 1901, he had said that certain specimens which he was collecting were the property of the nation, and Mr Foxton [Minister for Home Affairs] had repeated the same thing in 1903. The present Secretary for Public Lands had also told them that Dr Roth informed him that his collection of curios was the property of the country, and that he had never sold a curio in his life ... He would ask the Minister whether he had made any effort to discover the truth of the charge made in regard to the sale of curios, because only yesterday a wire was sent to the curator of the Sydney Museum on that subject ... (QPD 1905:1338).

The Member for Barcoo also thought there should be an inquiry:

> There was a good deal in the Premier's interjection that certain people were after Dr Roth's position. Many of the people who wished to see it abolished were people who had employed the blacks before Roth's appointment without paying them anything in return. Dr

Roth insisted on many station managers and beche-de-mer gatherers paying aboriginals for the work they did, and those persons were responsible for many of the charges that had been made against Dr Roth. Dr Roth was no friend of his, but he knew what had happened in various parts of the State before Dr Roth was appointed, and since his appointment the sub-protectors had taken a great deal of trouble in regard to the agreements under which the aboriginals worked (QPD 1905:1340).

The most vocal of the troublemakers had vested interests. They were two Parliamentarians, JH Hargreaves (Member for Cook) and J Forsyth (Member for Carpentaria), along with Charles Patching Jr (solicitor), George R Hepburn (Cooktown manager for Burns Philp), A Romano (a bêche-de-mer fisherman) and a Mr Owens (publican). At first sight the connecting link is not obvious. But Hepburn had differences with Roth over Indigenous labour on bêche-de-mer boats, some of which were owned by Burns Philp; and the head of their Brisbane office was none other than Forsyth, the Member for Carpentaria. The publican, Owens, was a licensee of one of Burns Philp's hotels.

Roth also confronted an unsympathetic political climate. The Member for Bourke, for example: 'thought Roth knew very little about Aborigines of Queensland, ... He [the Member for Bourke] thought the best way of treating the blacks was to gather them all together and put them on Government reserves' (QPD 1905:1339). The Member for Clermont thought the telegram from the Australian Museum gave sufficient reason to inquire into Roth's actions: 'That wire showed that Dr Roth had sold 2,000 specimens to the Sydney Museum. It was quite possible that the doctor had a collection of his own; but he distinctly told the Upper House that it was part of his business to collect curios, and those curios should therefore be the property of the State...' (QPD 1905:1339). The *Brisbane Courier* of 31 October 1905 commented: 'some explanation should be made as to why a proportion of the curios should have found their way to a Southern Museum to the number of 2,000, whilst the Queensland Museum has to be satisfied with some 300'. And the headline in the tabloid *Sydney Truth* of Sunday, 26 November 1905, screamed: 'THE DOCTOR ROTH SCANDAL SALE OF ABORIGINAL SPECIMENS TO THE SYDNEY MUSEUM (From our Own Correspondent) Curator admits buying specimens for the Museum but won't give list or prices without trustees' consent'. In this the Member for Clermont is quoted: '[Dr Roth] ... had an agreement with the Government that all specimens collected should belong to the State. Instead of answering the question, Dr Roth sheltered himself behind the result of a misapprehension ...'

In the subsequent Parliamentary inquiry Roth was found innocent of all charges, but no further mention was made of the collection at the Australian Museum. Roth said:

> I am well aware that the general opposition to my administration, and to myself personally, is mainly due to my interference with what has for many years past become considered a vested interest in the flesh and blood of the native.[5]

While some of Roth's actions, attitudes and language when writing about Aboriginal people are paternalistic and unacceptable now, he was a man ahead of his time. In an age when Indigenous peoples were being exploited and killed he actively defended their rights, protecting them from unscrupulous employers, making every effort to change the attitudes of officials who had close dealings with Aboriginal people and recording what he identified as a rich culture of a people under threat. The legacy he left for future generations is a unique resource of material relating to the traditional life of the Aboriginal people of a vast region of Queensland. Roth resigned from the post of Chief Protector of Aboriginals on 10 June 1906.

Notes

1. Letter from WE Roth to Baldwin Spencer, Copyright Manuscript Collections, Pitt Rivers Museum, University of Oxford.
2. Letter from Police Commissioner to Roth, 4 January 1898, Mitchell Library, Sydney.
3. Letter from Roth to Spencer, Cooktown, 10 May 1898, Copyright Manuscript Collections, Pitt Rivers Museum, University of Oxford.
4. Letter from Roth, 26 January 1905, Australian Museum Archives, Sydney.
5. Reports by the Under Secretary for Public Lands and Dr Roth re complaints against Dr Roth, Chief Protector of Aboriginals (nd 1905/1906?), Mitchell Library, Sydney.

Works Cited

Khan, K (2004) *Catalogue of the Roth Collection of Aboriginal Artefacts from North Queensland*, Vol 4, Technical Reports of the Australian Museum, No 18, Sydney: Australian Museum

———. (2003) *Catalogue of the Roth Collection of Aboriginal Artefacts from North Queensland*, Vol 3, Technical Reports of the Australian Museum, No 17, Sydney: Australian Museum

———. (1996) *Catalogue of the Roth Collection of Aboriginal Artefacts from North Queensland*, Vol 2, Technical Reports of the Australian Museum, No 12, Sydney: Australian Museum

———. (1993) *Catalogue of the Roth Collection of Aboriginal Artefacts from North Queensland*, Vol 1, Technical Reports of the Australian Museum, No 10, Sydney: Australian Museum

Queensland Parliamentary Debates (QPD) (1905) Legislative Assembly, 25 October, Brisbane George Arthur Vaughan

Roth, WE (1910) *North Queensland Ethnography Bulletins 14–18*, Records of the Australian Museum 8(1)

———. (1909) *North Queensland Ethnography Bulletins 12–13*, Records of the Australian Museum 7(3–4)

———. (1908) *North Queensland Ethnography Bulletins 10–11*, Records of the Australian Museum 7(1–2)

———. (1907) *North Queensland Ethnography Bulletin 9*, Records of the Australian Museum 6(5)

———. (1905) *North Queensland Ethnography Bulletin 8*, Brisbane: Government Printer

———. (1904) *North Queensland Ethnography Bulletin 7*, Brisbane: Government Printer

———. (1903) *North Queensland Ethnography Bulletins 5–6*, Brisbane: Government Printer

———. (1902) *North Queensland Ethnography Bulletin 4*, Brisbane: Government Printer

———. (1901) *North Queensland Ethnography Bulletins 1–3*, Brisbane: Government Printer

———. (1900) *Report of the Northern Protector of Aboriginals for 1899*, Brisbane: Government Printer, 1–15

———. (1898) *Report on Some Ethnological Notes on the Atherton Blacks*, Report to Commissioner of Police, unpublished mss, Mitchell Library, Sydney

———. (1897) *Ethnological Studies among the North-West-Central Queensland Aborigines*, Brisbane: Government Printer

CHAPTER 12

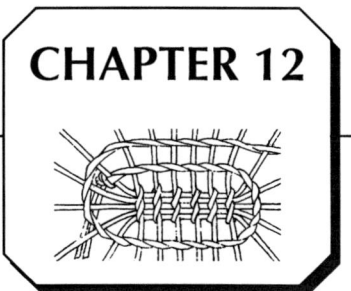

Naked Shame: Nation, Science and Indigenous Knowledge in Walter Roth's Interventions into Frontier Sexualities

Ann McGrath

When Walter E Roth, one of Queensland's founding Protectors of Aborigines, arranged outdoor photographs of an Aboriginal couple near a northern Aboriginal community, he saw it as a method of recording scientific evidence. Two photographs were deployed, however, as part of a contest between regional white men living on a cross-cultural frontier and metropolitan bureaucrats answerable to 'the British Empire'. Social engineers like Roth were seeking to prevent the exploitation and corruption of Aboriginal people. But male colonisers in less developed zones panicked at the prospect of losing easy access to cheap labour, including sexual services. Both categories of white men[1] wanted to assert superior rights to the governance of, and to intimate knowledge of, Queensland's indigenous people – especially of the women.

The photographs in question were of an Aboriginal man and woman allegedly 'in coitus'. In his 1897 *Ethnological Studies among the North-West-Central Queensland Aborigines*, published by the Queensland government, Roth described this subject as an 'interesting position' and 'the peculiar method of copulation in vogue throughout all these tribes' (Roth 1897:179, Fig 433, Plate XXIV). The couple's white employer, who spoke their language fluently – and who, as landholder and resource supplier, had significant sway over them – had assisted in the negotiations.[2] In the proto-anthropological style of the day, the photographs were impersonal, with no clan, location or individual names specified.

The only report of indigenous participants' responses is from Roth. Defending his actions, he stated:

> an aged married couple agreed to posture for me... Although half-civilised, they were a bit afraid of the camera at first, but could hardly refrain from laughing at the idea of my wanting to see them in the position asked for. However, Mr .... [their employer] promised them that I would give them money and tobacco etc. (I think flour) which I did – they were both contented.[3]

While the exchange items were standard, the required task was not. Today, the case could be read as an emblematic example of coloniser intrusiveness – of treating indigenous people more like specimens than people. Since the onset of British colonisation of their land, the local indigenous people lacked rights to their land, property, and personal and family autonomy. In the early 1900s, in a white male political milieu lacking any form of indigenous representation, the photograph scandal allowed easy ridicule. To contemporary and current audiences, the photos raise the problematic issues of the distinction between 'science' and 'pornography', the politics of data collection versus protection. What, indeed, was the difference between what Roth called 'ethno-pornography' and salacious 'pornography'? Did native sexuality not deserve the 'privacy' accorded white sexuality?

Metropolitan Interventions and Democratic Contests

At the beginnings of Australian nationhood, the politics of this controversy exposed deep tensions at the heart of an evolving colonising society. Queensland's new Aboriginal policy was considered a progressive development towards curbing the inhumanity of colonialism. Answerable to the Commissioner of Police, with local policemen as 'protectors', Roth's department had staff, a budget and an act to administer. Under the 1897 *Aborigines Protection and Prevention of the Sale of Opium Act*, the economic, social and sexual relations of the frontier were to be scrutinised by government authorities for 'protective purposes'. Roth and fellow Protector Archibald Meston paradoxically wanted to 'preserve the race' before it died out. Humanitarians had been appalled by the abuses committed by white and Asian men against Aboriginal people, including labour exploitation, sexual assault on minors, spreading venereal disease, the impregnation of Aboriginal women and the fathers' desertion of families without any support (Kidd 1997).

Tightened further after 1900, the Act's regulations required a licence for any employment of Aborigines.[4] The Act was particularly targeted to protect Aboriginal women from 'moral danger' – or sexual exploitation by Asian and white men. Police were authorised to scrutinise all cohabitation by non-indigenous men with Indigenous women. The Chief Protector's permission had to be sought for legal marriage. It was often refused and the authorities could also 'remove' Aborigines 'for their own protection'. Roth's officers routinely relocated Aboriginal females into government or mission-controlled employment and residency. High coloniser demand for sexual relations with Indigenous women made such regulations impossible to police. In an uncharacteristically defeatist tone for his administrative correspondence, Roth lamented: 'the whole subject is one difficult to cope with'.[5]

The protection legislation was spectacularly unpopular with white frontiersmen. Some were educated middle- and upper-class employers; most were semi-literate miners and casual bush workers. They especially resented government interference in their free access to indigenous female and male labour. Now their employment was regulated, wages were paid and virtually all association with Aboriginal women was criminalised. The policies drastically disrupted white men's everyday behaviour, their social networks and the de facto wives and children that constituted their mixed European and indigenous families. Those who resisted the new order, and the fracture of their families that it implied, faced prison sentences. Asian and Pacific Island men, rendered outsiders to the new nation, resisted the Act by engaging lawyers and clergy to negotiate marriage permissions and by successfully fighting cohabitation charges in court (McGrath 2003).[6]

During 1902 and 1903, local white men of cattle and mining country met in Maytown while coastal workers gathered in Port Douglas; further public meetings and petitions followed. The Member for Cook, John Hamilton, was besieged by complaints from pastoralists and a range of other white men, most of whom employed Aboriginal labour, but who resented being forced by the government to pay them.[7] Roth became the prime target of many protests and petitions, accompanied by dire warnings of economic disaster on the frontier. The removal of Pacific Island labourers due to the *Immigration Restriction Act* of 1901 was straining the labour market (Saunders 1982; Moore, Leckie & Munro 1990). Local employers claimed that since the Aboriginal regulations were introduced, they could not get any good labour. The government's 'foreign interference' was causing Aborigines to become 'worthless and unworkable'. 'Wandering blacks' would consequently kill or disturb the cattle and livestock.[8]

White employers argued that the regulations had caused starvation and opium addiction for Aborigines, and that 'fornication' was increasing. While Roth dismissed such claims, the outlawing and displacement of longer-term relationships between non-indigenous men and Aboriginal women probably did cause the casual sexual trade to increase. By distinguishing longer-term relations with Aboriginal women from 'fornication', these northern men indirectly suggested that they possessed their own moral codes.[9]

Roth was impatient with the often semi-literate, itinerant campaigners, viewing them as peddlers of vice. They had a 'vested interest in the flesh and blood of the native' and monopolised Aboriginal labour and indigenous women (*Queensland Parliamentary Papers* 1904; Khan 1993:15; Ellinghaus 2003).[10] In December 1903, Roth retorted that if the Act was causing too many problems with Aboriginal insubordination, the northern white men should employ white men. This must have infuriated the local white frontiersmen, who presumed extremely cheap labour and complementary sex was their right as colonisers Roth could not have anticipated just how deeply they would resent his interference in their most intimate relations, nor how determined they would be to 'vindicate' their 'character' against his accusations.[11]

In communicating with other senior administrators, Roth shared his disdain for the lowbrow lives and cross-racial families of his white detractors. Of one man, he noted 'reputedly father of half-caste child, removal to Reformatory been authorized'. He complained one of men owed him money and another he derogatively classed as a 'kombo' who had asked for permission to marry 'his black paramour'. In order for a man to obtain permission to marry, Roth had to rule on his 'good character', yet to Roth, these men's relationships with Aboriginal women already discredited them.[12] Roth did not see himself as breaking up 'families', for he did not think white men could act as legitimate 'protectors' of Aboriginal people. Under the new regime, it was only the government who stood as 'protector', family patriarch and father of the children (Grimshaw, Lake, McGrath & Quartly 1994:Chapter 12). Aboriginal administrators and the white male employers and cohabitors struggled for authority over blacks, and even over who was truly British. Amidst divergent value systems or 'moral economies', both coloniser groups were struggling to protect their private lives and public reputations.

Through the newspapers and by petitioning to local politicians, northern white men conducted a personal war against Roth's character and credibility. They mocked what they saw as Roth's inhumane pursuit of scientific research above practical health assistance to Aborigines. They laughed at Roth's gullibility in accepting some Aboriginal stories – a favourite cited was that crocodiles could not physically swim upstream.[13]

The circulation of these jokes in newspapers revealed a contest of knowledges taking place between white men over Aboriginal belief systems and the bush environment. Although 'high society' derided the white frontiersmen's associations with Aborigines, Roth's ethnographic knowledge won him international acclaim and prestigious invitations (Reynolds, Foreward in WE Roth 1984). This engendered jealousy amongst the white men who lived alongside Aborigines. In order to negotiate their cross-cultural worlds, they had accumulated linguistic and social knowledge of indigenous culture.

Since his Aboriginal informants anticipated benefits or punishments from him or his officers, Roth had the upper hand in gaining their cooperation. He was a man of the metropole who travelled to the periphery only for brief visits. Nonetheless, he may have impressed Aboriginal people with his keen ear for languages, his interest in their words and meanings, their games and beliefs, and his talent for line drawing. His interest in 'nudes' was more contentious.[14]

Roth was injudicious in classifying his studies of sexual, reproductive and other bodily rituals and behaviours as 'ethno-pornography'. The furore over the photos took until 1902 to erupt and it was not until 1904 – with Roth called away as a national expert to conduct a significant enquiry into the troubled conditions of Aborigines in Western Australia (see Chapter 13 in this volume) – that the scandal reached its peak. Previous accusations against Roth as a selfish doctor or a foolhardy bushman paled in comparison to the implication that he was a pornographic photographer.[15]

The photographs had been kept from the public, secreted in the government Archives. However, under the guise of looking for agricultural photographs of cocoa palms, the Parliamentarian John Hamilton 'found' and 'borrowed' Roth's photographs. Hamilton alleged that the photographs 'would disgrace a common Port Said exhibition'. This port of call – encountered by British residents on their journeys from their home country via the Suez Canal – was known for its explicit displays of visual pornography and prostitution. In the 1900s, British men preferred to associate explicit pornography with the Orient or the Middle East. However, men's clubs for the upper classes, like Brisbane's Johnsonian Club, created ordained zones where sexually explicit matters – albeit about 'primitive peoples' – could be dealt with in a 'scientific' fashion. Indeed, along with other ethnographic photographs, Roth had shown this 'copulation' negative to his Johnsonian Club audience.[16]

Amongst the wider Queensland public, rumours soon spread about the photographs. One rumour was that Roth 'forced' an elderly couple under his jurisdiction to humiliate themselves. Another was that a young girl was being raped in the photograph. Worse still, it was allegedly a girl whom Roth had 'abducted' from her parents. While the woman does look younger than the man in the photographs, such age differences were not uncommon in indigenous marriages, and the woman was in any case old enough to have had children. The abduction rumour, however, was a particularly subversive polemic. It provided a troubling critique of the humanitarian and state discourses and policy implementations that branded ordinary white men as the abductors of underage Aboriginal girls. Instead the rumour pointed the finger at Roth's Aborigines' Department as the real abductor. Under the Act, the state had wide new powers of 'removal' of girls and women, and it had already started to act on these.[17]

Reasonably enough, contemporary critics asked: if Aboriginals are humans treated as animals, how can this be 'protection'? Anonymous ethnologists cited in Parliament described the photographs as 'terrible', 'disgusting'. One expert stated: 'Those pictures haunt me'. In Parliament, the photographs were described as 'disgusting, immoral', and the sexual position depicted as 'unnatural', 'filthy' and obscene. The images not only offended decent society, they were 'grossly indecent'. For offending morality and 'decency', Roth, the policeman of other men's sexual behaviours, was now rendered the transgressor, the offender against morality and 'decency'. As one 'ethnologist' (anonymous) commented: 'What manner of man took these? He ought to be in gaol'. Hamilton agreed: 'Any Queensland Judge would reward such an offence with imprisonment in St. Helena'.[18] The very men threatened with gaol for living with Aboriginal women had now caught out the 'Protector'. His moral demise would be their moral victory.

Although Hamilton had circulated them freely, he stated in Parliament that the photos violated the 'shame and modesty of the women' and 'outraged' the feelings of the Aboriginal men (*QPD* 1904:578).[19] While we lack indigenous evidence, it is likely the photos would have caused shame. Imagine that a photograph of yourself or your relatives copulating was circulating in parliament, mocked by male politicians. Perhaps the subjects' cultural and physical remoteness, and lack of inclusion in democratic processes, plus their lack of access to literacy and newspapers, protected them from such knowledge. But we cannot be sure. The subjects' clans were more accustomed to receiving trade goods when permitting *white* men to engage in sex with an Aboriginal woman. They undoubtedly had their own powerful stories circulating about the white government boss who had asked to see an indigenous couple having sex.

In the wake of the photograph scandal, Hamilton called for Roth's sacking. He vilified Roth in every conceivable way, concluding with a derogatory comment about his Hungarian origins. The public furore built such momentum that it would have been difficult for Roth to continue to work in Queensland. While an enquiry into the photographs exonerated him, and he was promoted to a senior position in Brisbane, very soon afterwards he quit Queensland for a distant government job in British Guyana.[20]

The Photographs as Science

Why had Roth taken the photographs in the first place? He explained to the local Bishop of Carpentaria that he was documenting the 'natural postures which any anthropologist makes enquiry about, with a view to ascertaining connections (if any) between the highest apes and the lowest types of man'.[21] Indeed, he also recorded bodily postures relating to defecation, childbirth and a wide range of other practices. As Roth's ethnographic documentation and collections began when he was Government Medical Officer, his anatomical studies were medically objectified. When he was elevated to Chief Protector, he was responsible not only for bodily health but also social morality. In the light of his new role as 'protector', the context of such photographs therefore shifted out of the realm of 'science' and its notions of objective knowledge, and entered the role of moral welfare and ethics.[22] While confident at line drawing illustrations, Roth's photographic techniques troubled him. Some years before the scandal, he had written: 'I still am very bad at printing, and am not certain as yet whether the fault lies in the light, the chemicals, the climate, or in my own ignorance' (quoted in Khan 1993:13–14).[23]

Roth's naivety about the volatile nature of his portfolio was far more damaging than any technical ignorance. The study of Ethnology, his driving passion, was located within the contemporary Darwinian framework that married it with the 'natural sciences'. Roth was operating within a value system acquired through both his family's medical circles and his own superior Oxford and European education, involving training, approval and examination. Amongst the prestigious letters after his name were BA Oxon, MRCS Eng, LRCP Lon, JP Qu, late Nat. Science Demy of Magdalen College, Oxford.[24] To Roth, being both scientist and Protector was unproblematic. In the contemporary schema of imperial authority, they seemed to complement each other well. His authority enabled him to control Aborigines and to obtain research access to remote peoples.[25] He also wanted to assist the 'race' to survive. Most excitingly, he could ascertain the most intimate details of their lives, which could debunk current theories of male subincision and fertility control, make a contribution to science and impress his European scientist peers.

According to Roth, the photographs were to be used to illustrate an ethnographic study of the North West Central District of Queensland to be published in the Bulletin of the Berlin Anthropological Society. While he had earlier presented a paper to the Society graphically describing this sexual position, his colleagues had expressed doubt about the sexual position's viability. He thus needed the posed photographs to prove ethnological facts in this international academic context. In a 1904 letter defending his actions to Bishop White, the Anglican Bishop of the Carpentaria region, Roth explained that the 'description and illustration of the posture assumed in the sexual act was of the highest anthropological interest'.[26]

During the early 1900s, Walter Roth was esteemed by the upper echelons of white society – people in government and science, locally and internationally. Hailing from a highly educated, high-achieving family, he was well connected and knew how to climb the ladder of recognition and advancement. Roth had published his lengthy study of the North West Central Queensland Aborigines in 1897, dedicating it to Sir Horace Tozer, Home Secretary and Acting Premier of Queensland, and praising him for his efforts to 'ameliorate the condition of the Queensland Aboriginal'. The study impressed the Police Commissioner, William Edward Parry-Okeden, whose patronage assisted Roth's advancing to the position of Northern Protector. The book contained 438 illustrations – most Roth's own line drawings. When first tabled in Parliament, Roth's ethnological bulletins drew little attention. The first series was included in the *Queensland Parliamentary Papers* of 1901. Photographs showed full-frontal naked Aboriginal families hunting and more discreet images of fertility-related events, such as women's birth positions (Roth 1897).

Following strong advice from nervous government officials, readers of the 1897 publication were warned that Chapter XIII was 'far from suitable for the general lay reader'. Roth reasoned – albeit weakly – that its placement at the end would protect any reader 'unwittingly' encountering it (Roth 1897:vi, Chapter XIII). At the opening of the chapter, he adds an 'Author's Note' stating that it is 'not suitable for perusal by the general lay reader' (Roth 1897:169). I suspect he may have meant especially by white women. Roth included one plate of line drawings to illustrate Chapter XIII (Roth 1897:Plate XXIV). The illustration of the coital position to which he refers is very small – 1 cm × 1.3 cm – and juxtaposed with birth scenes, diagrams of painted bodies, drastic penis incisions and acrobatic genital operations.

In 1902, J Hamilton, Member for Cook, demanded an enquiry into the photographs 'in the interests of the public'. Hamilton called for Roth's sacking, considering that to allow an officer who did 'that sort of thing' to remain in the service would disgrace his chief. He judged Roth of being 'guilty of taking photographs of male and female aboriginals' in the 'most indecent positions'.[27] When Hamilton passed around that 'dirty photograph' to his white male Parliamentary colleagues, they were primed to leer and guffaw. It was the 'dirt' Hamilton needed to discredit Roth once and for all.

Roth's 1903 response was published in *Hansard* the following year: Roth was 'not ashamed to state that I did take the photograph shown by the Hon Member for Cook to members of the House, a photograph of which there is an identical illustration in my "Ethnological Studies" published by the Queensland Govt some five years ago'. It had been presented to Parliament; and, as if to boost his imperial credentials, Roth added that a copy had 'since been graciously accepted by the son of my Sovereign, HRH the Prince of Wales'.[28] He must have known this was not a photograph, but a line drawing, and hence hardly 'identical'.

Ethnology had a certain urgency at the time, due to its crucial value in informing imperial governance. Primitive societies were also thought to reveal remnants of 'primitive social organisation' and thus explain the historical story of the evolution of Western societies to their modern form. Around the turn of the century, Crawley's *Mystic Rose* and McLennan's *Primitive Marriage* synthesised fragments from so-called primitive cultures around the world to find evidence of 'primitive remnants' of group marriage. Such scholars used this to debate the origins of modern monogamous marriage and the 'civilised' social order. Premised upon theories of social evolution, these discourses were significant contributions to early sociology (Crawley 1902; McLennan 1970).

Roth's ethnological *Bulletins* tackled themes of marriage and betrothal in traditional society. With an eye to regional variations, he explained promised marriage practices, negotiations in which women organised the bestowal of a spouse, ritual deflowering – 'first fruit' as he called it – and marriage by capture. Roth's retellings also played on contemporary white male humour around the subject of marriage; he thus quips that one man is a 'Lothario' and another a woman's 'lord and master' (Roth 1908).

Roth also saw his photographs as vital evidence that disproved current international theories that penile mutilation or 'subincision' prevented procreation and fertilisation. The relevant section of his book is entitled 'The Commonly-alleged Object of Introcision Discussed'.[29] One of his arguments relied partly upon 'the peculiar method of copulation in vogue throughout all these tribes'. He described how the man kneels and then pulls the prone woman onto him. Roth argued that this position ensures the semen will be discharged, as he put it, 'into its proper quarter' (Roth 1897:179).[30] His sketch of the position is in the same simple style as his other copious ethnographic drawings. The grainy, poorly framed photographs provided little additional detail or insight into the sexual position. Yet, unhampered by artistic enhancement, to all appearances this was close to a real-life view of a couple having sex. Somehow these pieces of shiny photographic paper created a less than comforting form of the imperial gaze.

Conclusion

To Roth, his Queensland photos were purely 'scientific'; yet he was gathering 'evidence' in the ethnographic style, just as he would gather over 2,000 Aboriginal artefacts. Like his vast artefact collection, Roth saw his data collection activities as a service to Western knowledge and thus as a morally defensible action. The photograph scandal continues to raise complex questions about paradigms of 'science', their relation to colonialism, the marriage of scientific/academic with the bureaucratic work that went with protection, policing and nation-building (see McGrath 2003).

Whilst the controversy was orchestrated by a clever political campaign by frontier lobbyists who resented the Aborigines Act and its moral, social and sexual policing, contemporaries appeared genuinely offended. The photographs created volatile debate amongst the white community about community morals. Where exactly were the boundaries of decency so disturbingly transgressed? What exactly was the main cause of offence? Was it the fact that the couple did not look young, plump and alluring according to the tastes of the day? Or that they were black? Were rough frontiersmen affronted by the sight of an Aboriginal woman having sex with a black man? Or was it the unfamiliar sexual position which contemporaries believed to be 'abnormal'?

If both bodies were white, they would be classed as illicit pornography. If one had been white and the other Aboriginal, the photo would most likely have represented an illegal act and would have constituted criminal evidence. Studying the savage thus released the scientist from the ethical and privacy codes which applied to white society. In gathering what they saw as vital evidence, few ethnographers worried about offending the subject's social codes.

While Roth effectively navigated the perils of hierarchy, he missed the greater perils of resistance by members of an evolving Anglo-Celt democracy and the explosive power of a photograph. While only an educated specialist few might read his ethnological *Bulletins*, a photograph could be passed around, reproduced, scoffed and scorned at. It became a weapon in a contest for frontier sexual services. It also became a moral contest between men – men of the frontier versus men of the metropole, and implicitly also between metropolitan education versus 'frontier' and indigenous knowledge.

Whether entirely self-serving, unscrupulous or highly principled, the reputations of white frontiersmen had been comprehensively tarnished by the implementation of Queensland's new legislation. Some were fined; many served jail sentences. Overall the coloniser state categorised their actions as bad for the nation and for Aborigines. They complained – not unreasonably – that Roth had defamed them and had taken away their children.[31] Through proving that Roth had transgressed wider social values regarding sexual intimacy, and public office, frontiersmen could assert that their own codes of values and principles were superior. They knew what was decent and what was not. Compared with the explicit evidence of the pornographic 'protector', they attested that they were not essentially 'immoral' after all.

Behind the whole episode was white men's deep resentment over Roth's surveillance of their sexual morality – their sexual and marital lives with indigenous women. This might explain why the only strong public support Roth received over the 'pornographic photos' was from Christian leaders such as Bishop White of Carpentaria, who favoured segregating Aborigines from 'immoral' white men.[32] Contrasted with Roth's behaviour, however, frontiersmen were able to portray their own dealings with indigenous people as relatively decent and honourable. At stake was a conflict of authority over government interventions in intimate relations and privacy.

Roth might have also thought more carefully about the dubious values of upper-class white men. His work on 'ethno-pornography' – along with photographs – was eventually republished in R Burton's 1935 subscriber edition for metropolitan masturbation, *Venus Oceanica*. Its lurid photographs of 'available' 'native' women came replete with inviting captions. The book's cheap masquerade as science renders the product particularly distasteful. Paradoxically, in the context of a professional man supposedly devoted to imposing new 'civilised' standards of sexual morality on the frontier, I suspect Roth would have been embarrassed by this later use of his scientific research.

Unlike the photos in *Venus Oceanica*, Roth's photos did not declare that 'native' women were freely available to white men. Rather, his photographs confronted them with very explicit evidence of their main form of sexual competition – indigenous men. While penile mutilation and potency were disturbing in a different way, their sexual access to Aboriginal women and knowledge of different techniques was confrontational. The photo may have also reminded white men of their own fears of public exposure regarding their illicit sexual relations with indigenous women.

During the 1900s, in Australia's early nationhood, the photographic scandal revealed the tensions in colonial democracy and the competing acquisitiveness of its stakeholders. In undermining the coloniser state's attempts to curb open sexual associations of white men and Aboriginal women, Roth's demise represented a triumph of frontier values and *laissez faire*. The colonial lower classes and wealthier frontiersmen temporarily formed themselves into a kind of proto-nationalist group which refused to accept assault on their characters and asserted their own lifestyles of cultural boundary-crossing and 'local' moral systems. Albeit temporarily, they triumphed over middle-class humanitarian interventionism and science. As the *North Queensland Herald* commented in 1906, Roth's successor Richard Howard possessed acceptable local knowledge credentials: 'What he did not know about bush and black's lore is not worth going out of one's way to enquire' (quoted in Kidd 1997:59).[33] Yet, as the local journalist jokily remarked, 'Long Dick' 'will never photograph them' (quoted in Kidd 1997:59). [34]

In exposing those photographic plates to the strong North Queensland light, we have seen how Roth had made himself as well as his 'subjects' vulnerable. Yet Roth maintained a clear conscience, having been 'guilty of no conduct unworthy of a gentleman and a man of honour'.[35] His 'innocence' at this ethnological moment was not widely agreed, for not all white men belonged to the white 'gentleman' class or understood the scientific intelligentsia. More importantly, the photos of indigenous heterosexual coitus heightened many of the anxieties intrinsic to responsible nationhood and to colonial manhood.[36] Rendered all too public in parliament – that masculinist centrepiece of colonising democracy – these intimate sepia images served to expose some of the most shameful secrets and deepest moral and intellectual struggles of Queensland's frontiers.

Acknowledgments

For generous and valuable assistance with additional sources, I thank John Mulvaney, Kate Khan and Bruce Rigsby.

Notes

1. *A note on terminology*: While aware of the valuable work on the social construction of whiteness, I consider the term 'white men' a useful distinguishing category. 'Anglo-Celt' is not appropriate, as Roth was actually of Hungarian origin and many other colonisers who would class themselves as 'white' were similarly from various

European countries. 'British' or 'European' offers an alternative; however, these still read as code for 'white' and may be deceptive in the case of the men who were second- or third-generation Australian residents. Might they not be 'white Australians'? In other words, nationalistic identities then become contested; at what point did such groups class themselves as 'Australian' or 'colonial' rather than 'British'? Prior to federation in 1901, birthplace and status were officially derived from colony of origin. A man was therefore a 'native Queenslander', though also a subject of the British crown. The term 'colonisers', which I often use as a category, can also be deceptive because we then enter debates about whether Asians and Pacific Islanders were colonisers in relation to control of indigenous peoples. I also use the term 'Indigenous peoples' and 'Aborigines' because the exact clans we are referring to are not clear-cut from my investigations. Roth himself made mistakes in this regard, and some identities continue to be currently contested in Native Title litigation. For a discussion of whiteness, see Dyer 1997; Stoler 1995, p 102 and passim; Moreton-Robinson 2004.
2. Walter E Roth to Bishop White, 19 June 1904, Queensland State Archives (QSA) SA/58850.
3. *Ibid.*
4. See also Amendment to 'The Aboriginals Protection and Restriction of the Sale of Opium Act 1897', Supplement to *Queensland Government Gazette*, 16 May 1902, no 146.
5. Roth report 1904, 3rd session, *Queensland Parliamentary Papers*, p 2 of his report. For a discussion of the policy and white men's reactions, see Henningham 1999.
6. WG Stewart Russell, Yelvertoft to FW Briggs, 27 March 1904, QSA A/58850.
7. For examples, see Dickson to Hamilton, 29 October 1902; Dallachy to Under Secretary, 15 July 1901; QSA A/58850; Glissan to Briggs, QSA A/58850. Under secretary to comsnr police, 10 Oct 1901 QSA Pol J 1
8. Russell to Briggs, Gregory Downs, QSA A/58850; AN Glissan to Briggs, 25 March 1904, QSA A/58850; see also various letters in QSA Pol J 16.
9. See file QSA A/548850.
10. See Annual Report of the Northern Protector of Aborigines for 1901; *Queensland Parliamentary Papers* 1, 1902; Annual Report of the Northern Protector of Aborigines for 1900, *Queensland Votes and Proceedings*, 4(2), 1901.
11. W Dallacy to Under Secretary, 15 July 1901, and a range of others in same file: QSA A/58850.
12. Complaints and rejoinders, QSA A/58850; Roth Report, pp 847–73 (also p 2), *Queensland Parliamentary Papers*, 1904.
13. Hamilton to Minister for Lands, 28 July 1904, QSA A/58850; summarises these allegations and gathers a lot of 'evidence' from fellow whites and from Aborigines that Roth's ethnography is fallacious; for example, 'This tale was received by the blacks with shrieks of laughter and the following comments were made by them'. He also cites Hansard p 578; 585. Other relevant clippings and letters are contained in the file.

> The old King – 'Dr Roth is a b----fool to believe it'.
>
> Old Sandy a Koko Bunda Gungi – 'the Dr. is no good to say such things. He will make white men think black fellow altogether cranky'... and it continues with other examples.

14. Hamilton's allegations imply that Aboriginal people detested Roth. The Protector for the southern region stated, 'If Dr. Roth dealt less with nude photographs of aboriginal women, he would be held in more respect, by the blacks, as both men and women resent it in a very decided manner'. Hamilton to Hon Minister for Lands,

28 July 1904, QSA A/58850. Although Hamilton was extreme in campaigning against Roth, it appears he was representing a wide constituency and was not exaggerating their high levels of concern.
15. Dickson to Hamilton, 29 October 1902; Dallachy to Under Secretary, 15 July 1901; QSA A/58850. (See Chapter 13 in this volume regarding the Western Australian enquiry.)
16. Roth to Bishop White, 19 June 1904, QSA A/58850; Roth to R Etheridge, Curator Australian Museum, Sydney, 1 May 1904; 18 May 1904. Records of The Australian Museum, Sydney, R16; R18. Roth states he was planning a lecture on 7 May with 180 to 200 slides for a magic-lantern slide show. He seems to be seeking advice on stone tools for publication of a manuscript. He also requests to borrow a slide from the Australian Museum – one of an introcised penis.
17. Hamilton to Minister for Lands, 28 July 1904, QSA A/58850; See Kidd 1997. See also QSA A/58764, which contains discussions regarding the introduction and function of the Act relating to marriage, and debates regarding 'moral wrongs' in relation to Aborigines and marriage.
18. Hamilton to Minister for Lands, 14 June 1904, QSA A/58850, p 3.
19. Hamilton to Minister for Lands, 14 June 1904, QSA A/58850.
20. Here he held several senior government positions and was best known for setting up the Georgetown Museum, where he left an important collection before the Museum was destroyed by fire. The later museum was named in his honour. According to British author Evelyn Waugh, who met Roth in 1933, he was 'an opinionated and rather disagreeable old man' who conducted foolhardy expeditions up country where he nearly killed himself. We should not judge his personality on this meeting with Roth as a 72-year-old, in what was to be his dying year. His relationship with Spencer and other previous Oxford colleagues during his Queensland years suggests a contented man who remembered his friends fondly. Roth to Spencer, 19 Jan 1898, Spencer Papers, Pitt Rivers Museum. McDougall 1998:1; see also McDougall 2000.
21. Roth to Bishop White, 19 June 1904, QSA/58850.
22. Usually Roth differentiates districts – eg Boulia, Cloncurry, Leichardt etc. The chapter 'Ethno-pornography' discussed issues relating to puberty and initiation ceremonies involving genital mutilation for both women and men. Roth discusses marriage, betrothal, love charms, consanguinity, 'venery' pregnancy and labour, abortion, babyhood, menstruation and foul language.
23. Baldwin Spencer, a confidante and student at Oxford whilst Roth was there, suffered numerous photographic disasters and was beleaguered by the effects of heat, humidity, sand, wasted films and expeditions requiring heavy photographic equipment, yet from the 1890s he produced some stunning ethnographic portraits and learnt from other keen Melbourne-based photographers (Mulvaney 1982). It is worth noting that during his career, Roth took some excellent photographs of various northern Aboriginal people.
24. Demy was a kind of Graduate Fellow at Magdalen College.
25. Roth to Spencer, 19 Jan 1898, Spencer Papers, Pitt Rivers Museum.
26. Roth to White, 19 June 1904, QSA A/58850. White did not give Roth a full vote of confidence in his own letter; see White to Roth, 3 June 1904 in QSA A/58850. 'Though very repellent to my own ideas I can imagine a right minded man with other ideas and training to my own considering himself justified in photographing for special medical or genuinely scientific purposes every natural action of the blacks but to force them to the indecency of an unnatural publicity in order to photograph them under such circumstances would to my mind be a betrayal of trust on the part of the Protector and an act of which I cannot believe you capable'.
27. Roth to Under Secretary, 27 February 1903, and Roth to Bishop White, 19 June 1904.

28. Roth to Under Secretary, 27 February 1903, p 2.
29. The term 'subincision' is most often used now, whereas in 1904 the operation was also referred to as Sturt's Terrible Rite.
30. Roth to Bishop White, 19 June 1904, QSA A/58850.
31. Hamilton to Minister for Lands, 28 July 1904, QSA A/58850.
32. Roth wrote a range of glowing letters and annual reports regarding Gribble's Yarrabah Mission. For example, Roth to Under Secretary, 9 Oct 1905, QSA A/58850.
33. From *North Queensland Herald*, 29 October 1906.
34. *Ibid.*
35. Roth to Bishop White, 19 June 1904, QSA/A 58850.
36. Marilyn Lake (1998) pursued female anxiety in her articles about white women attempting to tame the uncivilised white men of the frontier. Her recent work in progress innovatively explores male colonising anxieties.

Works Cited

Crawley, E (1902) *The Mystic Rose: A Study of Primitive Marriage*, London: Macmillan

Dyer, Richard (1997) *White*, London: Routledge

Ellinghaus, K (2003) 'Absorbing the "Aboriginal problem": controlling interracial marriage in Australia in the late 19th and early 20th centuries', *Aboriginal History* 27, 197–99

Grimshaw, P, Lake, M, McGrath, A and Quartly, M (1994) *Creating a Nation*, Ringwood: Penguin/McPhee Gribble

Henningham, Nikki (1999) '"Due consideration and kindness": interracial marriage in North Queensland, 1890–1920', in Damousi, J and Ellinghaus, K (eds), *Citizenship, Women and Social Justice: International Historical Perspectives*, Melbourne: History Department, University of Melbourne, 61–70

Khan, K (1993) *Catalogue of the Roth Collection of Aboriginal Artefacts from North Queensland*, vol 1, Sydney: Australian Museum

Kidd, R (1997) *The Way We Civilise: Aboriginal Affairs – the Untold Story*, St Lucia: University of Queensland Press

Lake, Marilyn (1998) 'Frontier feminism and the marauding white man', in Midgeley, C (ed), *Gender and Imperialism*, Manchester: Manchester University Press 123–36

McDougall, R (2000) 'Wilson Harris on the frontiers of myth criticism 1978–1983', *Journal of Caribbean Literatures* 2(1–3), 109–21

———. (1998) 'Walter Roth, Wilson Harris, and a Caribbean/Postcolonial theory of Modernism', *University of Toronto Quarterly* 67(2), 567–91

McGrath, A (2003) 'The golden thread of kinship: mixed marriages between Asians and Aboriginals during Australia's federation era', in Edwards, P & Shen, Y (eds), *Lost in the Whitewash*, Canberra: Humanities Research Centre

McLennan, John F (1970) (first published Edinburgh 1865) *Primitive Marriage: An Inquiry into the Origin of the Form of Capture in Marriage Ceremonies*, Chicago: University of Chicago Press

Moore, Clive, Leckie, Jacqueline and Munro, Doug (1990) *Labour in the South Pacific*, Townsville: James Cook University

Moreton-Robinson, Aileen (ed) (2004) *Whitening Race: Essays in Social and Cultural Criticism*, Canberra: Aboriginal Studies Press

Mulvaney, J (1982) 'Walter Baldwin Spencer', in *The Aboriginal photographs of Baldwin Spencer*. Edited by R Vanderwal, pp vii–x. Melbourne: John Currey, O'Neil

Queensland Parliamentary Papers (1904) 'Charge against Dr Roth, Chief Protector of Aboriginals, by Mr J. Hamilton, Member for Cook', Queensland State Archives Item ID337171, Batch file

Roth, Walter E (1984) *The Queensland Aborigines*, vol 1, facsimile, Hesperian Press

Roth, Walter E (1908) 'Marriage ceremonies and infant life', *North Queensland Ethnography Bulletin No 10, Records of the Australian Museum* 7(1)Sydney
———. (1897) *Ethnological Studies among the North-West-Central Queensland Aborigines*, Queensland's Agent-General, London
Saunders, Kay (1982) *Workers in Bondage: The Origins and Bases of Unfree Labour in Queensland, 1824–1916*, St Lucia: University of Queensland Press
Stoler, Ann Laura (1997) 'Sexual affronts and racial frontiers: European identities and the cultural politics of exclusion in colonial Southeast Asia' in Cooper, F and Stoler, A (eds), *Tensions of Empire: Colonial Cultures in a Bourgeois World*, Berkeley: University of California
———. (1995) *Race and the Education of Desire*, Durham: Duke University Press

CHAPTER 13

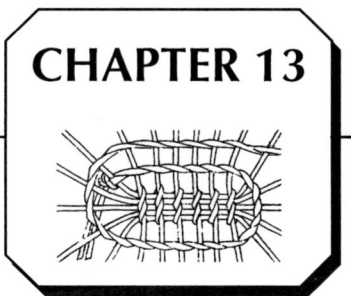

Walter Edmund Roth: Royal Commissioner of Western Australia, 1904

Geoffrey Gray

At the end of the 19th century there was an increasing belief that anthropology could help in the welfare and amelioration of colonised peoples. It was a period when anthropology was wide ranging in its interests – encompassing prehistoric archaeology, material culture and physical anthropology. It was driven by evolutionary theories but also mediated by diffusionist ideas about origins and the spread of cultural traits. Its practitioners were predominantly medical men and lawyers, but missionaries also contributed to the development of anthropological theories about origins and religious beliefs. In Australia the pre-eminent anthropologist at the time was the Melbourne-based Baldwin Spencer, Professor of Biology at the University of Melbourne. Spencer was at the forefront of presenting anthropology as a reformist discipline capable of assisting governments in the more efficient governance of its indigenous populations. Walter Edmund Roth was another figure in this tradition. Both Spencer and Roth had trained under Henry Balfour at Oxford before pursuing their separate careers, which brought them both to Australia, and to a professional interest in Aboriginal people (see Chapter 6 in this volume). Both men were appointed Protectors of Aborigines, Roth in Queensland, Spencer in the Northern Territory. This gave them a certain authority with government when it came to matters dealing with the control, care and welfare of Aboriginal people.

The Situation in Western Australia before the Royal Commission

In the latter years of the 19th century the treatment and conditions of Aboriginal people had been a source of concern for humanitarians not only in Western Australia but also on the east coast as well as in Britain. There was particular concern over the clashes in northwest Western Australia between Aborigines and pastoralists, mainly over cattle killing. Legislation passed in 1883 and 1892 increased the penalty for cattle killing to three years' imprisonment with whipping. As the killing of one beast would implicate many people, this legislation enabled the wholesale removal of Aboriginal people from troublesome areas. Police could claim a standard sum of money for rations for Aboriginal prisoners, which encouraged wholesale arrests for cattle killing and subsequent fiddling of claims for out-of-pocket expenses in bringing Aboriginal people to trial. The well-known Western Australian historian Geoffrey Bolton suggests that this may have made for speedier peace in the frontier districts, as it reduced the temptation for pastoralists to take the law into their own hands. In addition, it resulted in regular patrols by the police (Bolton 1981). The pastoralists, however, were not happy with the system. They complained that many offenders were discharged without trial, soon to be rounded up again for the crime of cattle killing. Only the police were happy with the system, as they were often the financial beneficiaries, recipients of the so-called 'blood-money'.

Employment of Aboriginal people was supported by government, but there was growing opposition from white workers, who increasingly viewed Aboriginal people as a source of competition. Politicians who represented electorates where Aboriginal labour presented a threat supported measures that would restrict the employment of Aborigines. Peter Biskup, in his wonderful study of Western Australian Aboriginal policy between 1898 and 1954, comments:

> Ironically, the area in which Aboriginal employment conditions were most open to criticism was the northwest pastoral industry, for which reliable and competent white labour was not sufficiently available. ... [T]he colonial parliament dominated by pastoral and rural interests, passed several acts which gave the pastoralists a decisive say in most matters affecting the employment of aborigines. After the abolition of the Aborigines Protection Board, which they regarded as yet another victory for the pastoralists, the humanitarians took the offensive. The campaign was well organised, and the press in eastern Australia and Great Britain were never short of a good copy about 'slavery under British flag in Western Australia'. The campaign was given further impetus by the establishment of the Commonwealth of Australia, for after 1901

adverse publicity overseas was a matter which concerned all Australians (1973:57).

The Aborigines Protection Board was replaced on 1 April 1898 by the Aborigines Department, which took responsibility for the administration of Aboriginal affairs. The Premier, John Forrest, Minister in charge of the Aborigines Department, repealed s.70 of the 1889 Constitution Act which guaranteed the old Aborigines Protection Board an annual grant of £5,000 or 1% of gross colonial revenue, whichever was greater. Biskup considers the repeal of s.70 a retrograde step which augured ill for the colony's Aboriginal population. 'The fields to be affected most by the resulting reduction in expenditure were the system of travelling inspectors, distribution of relief and mission subsidies'. Protectorship became part-time, in a sense an unpaid job, 'regarded by some officials as an irksome addition to their manifold duties'. Administratively the system did not work very well, and relations between government and missions deteriorated (Biskup 1973:46–50).

In September 1902 there was a call for a Royal Commission to inquire into all aspects of Aboriginal administration. The following month the *Morning Herald* editorialised that an inquiry should be entrusted to an 'independent expert', preferably the Queensland Assistant Protector of Aborigines, Walter Roth. Biskup makes the argument that criticism in the London *Times* was sufficient challenge to a government which claimed to subscribe to liberal ideals, and which it could hardly ignore. Appointment of a local Royal Commissioner would only add to the belief that the West Australian government was not serious about Aboriginal policy.

Appointment of Roth as Commissioner

Roth had been approached in April 1904 by the Premier, Walter James, to undertake a survey of Aboriginal administration. On 31 August the Governor of Western Australia, Admiral Sir Frederick George Denham Bedford, appointed Roth as Commissioner, specifically to enquire into:

1. the administration of the Aborigines Department;
2. the employment of aboriginal natives under contracts of service and indentures of apprenticeship;
3. employment of aboriginal natives in the pearl shell fishery and otherwise on boats;
4. the native police system;
5. the treatment of aboriginal prisoners;
6. the distribution of relief; and
7. generally into the treatment of the aboriginal and half-caste inhabitants of the State.[1]

During the lifetime of the Commission, Roth was appointed a Protector of Aborigines; and government officers and other persons within the State were commanded, by the Governor, to be of assistance in the execution of his commission.

The Queensland Government raised no objection to Roth's appointment other than ensuring the Western Australian government would provide financial remuneration to Roth and cover his expenses. In Western Australia, however, Roth's appointment was contentious – mainly because of his campaign against the maltreatment of Aborigines in Queensland and his scientific studies in ethnology. The motives for this work had been brought into question by some members of the West Australian Parliament, who made comment about its sexual nature. The problem of pornography and ethnographic description at the turn of the century is never far from the surface, and Roth provides an example of the problem (Stocking 1995:3–14)[2] (see Chapters 12 and 15 in this volume). Perhaps in response to these allegations Roth sent over to the Premier of Western Australia copies of his 'last five Annual Reports as Northern Protector' of Queensland, with the comment 'understanding that you are interested in the welfare and amelioration of the autochthonous population',[3] and to underline his scientific credentials. Having made the appointment, the West Australian government was keen for Roth to start as soon as possible. He was met at Fremantle on 25 August 1904 by the Protector of Aborigines, Henry Prinsep.[4]

Prinsep was born in Calcutta, where his father had been Advocate-General in the Bengal government, and he had received most of his education in England. He joined the West Australian colonial service in 1872 and was Under Secretary of Mines at the time of his appointment as Chief Protector. Prinsep complained about the lack of support by government. He maintained he was not consulted over the establishment or the terms of the Royal Commission. It is little wonder that Prinsep was described as lacking forcefulness and knowing little 'about Aborigines'. Moreover the position of Chief Protector had no legal status and received limited and conditional support from the Minister (Biskup 1973:54–55). What these two discussed is unknown but Prinsep later claimed that Roth's recommendations showed that he had taken Prinsep's advice.

At Work

Roth travelled to the north-west accompanied by VS Hartrick from the Department of Education, who acted as typist and note taker.[5] It is unclear whether Roth was expected to cover all of Western Australia;

there was some ambiguity in the terms of his appointment, although probably it was intended to cover the administration of Aborigines in all parts of the state. In any case, Roth concentrated on the northern and north-west areas, which seems to have satisfied the government and perhaps was the area of its main concern. He also limited himself to investigating only those occurrences of mistreatment within the previous three years.[6]

It is difficult to ascertain how Roth worked, as the archival material is limited, sparse and fragmented. He was very critical of police behaviour. There is the example of the alleged murder by a policeman of an Aboriginal witness, which provides some insight. This allegation was hotly disputed by the Police Commissioner, Frederick Arthur Hare. He stated that Roth made the charge based on 'the statement of a native who, it appears, he could scarcely understand, and who, in fact could not give any information regarding the constables who were supposed to have performed the alleged deed'. It was Hare's opinion that it was 'most unlikely and most improbable that a constable would take that action in front of a body of native prisoners and witnesses, knowing full well, that in the course of time, evidence would be forthcoming which would render him liable to punishment for his action'.[7] Aboriginal people had told Roth that information from Aboriginal witnesses, usually women (often the wives of the accused), was obtained at the point of a rifle. Roth heard that many of these women were young, chained like the men and often subject to rape.[8]

Roth delivered his report to the Parliament on 29 December 1904. He examined 110 witnesses, of whom 40 were police, 14 were pastoralists and 2 were Aboriginal prisoners. He also interviewed clergymen, magistrates, stockmen and some Aboriginal witnesses. The report was accepted by Parliament at the end of January 1905.

Recommendations

Prinsep, as we have seen, hailed Roth's report as vindication for all his requests of previous years. Late in 1900 Prinsep had put before Forrest a range of reforms to amend the 1886 *Aborigines Protection Act*. The proposal envisaged the introduction of employment permits, the creation of Aboriginal reserves to which any Aborigines 'not fully employed' (that is, lacking an employment permit) could be removed, and the establishment of 'white reserves' from which Aborigines not employed by trustworthy persons could be excluded. He also proposed to give the Chief Protector the right to remove an Aboriginal child up to the age of 16 'from any place and cause him to reside in any other place' (Biskup 1973:50). Prinsep noted Roth's suggestion that in each district there should be a government agent directly responsible to head office. He told his Minister that he had promoted such an idea himself, and that Roth had accepted his advice. Only through this structure, Prinsep declared, could the abuse be contained (Biskup 1973:50). It would also enable Aboriginal offenders to have representation in court.

In fact all of Roth's recommendations (except those few with which he disagreed), Prinsep claimed might have been sourced to him. He disagreed with Roth over the payment of wages to Aboriginal workers: 'it would be better to omit ... the payment of wages to working aborigines, except in those districts where there may be aborigines who have become so civilised as to be virtually on a par with a labouring white man'.[9] Nor was he in favour of labour contracts, rather resorting to the idea that regular inspection and constant supervision would be more effective in controlling the distribution of rations and the poor treatment of Aboriginal workers. So long as the police did not have this responsibility!

Roth particularly disapproved of the system allowing police to claim money for rations to Aboriginal prisoners, and objected strongly to the use of neck chains and the practice of yoking such prisoners. Aboriginal prisoners and witnesses, almost all associated with cattle killing, were brought to trial neck-chained. Roth considered this a practice that should be discontinued, suggesting that handcuffs be used instead. In conformity with Roth's recommendations the government of Western Australia imposed a ban on these practices. But it was ignored with impunity. Neck chaining was not made illegal, although it was initially incorporated in the changed Police Regulations of 1905. It was still in practice as late as 1946, when an Aboriginal man was brought in from Laverton, and there are reports suggesting that the practice went on even longer.

Roth also recommended that large hunting reserves be created on the margins of pastoral settlement. These reserves would provide an environment in which it would be easier to preserve Aborigines' traditional way of life and divert them from cattle spearing. Roth may have been influenced by the policies pursued by the United States and Canada with respect to American First Nations peoples, which had been ventilated in Western Australia before his arrival. It was hardly practical in the circumstances, for it ignored the effect of pastoralism on the native game and Aboriginal waterholes.

The maximum size for an Aboriginal reserve had been set at 800 hectares, suitable for the Moola Bulla Native Settlement and Violet Valley Feeding Depot both established as reserves in the first few years after Roth's report. Moola Bulla had a twofold aim: its primary purpose was to act as a buffer between the 'semi-nomadic aborigines' and the marginal pastoral regions – that is, put an end to cattle killing; its subsidiary purpose was to 'civilise' the local Aboriginal people. But the notion of a cash wage was dropped, as was Roth's proposal for large hunting reserves.

Concerned for the morals of Aboriginal people, Roth also recommended that the Chief Protector should have legal guardianship over all Aboriginal and 'half-caste' children under 18, and that steps should be taken to prevent 'Europeans' (a generic term for white people) and 'Asians' (by which he meant Malays and Japanese) from sexual intercourse with Aboriginal women. He recommended that the police be given the right to order pearling crews back to their boats, and that small reserves be set aside where alone the pearling crews could land to collect wood and replenish their water supplies. This recommendation was intended to check the increase of children of mixed descent as well as curbing the spread of venereal disease.

Thus, while recommendations offering Aboriginal people the possibility of participating in Western Australian economic and social life were dropped, those recommendations giving the Chief Protector greater powers were endorsed in their entirety. He and his officers (often police) were vested with autocratic powers. The Chief Protector could exercise the right of control over any property belonging to an Aboriginal or part-Aboriginal person; he could order the removal of any unemployed Aboriginal person to a reserve; he could declare specific areas out of bounds to Aboriginal people; and he alone could regulate the employment of Aboriginal people, fix conditions and issue permits to employ Aboriginal labour. A consequence was that all Aboriginal people and people of Aboriginal descent were placed under surveillance by the state. Stephen Kinnane in his recent book *Shadow Lines* writes that 'At the core of the corruption revealed by Roth's Commission was the heightened vulnerability of Aboriginal women and children. Infuriatingly, the resulting legislation, with its aim of widespread removal of children, would do unprecedented damage to a society already under attack' (2003:36). Kinnane's grandmother was removed under this legislation.

Responses by Government Bureaucracies

The Chief Commissioner of Police, the Magistracy, the Comptroller of Prisons, the District Medical Officer supported by the Principal Medical Officer and members of the pastoral and pearling industry all objected to those recommendations (and 'evidence') which affected their particular interests. Roth was variously described as 'ignorant of natives or their customs', lacking in experience of the north-west, unable to master the whole question in the short time available and, of course, biased. He was accused of 'exaggeration and error' and so on.[10] It was also said that he had refused to talk with representatives of the pearling industry and had instead approached the 'scum' and 'riff-raff' of the north to 'secure evidence'. Roth was particularly critical of the police and their methods; and this led to a lengthy exchange between Hare and the Colonial Secretary, to Hare's suspension and later to Roth's apology.[11] Hare conducted his own investigation in an attempt to clear his officers and men.[12]

At Broome Gaol prisoners were kept in neck chains for the duration of their sentence. Prisoners were chained twenty-four hours a day; when they worked outside the gaol they were chained as well. Roth had recommended that a corrugated iron fence be placed round the compound, allowing prisoners freedom from their chains. But the District Medical Officer defended the practice, criticising both Roth's medical knowledge and his 'woeful lack of knowledge of anatomical mechanics'. His opposition was based on his view that a 'real wild aborigine' could easily slip out of wrist cuffs, or free himself from a belt round the waist which would restrict the natural expansion of the stomach and thus deny the prisoner the opportunity to fill up on water while working in the heat: neck chains were the only solution. Furthermore, it required only an elementary knowledge of human anatomy, the District Medical Officer said, to realise that 'if a certain weight has to be carried all day it is much more easily borne on the shoulders than at the extremities of the limbs'. A neck chain weighed between 2.2 lb (1 kg) and 5 lb (2.5 kg). Wounds or sores from carrying such a weight were unknown to the DMO; in fact, he said, 'the prisoners themselves prefer the neck chains'. His objection to the proposed corrugated iron fence rested on the location of the gaol: 'our gaol here is placed on the very hottest spot in the townsite & to enclose this narrow strip of burning sandhill with a fence would exclude what little breeze the inmates get'. The suggestion was obvious evidence of Roth's 'thoughtlessness'. He concluded: some 'hundreds of black prisoners have passed through Broome Gaol during the last few years and their physique on leaving has been incomparably better ... than on their first arrival'.[13]

Conclusion

Geoffrey Bolton argues that the thrust of the Royal Commission and of all the debate about Aboriginal policy leading up to it was toward solving the problems of the north and bringing settler-Aboriginal relations more effectively within the rule of law. Consequences such as those mentioned by Kinnane were, Bolton maintains, unintended. Biskup is less forgiving at least of the Western Australian Government. Those recommendations by Roth that addressed some of the most shameful aspects of Aboriginal treatment were ignored and the government continued to conduct itself much as it had in the past. While much of what Roth recommended on the surface ameliorated the hardship of Aboriginal people and attempted to modernise the 1886 Act, he was largely unsuccessful with the main issues (wages, evidence, due process, etc); and his lasting legacy has been the removal of Aboriginal children. In the long term the lives of Aboriginal people were worsened as a result of Roth's Commission and the subsequent legislation passed by Parliament. It is unlikely that he envisaged such an outcome.

There is little doubt that the Western Australian Government was under both local and international pressure about the treatment and conditions of Aboriginal people, particularly in the pastoral north. It is equally clear that, in the circumstances, a local appointment would not quell criticism from humanitarian bodies. Roth was appointed because he was an outsider, a medical doctor who had experience with Aboriginal people, ordinary settlers and scientists. Most of his recommendations drew from the 1897 Queensland *Aborigines Protection and Restriction of the Sale of Opium Act* and the amendment of 1901. This Act was considered at the time to be most enlightened regarding the administration of Aborigines and was the benchmark for legislation. The Western Australian Act follows the Queensland Act. The wide definition of Aboriginal in the Queensland Act was adopted by the WA Act, *inter alia*: 'Every person who is (a) an Aboriginal inhabitant of Queensland; or (b) a half-caste who … is living with an Aboriginal wife or husband or child; or (c) a half-caste who … habitually lives or associates with Aboriginals; shall be deemed to be Aboriginal within the meaning of the Act' (McCorquodale 1987:55, 95). Certainly the Queensland Act enabled greater control and supervision of Aboriginal and 'part-Aboriginal'[14] people; and this was recommended by Roth and implemented in the 1905 West Australian Act, as well as being enhanced by later parliamentary Acts.

Payment of wages, the poor treatment and conditions of indigenous labour, the problem of miscegenation and the population increase of half-castes bedevilled colonial administrators at the turn of the 20th century. Such problems were addressed through structural change in colonial administration. It was not until the new discipline of social anthropology, practised and promoted by Malinowski and Radcliffe-Brown, that colonised peoples were included in the changes, not as active participants but as scientific objects to be described and analysed as a way of assisting the colonial administration with its governance of indigenous peoples. Roth represented a certain thinking about native peoples, underlined by a humanitarianism that Les Hiatt (1996) regards as a feature of ethnographic thinking at the time. Debates about the value of anthropological knowledge in colonial administration were marginal at this time.

Roth concluded his report by stating that while there was, generally speaking, no 'actual physical cruelty' directed toward Aboriginal people, 'the wrongs and injustices taking place in [settled] areas, and the cruelties and abuses met with in the unsettled areas cannot be longer hidden or tolerated'.[15] This hope was unmet.

Notes

1. State Records Office, Western Australia (hereafter SROWA):ACC 1820, 1714/04.
2. Specifically 'Ethnopornographia' in Burton 1935.
3. Roth to Premier, 1 July 1904, SROWA:1820, 1714/04.
4. Under Secretary to Roth, 5 August 1904; Memo to Premier, 23 August 1904, SROWA:1820, 1714/04.
5. SROWA:1820, 1714/04.
6. *Royal Commission on the Condition of the Natives*, December 1904, p 1.
7. Reported in *The West Australian*, 1 February 1905.
8. See Gammage 1998 for a detailed account of the behaviour of Native Police in similar situations in New Guinea.
9. Reported in *The West Australian*, 2 February 1905.
10. SROWA:ACC 1820, various files.
11. See SROWA:1820, 341/1905.
12. Various, SROWA:ACC 1820, 2681/1905. These matters have been dealt with by Biskup (1973:59–65) and Rowley (1971/72:190–94).
13. District Medical Officer to Principal Medical Officer, 16 February 1905, SROWA: ACC 1820, CSO 934/1905.
14. I know this term and the term 'half-caste' are offensive to many Aboriginal people, but the category of people covered by this term was of considerable interest to Australian State and Federal governments in the latter half of the 19th century. I mean no offence by employing these terms.
15. Roth, *Royal Commission on the Condition of the Natives*, 29 December 1904, p 32.

Works Cited

Biskup, Peter (1973) *Not Slaves Not Citizens. The Aboriginal Problem in Western Australia 1898–1954*, St Lucia: University of Queensland Press

Bolton, Geoffrey (1981) 'Black and white after 1897', in Stannage, Tom (ed), *A New History of Western Australia*, Nedlands: University of Western Australia Press, 129–31

Burton, Ronald (1935) *Venus Oceania*, New York: Oceania Research Press

Gammage, Bill (1998) *The Sky Travellers: Journeys in New Guinea, 1938–1939*, Melbourne: The Miegunyah Press

Hiatt, LR (1996) *Arguments About Aborigines: Australia and the Evolution of Anthropology*, Melbourne: Cambridge University Press

Kinnane, Stephen (2003) *Shadow Lines*, Fremantle: Fremantle Press

McCorquodale, John (1987) *Aborigines and the Law: A Digest*, Canberra: Aboriginal Studies Press

Rowley, CD (1971/72) *The Destruction of Aboriginal Society*, Ringwood: Penguin
Stocking, George (1995) *After Tylor: British Social Anthropology, 1888–1951*, Madison: University of Wisconsin Press
Tod Woenne, Susan (1979) '"The true state of affairs": commissions of inquiry concerning Western Australian Aborigines', in Berndt, Ronald M and Berndt, Catherine H (eds), *Aborigines of the West: Their Past and Their Present*, Nedlands: University of Western Australia Press, 324–56

CHAPTER 14

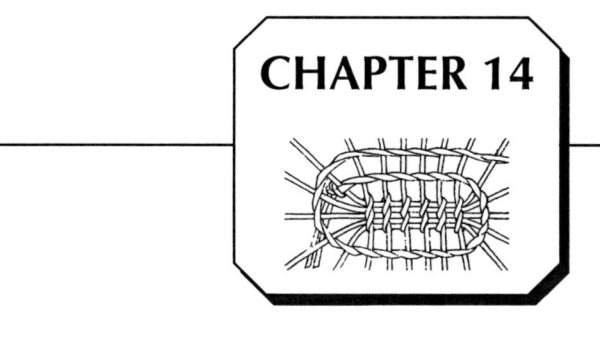

Walter Roth and Ethno-Pornography

Helen Pringle

This paper discusses some matters which would have been of intimate and personal concern to the affected people. The matters are already in the public domain, but readers are asked to use their discretion before reading this paper.

In various international human rights documents concerned with the problem of female genital cutting, the practice of 'introcision' of women is noted as current practice among Australian Aborigines.[1] The source of such reports can be traced to Walter Roth's *Ethnological Studies among the North-West-Central Queensland Aborigines* (1897). Roth's accounts of introcision were compiled during his time as a doctor in the Boulia area of Queensland in the 1890s.

In this chapter, I explore Roth's accounts of introcision, and relate them to an episode in which Roth was accused of taking photographs of Aborigines having sexual intercourse. In 1904 and 1905, speeches in the Queensland Parliament on this and other aspects of Roth's work were said to form 'a pile as high as the Eiffel Tower',[2] and the episode played a part in Roth's resignation as Protector and his departure for British Guiana in 1905. Roth took the photographs to support his more theoretical conjecture that the genital cutting of Aboriginal men was intended as a mimicry of the vulva, rather than being designed to prevent procreation, as many of his contemporaries had hypothesised. In order to illustrate that insemination by an introcised man was possible, Roth 'paid' an Aboriginal couple to demonstrate a sexual position which he photographed. I return to this episode at the end of the chapter.

I would emphasise at the outset that whether the cutting of women is or was a widespread ritual practice among Aborigines in North West Queensland, and the form it might have taken, is open to argument. My chapter is a commentary on *Roth's* accounts of Aboriginal ritual practices, not on those ritual practices themselves, of which I claim no knowledge.

Roth and the Practice of 'Introcision'

Roth explored in some detail what he called 'introcision' in the chapter of *Ethnological Studies* entitled 'Ethno-pornography'. In the book's Preface, Roth notes of this final chapter, 'I am well aware that it is far from suitable for the general lay reader; the subject matter, however, being essential to a scientific account of these aboriginals, I have decided upon its publication, at the same time placing it at the very last, in the hope that those who do not wish to peruse its pages need not unwittingly find themselves doing so' (Roth 1897:v–vi). Roth also placed an Author's Note at the head of the last chapter, warning, 'The following chapter is not suitable for perusal by the general lay reader' (Roth 1897:169).

When the book was sent to the printer, the Government Printing Officer was so concerned that he sent a memo to the then Under Secretary of the Home Department, Sir Horace Tozer, inquiring: 'You are doubtless aware that the last chapter – ch:xiii and the last plate (pl. xxlv) deal with indelicate subjects, is it likely they may be in violation of the Indecent Advertisements Acts, and, if they are, is the author's note, at the head of the chapter, a sufficient protection?' Sir Horace replied in Pauline mode: 'To the pure all things are pure. The impure will never pay 10s for this book'.[3] The book is dedicated by Roth to Tozer, by then Acting Premier of Queensland, in appreciation of his efforts to 'ameliorate the condition of the Queensland Aboriginal'. Roth later explained to Baldwin Spencer that:

> the government originally intended omitting the last chapter, with accompanying plate, and publishing it separately for special distribution to certain people only – mainly for the purpose of drawing attention to the present condition of certain of the aborigines in view of the legislation proposal to be enforced. The ordinary reading public had in a sense to be protected by being told that such and such a chapter was obscene, and that they could please themselves if they chose to read it. And after all, scientific and interesting as these particulars are to men like us, they are certainly not so to the general lay reader (in McDougall 2002:fn 29).

The topics covered in Roth's 'indelicate' last chapter include initiation rites of men and women, marriage, betrothal, love charms, venery, pregnancy and labour, abortion, babyhood, menstruation, micturition and defecation, and finally, foul language. Few of these subjects fall (or fell) within usual understandings of 'pornography'. Indeed, Roth begins the final chapter with a consideration of social rank. He ends the chapter (and the book) with the sentence, 'I have no evidence as to any practice of masturbation or sodomy anywhere among the North-West-Central Queensland aboriginals' (Roth 1897:184).

Initiation practices are at the centre of Roth's final chapter. According to Roth, both men and women in North West Queensland were subject to genital cutting at around puberty. He details the cutting of women in his account of the first ceremonial stage among the Pitta-Pitta around Boulia:

> Two or three men manage to get the young woman, when thus ripe enough, all alone by herself away in the bush, and, throwing her down, one of them forcibly enlarges the vaginal orifice by tearing it downwards with the first three fingers wound round and round with opossum-string (*cf.* introcision in the male – sects. 317–322). Other men come forwards from all directions, and the struggling victim has to submit in rotation to promiscuous coition with all the 'bucks' present: should any sick individual be in camp, he would drink the bloody semen collected from her subsequently in a koolamon (sect. 283) (Roth 1897:174).

Roth's final chapter contains several other accounts of initiation practices in North West Queensland. Roth writes that in the area around Glenormiston, a young woman is drawn away from a daytime corroboree and ambushed by several young men who cover her eyes 'so as to prevent her seeing the individual, probably a very old man, who is beckoned up from some hiding-place to come and operate directly everything is ready' (Roth 1897:174). Roth's third citation of the practice is among the Yaroinga in the Upper Georgina District (p 175), as illustrated in Figure 422 of *Ethnological Studies*. The other accounts concern the Kalkadoon (Kalkatungu) of the Leichhardt-Selwyn District, and the Birdsville area. In the survey of Birdsville, the cutting instrument is illustrated in Figure 424 of the book, described by Roth as 'a wooden stick of very hard wood about two feet long, with a representation of the extremity of a life-sized penis rudely carved at the top, and thinner all the way down to the handle' (p 175).

It is not clear upon what kind of evidence these accounts are based. In the Preface to *Ethnological Studies*, Roth writes that mastery of the local language is necessary in order to study societies properly, and he emphasises his opportunities for anthropological inquiry as hospital surgeon. But he also notes that his information on progression through the two upper degrees of social rank in the area is 'meagre'. Roth explains that 'the aboriginals were always very chary of imparting information concerning these higher grades even to me who had become intimately connected with them through a knowledge of their written and sign languages and other causes'. I should note that Roth was rather more modest about his possession of such knowledge when he spoke to a Committee of the Queensland Parliament on amendments to the 1897 *Aboriginals Protection and Restriction of the Sale of Opium Act*.[4]

In *Ethnological Studies*, Roth adds that other difficulties in collecting accurate information stem from the onslaught of European civilisation in the area:

> with the gradual depletion of the aboriginal population, the initiation ceremonies of the higher ranks are gradually becoming obsolete, those for the females especially being already very marked; that individuals belonging to the higher grades and consequently older people are not too commonly met with; and that no one is allowed to be present or to assist in the initiation of any degree higher than that of which he is himself a member. As far as my personal knowledge goes, in North-West-Central Queensland the procedures of the first and second degrees only are permitted to be viewed by Europeans (Roth 1897:169).

Throughout his official reports as Protector, Roth was forthright about the 'depletion' of the Aboriginal population by guns and disease. The area around Boulia had been 'depleted' by Alexander Kennedy and his good friend Police Sub-Inspector Frederick Urquhart.[5] Kennedy's biographer and friend, Hudson Fysh, argued that the power of the Kalkadoon, who had caused Kennedy 'so much concern', had been 'finally broken' by 1885 (Fysh 1950:117).[6] A powerful picture of Aborigines around Carandotta was sent to the Colonial Secretary in 1892 by BH Purcell, who noted rampant syphilis among children, and among women deliberately infected by white travellers. Purcell reported seeing 'men and women, their faces sunken in, their bodies so shrunken, and eyes so small and far back in their heads that at first sight they appeared like mummies of centuries gone by walking about the camps'.[7]

Even allowing for possible exaggeration in the reports of Purcell and others, Roth's accounts of introcision could refer only to a small and apparently diminishing number of Aborigines. I think it wise in this context to be cautious as to the extent to which Roth's accounts of initiation ceremonies were based on direct observation. Moreover, Roth regularly used material on Aboriginal practices given to him by those he called 'old hands', meaning white station owners.[8]

Roth admits in *Ethnological Studies* that he was excluded from viewing parts of the ceremonies he describes. He noted elsewhere one of the reasons for this exclusion:

> I have been present at initiation ceremonies on the East Coast (Princess Charlotte Bay, McIvor River, etc.), and several [*Roth's footnote:* For descriptions see *Ethnol. Studies*, etc., 1897 – Sects. 299 to 315] in the North-Western Districts; I cannot say that I have been initiated into the latter, for the very good reason that I was not prepared to submit myself to the necessary sexual mutilation, an ordeal to which I am not aware that any European, however keen on Anthropological Science, has hitherto allowed himself to be subjected (Roth 1909:166).

Throughout the final chapter of *Ethnological Studies*, there is significant confusion as to what exactly Roth saw for himself, and I am not convinced that the confusion is accidental.

Roth's accounts of introcision are shot through with this obfuscation. For example, take Roth's 'description' of genital cutting in the Glenormiston area: 'her thighs are now drawn apart and her eyes covered so as to prevent her seeing the individual, *probably* a very old man [my emphasis], who is beckoned up from some hiding-place to come and operate directly everything is ready' (Roth 1897:174). Again, in writing of the preliminary initiation of boys in the Cloncurry District, Roth notes, 'This first ceremonial *may be described* somewhat on the following lines [my emphasis]' (p 173). When Roth comes to mention the higher stages of initiation, he notes, 'Particulars of these are not so easily procurable as those of the preceding, and the following comprises the information which can be depended upon. Both initiation rites *would appear* [my emphasis] to take place on the same occasions as when a novitiate is made a *kati-kati maro*' (p 177). Roth says very little about these higher stages other than that they involve body paint and ornamentation. He writes, 'Among the Kalkadoon, with the male, the third grade is constituted *apparently* [my emphasis] by the operation of introcision, or *yel-la*' (p 177).

The frequency of such tentativeness in Roth's work should restrain us from too readily concluding that his accounts are a simple transcription of ritual practice. Roth's accounts of introcision are driven by preconceived conjecture more than they are based on his own detailed empirical observation.

Roth's Thesis of Mimetic 'Introcision'

Roth's focus in the last chapter of *Ethnological Studies* is on what he calls 'this locally-universal practice of lacerating the vaginal orifice, i.e., female introcision (sect. 316)'. However, his accounts of 'female introcision' need to be read in the context of his curiosity about the 'introcision' of young men. After picturing the initiation of young women into sexual life, Roth comes a few pages later to discuss what was at the time known as 'Sturt's terrible rite' – 'whistling', or, sometimes, (artificial) hypospadias. Most contemporary European writers on the genital cutting of Aboriginal men preferred the term 'subincision'. However, Roth adopted the term 'introcision' precisely in order to assimilate male and female genital cutting. As he notes, 'I have designedly introduced the term "introcision", because of, and so as to include, the corresponding mutilation of the females (sect. 305–309)' (Roth 1897:177).

Roth explains that the introcision of men takes place subsequent to circumcision, and involves 'the permanent opening up of a more or less considerable extent of the penile portion of the urethra by incision commencing at the external urinary meatus' (Roth 1897:177). Figure 429 of *Ethnological Studies* is a sketch of a post-introcision penis, and Roth was apparently aware of the effects of the cutting, particularly in the way it made it difficult for subincised men to ride horses, and made them more vulnerable to virulent strains of venereal disease. However, it is clear that Roth did not witness the ceremony he describes, as can be seen from this passage in the book:

> No females, and no males who have not already been themselves introcised, are on any account allowed to witness the ordeal, the sight of which would probably confirm any determination of their part to exile themselves with a view to escaping it: thus, in the Cloncurry District, I came here and there across an appreciable number of Pitta-Pitta and other Boulia Districts males, who admittedly had left their own tribe on this account (Roth 1897:177–78).

Notwithstanding this admission that he had not viewed the 'ordeal', Roth goes on to give a detailed description of it among the Pitta-Pitta. In order to cement his conjecture of its mimetic identity with the vaginal laceration of women, Roth deems it necessary to present this detailed account of the introcision of men:

> One of the elders will lie face downwards on the ground, a slight excavation having been made there to receive the protuberance of the stomach, and upon this individual's back the victim is laid, face up, *very much after the style of the first female initiation ceremony among the Yaroinga* (sect. 306 [figure 422]): his limbs are held in position by various assistants, and his body fixed by another who sits astride [my emphasis] (Roth 1897:178).

Even if we were to assume the fidelity of Roth's accounts to ritual practice, the connection between the subincision of men and the cutting of women is not at all obvious. Take, for example, Roth's comment:

'the forcible laceration and enlargement of the vaginal orifice, i.e., female-introcision'. Roth's use of 'i.e.' in this comment is tendentious, linking as it does the genital cutting of women to introcision of men as if the connection were uncontroversial. Roth's coining of the word 'introcision' is designed to support his own explanation of the genital cutting of *men*, and to counter the hypothesis that such cutting is a contraceptive measure to limit population and thereby limit the demand for food.[9]

Roth argues that the introcision of men is not necessary to inhibit procreation, as the supply of food to progenitors is not affected by the number of their offspring under paedomatronymic principles; at any rate, he notes, such principles operate even where cutting is not performed. Hence, says Roth, introcision could hardly be effective as a means of contraception. His view is that the ritual is universal in the North West Queensland area: 'The information which on the one hand I have obtained from those reliable, and on the other which I have collected from the dozens upon dozens of personal examinations of my own, is conclusive concerning this matter of every adult male being so mutilated' (Roth 1897:180).

Moreover, Roth argues, the cutting of men's penises could not act to prevent fertilisation, given the 'peculiar method of copulation in vogue' in these districts. In order to counter the explanation of male genital cutting as prophylactic, Roth sets out in detail this 'peculiar method of copulation', as well as providing a sketch in Figure 433 of *Ethnological Studies*. His account runs thus:

> The female lies on her back on the ground, while the male with open thighs sits on his heels close in front: he now pulls her towards him, and raising her buttocks drags them into the inner aspects of his own thighs, her legs clutching him round the flanks (Fig. 433), while he arranges with his hands the toilette of her perineum and the insertion of his penis. In this position the vaginal orifice, already enlarged by the general laceration at initiation (sects. 305–309), is actually immediately beneath and in close contact with the basal portion of the penis, and it is certainly therefore a matter of impossibility to conceive the semen as being discharged for the most part anywhere but into its proper quarter (Roth 1897:179).

Roth notes that genital cutting of women is only practised where male introcision is practised, and that both men and women must undergo the 'ordeal' as 'an indispensable preliminary to marriage' (Roth 1897:179). He continues with the conjecture:

> It is possible that the cutting of the perineum and general laceration, &c., of the female was originally a matter of convenience for the male, the mutilation in her case subsequently coming to signify her fitness,

capability, or experience, in the art of the full enjoyment of copulation, and that, on the principle of a form of mimicry, the analogous sign was inflicted on the male to denote corresponding fitness on his part. With this hypothesis, it is interesting to note that in the Pitta-Pitta and cognate Boulia District dialects the term used to describe the introcised penis denotes etymologically the one with a vulva or 'slit' (see *me-ko ma-ro* in the Pitta-Pitta vocabulary, sect. 44) (Roth 1897:180).

This passage from *Ethnological Studies* reflects Roth's central point: to show that introcision is not performed on men so as to inhibit conception, and that the introcised penis is a mimicry of the vulva, denoting fitness for marriage.[10] In order to support his view against the common argument concerning the efficacy of the introcised penis in inhibiting procreation, Roth produced what he imagined to be a trump card: photographs of an Aboriginal couple engaged in 'the peculiar method of copulation'. These were the photographs at the centre of the scandal in Roth's term as Protector, and it is with the incident of the photos that I conclude.

The Scandal of Roth's Photos

The complaint against Roth in regard to the photographs was not the only matter in dispute during and at the end of his term as Chief Protector. Roth's perceived animosity to the interests of some white settlers, or as one complainant noted, Roth's 'Pecksniffian sympathy for the poor Blacks', provoked much opposition.[11] There is, however, little doubt that some complaints against Roth were well founded – for example, his disposition of artefacts collected in his official capacity.[12] Moreover, Roth had previously been in trouble over his photography. Questions had been raised in the Queensland Parliament in 1902 about photographs he had taken of some Aboriginal women; Mr Dunsford MP claimed (rightly it appears) that the women in the photographs produced by Roth in order to attest to their good health had in fact died shortly after the photographs were taken.[13]

Questions about Roth's photographs of an Aboriginal couple having sex were first raised in Parliament in 1904. Roth claimed in his defence that the photographs at issue were identical to Figure 433 of *Ethnological Studies*. And, he maintained, the book had been sent to the Prince of Wales – thus attesting to its respectability. In response, the indefatigable MP Mr Hamilton claimed that the diagrams were not included in the copy sent to the Prince of Wales, and that the Prince most likely did not read the book anyway. Indeed, Hamilton mused, 'the Prince probably never saw or heard of it, and for the sake of Queensland, it is to be hoped he never will'. Hamilton continued that 'a mere glance at which would be a cause of shame and disgust, to any respectable man, leaving all types of womanhood out of the question'. He concluded that 'to Queenslanders, it will be some consolation to know that Hungary is responsible for [Roth's] existence, and that Britain is mercifully free from any liability in the transaction'.[14]

Roth's defence of his photograph on the ground that it was the same as the sketch of Figure 433 in his book raises the question of why he would need the photographs. In reply to a request for explanation from his friend the Bishop of Carpentaria, Roth wrote:

> The description and illustration of the posture assumed in the sexual act was of the highest anthropological interest in that it in large measure defended my thesis that the mutilation known as Sturt's terrible rite, or sub-incision (by Professor Stirling) or intro-cision (by myself) did *not* act as had hitherto been supposed as a preventive to procreation.
>
> ... The photograph was taken for purely scientific purposes only and is one of a series (defecation, micturition, tree climbing, sitting, standing) of natural postures which every anthropologist makes inquiry about, with a view to ascertaining the connections (if any) between the highest apes and the lowest types of man.[15]

In writing to Bishop White, Roth noted that he first saw 'this peculiar method of copulation' in 1894:

> but knowing the natural modesty of the savage, which I have invariably admired and respected, and knowing that I should lose their respect were I to attempt to put any of these uncivilised blacks in the position necessary to take the required photograph, I made a sketch (which as I have already stated, was subsequently published) and put the matter out of my mind.[16]

Roth noted to Bishop White that when *Ethnological Studies* was published, he had received written and oral communications doubting that such a posture of copulation was physically possible. In the meantime, he said, he had found the same posture everywhere: 'I thereupon informed my scientific friends of the very interesting corollary that the sexual mutilation now met with [in certain parts of Australia] was probably traditionally practised throughout the entire Continent'.[17] That is, for Roth, the incidence of the posture in certain areas was the sign that the subincision of men had originally been practised there despite its contemporary absence. Hence the perceived necessity to photograph the 'peculiar method'.

According to Roth, his scientific opportunity came in 1900 or 1901, when an aged married couple on a station 'agreed to posture for me'. Roth wrote to White that the woman was the mother of children, presumably so as to emphasise the scientific rather than prurient character of his photography:

> Although half-civilised, they were a bit afraid of the camera at first, but could hardly refrain from laughing at the idea of my wanting to see them in the position asked for. However Mr. ... promised them I would give them money and tobacco etc. (I think flour) which I did – they were both contented. Considering the scandal which certain individuals have been trying to sow, I am indeed thankful that, if called upon, I can thus bring forward a European witness who was with me at the time in question.[18]

Roth concluded, 'I have been guilty of no conduct unworthy of a gentleman and a man of honour'.

Conclusion

The scandal of Roth's photographs of 'the peculiar method of copulation' did not concern an isolated indiscretion but was related to the very core of his anthropological speculations. Roth considered his photography as a scientific exercise designed to uphold his conjecture about introcision in the Boulia area – and in turn, about ritual and customs over the entire Australian continent. On the other hand, Roth's curiosity was continuous with a practice noted by Herbert Basedow (1927:151): 'it is a well-known fact that men of low moral character used to make a habit of giving quantities of rum, gin, and other spirituous liquors to the natives who would then, in a semi-intoxicated condition, be persuaded or forced to perform in a way which may have satisfied the lustful humour of the white villain, but was opposed entirely to the sense of decency and modesty of a primitive people'. Roth's speculations participated in the genre of ethno-pornography, and were not simply a meditation on the genre.

Notes

1. See in particular OHCHR Fact Sheet no 23.
2. In the words of Mr Lesina, *QPD*, 24 November 1905, 1810.
3. Memo from Government Printing Office to Under Secretary of the Home Department, 13 October 1897, with note by Sir Horace Tozer, 16 October 1897, Queensland State Archives (hereafter QSA) A/58550.
4. *QPD*, lxxxvii (1901), 1135–45, esp 1138.
5. I am grateful to Iain Davidson for emphasising this background to Roth's work.
6. Fysh noted that the Kalkadoon became 'the subject of a brilliant study by Walter E Roth', whose work he had used in his biography of Kennedy (Fysh 1950:127).
7. BH Purcell, 'The general condition of Aborigines in the Western and Northern parts of this Colony', QSA Col/A717 in letter no 14199 of 1892. Most of this report is reprinted in Evans *et al* 1988:386–88; my transcription of the report differs slightly.

8. For example, see Roth's Report (as Protector of Rockhampton) to the Commissioner of Police, 6 July 1898, QSA A/19898 [Roth Estrays].
9. Basedow (1927) provides a detailed summary of then contemporary perspectives on the contraceptive purpose of the practice. For a sense of more recent controversies on this question, see Cawte *et al* (1966), Singer and Desole (1967), and Cawte (1968). However, the question of the character and purpose of subincision is well outside the scope of this chapter on Roth.
10. However, as Spencer and Gillen (1899:263) responded to Roth on this point: 'This still leaves unexplained the mutilation of the women, and it would seem to be almost simpler to imagine that this was a consequence of the mutilation of the men'.
11. FW Briggs to Minister for Lands, 25 March 1905, QSA A/58927.
12. See 'Revelations – The Ethnological Specimens sold to Sydney Museum – Complete Official List – Giving Dates and Localities', *Truth Sunday*, 15 April 1906, clipping in QSA HOM/J20 1906/10295, and QSA HOM/J20 1906/10754.
13. Question to Home Secretary re 'Photographing of Gins', *QPD* xc (1902), 904; see also question of Mr Hamilton, 28 October 1902, *QPD*, xc, 958.
14. Mr Hamilton to Minister for Lands, 13 June 1904, *QPD*, xcii (1904), 578–89.
15. Roth to White, 19 June 1904, QSA A/58850, tabled in *QPD*, xcii, 13 July 1904, 585. Bishop White wrote to Roth on 3 June 1904, and Roth's reply is dated 19 June 1904. White telegrammed that he was satisfied with Roth's explanation, letter of 8 July 1904.
16. Roth to White, 19 June 1904, QSA A/58850.
17. *Ibid.*
18. *Ibid.*

Works Cited

Basedow, H (1927) 'Subincision and kindred rites of the Australian Aboriginal', *Journal of the Royal Anthropological Society* 57, 123–56

Cawte, JE (1968) 'Further comment on the Australian subincision ceremony', *American Anthropologist* ns 70(5), 961–64

Cawte, JE, Djagamara, N and Barrett, MJ (1966) 'The meaning of subincision of the urethra to Aboriginal Australians', *British Journal of Medical Psychology* 39, 245–53

Evans, R, Saunders, K and Cronin, K (1988) *Race Relations in Colonial Queensland: A History of Exclusion, Exploitation and Extermination*, 2nd ed, Brisbane: University of Queensland Press

Fysh, WH (1950 [1933]) *Taming the North*, 2nd edn, Sydney: Angus & Robertson

McDougall, R (2002) 'Walter and Henry Ling Roth: "on the signification of couvade": the place of Australia and British Guiana in the *fin de siècle* debate concerning the history of humanity', *Australian Cultural History* 21, 61–67

Office of the High Commissioner for Human Rights (OHCHR), Fact Sheet 23, *Harmful Traditional Practices Affecting the Health of Women and Children*, at www.unhchr.ch/html/menu6/2/fs23.htm

Queensland Parliamentary Debates (*QPD*) (1901–5) Brisbane: Government Printer

Roth, WE (1909) 'On certain initiation ceremonies', *North Queensland Ethnography Bulletin No 12, Records of the Australian Museum* 7(3–4)

———. (1897) *Ethnological Studies among the North-West-Central Queensland Aborigines*, Brisbane: Government Printer

Singer, P and Desole, DE (1967) 'The Australian subincision ceremony reconsidered: vaginal envy or kangaroo bifid penis envy', *American Anthropologist* ns 69(3/4), 355–58

Spencer, B and Gillen, FJ (1899) *The Native Tribes of Central Australia*, London: Macmillan

PART 5

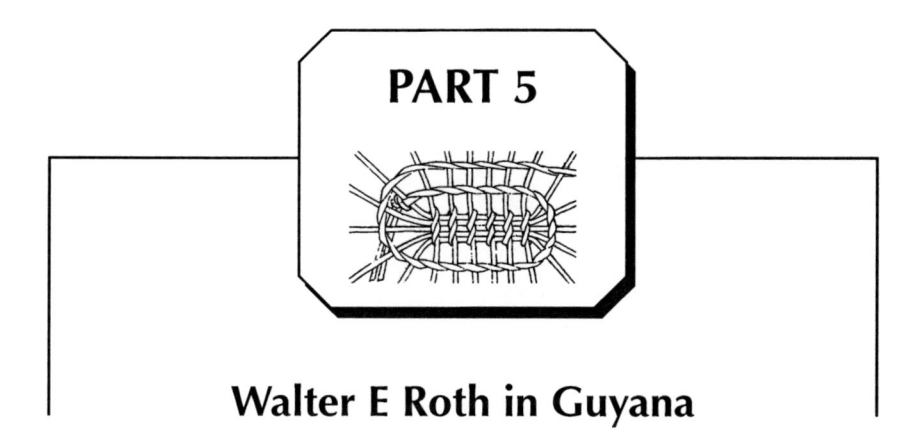

Walter E Roth in Guyana

CHAPTER 15

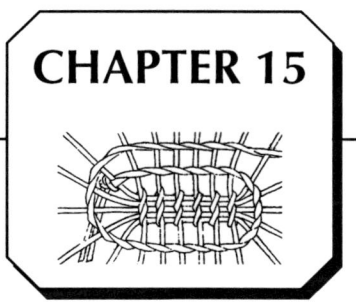

An Indigenous Compendium: Walter E Roth and the Ethnology of British Guiana

Neil L Whitehead

This chapter examines the major ethnological works and intellectual context of Walter E Roth in the colony of British Guiana[1] from 1906, when he transferred to British Guiana, being assigned as the Stipendiary Magistrate and Medical Officer of the Pomeroon District in the north-west region of the colony. He later moved to the Demerara River District, near the capital Georgetown, in the same capacities as magistrate and medic.

In this period he led three expeditions into the interior of British Guiana, the first to headwaters of the Barima River, the second to Mount Roraima, at the intersection of the borders of Brazil, British Guiana and Venezuela, and the third to the upper Essequibo, a description of which appears in the preface to his volume *Additional Studies of the Arts, Crafts, and Customs of the Guiana Indians* (1929). Important though these journeys were for his ethnological collations they did not represent a sustained residency in the interior or among native people themselves, and this marks Roth off from other contemporaries who may not now have the same degree of academic lustre but nonetheless more exactly fulfilled the anthropological ideal of fieldwork.[2] Roth openly noted in the Preface to *Additional Studies* that:

> As a matter of fact, during the whole month spent with the Indians it was a case of sign language and pencil or water-color drawing... All the same, it sometimes seemed quite uncanny to hear my own voice, which,

for what reason I know not, I was almost afraid to use. I was absolutely and indeed alone with these people [the Taruma], but as usual quite content and happy (Roth 1929:v).

Roth retired from the Colonial Service in British Guiana in 1928 and became Curator of the Museum of the Royal Agricultural and Commercial Society in Georgetown, which now bears his name.[3] He was awarded honorary fellowships by the Royal Anthropological Institute and the American Anthropological Association in 1932. He died the following year aged 70.

Undoubtedly Roth produced a series of important ethnological works about the native peoples of the colony, as well as making some key translations of Dutch and German materials relating to the early occupation and later exploration of the interior region, a task which occupied his spare time while acting as a magistrate. However, Roth was not the only early ethnologist of this region and the relationship of his compendia of folklore, animism, arts, crafts and customs (all issued by the US Bureau of Ethnology) to the work of other contemporary observers with anthropological pretension needs to be carefully considered. In this context the place of Walter Roth and his works for the self-imagining and fashioning of the space of 'Guiana' is also significant, particularly in light of his translation work.

Imperial Anthropology and Colonial Culture

In order to understand the place of Walter Roth in the emergence of anthropology[4] in British Guiana it is first necessary to set anthropology itself within the broader frame of imperial consolidation in the later 19th century. In its early colonial guise ethnological writing was often indistinguishable from travelogue more generally, being part of the authenticating apparatus of the travel genre as a whole (see the essays in Hulme & Youngs 2002).

A central element in this imperial gaze was the lens of 'Science', which made the otherwise individual and idiosyncratic observer a source of credible and possibly profitable information. As a result travel writing in this period, even in its ethnological format, is as much concerned with consolidation of empire as it is with the exploration and discovery of new lands and peoples. Indeed the tenor of some of these writings suggests that such discovery, with all its attendant romantic overtones, should now be supplanted by the stolid if solid work of colonial development. In this context ethnological writing has a special importance, since it represents a conscious attempt to marshal and understand the human resources of the colony.

Figure 15.1 The Walter Roth Museum, 61 Main Street, Georgetown, Guyana

'Travel' itself, as a concept, also gains a distinct meaning in this period. The major work of exploration having been done, it now remained only to flesh out and precisely delineate the nature of colonial possession. In this way extended residency abroad became equivalent to the 'explorations' of old. The heroic individual, as with Alexander Humboldt in South America, or Mungo Park in Africa, was gradually replaced by the government-sponsored expeditionary or field officer, and the tales of close encounter or exotic captivity among wild savages, were now echoed in more controlled interviews with pacified or dependant colonial subjects in the making, as was the case for Walter Roth.

Organisations like the Royal Anthropological Institute or the Royal Geographical Society played a significant role in promoting a broad but scientifically disciplined interest in ethnological facts, geographical exploration and natural history. Indeed interest in natural history was no less linked to imperial expansion than the more obvious connection between cartography and colonial possession, and was itself incompletely separated from 'moral' history that in turn comprised ethnology. Plant collecting in particular was an important source of potential profit from journeys otherwise redundant in cartographical terms. The journeys of British botanists to South America, such as Henry Bates, who was to become the Assistant Secretary of the Royal Geographical Society, were notoriously the source of much economically important information.[5]

Ethnology thus sat uneasily alongside the category of natural science, both because comparative cultural or biological study was itself still limited, and also because the primitive condition of indigenous society was implicitly seen as evidence of its naturalness. In this way ethnological writing, as much as the better known botanical and zoological materials, came to be expressive of the imperial scientific gaze.

Walter Roth's cladistic approach to the arts, crafts, customs, animism and folklore of the native population of Guyana[6] perfectly expresses this intellectual and representational context, since unlike his missionary predecessors he himself had no particular claim to intimate knowledge of native life or long-term residence in the 'bush'. Indeed Roth himself invokes exactly this conjuncture as the reason for his labours:

> There is still a vast amount of field work to be undertaken, not only there [the interior of British Guiana], but in Surinam and Cayenne [French Guiana], and if haste be not made, the information which it is possible to glean will probably be lost forever (Roth 1924:Preface).

Such attitudes went on to inform the tradition of Malinowskian-style fieldwork – a heroic endeavour that pictured the ethnographer snatching the last vestiges of the primitive from the jaws of a voracious modernity.[7] Indeed Roth himself invokes the First World War, noting that it delayed the production of the first volume, but also that in its wake:

> The so-called opening up of the country for the trader, the rancher, the timber getter, the balata and the rubber bleeder, *et hoc genus omne*, may or may not exert a beneficial influence on the welfare of the Creole, the Negro, and the European; but for the aboriginal Indian it means ruin, degradation, and disappearance (Roth 1924:Preface).

Roth provides a vignette from his Rupununi expedition in 1925 that perfectly illustrates the impact of such sentiments on his reactions and interactions with the native population:

> By midday we reached the Wapishana village of Sand Creek, but so changed that I hardly recognized it. I remembered a model garden city; I returned to find a miniature east-end slum. Instead of the houses being scattered over the savannah from 50 to a couple of hundred yards apart, an arrangement that afforded their occupants opportunity for privacy in their ablutions, etc., and so encouraged modesty and decency, that allowed them to spend their lives in the normal Indian secluded manner, and so helped each to mind his own business and prevent wrangling – the buildings are now all huddled together around a central modernized joss-house, and form an excellent nidus for the dissemination of disease, filth, and scandal. What is worse, considering their position in life, everyone wears clothes; even the toddling infant has to be covered. And yet clothes are not worn

for decency's sake, but for something akin to mimicry and swank, because underneath their European habiliments, the sexes sport the red-cloth lap and beaded apron, respectively. Talismans and charms continue to be employed and the filing of incisor teeth is still in vogue (Roth 1929:vii).

The veneer of modernity and civilisation thus obscured the still primitive and secretive savage, whose lack of physical hygiene becomes equated with the absence of moral virtue as well. Roth returns to this theme, just as he returns to Sand Creek later in his journey, bewailing the 'wages squandered' on clothing and drink with a resulting neglect of farming and even suggesting that the headman is colluding with Brazilian slavers. Roth also notes that Sandy, his dependable Makushi guide, was coughing up blood and therefore that his services had to be dispensed with. But Roth fails to acknowledge that the source of illness was likely himself or other Europeans, and that the colonial presence generally was itself the cause for the 'degeneration' in the native condition he diligently recorded in his compendia.

In contrast to the Makushi Roth saw the Waiwai as:

a delightful and charming set of people – clean, industrious, and happy. It was the first occasion that I had come across Indians whistling while they work. The distance of their native haunts from the centers of civilization has so far saved them from being interfered with by the missionary, rancher and balata bleeder: at present they are moral, and during the whole of my stay among them, I saw no drinking. Smoking was unusual (Roth 1929:x)

This aesthetic of nostalgic remorse for the 'former savage' is of course evident in colonial writing worldwide, as it was in other contemporary ethnological observations of British Guiana. Henry Kirke,[8] like Roth a Stipendiary Magistrate, was resident in Georgetown and the Berbice River. He writes:

Colonies change so rapidly, both as to men, manners and customs, that the colony of British Guiana when I left it was totally different from the colony as I had found it. The land itself had changed; old landmarks had disappeared, and new ones sprung up... railways and steam vessels are now hurrying through vast territories only known twenty years ago to the fierce Carib and Arawak; gold diggers and diamond searchers are swarming up every great river and gloomy creek, and the whole face of the country is being rapidly changed. The old quaint manners and habits have disappeared; the old legends are vanishing; the people dress and talk as others; the electric light illuminates their houses... the silk chimney pot of civilization is constantly in evidence; and they are as other men. The world is gradually acquiring a painful similarity; in a few hundred years every one will dress alike and speak the same language, and the human race will be reduced to one dull commonplace level of uniformity (Kirke 1898:1–2).

But such sentiments all too easily overlook the earlier onset of modernity under the Dutch and Spanish, who from the 16th century had been closely engaged with the native population and had substantively changed the conditions of native life (see Whitehead 1999a, 1999b, 1999c). Moreover, the very same conditions of mobility and communication that heralded the coming of 'one dull commonplace level of uniformity' also permitted the kind of intrusive ethnology that underlay the fieldwork ideal.

In this light Walter Roth certainly raised ethnological observation from the level of mere travel tale to that of science through his systematic and exhaustive compendia, derived from the works of earlier travellers and discoverers. He also saw the need to combine such ethnological sources with direct experience of native life – although this was not the dialogical encounter that later anthropologists, such as John Gillin or William Farabee,[9] espoused. No doubt this was a large part of the reason that Roth was not really considered part of the circuit of professional (or professionalising) anthropologists; and Melville Herskovits, a noted figure in the anthropology of the Caribbean and peoples of African heritage, notes as much in his obituary of Roth for the *American Anthropologist*:

> His ability as an artist will be at once apparent to anthropologists when it is stated that the large number of plates reproducing details of Guiana Indian basketry published in the 38th Annual Report of the Bureau of American Ethnology were drawn by him. In spite of the fact that his work never took him into the centers of learning, he did not lack recognition. He was President of the Anthropological Section of the British Association for the Advancement of Science (1902) in Hobart, Tasmania; in the same year he was elected honorary Corresponding Member of the Berlin Anthropological Society. Two years later he was chosen an honorary Corresponding Member of the Royal Anthropological Institute, which organization awarded him honorary Fellowship in 1932. The same year, a similar honor was bestowed on him by the American Anthropological Association (Herskovits 1934:268–69).

In the eyes of his contemporaries Roth thus appeared as not quite a proper anthropologist; and Herskovits implies this in his footnote to the obituary, where he acknowledges his reliance on both the obituary for Roth that appeared in the Georgetown *Daily Chronicle* of 6 April 1933 and 'much supplementary material' on Roth's life and publications. In short the academy wished to claim him but did so at arm's length as he did not conform to the emergent image of the ethnographer-anthropologist, at least in his Guyana work.[10]

The character of Roth's ethnological works is best conveyed by the term 'compendium', for he garnered the majority of his information from published sources and arranged that information according to a rigorous scheme. This schematic featured both synthetic chapters

Figure 15.2 Illustration of basketry (Drawn by Walter Roth)

that classified forms of material culture according to usages and technologies for their manufacture, as well as according to the form of materials used in manufacture. In turn each paragraph in the work was assigned a number so that reference could be made either following the pagination or according to this enumeration of paragraphs. For example, the chapters in *Arts, Crafts, and Customs* begin with consideration of tools made with 'Fire, Stone, Timber… ', 'Gums, Wax, Oils and Pigments' and 'Twines, Cords and Bands'. Some items of material culture received particular attention – baby slings, string games, narcotics – but this is then mixed in with other cultural forms such as 'salutations'. The choice of such classifications for the various topics seems arbitrary as no more fundamental scheme is at play in guiding the selection of the groupings for his source materials.

In Roth's work *An Inquiry into the Animism and Folk-Lore of the Guiana Indians* (1915) much the same is true. Tales, legends, myths and stories are taken from the context of their telling and classified according to their thematic elements. Heroes, cults, fetishes, creation stories, dreams and a whole suite of spirit entities of earth, water, sky and land thus feature as chapter headings alongside consideration of taboos, omens, charms, curing and killing (see discussion of *kanaimà* below). The final part of the work collates 'miscellaneous' materials, including those that indicate change and syncretism of ideas and beliefs.

The underlying difficulty in using Roth's work is the arbitrary nature of these categories – certainly just about everything is there, but where it is discussed in the volumes, and why there rather than elsewhere, are issues Roth never broaches. This perhaps is the key reason why his compendia did not establish him in the world of professional anthropologists. The compendia are faintly antiquarian in their approach, stressing the curious over the meaningful, and are silent on issues as to how human behaviours, evidenced in the material and intellectual cultural practices listed, might be understood. Compendia create an air of overwhelming authority through iteration, but they are necessarily selective as well, and the principles which guide such selections profoundly influence the implicit meanings of the work as a whole.[11]

Certainly such an approach relates strongly to the idea that the central task of ethnology (if not anthropology) was to salvage as much as possible of 'primitive' culture from the wreckage of modernity. However, indigenous survival and persistence through the 20th century rendered such an exercise obsolete. There is no doubt that Roth's compendia are highly fascinating and useful historical reflections of his time. They also offer a handy short cut to the harried academic in search of references and illustrations of native culture in north-eastern South America. But nagging issues as to the reasons and consequences for the profound changes that were occurring, and that are the occasion for the volumes, are never addressed directly in the compendia themselves.

The Cultural Politics of Ethnology in Colonial Guiana

When Roth arrived in British Guiana in 1906 he found an already developed tradition of writing about the native population. In particular the works of Rev William Brett, Sir Everard Im Thurn, Charles Barrington-Brown, Richard Schomburgk and Sir Robert Schomburgk were an established part of the literary and ethnological field into which Roth entered. The earlier writings of William Hilhouse and the Schomburgk brothers were of less contemporary relevance, but Roth's translation of some of the Schomburgks' writings clearly acknowledges their priority in this field. Hilhouse makes for an instructive comparison with Roth, since he too was appointed 'Protector' of the Indians in Guiana, in the 1830s, and his advocacy for them led him into controversy and conflict with the local colonists, somewhat as in the case of Roth in Australia (see Chapters 11, 12 and 14 in this volume).

However, Roth's most immediate literary and ethnological competitors were the missionaries Brett and Im Thurn and the 'field specialist' Barrington-Brown. Although their works were of a previous generation, published in the period 1868–83, they effectively set the agenda for at least a preliminary understanding of the character and distribution of the native population. Among the three authors there were clear differences in literary style and ethnological purpose. Brett (1868, 1881) concerned himself with a spiritual and poetic vision of the Indian, offering portraits of tribal characteristics and lifestyle alongside extensive recording of folklore and myth.[12] For Im Thurn (1883) the analysis of society, politics and power, as befitting a future President of the Royal Anthropological Institute, was the principal concern. As a fellow government employee, Roth was probably intellectually closer to Barrington-Brown, who had parlayed his extensive interior travels into a memoir of indigenous encounters.[13] Roth however saw the importance of a systematic approach to ethnological data where Barrington-Brown and Brett did not; and this made Im Thurn his principal competitor in terms of intellectual legacies in the ethnology of British Guiana.

Kanaimà in Colonial Ethnologies

In order to appreciate the dynamics of such cultural politics it is appropriate to consider a key topic for both Im Thurn and Roth, the *kanaimà* complex. *Kanaimà* received chapter-length attention in Roth's *Animism and Folk-lore* but it is unclear why Roth utterly ignored Im Thurn's copious discussion in *Among the Indians of Guiana* (Im Thurn 1883:328–40) – the more so since he relied extensively on all the other key sources, including Barrington-Brown, Brett, Hilhouse and the Schomburgks. In this context it is perhaps relevant to note that Roth's works were published by the US Bureau of Ethnology, not the Royal Anthropological Institute or some other British institution. Indeed, as he explicitly states, his 1926 expedition to southern British Guiana was 'on behalf of the United States Government' (1929:v) rather than any British organisation. The absent-minded nature of imperialism in British Guiana[14] and the proximity of the United States no doubt contributed to this, as did Roth's friendship with J Walter Fewkes.[15] But Roth's possible disenchantment with the British imperial vision itself also may have played into the decision, silently reflected in his erasure of Sir Everard Im Thurn, future Governor of Fiji, from this important aspect of his ethnological compendium on the folklore of the 'Guiana Indians'. In turn Im Thurn's Presidency of the Royal Anthropological Institute, as well as his curatorship of the Museum of the Royal Agricultural and Commercial Society in the 1880s through the patronage of Sir Joseph Hooker (see note 5), reflects this gulf in scholarly credential between the compendia of the medico-magistrate Walter Roth and the field observations and theoretical forays of the politically powerful priest Sir Everard Im Thurn.

These differing orientations to the politics of colonial rule also are evident in the development of the Walter Roth Museum of Anthropology.

This was the first museum of anthropology in the English-speaking Caribbean and was founded in 1974, after independence from Britain. The name of the museum, which prominently featured the collections of the Guyanese archaeologist Denis Williams, was chosen partly in recognition of Roth's lukewarm regard for the pretensions of imperial rule, if not of the potential beneficence of an enlightened colonialism.[16] After all Roth came with mildly 'radical-liberal' baggage from Australia. Roth was a doctor in the Boulia area of Queensland in the 1890s, and was later Northern Protector of Aborigines and then Chief Protector of Aborigines in Queensland.[17] However, as Helen Pringle writes:

> If he is known at all today, Roth would be recognised as a figure in the story of the removal of Walter told by Robert Manne, *In Denial: The Stolen Generations and the Right*, Australian Quarterly Essay no. 1 (2001), pp. 7–10. It was also during Roth's term as Protector that Aboriginal children began to be removed to Barambah… It seems to me, from an examination of the records of Roth's term as Protector, that the children of Aboriginal women and non-white men were particularly vulnerable to removal orders [at this time]… (pers comm).

It would not have been unusual for a medically trained government functionary to have viewed the missionary effort as somewhat anachronistic in a world where concerns of 'public health' and 'education', not redemption and salvation, had become the hallmarks of progressive thinking, as is reflected in Roth's account of the Wapishana at Sand Creek quoted earlier. Whatever further biographical research might reveal on this issue, it is at least clear that Roth's ethnological compendia suffered for the exclusion of Im Thurn's work, at least on the question of *kanaimà*, a form of assault sorcery. The term invokes truly strange and troubling acts. In both the colonial literature and native oral testimony, it refers to the killing of individuals by dark shamans (or sorcerers) through the violent physical mutilation of the mouth and anus, into which are inserted various magical objects. The killers are then mystically enjoined to return to the dead body of the victim in order to drink the juices of putrefaction and to thereby transform themselves on a spiritual plane (see Whitehead 2002).

Kanaimà has been discussed in colonial sources since at least the early 19th century and this reflected the way in which the topic was seen as indicative of the still-lingering savagery of the native population of the deep interior. In this way descriptions of encounter with, or new knowledge about, *kanaimà* ritual also became tokens of an author's own credibility as a genuine 'explorer' or 'ethnologist'. However, in these works *kanaimà* is assimilated to revenge more generally, and this meant that a vast array of different kinds of death are attributed to *kanaimà* when they may not have been ritual killings at all. Inevitably the nature of *kanaimà* deaths thus appeared quite obscure; and the claim that a killing was the work of *kanaimà* was seen as more the superstitious invocation of a spirit-ghoul than a reference to a distinct and ritually significant mode of death.

With more systematic ethnological recording, and particularly after Im Thurn's theoretical readings, *kanaimà* transmutes in the colonial sources into a functionalist mechanism for sustaining social order; and the killing becomes a kind of 'jungle justice' which, in the absence of the Hobbesian state and its police, regulates and punishes the 'criminal'. As a result, the symbolic and ritual meanings of *kanaimà* were effectively ignored, or were understood as an unfortunate welling up of native savagery.

The colonial gaze that produced this ethnological and literary view of *kanaimà* certainly serviced the project of colonial administration. But, even if the cultural importance of *kanaimà* was reflected in the attention both Roth and Im Thurn gave it, colonial representations always emphasised apparent juridical features to *kanaimà*, picturing it as a codified system of revenge – a *lex talionsis*. The physically violent nature of *kanaimà* killing and its connection to notions of revenge obscured its occult meanings for the colonial commentator. Instead *kanaimà* served as an answer to the puzzle of how native society might regulate itself in the absence of formal institutions of law or criminal justice.[18] Nonetheless *kanaimà* proved sufficiently elusive as an object of scientific contemplation that it did not become a basis for the campaigns of cultural extirpation associated with other dramatised cultural practices, such as cannibalism. This elusiveness, coupled with pervasive native reference to *kanaimà*, meant that *kanaimà* required some codification; and so the legalistic interpretation was pursued by the major missionary and ethnological writers – Brett, Im Thurn, Roth and Gillin.

The ferocity and horrific mutilations of a *kanaimà* attack were impossible to ignore. But they were seen as an almost laudable aspect of the rigour of native 'justice', provoking Im Thurn to make favourable comparison with 'tribal' Saxon and Judaic ideas of retaliation and recompense. The profound spirituality of *kanaimà* was erased through its presentation as a folkloric belief, akin to the vampire or werewolf. The beneficial effects of *kanaimà* in producing social order were identified in both its proto-legal functions and their supposed consequences – the sustaining of social distance and of the particularity of 'tribal' identity. This analysis is given persistent emphasis by Im Thurn and was taken up by both Roth and Gillin, to the point that *kanaimà* becomes a particular instance of legal systems founded on retribution and punishment – the only difference from 'white society' being that it is the retributive force of government and society, rather than of family, which is expressed in the latter case.[19]

This literary and observational process was underwritten by a high degree of intertextuality among colonial and modern authors. Certain key accounts, especially that of Roth, have been constantly recycled, progressively constricting the interpretive space for subsequent new descriptions or information. With the publication of Roth's account, the colonial imagining of *kanaimà* becomes embalmed in the ethnological record, and later writings have largely failed to escape this rendition.

In *The Folk-lore and Animism of the Guiana Indians*, Chapter XVIII is dedicated to a discussion of 'Kanaimà; the invisible or broken arrow'. Significantly, although Roth had collated and (presumably) read all the reports that were extant, he chooses not to represent *kanaimà* as anything more than a principle of revenge performed with somewhat excessive alacrity. References to the poetics of *kanaimà* mutilation are largely confined to observation of injuries to the mouth, the use of poisons and the shape-shifting proclivities of *kanaimà* assassins. Roth reviewed materials that contain considerably more information than this.

Roth's collation therefore represented a very lacklustre attempt to order the data. He apparently never interviewed a *kanaimà* practitioner directly, nor (like many of the earlier commentators) did he encounter any victims. As a result he was unable to synthesise and weigh the various elements of ritual practice he collated in a way that might reflect the relationship of *kanaimà* killing to the wider field of cosmology, myth and ritual. In short his handling of this crucial issue reflects all the drawbacks to compendium form that I discussed earlier.

No less curious is his failure to mention Im Thurn's (1883) extensive discussion of 'kenaimas'. Given Roth's subsequent high reputation as a 'father of ethnology in British Guiana',[20] and given that it is far easier to obtain library access to or even a reprint of his collations for the Bureau of American Ethnology than it is Im Thurn's volume, it is Roth's work that became the rather hackneyed starting point for many discussions of the native people of the region. As a direct result subsequent ethnographic interest in the *kanaimà* was minimal, even when the practice was reported.

Roth (1915:359) did collect some new information from the Pomeroon Karinya on the use of *massi* poison by *kanaimàs*, but he seems to have conflated these materials with ideas about *kanaimà* initiation techniques. Overall, by separating his discussion of *kanaimà* from that of curing shamanism or *piya*, Roth ends up with a less convincing account than that of Im Thurn, who appears to have appreciated the importance of this connection. Roth simply assimilates *kanaimà* to modes of vengeance and so misses its much more important shamanic dimension. Where accounts of particular *kanaimàs* were available he treats them as examples of mercenary vengeance killings; and so the image of free-ranging, if 'legitimate', assassin becomes the key anthropological motif for *kanaimà* in the regional literature.

Roth (1915:355) also notes that 'I can not recall at present a single instance of Kanaima culled from the literature dealing with Cayenne, Surinam or the Orinoco region'. However, although he refers to the work of the Penard brothers, he apparently did not read it carefully (see note 22), for they do include a number of references to *kanaimà* among the Surinam Karinya (1907:I, 70–74; III, 77–78), which he omits. At the very least, then, Roth's compendia are not exhaustive in the way that they might first appear to be. Accordingly, Im Thurn's relevance to the advent of modern categories of anthropological thought is somewhat perversely shown by the fact that his synthesis of material on *kanaimà* was totally ignored by Roth in his allegedly definitive compendium of materials on the native peoples of the region. One can only presume that some 'professional' consideration was involved here. Im Thurn himself borrowed an illustration of a Makushi shaman from Jules Crevaux, whom he had met in British Guiana.[21] This same illustration Roth correctly reattributes to Crevaux, passing over Im Thurn's lapse in silence.

None of this amounts to a suggestion of overt personal antipathy to Im Thurn by Roth. But such lapses and oversights are often revealing

Figure 15.3 Jules Crevaux's illustration of a Makushi shaman

of other kinds of cultural process than those that are apparent. In this way the cultural dynamics of Roth's ethnology were quite different from those of Im Thurn, and even antipathetic to the larger goal of anthropological interpretation. At least in the case of *kanaimà*, the compendia of Roth were misleading and distracted attention from what has proved to be a fundamental reality of native life – both then and up to the present day.

Walter Roth and the Imagination of Guiana

Nonetheless, the presence of the Roth clan in Guyana has been significant and persistent in many ways. In 1993 I met Johnny Roth, the son of John Roth and grandson of Walter's son Vincent. Johnny told me that Vincent was involved in a shoot-out at the bar in Monkey Mountain, in a dispute over diamonds back in the 1920s. Johnny himself was educated in Brazil until he was 12 years old. His mother was Makushi and he has married a Makushi himself. He told me that he had found *kanaimà* ritual vessels many times in his prospecting for gold and diamonds.

Henry Roth, Vincent's brother, wrote for the Guyanese journal *Timehri* in 1950 on the topic of *kanaimà*. His attitudes seem to very much reflect the distinction between the scholar and the man of experience, somewhat echoing the contrast between Walter and Im Thurn in earlier times. As a government officer in the Rupununi district in the period after John Gillin's fieldwork, Henry eschews all pretence at anthropological expertise, although he says, 'I think I can say I should know the subject *as much as the other man*'. The result is a matter-of-fact summary of all the salient features of *kanaimà* and an untroubled affirmation of 'real' *kanaimà*, since 'Any *Old-Timers* from the Demerara and Berbice rivers can vouch for the corporeal existence of the Kanaimas' (H Roth 1950:25–26).

However, Walter Roth's overarching influence in the imagination of the space of 'Guiana' remains pre-eminent, not just because of the way in which the compendia make evident the complexity and richness of native life, but also for the way in which that is given a geographical reality. In fact, this cultural area typology and geographical space was precisely co-extensive with the practice of *kanaimà*, which was generally seen as unique to 'Guiana', though not quite as restricted as Roth thought in suggesting that it did not occur in Surinam or Cayenne. In other ways too Roth was quite overt in creating the space of 'Guiana', writing in the Preface to *Animism and Folk-Lore* that:

> As the work progressed, I recognized that, for the proper comprehension of my subject, it was necessary to make inquiry concerning the Indians

of Venezuela, Surinam, Cayenne, with the result that the area to be reviewed comprised practically that portion of the South American continent bounded, roughly speaking, by the Atlantic seaboard, the Orinoco, and the northern limits of the watershed of the Rio Negro, and the lower Amazon; and it was not long before I realized that for the proper study of the Arawaks and Caribs I had to include that of the now almost extinct Antilleans (Roth 1915:Preface).

The materials in the compendia lacked any real historiographical weighting, and sources from widely different time periods appear side by side without any consideration of how historical change may have affected the cultural practices under discussion. Yet Roth was not unaware of the significance of change. So it must be inferred that he simply did not know how to write it into his ethnological methodology, given the priority he gave to the salvage of cultural practices he understood to be fast disappearing. In this he was hardly alone. Bronislaw Malinowski explicitly launched his program of 'fieldwork' by eschewing the necessity for any historical understanding, which was anyway impossible amongst 'illiterate' cultures. In this light Roth's excellent translations of Adriaan van Berkel's account of 17th century Berbice and Surinam, as well as his translation of Richard Schomburgk's travel accounts, seem more related to his command of the German and Dutch language than to any program of ethnohistorical intent.[22]

Nonetheless, Roth's compendia anticipated and may even have inspired to some degree Julian Steward's editing of the *Handbook of South American Indians* (1946). Both were issued by the Bureau of American Ethnology. The *Handbook* is a massive seven-volume collaborative work in which, as in Roth's compendia, the essays synthesise vast quantities of ethnological data ranging over many hundreds of years. The same problems apparent in Roth's compendia resurface in the *Handbook*, particularly the conflation of geographical and cultural distributions. Nonetheless, it is notable that 'Guiana' is a distinct region in the *Handbook* and the influence of Roth's work seems undeniable here. Roth may be rightly criticised with hindsight, but he very much exemplified the best working methods of his day.

On a more personal note I will say that his interest in and dedicated scholarship with regard to native peoples in Guayana has been inspirational. Roth's works have been heavily used by myself and others notwithstanding the limitations indicated. No scholar can anticipate the needs and obsessions of future generations, and the fact that Roth's compendia remain essential for any burgeoning scholar of the region is an eloquent testimony to the intellectual vigour and discipline of this most fascinating man, who justly holds a pre-eminent position in the ethnology of South America. Moreover, his romantic sensibilities may still lure us to the forests of Guyana:

> The call of the wild can never be stilled in me, and thus it came to pass that on taking farewell of poor old Sandy [his Makushi guide in 1926], whom I never expect to see again in the flesh, we arranged to meet 'some day' in the future and fish and hunt together in the happy hunting grounds beyond the Taruma and Waiwai (Roth 1929:xi).

There I hope to see them both.

Notes

1. The term 'Guyana' refers to the independent country formerly known as 'British Guiana'; the term 'Guianas' is used to refer collectively to the colonial enclaves of British Guiana, Surinam and Guyane (or French Guiana). Some writers also use the term 'Guianas' to refer to the territories of those colonial enclaves, plus the regions of Brazil and Venezuela that lie south of the Orinoco and north of the Amazon; contemporary usage names this geographical region as 'Guayana', which is also the Spanish-language term.
2. Roth also characterised the Makushi of the interior in a way that suggests rather less empathy for actual natives than for his own idealised version of them. Of his expedition to the Rupununi he notes:

    > At Annai I succeeded in enlisting the services of six of the least drunken and degenerate Makushi as boat hands. ... Within another week I was ... only too glad to be rid of my boat hands, who were now paid off. They had given me no end of trouble; one had absconded with his advance, while all the others, Sandy excepted, has [sic] lost a day in getting drunk at an evening drinking party that they had visited without my permission or knowledge (1929:vi).

3. In 1980 the ethnographic collections of Dr Walter Roth, Mr JJ Quelch and Sir Everard Im Thurn were transferred to the Walter Roth Museum from the Guyana Museum, which had replaced the Museum of the Royal Agricultural and Commercial Society on independence from Britain in 1956. The Walter Roth Museum was opened to the public in 1982. The Museum's collections include excavated artefacts from all of the 10 Administrative Regions of Guyana as well as items of material culture donated by various anthropologists.
4. Anthropology here should be understood as that professional activity which emerged at the end of the 19th century; ethnology is considerably older than this, being an aspect of inter-group relations for many past cultures and times, particularly associated with imperial or state power as a means of ordering cultural groupings.
5. Among such entrepreneurial scientists were Sir Clements R Markham, botanist and senior official of the India office, as well as Sir Joseph D Hooker, director of Kew Gardens, and Henry Ridley, director of the Singapore Botanical Gardens. Markham was involved in promoting the cultivation of the rubber plant varieties *Hevea brasiliensis* and *Castilla moraceae* and in 1875 and 1876 the botanist Robert Cross was sent to Central and South America to collect specimens and report on their requirements regarding climate and soil. The plants and seeds that he brought back, along with the others, were distributed through the Botanical Gardens at Kew to the colonies

An Indigenous Compendium | 251

of Ceylon, India and Malaya, and from there throughout the east. *Hevea brasiliensis* proved to be by far the most successful rubber plant, and it became the preferred variety, contributing directly to the collapse of the South American rubber industry at the beginning of the 20th century. Notably, this legacy of 'bio-piracy' is still an active consideration in the politics of botanical research in South America today.

6. Roth used the term 'Guiana Indians' and understood by that, given his source material, to be the geographical space bounded by the Atlantic, the Amazon and the Orinoco.
7. The irony here is that Bronislaw Malinowski, like Walter Roth, came from a Jewish immigrant background and although his field methods went on to become the professional standard, like Roth, he was never part of the British establishment – as, say, Sir Edward Evans-Pritchard was.
8. Henry Kirke (1842–1925) was educated from 1860 to 1866 at Wadham College, Oxford, and was then called to the Bar at the Inner Temple in 1868. He was successively Sheriff of Demerara, Police Magistrate of Georgetown, Supreme Court Judge in British Guiana, Attorney-General of Jamaica and Magistrate for Derbyshire. He was author of *Twenty-five Years in British Guiana* (1898).
9. William Farabee published *The Central Caribs* (Philadelphia: The University Museum) in 1924 and John Gillin published *The Barama River Caribs of British Guiana* (Papers of the Peabody Museum, XIV [2]. Cambridge [Mass.]: Peabody Museum) in 1936. Farabee worked in the far south of the colony and Gillin in the north-west, both regions to which Roth had also journeyed.
10. Herskovits certainly suggests that his reports on native peoples in Australia had a greater impact on academic enquiry, quoting the 1905 comment of NW Thomas in *Man* 5(16), 30: 'Great as is the value of the work done by Messrs Spencer and Gillen, that done by Dr Roth is a more than dangerous rival in respect of information on ethnographical questions'.
11. The arbitrary nature of such exercises is very evident in the instability between other forms of categorical iteration, such as in encyclopedias or dictionaries. Other all-encompassing compendia of native people in the Guyana region were made by Raymond Breton (1665–66) and Wilhelm Ahlbrinck (1931) and most recently by Lal Balkaran (2002). These all happily conflate ethnological observation, linguistic practice and historical context, much as did Roth.
12. Some of these materials became the basis for a volume of poetry by Brett in which these materials were retold in verse form; see his 1880 volume, *Legends and Myths of the Aboriginal Indians of British Guiana*.
13. See his *Canoe and Camp Life in British Guiana* (1877). Barrington-Brown was a prominent figure in the life of the colony of British Guiana in his capacity as Government Surveyor. He was also professionally accomplished as a geologist and well reputed as an explorer. In these ways he is very much an example of the strength and limits of the imperialist class of his era – literate but not literary, an explorer but not a discoverer, a field geologist but not a scientific innovator.
14. See Peter Rivière's discussion of this in *Absent Minded Imperialism: Britain and the Expansion of Empire in Nineteenth-century Brazil* (London: IB Tauris & Co, 1995).
15. In 1895 Fewkes embarked on various archaeological explorations for the Smithsonian's Bureau of American Ethnology, and in 1918 was appointed chief of the Bureau. He was particularly interested in the prehistoric inhabitants of the island of Puerto Rico, which became a possession of the United States as a result of the Spanish-American war. He excavated a number of sites in Puerto Rico and extended his research to neighbouring islands such as Haiti, Cuba, Trinidad and the Lesser Antilles, resulting in the work *Aborigines of Porto Rico and Neighboring Islands* (1907).

Jesse Fewkes retired from the Smithsonian Institution in 1928 and died two years later, just before Walter Roth. Roth mentions Fewkes as a personal friend and quotes his letter to him describing his expedition to the south of British Guiana in January–July 1925 in *Additional Studies* (1929:v–xi), and this connection does much to explain Roth's orientation to the US academic context.

16. This positive evaluation of Roth by the Peoples National Congress government was also informed by a rejection of more establishment figures, such as Im Thurn. Early in my acquaintance with the Director of the Walter Roth Museum, Denis Williams, I was told an anecdote about Im Thurn in order to underline the way in which Roth, and the continuing presence of his descendants in Guyana, made him part of the nationalist vision of the PNC leadership. In contrast to Roth's public concern for native welfare, Williams suggested, Im Thurn was more interested in sustaining the image of British imperialism.

    As evidence of this I was given a photocopy of the marked-up author's proofs for the first page of Chapter 1 of Im Thurn's *Among the Indians of Guiana* (1883), deposited in the National Anthropological Archives held at the museum. From this it was evident that Im Thurn had decided to erase a highly contentious reference to the actions of British colonists in Australia, as part of an opening discussion of the proper framework for colonial development of native populations under British rule; the inference being that this was evidence of a cover-up by Im Thurn of the crimes of colonialism. The excised passage reads: '[in Australia] not so many years ago there were cases in which the natives were shot down to satisfy the provision of meat for the dogs and others in which, when the natives were found troublesome in the district, strychnine was put in the well from which they drank, and so their numbers were lessened'.

17. In this light it is appropriate to note that Roth enthusiastically applied his medical training to the project of governmentality through his publications *The Elements of School Hygiene: for the Use of Teachers in Schools* (London: Baillière, Tindall and Cox, 1886), *Notes on Government, Morals, and Crime* (Brisbane: GA Vaughan, Govt Printer, 1906) and *Theatre Hygiene: A Scheme for the Study of a Somewhat Neglected Department of the Public Health* (London: Baillière, Tindall and Cox, 1888). See also Chapter 1 in this volume on Walter's upbringing in the liberal family of Mathias Roth, which stresses his exposure to European culture more widely and a resulting distancing from the mainstream of British colonial culture, since Mathias was both Jewish and a Hungarian immigrant.

18. As Thomas (1994:127) has pointed out with regard to British missionary efforts elsewhere, each mission 'field' was apt to dramatise certain key cultural practices – such as headhunting, cannibalism or widow burning – in order to provide an index of growing evangelical success. As a result these kinds of representation tend also to present the cultural practice in question as on the verge of extinction. This was very much how shamanism generally, including *kanaimà*, were presented.

19. Im Thurn here anticipates Evans-Pritchard's (1937) classic work on Azande sorcery since, as in the Azande case, the ethnology of *kanaimà* shamanism ultimately and comfortingly 'reveals' it as a system of justice and legality. In this way the cultural force of *kanaimà*, which so manifestly entrances and troubles the colonial imagination, is shown to be a matter of the ineffable and irrational nature of colonial subjects. That primitive mystery is then made less threatening through the 'science' of ethnological description which sanitises barbarous practice through its selective re-presentation in familiar, intelligible and comforting terms – as a form of law and order.

20. According to the obituary in the Georgetown *Daily Chronicle*, 6 April 1933.

21. The frontispiece illustration (Plate 1) to *Among the Indians of Guiana* (1883) shows a seated man in full feather regalia to which Im Thurn gave the caption 'A Macusi

Indian in full dancing dress'; however the original photograph from which this illustration is obviously derived actually appears in Jules Crevaux's *Voyages dans L'Amerique du Sud* (1883:117), itself a compilation of materials published earlier in the travel magazine *Tour de Monde*. This is despite the fact that Crevaux speaks warmly of his encounter with Im Thurn in British Guiana in July 1878 (Crevaux 1883:140) and that Im Thurn brazenly claims that all the illustrations (except those otherwise indicated) are 'from my own sketches' (1883:viii).
22. Roth tells us in *Additional Studies* (1929:v) that he learnt Dutch specifically in order to be able to read relevant sources in that language. This may well be a reason why he did not include all relevant references from the works of the Penard brothers in his earlier work.

Works Cited

Ahlbrinck, Wilhelm (1931) *Encyclopaedie der Karaïben, behelzend taal, zeden en gewoonten dezer Indianen*, Amsterdam: Koninklijke Akademie van Wetenschappen

Balkaran, Lal (2002) *Dictionary of the Guyanese Amerindians and Other South American Tribes. An A-Z Guide To Their Anthropology, Cosmology, Culture, Exploration, History, Geography, Legend, Folklore and Myth*, Ontario: LBA Publications

Breton, Raymond (1666) *Dictionaire françois-caraibe*, Auxerre: Gilles Bouquet

———. (1665) *Dictionaire caraibe-françois: meslé de quantité de remarques historiques pour l'esclaircissement de la langue*, Auxerre: Gilles Bouquet

Brett, William H (1881) *Mission Work in the Forests of Guiana*, London/New York: Society for Promoting Christian Knowledge/E & JB Young & Co

———. (1880) *Legends and Myths of the Aboriginal Indians of British Guiana*, London: William Wells Gardner

———. (1868) *The Indian Tribes of Guiana*, London: Bell & Daldy

Barrington-Brown, C (1877) *Canoe and Camp Life in British Guiana*, London: Edward Stanford

Crevaux, Jules (1883) *Voyages dans L'Amérique du Sud*, Paris: Hachette

Herskovits, Melville J (1934) 'Walter E. Roth', *American Anthropologist* 36, 266–69

Hilhouse, William (1825) *Indian Notices*, Printed for the Author

Hulme, Peter and Youngs, Timothy (2002) *The Cambridge Companion to Travel Writing*, Cambridge: Cambridge University Press

Im Thurn, E (1883) *Among the Indians of Guiana*, London: Kegan, Paul, Trench and Co

Kirke, Henry (1898) *Twenty-five Years in British Guiana*, London: Sampson Low, Marston and Company

Penard, FP and Penard, AP (1907) *De Menschetende Aanbidders der Zonneslang*, Paramaribo: privately published

Roth, Henry (1950) 'The Kanaima', *Timehri* 29, 25–26

Roth, Walter E (1948) *Adriaan van Berkel's Travels in South America between the Berbice and Essequibo Rivers and in Surinam, 1670–1689*, Georgetown: Daily Chronicle

———. (1929) *Additional Studies of the Arts, Crafts, and Customs of the Guiana Indians, With Special Reference to Those of Southern Guiana*, Bulletin of the Bureau of American Ethnology, 91, Washington: US Government Printing Office

———. (1924) *An Introductory Study of the Arts, Crafts, and Customs of the Guiana Indians*, 38th annual report of the Bureau of American Ethnology, 1916–17, Washington: Smithsonian Institution

———. (1922) *Richard Schomburgk's Travels in British Guiana, 1840–1844*, Georgetown: Daily Chronicle

Roth, Walter E (1915) *An Inquiry into the Animism and Folk-Lore of the Guiana Indians*, 30th annual report of the Bureau of American Ethnology, 1908–09, Washington: Smithsonian Institution

Steward, Julian Haynes (1946) *Handbook of South American Indians (7 vols.)*, Bulletin of the Bureau of American Ethnology, 143, Washington: US Government Printing Office

Thomas, Nicholas (1994) *Colonialism's Culture. Anthropology, Travel and Government*, Princeton: Princeton University Press

Whitehead, Neil L (2002) *Dark Shamans. Kanaimà and the Poetics of Violent Death*, Durham: Duke University Press

———. (1999a) 'The crises and transformations of invaded societies (1492–1580) – The Caribbean', in Salomon, F and Schwartz, S (eds), *The Cambridge History of Native American Peoples, III (1)*, Cambridge: Cambridge University Press, 864–903

———. (1999b) 'Lowland peoples confront colonial regimes in Northern South America, 1550–1900', in Salomon, F and Schwartz, S (eds), *The Cambridge History of Native American Peoples, III (2)*, Cambridge: Cambridge University Press, 382–441

———. (1999c) 'Native society and the European occupation of the Caribbean islands and coastal Tierra Firme, 1492–1650', in Damas, C and Emmer, P (eds), *A General History of the Caribbean,* Vol III, London and Basingstoke: UNESCO Publications, 180–200

CHAPTER 16

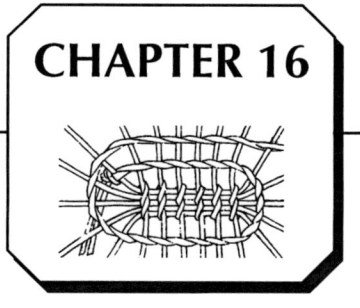

'Protector of Indians': Assessing Walter Roth's Legacy in Policy Towards Amerindians in Guyana

Janette Bulkan and Arif Bulkan

Walter Roth's first official posting in British Guiana in 1907 was as the Government Medical Officer, Magistrate and Protector of Indians in the Pomeroon District, an area that, one century later, still demarcates the westernmost extent of African and East Indian settlement of the coastal plain (coterminous with rice and, formerly, plantation cultivation of sugar and other export crops). The coastal road ends at the market village named Charity, on the Pomeroon River, which remains the fluvial gateway to the Amerindian peoples of the North West District, who were the first subjects of Roth's investigations.

Roth seems not to have dwelled upon the setbacks of his professional life in Australia but embraced with alacrity the challenges of this new world, which included the discomforts of the (still) mosquito-infested locale and having to write at night by hurricane lamplight. He continued his lifelong labours as a colonial civil servant and, concomitantly, catalogued the material culture, social structure and beliefs of indigenous peoples on this other side of the world.

Guyana and Australia, subject to the same colonial gaze, provide another example of the similarities in colonial forms of rule across antipodean territories. Long before Roth's arrival, colonial administrators were transferred from one colony to another; from 1902 protectionist legislation was passed for indigenous people in British Guiana; plant material was moved among tropical territories and the same assemblage of trees and ornamentals were planted in colonial botanic gardens, for example. Incidentally, in Guyana the term 'aboriginal' was used interchangeably with 'Indian' but from the beginning of the 20th century, both terms were eventually superseded by the increasing use of the term 'Amerindian' – a contraction of 'American' and 'Indian' – no doubt impelled by the need to differentiate indigenous peoples from the significant East Indian indentured immigration into Guyana in the second half of the 19th century.

Today, Roth is more remembered internationally for the impressive body of original ethnological work and translations into English of the manuscripts or publications of eminent contemporaries and earlier historical writers working in the same Guyana culture area (Collins 1971). Another part of his legacy, with more lasting impact in Guyana, was arguably his work in drawing up the *Aboriginal Indians Protection Ordinance*, Number 28 of 1910, based on his experience as former Chief Protector of Aboriginals in Queensland, Australia, and 'designed to protect the Indians from exploitation' (Menezes 1988). This chapter examines the policy framework crafted by Roth and used in State dealings with Guyana's indigenous peoples up to the present, and reflects upon the fate of that legislation now. It hardly needs restating that the 1910 Ordinance needs to be considered in relation to the colonial context in which it was drawn up and implemented, and not in comparison with contemporary mores.

We make two major points about Roth's public service in British Guiana. The first is that an unintended consequence of its overtly protectionist project was that the 1910 Ordinance codified in law the racialisation of colonial society and infantilisation of its first peoples, forming a legacy that endures into the present. This hardening of ethnic categories is as problematic for contemporary Amerindians as for the majority society, now comprised of ethnic East Indians and Africans, and persons of 'mixed' descent, who, taken together with Amerindians, form the bulk of the population of the Guyanese nation state. However, equally as important is giving due recognition to the ethos of the *fin de siècle* era which both shaped and was shaped by Walter Roth: a common thread running through colonial administrative policies was the notion that indigenous peoples were on the verge of extinction, necessitating the preservation of remnant groups. Territorial reservations, however problematic today – often interpreted as connoting the essentialisation of indigenous peoples, in much the same way as the fictive notion of untouched wilderness – in point of fact provided the requisite space for small isolated groups to recoup. They became, over time, a base from which to negotiate their interactions with the State, other citizens and capitalist enterprises intent on extracting both indigenous knowledge of and the natural resources from indigenous lands.

While Roth's 1910 Ordinance is routinely excoriated as flawed, it provided an opportunity for 'time-out', so that in this century intact indigenous communities in Guyana were able to contribute significantly in the process of the revision of the Amerindian Act of 1951. However, limited the 1910 Ordinance now seems to indigenous rights' activists and others, State recognition of their 'first nations' status and land rights claims – much in advance of the situation of indigenous peoples in contiguous Suriname, French Guiana or Brazil – is attributable in part to Roth's public policy and ethnographic work. Roth's legacy, then, while mixed, can indubitably be credited with helping to safeguard the survival of intact Guyanese Amerindian societies into the 21st century.

Racialisation Through Registration

During six years of sharing an office and working in the Amerindian Research Unit of the University of Guyana, Janette Bulkan heard many stories of Pomeroon River Amerindian communities from a colleague who was Arawak from Kabakaburi Mission, 16 miles upriver of Charity on the Pomeroon River. Like many coastal Amerindians, this Arawak colleague was phenotypically less 'pure' (browner in complexion, taller and slimmer) when measured against the standard prototype of Arawak or Carib in Guyana, aptly described by anthropologist Lee Drummond as 'the multiracial emigrant society *par excellence*' (Drummond 1977a). The story which most saddened her in its recounting was the local captain's (village leader) refusal in the early 1950s to register her father as an Arawak, on account of his curly (signifying 'negroid') hair. Only persons registered as *bona fide* Amerindians could remain within the titled Kabakaburi land area, so her parents had to relocate their home to just outside the reservation's boundaries, the physical separation underlining social distancing.

The practice of registration of Amerindians as a prerequisite for determining eligibility to live within a reservation area – a registration largely based on phenotype – was one of the new features in the 1910 Aboriginal Protection Ordinance, crafted by Roth. In the Kabakaburi case mentioned, the Captain's denial of Amerindian ethnic status to a fellow villager was based on a personal grudge. However, that grudge could be acted upon, as it was located within an ideological system which simultaneously privileged Government-appointed captains or village chiefs and a putative ethnic purity, while maintaining an ambivalent relationship to the larger Creole society that pressed in upon it. Among Drummond's insights was his convincing linking of contemporary attitudes towards and patterns of Amerindian ethnic residency and descent rules to a colonial vision that both preceded and included Roth. That colonial vision was of a racialised landscape, in which an indigenous association with the vast interior was buttressed by laws passed after the emancipation of slaves in 1834 that effectively denied freed slaves the option of residing away from the densely settled coastal plain. Indigenous society was viewed as being on the way to extinction. In Drummond's words, 'Brett [one of the first Anglican priests sent to British Guiana and stationed in the Pomeroon River in the 1840s] described the decline and imminent extinction of the Arawak "families". Roth … treated the families in the manner of archaeological artifacts, pieces of salvage ethnography he had snatched from the maw of history' (Drummond 1977b:310–11). The intent behind the 1910 Ordinance, in turn, can be seen as salvage public policy.

The Move to Protectionism

The impulses behind the pan-colonial move to protectionism (including spatial and racial segregation of indigenous peoples) ranged from concern over demographic decline and the often catastrophic impact of cultural contact to blatant appropriation of indigenous homelands by interest groups backed by the power of the State. Local experiences tended to reflect the desirability of indigenous lands to powerful interests. The mainstay of the British Guiana economy was plantation production of agricultural commodities located on the coastal plain. Over time, resource extractive industries – minerals, principally bauxite, gold and diamonds; and timber and non-timber forest products – led to penetration of indigenous homelands by elements of the dominant society. However, resource extractive enterprises occurred in waves, were seldom associated with permanent settlement by outsiders and were framed by colonial rules and regulations relating to mining, forestry, balata latex extraction and so on. In contrast, indigenous people fared worse in the more aggressive context of settler societies like the US and Australia, characterised by capitalist penetration and more permanent settlement in indigenous homelands. Reflecting on the relationship between the Empire and Nature, William Adams described the more brutal end of the continuum in which 'settler societies had established their own, internal, forms of colonialism in order to dominate indigenous minorities, or profoundly suppress majorities … herded into isolated fragments of their former terrain, on "reservations", "missions" or "tribal lands", administered with a complex mix of brute exploitation, paternalistic exhortation and racist disdain' (Adams 2003:6).

In the case of Guyana, colonial concern to cordon off indigenous societies from the gold industry in particular at the turn of the 20th century was a key motivation for protectionist legislation. Since all lands were designated as Crown lands at the time, concession and grant allocation of Amerindian homelands to outsiders could have proceeded apace, with little regard to pre-existing indigenous claims. However, the colonial State had relied heavily on Amerindian testimony and acceptance of British sovereignty to counter Venezuelan land claims to the Essequibo territory in the final decade of the 19th century. The reservation system that was instituted followed the pattern common to other British territories. It had preceded Roth; his contribution was in amplification and codification of the administrative details.

The 1902 Amerindian Ordinance

A strong vein of paternalism is very evident in the 1902 *Aboriginal Indians Protection Ordinance*, under which Amerindian districts and reservations were created, the latter on occupied Crown land, for the exclusive use of Amerindians. This statute was promulgated before Roth's arrival in the colony. The Ordinance created the position of 'Protector of Indians', which carried with it considerable powers over the lives of Amerindians, including powers to institute criminal proceedings on behalf of Amerindians, to monitor such proceedings on their behalf and to retain the services of counsel for such purposes. Curiously, though, the Ordinance made no mention of who bore the responsibility for paying for the services of any lawyer so retained. The Protector was also empowered to terminate at any time a contract for labour entered into by an Amerindian, and to make rules for the regulation and conduct of reservations. The Ordinance also established the post of 'Deputy Protector' and the bulk of these highly intrusive powers attached to that role too.

Supplementing the power of the Protector to directly regulate life on the reservations, the 1902 Ordinance implemented a thinly disguised system of indirect rule, in the form of captains and constables, who were appointed to serve in the districts. Although such appointments were to be made from among the Amerindians themselves, captains served at the pleasure of the Governor, were paid out of the public purse as the Governor saw fit and most importantly, had to report to the Protector or his deputy as required. In such a scenario, there was little room for independence, and in this way the hand of the Crown could extend even onto the most remote reservation.

Among the offences created by this Ordinance was a curious one that penalised 'enticing away or cohabiting with' the wife of an Indian.

The only scenario in which a married woman could form a new liaison was if her husband first deserted her. Notably, the man was not similarly constrained, and could have multiple (or successive) partners with impunity. Punishment for breach of this prohibition was substantial, and included imprisonment for up to three months.

In consonance with the era, this paternalism towards Amerindians, though belated and certainly self-serving, manifested itself in a highly intrusive manner. Amerindians were now relegated to the status of wards of the State, consigned to reserves and liable to the rules and regulations of a benevolent overlord. Even personal matters were not inviolable, and their employment or social liaisons (in the case of women) could be summarily terminated without their consent.

The 1910 Ordinance

Walter Roth is widely credited with authorship of the 1910 Ordinance, which took the place of the 1902 Ordinance. The fruit of Roth's efforts, the *Aboriginal Indians Protection Ordinance* enacted in 1910, was detailed and far more widely embracing than its predecessor, though the influence of the latter's underlying philosophy was unmistakable. Indeed, several more provisions were included in Roth's handiwork that underscored what was then the prevailing perception that Amerindians were inferior and incapable of regulating their own lives, even though the State had relied heavily on their testimony in presenting its case before an international tribunal charged with settling the boundary with Venezuela in the final years of the 19th century.

To begin with, several elements of the 1902 legislation were retained, such as the position of Protector of Indians with all its powers over Amerindians, the system of captains who were to police the reservations and the offence relating to wives of Amerindian men. Most critically, the approach of reserving lands for Amerindians, who were to be kept separate and apart from the rest of the population, was retained intact. The colonial practices of cordoning off peoples or selected lands by executive fiat have been reappraised in many recent studies (Adams & Mulligan 2003). The prevailing ethos also underlies the 1910 legislation, which empowered the Governor to declare any portion of unoccupied Crown lands as a reservation. Although this policy is still viewed in some quarters as an expression of the Crown's desire to keep areas inviolable from the development of the interior, and preserved for the use and benefit of Amerindians, such a rationale is belied by the specifics of the legislation. The Governor was empowered to declare reservations in his sole discretion, which meant that conservation or protectionist concerns could be trumped by economic considerations regarding any decision as to when or how land should be allocated. Moreover, the Governor's unfettered power to 'de-reserve' areas, or to alter the boundaries of reservations, meant that areas kept separate and apart for use by Amerindians could be instantly reclaimed for resource extraction, should the need arise (*AIPO* 1910:section 4).

With regard to the reservation system, however, the 1910 Ordinance took the protectionist stance considerably further. Whereas under the earlier statute non-Amerindians were merely prohibited from acquiring or occupying land or entering upon reservations, henceforth the free movement of Amerindians within the districts was severely curtailed, as permission was now needed for them to be absent from reservations (*AIPO* 1910:sections 11, 15). As if this were not bad enough, the Governor could cause an Amerindian within a district to be removed and kept within a reservation, or removed to another district altogether (*AIPO* 1910:section 10). Ultimately, it was the Crown, through regulations issued by the Governor and implemented by a superintendent, and not the inhabitants themselves, who determined the conditions for access onto a reserve (*AIPO* 1910:sections 8[c], 14).

There were also a host of other provisions, many in the spirit of the paternalistic approach, which had the inevitable effect of whittling away at the freedom of these once sovereign peoples. The power of the Protector to terminate contracts of labour entered into by Amerindians[1] was retained, adorned with drastic embellishments. Employment of Amerindians could only take place with the permission of the Protector, and this applied even to employment relationships existing before the Ordinance (*AIPO* 1910:section 20). Permits were only valid for six months, and had to be renewed upon application to the Protector, who of course had the power to revoke the permission at any time and dispatch the employee to a reservation (*AIPO* 1910:section 21). Written agreements were also required, to be effected in the presence of the Protector, a justice of the peace or a police constable (*AIPO* 1910:section 23). Finally, breach of these provisions attracted stiff penalties, and the Protector had overall power to supervise the employment, which included inspecting the employee (*AIPO* 1910:section 24). While these provisions were admittedly designed to protect Amerindians from exploitation, they espoused indiscriminate powers, and it is not clear from the records how effective they were in practice. Certainly, in the post-independence period, and up to the end of the century – until which, remarkably, they survived – they were routinely ignored, and trotted out only by activists to bemoan the plight of Guyana's native peoples.

In the spirit of the provisions relating to employment was a clause added in the 1910 legislation that conferred upon the Protector sweeping powers relating to Amerindian property, both movable and immovable.

This clause empowered him to take possession of Amerindian property and sell or dispose of it as he saw fit. Subsidiary powers related to the instituting of legal action for the recovery of property, or damages related thereto, and to appointment of an attorney or agent to act on behalf of the Amerindian owner. In fact, the rather loose drafting of the provision, by empowering the Protector to 'exercise in the name of an Indian any power which the Indian might exercise for his own benefit' (*AIPO* 1910:section 17), was a veritable carte blanche for Protectors over the property of Amerindians. Significantly, these powers could be exercised without the consent of the Amerindian owner, if necessary for the 'due preservation of the property' (*AIPO* 1910:section 17).

Many of the offences of the previous Ordinance were retained, supplemented by additional ones designed to give force to the various provisions of the new law. One in particular, however, deserves mention, and that concerns the extensive prohibitions implemented in 1910 relating to the consumption of alcohol by indigenous peoples (*AIPO* 1910:Part V). This was certainly not unique to British Guiana,[2] and reflected a widely held opinion that Amerindians could not tolerate, or regulate, consumption of intoxicating drinks. Whatever the merit in such a view, the provisions of the law were particularly draconian. Non-Amerindians were prohibited from selling or otherwise supplying intoxicating liquor to Amerindians, and could face fines as well as forfeitures for breach of this prohibition. These prohibitions even extended to customary drinks such as *piwari*, and mere presence at a ceremony where such drinks were consumed constituted an offence, if occurring outside of a three-month period specified in the Ordinance. Amerindians found in a state of intoxication could be indefinitely detained until sober, in addition to facing other penalties relating to drunkenness. These powers could be exercised by any police or rural constable 'without process of law', which meant that no neutral arbiter such as magistrate or judge need sanction the arrest and detention. Compounding such an egregious invasion of personal liberty was the total discretion entrusted to the police, who alone could decide what amounted to intoxication and the length of any detention, without any clear guidelines or safeguards laid down in the Ordinance.

Rounding off these provisions was the extension of the powers granted to the Governor over Amerindians, not confined to those living on the reservations. As before, he was entrusted with appointing the Protector of Indians and his deputies as well as captains and constables, and could terminate all such appointments in his discretion. In addition, the 1910 Ordinance specified far more intrusive powers. While some of these covered relatively innocuous matters – for example, the Governor was entrusted with budgeting the spending of public moneys for Amerindians, defining the duties of the Protector, sub-protectors, superintendents, captains and constables, and making regulations governing entry onto a reserve by non-Amerindians – other powers contained far more sinister implications. Thus the Governor was empowered to make regulations providing for 'the care, custody and education of the children of aboriginals', 'the conditions on which aboriginal or half-caste children may be apprentice to, or placed in service with, suitable persons', 'the control of all Indians and half-castes residing upon a reserve' and the prohibition of 'any rites or customs of aboriginals' which he felt to be injurious to their welfare (*AIPO* 1910:section 8).

This Ordinance endured for another four decades. When it was finally replaced in 1951, the changes in the new legislation focused mainly on strengthening the internal governance provisions of the reservations, restyled 'villages, districts and areas'. Interestingly, the underlying paternalist philosophy survived, and all of Roth's provisions mentioned above – such as those relating to employment, property and the prohibition of alcohol – were retained. The powers of the Governor were also retained, along with the concept of the inviolability of the Amerindian areas – with access to be determined by the Crown through her various officials. Despite sporadic calls for the revision of the Amerindian Act following independence in 1966, this law remained in its original form down to the end of the century, the only major change occurring in 1976 when the Act was amended to confer land titles on 62 named villages. If nothing else then, Roth's changes in 1910 certainly had an enduring effect.

Consultations for a new Act were initiated in 2003, culminating in an entirely revised Amerindian Act in March 2006. Predictably, individual Amerindians as well as their representatives clamoured for the removal of many, if not all, of the 1902 and 1910 provisions. One notable exception, however, concerned those relating to intoxicating liquor. These provisions, undemocratic and archaic as they appear, were not rejected across the board, and both individuals as well as communities advocated for their retention. However, while the statutory prohibitions on alcohol have not been included in the revised Act, it is understood that village councils, in the exercise of their rule-making function, may regulate the sale of supply of intoxicants within the borders of their village.[3] This, essentially, is the approach of the new draft Act – to allow Amerindians to decide for themselves, by and through their own internal procedures. While the influence of the State on Amerindian communities is unmistakably present, the new approach focuses more on strengthening internal procedures of governance and accountability, as well as providing mechanisms for securing titles to land. No longer are Amerindians treated as separate or inferior in terms of their decision-making capacity, insofar as provisions impinging on their freedom to enter into employment, control of property, and control of Amerindian villages and districts have all been discarded.

Roth's Contribution

Guyanese Amerindians today have more secure land rights and legal protections than do indigenous peoples in neighbouring Suriname, French Guiana or Roraima State in Brazil. In spite of the heavy-handed provisions of the Amerindian Ordinances, they provided a secure basis for the protection and administration of intact Amerindian communities. It is not coincidental that Guyanese indigenous peoples have taken a lead role in pressing for reforms to the Amerindian Ordinances, and in lobbying the State to sign or ratify various international conventions relating to indigenous peoples. Walter Roth's work, in both ethnological and legal fields, was pivotal and his legacy can best be appreciated when the indigenous situation in Guyana is compared with those in adjoining territories.

Notes

1. First granted in 1902 by virtue of the *Aboriginal Indians Protection Ordinance*, section 6.
2. Other colonies, such as Canada, also prohibited native peoples from consuming and possessing intoxicating beverages.
3. Amerindian Act, #13 of 2006, s. 14.

Works Cited

Aboriginal Indians Protection Ordinance (AIPO), No 28 of 1910
Adams, William M (2003) 'Nature and the colonial mind', in Mulligan, M (ed), *Decolonizing Nature: Strategies for Conservation in a Post-colonial Era*, London: Earthscan Publications Ltd, 16–50
Collins, Carol (1971) 'A catalogue of the Roth Collection in the University of Guyana Library', ms, 32 pp
Drummond, Lee (1977a) 'On being Carib', in Basso, E (ed), *Carib Speaking Indians: Culture, Society and Language*, Tucson: University of Arizona Press, 76–88
——. (1977b) 'The outskirts of the earth: A study of Amerindian ethnicity on the Pomeroon River, Guyana', PhD dissertation, University of Chicago
Menezes, Mary Noel (1988) 'The Amerindians of Guyana: Original lords of the soil', *América Indígena* XLVIII(2), 353–76

PART 6

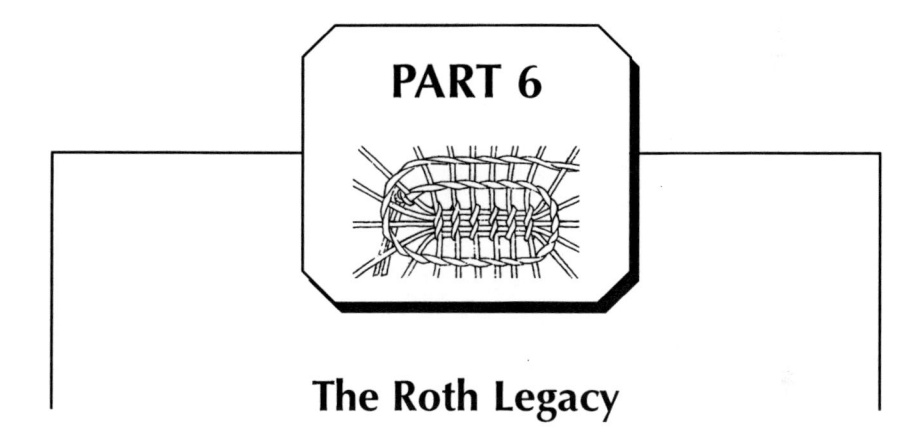

The Roth Legacy

CHAPTER 17

Vincent Roth: The Man, His Life and His Work

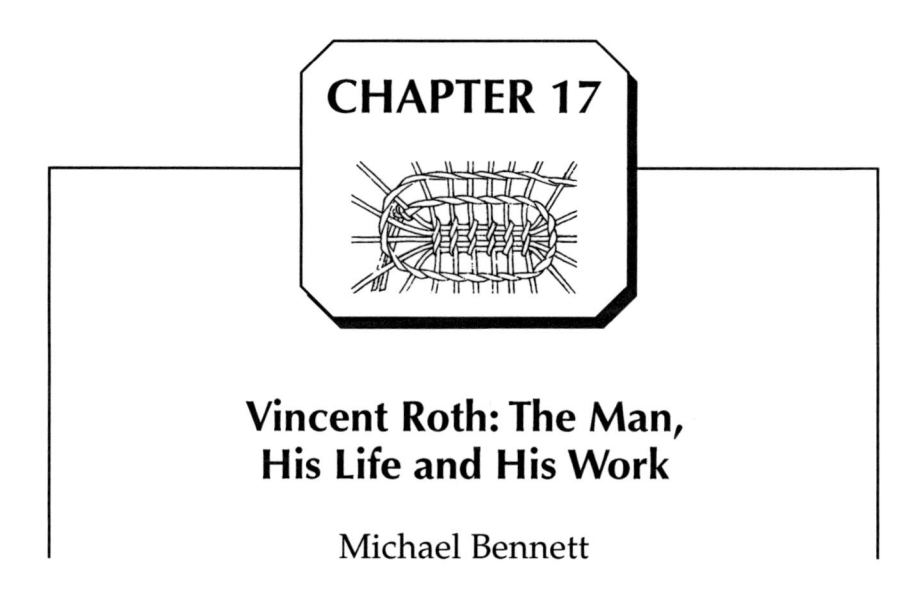

Michael Bennett

Vincent Roth (1889–1967) was placed in a convent at the age of 10 months following the death of his mother. Subsequently he was adopted by a maiden aunt in Scotland and spent his formative years in Scotland, Switzerland and Australia.

Taken to British Guiana by his father, Walter, in 1907, Vincent had to adapt to a completely new way of life in the Land of Six Peoples.

After a false start, Vincent devoted his working life to colonial administration in government service. He took a great interest in the people he met and their way of life, and spread his knowledge in later life by way of newspaper articles, books and radio broadcasts. He rebuilt the Georgetown Museum and became its curator, founded a zoo and was appointed to the Legislative Council.

Early Life

Vincent had a strange, some might say sad, childhood. He was born in Brisbane on 29 September 1889. Shortly after his birth the family moved to South Australia, and then again to Sydney. When he was about 10 months old his mother, Eva, took ill and died. His father, Walter, was in a quandary as to what to do, as he wanted to return to England to qualify as a doctor. After a long discussion with his brother Reuter, Walter decided to leave Vincent in the care of the nuns at the Parramatta Convent.

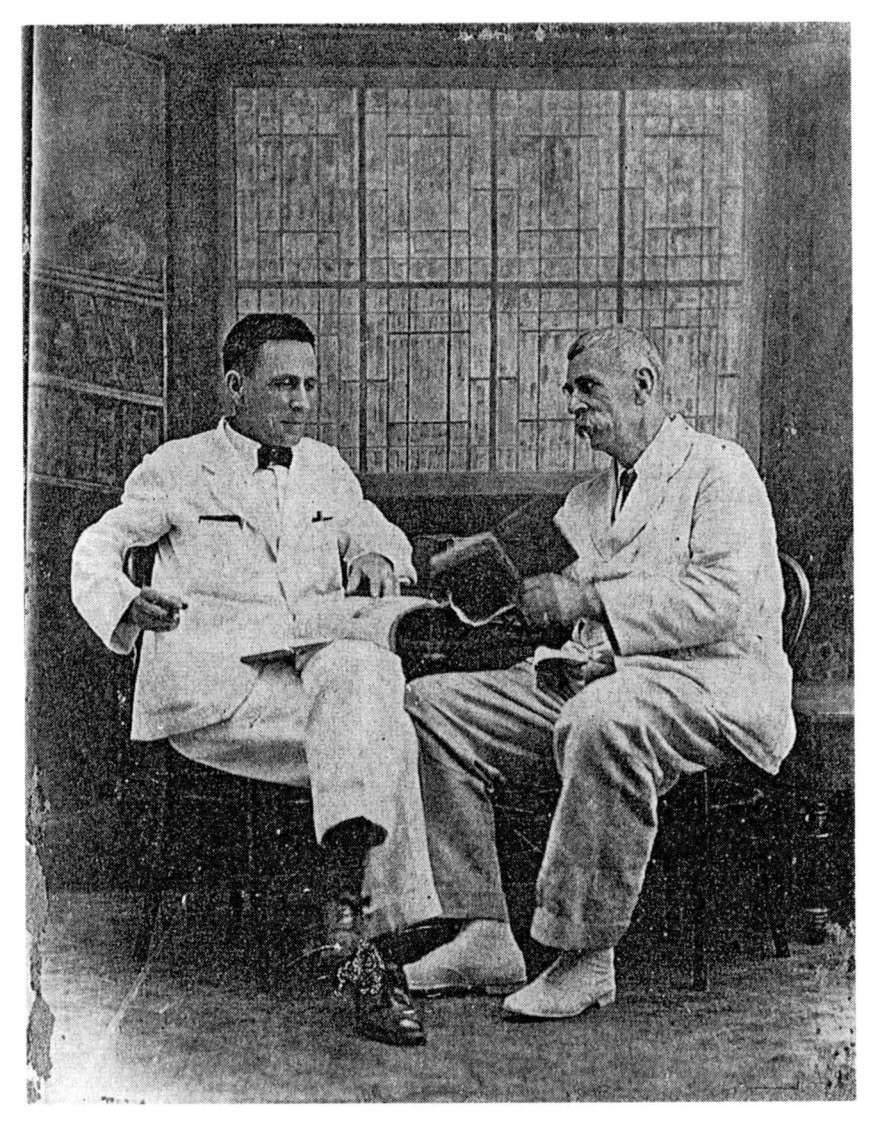

Figure 17.1 Vincent Roth (right) with Walter E Roth

Back in England Walter contacted Eva's family at Strathpeffer in Scotland, who were very keen to see the new addition to the family. Maggie Grant, a spinster, said she would love to bring up young Vincent as her own. Walter agreed to this and made arrangements for Reuter and his wife, who were planning a trip to Europe, to bring young Vincent with them.

Looking out of a bedroom window one day he was fascinated to see that a large construction project was under way: a railway line was being brought into the town. He spent many an hour in the garden watching the small trains of little dump trucks building the embankments and listening to the hooting of the construction locomotives. He became so enthusiastic that he cut out little flat models of them and pretended that he too was building a railway on the floor of the morning room. Vincent had not been long installed in his new home when his Grandmother Roth, retired in Divonne (France), said that she too would like to see her new grandson. But for some reason, perhaps due to the recent death of her husband, Vincent did not go to his grandmother's, and instead he was boarded out with a lady and her son in Geneva. After several years there his carer became ill, and so Vincent finally went to live with his grandmother and maiden aunt Julia.

Soon after his seventh birthday it was decided that Vincent's formal education should begin; and not long after this he found himself back in Strathpeffer with his Aunt Maggie, who ran a large boardinghouse for summer visitors to the spa village. At last Vincent was able to enter into some semblance of a normal family life, as here he had aunts, uncles and numerous cousins.

One event that Vincent looked forward to was the annual visit to Strathpeffer by the Bastock and Wombells Circus. A week before its arrival the village was placarded with gaily coloured posters depicting lions, elephants, beautiful scantily dressed ladies standing on horses similar pictures calculated to excite young minds. For several weeks after the departure of the show all Vincent's spare time was spent making cardboard models of the caravan cages with the animals inside. Model making was to be a hobby of Vincent's throughout his life.

When Vincent moved to Dingwall Academy his route from the station took him past a taxidermist. He was fascinated by the exhibits in the display window: fishing rods, fly hooks, shotguns, rifles, gaffs and landing nets. One day Vincent accosted the old man who was its owner, saying he was interested in bird-stuffing. To his surprise, he was accepted as an unpaid apprentice on Saturday afternoons. Thus was he introduced into the mysteries of skinning scalpels, arsenical soap, brain scoops, bone saws and glass eyes, which was to stand him in good stead for a life to be spent in the bush.

It was in Dingwall that Vincent heard a rumour that two elderly ladies had returned from a trip to Australia where they had met a Dr Walter Roth, the father of one of those 'Strathpeffer scamps'. Vincent asked his Aunt Maggie to arrange a meeting with the ladies. This was duly done, and during the conversation one of the ladies was heard to say 'and she is such a nice woman too'. So Vincent learnt that he had a stepmother, a subject never mentioned by his father in any letter to him or his aunt. Vincent immediately wrote to his father saying, now that he had a mother could he join them in Australia?

Family Life

Vincent thus was reunited with his father and met for the first time his new 'mother'. This probably was the time that he was first introduced to anthropology. One room in the family home at Sherwood in Queensland was known as 'Dad's Museum', but it was also used as an office, and as Vincent's study. The walls were lined with many shelved cupboards that contained the large collection of Aboriginal artefacts, tools, toys, weapons and household goods Walter had amassed in North Queensland – each well docketed and described – all overshadowed by a large bark canoe slung up in the roof of the short verandah outside the museum.

Vincent enrolled at Brisbane Grammar School and a new era in his life began. During term his daily routine was fairly consistent. He would get up about six o'clock and do schoolwork until breakfast. After breakfast he would write up his diary and practise the bugle, finishing in time to catch the 8.38 am from the nearby station to Brisbane. Once or twice a week there would be band practice during the lunch hour. After school, unless he went to see his father in his office, he caught the 4.10 pm train home. As soon as he got home he would polish his bugle, press his cadet uniform or develop photographs until suppertime, after which he would have an evening session with his tutor. Saturday mornings he would chop firewood, mow the lawn or perform some other household chore. He would then clean his rifle and perhaps do some modelling with his friends. On Sundays, after bringing his diary up to date he would write to his grandmother and Aunt Maggie. During the holidays he sailed on the Brisbane River with his friends, one of whose father owned a small yacht.

At the beginning of 1905 Vincent moved to Maryborough Grammar School. But in May the following year he received a letter from his father telling him to return home. His father, at this time, was being vilified in the national press regarding certain alleged offences in relation to Aborigines (see Chapters 11, 12 and 14 in this volume). To save his family any embarrassment, Walter decided to send Vincent with his stepmother to Tasmania to finish his education.

British Guiana

But then his father decided to leave Australia and to accept the post of Government Medical Officer and Magistrate in the Pomeroon District of British Guiana (now Guyana). Before 1831 the country consisted of three colonies. Essequibo lay to the west and was separated from Berbice by Demerara. Essequibo and Berbice were the first colonised by the Dutch. Demerara was developed later, and was occupied by the British, French, Dutch and finally the British again. To this day it is the only coastal strip of Guyana that is fully developed.

The first inhabitants were the Amerindian tribes, who are thought to have migrated east from Asia, through North and Central America to South America, where they spread out over the continent. In the 18th and 19th centuries there were many 'tribes'. But by the beginning of the 20th century there were less than a dozen remaining, the chief among which were the Akawaio, Wapisiana, Macusi, Arecuna, Warrau, Carib, Arawak, Patamona and, in the far south of the country, the Wai-Wai.

In the Dutch provinces Negro slaves were imported from Africa; and when slavery was abolished in 1834 the question arose as to who would take their place. Efforts were made to import free Negroes from the West Indies but this met with little success. Considerable numbers of Portuguese from Madeira were brought in then, but they found the climate and work too onerous; and those that did not fall sick and die drifted into the towns to become peddlers and small shopkeepers.

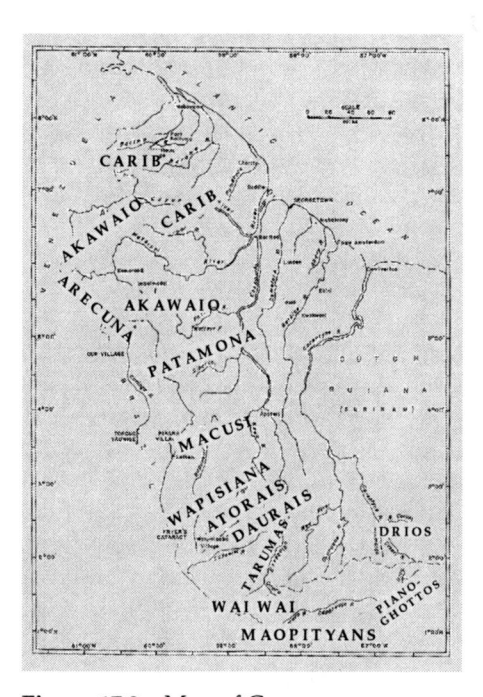

Figure 17.2 Map of Guyana

In Mauritius it was discovered that East Indians worked well in the cane fields. So recruitment began in Calcutta and Bombay for indentured labour. Soon boatloads of Indians began to arrive in the Colony. The final influx of cheap labour was from China. They founded a settlement at Hopetown on a creek off the Demerara River, some 20 miles south of Georgetown, from where they later spread through the Colony. Thus British Guiana became known as the Land of Six Peoples: Amerindians, Africans, Portuguese, Indians, Chinese and Europeans. Each brought their own language and culture, mosques, temples and churches (all built along the coastal fringe). English remained the official language.

A False Start

This was the world into which Vincent and his father arrived on 1 March 1907. After a few days in the capital they were taken to their new abode at Marlborough, on the Pomeroon. As they had on the ship, the pair would get up in the morning and do their club exercises and practise their step dancing. When his father was away performing his duties as Protector or collecting anthropological information, Vincent continued with shorthand and learning German, and reading Im Thurn's *Among the Indians of Guiana*. The rest of the day was spent in butterfly or insect hunting. He paid two boys one penny each for every 10 insects they caught. Apart from his father and the local parson, Vincent was the only European in the district. This brought him into close contact with Akawoio, Arawak and Warrau peoples.

After several months, however, Vincent told his father that he did not think that 'life in the bush' was for him. So it was decided that he would go to Georgetown and try his fortune with one of the large commercial firms.

A First Career

He settled for one as a junior reporter with the *Argosy*. His duties included daily police court reporting (which he did not like), revising district notes sent in by largely illiterate correspondents, punctuating cables and revising printed 'copy'. He also reviewed magazine articles. He visited the banks for the rates of exchange and the Lands and Mines Department for the gold returns. On one occasion the editor asked him to write up his own impressions of a court trial, from the point of view of a newcomer to the Colony, and Vincent was very proud when he saw the opening paragraphs of the article in the paper that were his own. But after seven weeks the work began to pall and he handed in his notice. The editor was sorry to lose him and said he would accept any articles that Vincent sent him.

Then Vincent went to see the Commissioner of the Lands and Mines Department, sensing that the life of a surveyor might offer what he was looking for. The Commissioner said he would be happy to offer him a job as soon as a vacancy occurred. Vincent returned to the Pomeroon, and started to accompany the Lands and Mines district surveyor on his rounds. The surveyor was a Creole who had been to England for his education. Vincent also accompanied his father when he held Court; and this was of use to him when he finally joined the Lands and Mines Department in February 1909, as Land Officer on the Demerara River, based at Christianburg.

His post incorporated the following offices: Land Officer, Government Surveyor, Sub-Protector of Indians, Deputy Officer in Charge of Navigation on the Essequibo and its tributaries, Commissary of Taxation, Inspector of Weights and Measures, Inspector of Schools, Inspector of Post Offices, President of the Local Board of Guardians, Justice of the Peace and Superintendent Registrar, which included the post of Marriage Officer and Gold Sub-warden. His district was about 250 miles long with an average width of 20 miles and a population of about 8,000. He held his first post at the age of 20.

One problem he encountered early in his career, when he was not so sure of the law he had to administer, concerned an old Indian and his family. He had four daughters, each with her man living with her, each in their own house round the old man's, on Crown Land. One had a full-blooded Indian, two had Negroes and the fourth an East Indian. The problem was that the two Negroes and the East Indian were trespassers: how could they put themselves in order without either giving up the girls and leaving the place, or taking the girls away from their parental home, or buying homesteads there (which in most cases would have interfered with the old man's rights as an aboriginal of the country)? In the case of the East Indian his house was sufficiently removed from the others to enable him to buy a homestead. With regard to the Negroes, Vincent put the problem to the Commissioner to solve.

His transfer to the more remote North West District, seven years later, brought him in contact with many more indigenous Amerindians; and he was able to study their customs and way of life in great detail. As there were no government rest houses, he spent his nights in their villages. Moving along the various trails and fields his eyes were constantly on the ground, not only looking out for deadly snakes, but alert also for shards of pottery, beads and other artefacts discarded by previous inhabitants. He produced drawings of all of his finds in great detail, having an artistic hand like his father, his Uncle Henry Ling and his Aunt Edith.

Most of the villages that Vincent visited were inhabited by Caribs. He noted that both sexes were on average taller than the Warraus and

Arawaks with whom he was better acquainted. All the men and most of the women were naked except for their 'laps', strips of red or yellow cloth passing under the body and over a belt of beads, the ends adorned with beads and cotton fringe hanging down before and behind. These have been called 'loincloths' by some travellers, which they are not, as they do not enfold the loins, only the crotch. The Caribs called this garment *camisiari*, probably a corruption of the Spanish *kamisa*.

One problem in these villages was that when the inhabitants were having a *paiwarri* drinking party, Negro 'pork-knockers' in the district would wait until it was well under way and then creep into the village to interfere with the womenfolk. Vincent would hold Court and punish the Negroes by either a fine or imprisonment depending on the severity of the case.

Vincent was also involved in attempts to curb *balata* smuggling, which was one of the main causes for concern in the North West District. In years gone by the forests of the district were most prolific in bulletwood trees, which was the source of the gum known as *balata* used extensively in the manufacture of machinery belting. The legal method of bleeding a bullet tree in the Colony was to cut notches around half the circumference but only as far up as the first branch. This would produce on average four to five gallons of latex. When the scars were thoroughly healed, in four to five years' time, the other half of the tree's circumference could be bled. The operation was then repeated at similar intervals. In Venezuela, however, it was the practice to fell the tree and bleed it along its entire length. By this method the yield for each tree was some 15 to 20 gallons. The latex was boiled and poured into condensed milk boxes to harden. Each block averaged 20 pounds of dried *balata*, and this block *balata* was known as 'Venezuelan Balata', distinguishing it from the 'Sheet Balata' prepared by lawful methods in British Guiana.

On the principle of 'getting rich' quickly the Venezuelan practice soon spread across the border. Block balata was smuggled out of the Colony then brought back to a British customs house where it was declared as 'Venezuelan Balata'. In order to stop the destruction of bullet trees, the government ordered that no block balata could enter the Colony and that possession of it was illegal. This had little effect, as the product was simply smuggled out to Venezuela and sold there. Efforts to catch the illicit bleeders continued with less rather than more success until, at length, the drop in the balata market brought the industry to a close around 1920.

During the Mazaruni gold and diamond rush in the late 1920s Vincent was stationed at a settlement called Kamakusa. The influx of miners into the district caused the owners of the boats that transported the 'pork-knockers' to build bigger and more powerful boats, and to overload them to a dangerous level, which led to many tragic accidents in the falls of the turbulent Mazaruni River. Vincent was very disturbed by these events and so set about revising the River Navigation Regulations, which were amended accordingly in an effort to prevent similar disasters.

The diamond rush, as might be expected, brought an influx of women, the majority of whom were politely called 'women of the fields'. Some did in fact buy mining privileges and had their own registered labourers. However, the majority of the women were prostitutes. In order to pay for their favours, many shopkeepers and their assistants engaged in petty crime whose presence encouraged shopkeepers and their assistants to engage in petty crime, stealing goods and money and, in some cases, even diamonds from their employers. The situation rapidly got out of hand, and some of the leading traders approached the Commissioner of Lands and Mines to place some restriction on women moving into the diamond fields. The Commissioner responded by stopping the issue of mining titles to women; and the Warden at Bartica, the gateway to the diamond fields, then refused female domestics to proceed up the Mazaruni. This led to another outcry from the traders, that their 'housekeepers' were prevented from returning to the district. So the Commissioner had to backtrack, allowing housekeepers and domestics to be registered with their employers. Vincent's task was to check that the employees were with their respective employers. But after a while it became too time-consuming, and the Warden-Magistrate decided that the government would not want him chasing prostitutes about the district.

A Second Career

When in 1935 he retired from Government Service due to ill health, Vincent joined a local newspaper as second editor, contributing articles and also writing books about the flora and fauna of the Colony. *Notes and Observations on Animal Life in British Guiana* was published in 1941 based on 30 years of living in the bush. The book contains 54 illustrations from photographs and drawings by the author. In the Foreword to *Notes and Observations on Fish Life in British Guiana* (1943), Vincent wrote, 'The kind reception afforded by the public to my "Animal Life in British Guiana", encouraged me to proceed with the compilation of a similar volume on the local fishes... The coloured frontispiece and all but three of the black-and-white illustrations are from my own paintings and drawings'.

He also made weekly radio broadcasts on these subjects. In 1943 he was one of the first nominated members of the Legislative Council to be appointed by the King. Vincent represented Mining and Interior Interests and, in 1947 when re-elected for a second term, Interior, Forestry and Mines.

In 1945 a disastrous fire caused devastation in the Georgetown city centre. One of the buildings destroyed was the Georgetown Museum (now known as the National Museum), of which Vincent was then the Curator, as his father was before him. Nothing could be saved, and Vincent was later responsible for rebuilding and restocking the museum. He made several scale models of the city before the fire. He also made and donated a set of panels of parquetry wainscoting in the Hall of Anthropology. Each panel consisted of over 2,400 pieces of wood donated by the Forestry Department: brown silverballi, manni, purpleheart and white cedar. The design depicted such items as canine genitalia in the centre, periwinkle shell at the ends and a Wapisiani circular basket. Sadly some of these panels are no longer on public view (it is assumed they were removed by a later administration). Having re-established the Museum, Vincent started a zoo in the Botanical Gardens. When anthropologists Clifford Evans and Betty Meggers from the Smithsonian Institution came to the Colony in 1952, Vincent acted as their guide and mentor. Sadly he did not live long enough to see the establishment of the Walter Roth Museum of Anthropology, where most of the Meggers' artefacts are now housed.

Works Cited

Im Thurn, Everard Ferdinand (1883) *Among the Indians of Guiana: Being Sketches, Chiefly Anthropologic from the Interior of British Guiana*, London: Kegan Paul & Co

Roth, Vincent (1943) *Notes and Observations on Fish Life in British Guiana 1907–1903*, Georgetown: Daily Chronicle

———. (1941) *Notes and Observations on Animal Life in British Guiana*, Georgetown: Daily Chronicle

CHAPTER 18

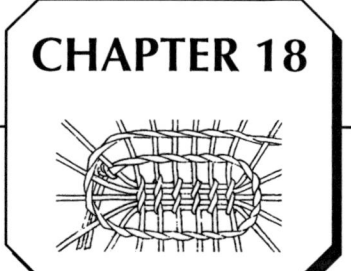

George Kingsley Roth and the Fijian Way of Life

Julian Croft

First a word of explanation. I am not an anthropologist, an historian or a political scientist. I came to my subject in a round-about way which needs a short explanation. I have spent my academic life as a literary critic, a teacher of literature and a literary historian. One of my subjects of research was (and still is) the Australian poet RD FitzGerald, who, as well as being a significant mid-20th century Australian poet, practised as a surveyor all his working life. He spent the middle 1930s in Fiji surveying boundaries for the Native Lands Commission, and in the 1980s, through my research for an edition of his work I read a number of books on Fiji of the 1930s, and particularly what informed the official policy on land holdings. One of the books I read was the second edition of George Kingsley Roth's *Fijian Way of Life*, published by Oxford University Press in Melbourne in 1973. I remembered it because it was redolent in style and tone of the kind of colonial administrative writing I had experienced when I taught at Fourah Bay College in Freetown, Sierra Leone, in the 1960s. That style is discursive, lucid, jargon-free and humane.

In 2001 Russell McDougall spoke to me about the work he was doing on Henry Ling Roth and his career in the old Empire and the new Commonwealth. He also mentioned Walter Roth in Queensland. The name was familiar, and I was sure I knew it was somehow related to Fiji, but these Roths seemed to be of another generation. Russell knew immediately the relationship between the Fiji Roth and his subjects. He was Henry Ling's son, about whom people seemed to know little, and there had been no interest expressed in him for the upcoming Roth

Figure 18.1 George Kingsley Roth (right) with Henry Ling Roth (Reproduced with the permission of Michael Bennett)

Family Conference in 2004 which provided the basis for this book. That surprised me at the time, as GK Roth had obviously had a long and distinguished career in Fijian colonial administration, and he had written many anthropological articles and some books, one of which I discovered on my own shelves after the conversation with Russell: *The Story of Fiji* (nd) written for schoolchildren and published by Oxford in Melbourne in the early 1960s, which I bought in Suva in 1963 on my first visit to the islands.

I then re-read parts of *Fijian Way of Life* for a collaborative project Russell and I had in mind (see Croft & McDougall 2005), and when I did, I read, possibly for the first time, but certainly with close attention this time, the Introduction to the second edition by GB Milner (Professor of Austronesian Studies, School of Oriental and African Studies, University of London) for some biographical information. There was little biographical information, however the introduction was a revelation. For here was a story which placed GK Roth right in the middle of one of the most important debates of the late 20th century: the colonial and postcolonial views on indigenous land rights and individual and communal identities.

Unfashionable Views

Writing in 1973 in the Introduction to the second edition of Roth's *Fijian Way of Life*, Milner made no bones about why the 1953 edition was being republished:

> The organisation of the Fijian Administration, as it is described in Chapter IV of this book, was the foundation on which post-war reconstruction and economic development had been put in hand. It was hoped that the new legislation and administrative changes would provide a firm basis for the growth of larger and stronger villages, and that it would stem the drift of young able-bodied Fijians into towns. Encouragement of communal enterprises run on traditional lines was to promote greater productivity and this in turn would facilitate the provision of better social services ...
> ... [In the 1960s] in a succession of articles and books the traditional policy of Fijian Administration described in this present book has been repeatedly attacked. It has been alleged, for instance, that it was founded on a misunderstanding of the structure of Fijian society and of the principles of land tenure in pre-European times. It was said that, serious as this was, matters were made worse by the lack of provision either for the diversity of social structure in different parts of Fiji, or for organic growth and demographic fluctuations. Instead, the social reality had been forced into a procrustean bed designed by misinformed administrators intent only on adhering to the dogma and orthodoxy established once and for all in the 1870s and the 1880s. The Fijian Administration was declared to be not only paternalistic in its approach but constrictive and inhibiting in its practice. It was accused of stifling all the natural Fijian enterprise, energy and initiative which, had there been less wrong-headed administrative meddling above and less executive muddling below, would soon have transformed the situation ...

and he concluded:

> ... It is not my purpose to list or examine all the charges that have been made against the Colonial policy and administration represented by Roth and Sukuna. They are dead and, in our iconoclastic age, it seems to be the favourite sport of many to belittle the achievements of the dead (Roth 1973:xxii–xxiii).

When I read this I knew that here was an answer to a question which had been worrying me for some time. When Russell first suggested I write something on GK Roth for the Roth Family Conference, and after I had established the outline of his biography, I turned to the histories and studies of Fijian colonial rule and found to my amazement that he did not appear in the indexes of most of them. How could this be? Now I had an answer. His opinions and actions as a colonial administrator were deeply unfashionable and, if Milner is to be followed, positively antipathetic to most writers from 1960 onwards. And why was this? We need now to turn to Roth's biography, his career as a colonial administrator, and the history of Fijian colonial administration to understand why his contribution was so important to that colony (and the nation as it is now), and so contested through active erasure over the last four decades.

Family Background

My main source for Roth's biography is the short summary provided by Michael Bennett to Russell McDougall in 2002. George Kingsley Roth was possibly named after Mary Kingsley, the African explorer and member of the equally interesting Kingsley family of writers and travellers, and it is a cipher for the closely knit sense of purpose and idealism which informed that generation of British imperialists. He was born in 1903 at Halifax in Yorkshire, where Henry Ling was Keeper of the Bankfield Museum. Both he and his brother Alfred attended the Hipperholme Grammar School, and then Liverpool University where Kingsley (as he seems to have been known in the family) graduated with Honours. His father had wanted him to go to Cambridge to read Anthropology under Henry's old friend Dr Alfred Haddon (1855–1940). Family finances would not stretch that far, and it was not until 1931 that he entered Christ's College, Cambridge, to complete a Diploma in Anthropology in 1933 under his college's tutor, Mr Grose, and later a Master of Science in 1937, which was awarded for two years of research.

Henry Ling died in 1925, and after his death Kingsley applied to the Colonial Office for a post in the Far East, and in 1929 he was offered a post as a District Officer in Fiji (as far east as it was possible to go). Apart from a period in 1937–38 in Zanzibar and various home leaves, Fiji was to be his home until he retired in 1957. He seems to have adjusted to Pacific life easily, possibly because of his academic interests. As his biographer notes, 'For a young expatriate life in Fiji could be lonely, the only leisure pursuits were drink, women or anthropology. Kingsley chose the last option' (Bennett nd). Perhaps this is an important point as to the enigma of his later reputation (or lack of it). Kingsley Roth was the first of a generation of professionally trained anthropologists, following in the footsteps of the enthusiasts of the late 19th century, of which his father was a splendid example. Nor did his formal training make him feel distinct from that previous generation. His *Fijian Way of Life* bears as its dedication the simple words *'In affectionate memory of my father H. Ling Roth'*. His meticulous accounts of the material culture of Fijians and their social practices in professional journals and in his major book and his ease with the language and its history are indicative of a close and lifelong observation of a society he felt it was his professional duty to nurture within the original terms of the Deed of Cession of the Fiji Islands to Queen Victoria in 1874.

In 1937 he married Jane Violet Coats, a New Zealander. They had no children, and his biographer notes that that may have been 'a joint decision ... as Kingsley suffered from chronic diabetes' (Bennett nd). His marriage coincided with his reassignment to Zanzibar, and on their return to Fiji immediately prior to World War Two, the Governor wanted Roth to transfer to Tonga. He refused, although this was apparently in the face of official policy which preferred that colonial officers move about; although Roth's biographer speculates that the Governor might have been uneasy with officers 'who had been in a particular location longer than they had and possibly knew more about the people and their customs than they did' (Bennett nd). Roth's deep and affectionate knowledge of the Fijian way of life may have been another negative for the post-1960 generation of scholars and commentators who were part of the debate on Fiji's future as a multiracial, pluralist, independent nation.

The Second World War was a stressful time in Fiji. For a few months in 1942 it looked as if a Japanese invasion was possible, and with it the breaking of sea contact between Australia and the United States. Mobilisation within Fiji and the presence of many foreign troops had a deep effect on traditional village life, as it did in many colonial traditional cultures in the Pacific. Arising from those changes was the challenge of post-war planning and a social programme to address wartime stresses. Roth was intimately part of that process, and his beliefs and the policies the Administration pursued (which were to be so roundly criticised later) are explained in detail in his major work.

In 1954 Roth was made Secretary for Fijian Affairs, a position which involved working with the indigenous arm of government which had been set up post-war. He was in this position until he retired in 1957. During his working life in Fiji Roth had kept up an active interest in field anthropology, publishing papers in important journals on many aspects of Fijian life: house building, tattooing, fire walking, pottery, the making of bark cloth. He had intended to use his retirement to write up more of this material but unfortunately he died at the early age of 57 in 1960. He was awarded the Order of the British Empire in 1954, and was made a Companion of the Order of St Michael and St George for his services to the Colonial Office in 1957.

Family members described him as 'the most kind, patient, and generous man one could wish to meet, willing to listen to anyone, an understanding man with a quick sense of humour' (Bennett nd). He seems to have had warm relations with the Fijian people, and, even to his critics – such as Spate in his 1959 report – Roth's view of Fijian society is understandable, though wrong and out of date (Spate 1959:7–8).

But why did such humane, considered and carefully researched views seem so totally right in 1953 (the year of *Fijian Way of Life*), and so totally wrong in 1959 (the year of the first of the revisionist reports)?

GK Roth in the Context of Fijian History

That has to do with Fijian history. The Fiji Islands came into the British Empire through a voluntary Deed of Cession negotiated by Sir Hercules Robinson, Governor of New South Wales, and the Fijian chief Cakobau in 1874. In it the Fijians asked for British external protection while having their customary law and the possession of their lands respected by the Crown. The Colonial Administrators would protect these interests while governing indirectly through a graduated series of indigenous officials. Generations of Fijians have since marvelled at this agreement when they looked beyond their shores to see what had happened in New Caledonia, Australia, Tahiti, New Zealand and Hawaii. It is, for us, paradoxical, that as the colourful (ie a racehorse-owning bon vivant) figure of Sir Hercules Robinson was negotiating this enlightened agreement, the indigenous inhabitants of his own colony were sinking into a state of landless anomie from which they have scarcely recovered.

The first Governor of Fiji, and the man who was to implement the Deed, was Sir Arthur Gordon, First Lord Stanmore, one of the luminaries of British colonial administration in the late 19th century. He too was a familiar figure to me. My first wife's great-grandfather had crossed swords with him when he was Governor of Mauritius in the early 1870s. Her ancestor, Adolphe de Plevitz, had successfully agitated for a Royal Commission into the treatment of indentured Indian labourers in the sugar plantations. Local planters tried to assassinate him, and although Gordon was sympathetic to the cause, he was not happy with the degree of local commotion caused by de Plevitz. The ancestor consequently left, and went, unfortunately, to Fiji, where to both men's dismay Gordon was appointed as Governor.

Gordon's liberal disposition was not tried so sorely in Fiji. He could implement the policies of the Deed without the resistance of a large body of planters who, as in the case of Mauritius, had been there for generations. Land was still mainly in Fijian hands; tribal war was waning; missionaries had introduced education and Christianity, which the Fijians seemed to have accepted enthusiastically; and in a few years Gordon was able to set up a robust network of governance through indirect rule (a model which was to be copied with some success in West Africa several decades later). He learnt the language, and he had an enthusiastic and very hard-working Colonial Secretary, Thurston, who later became Governor after Gordon left and went on to the more immediate problems of New Zealand and the Parihaka land rights crisis. Thurston consolidated Gordon's policies, and held the line against agitation from European entrepreneurs wanting easy access to Fijian land. Subsequent Governors from around the turn of the 20th century were not so sympathetic, and only intervention by Gordon, as Lord Stanmore, in the House of Lords in 1908, prevented major losses of land tenure. This was still the situation when Roth arrived in the colony in the late 1920s, but the attack on indigenous land tenure, together with a debate on restricting the privileges of the Fijian aristocracy, of breaking down Fijian communal identity to create a more individualistic Fijian more pliable to the needs of industrial capitalism, still occupied the minds of the 'progressive' colonists.

The great difference between the Fiji of Gordon and Thurston and that of Roth's time was the consequences of the introduction of Indian indentured labour to work the colonial copra and sugar plantations. Gordon's experience in Mauritius of the benefits of sugar and the fact that he would not have to call on Fiji labour or disturb their lands was behind his decision to encourage the importation of indentured labour from the subcontinent from the late 1870s onwards (Gillion 1977:2–3). By the time Roth arrived in the Colony, the indenture system had been abolished but the status and future of the Indians who remained in Fiji were undefined and destined to become a major political issue. By the end of the Second World War the Fiji Indians 'had been transformed from a collection of poor plantation labourers into a diversified ... community which was racked by disunity and conflict' (Gillion 1977: vii). They also outnumbered the indigenous Fijians whose land, custom and privileges depended on the continuance of European power (Gillion 1977:199).

Nothing is said of the Indian population in Roth's book, which, though striking, is defensible because the book is about the Fijian way of life, its traditions and its current organisation. Nevertheless, the 'Indian problem', as it was called would not go away, and it was the 'principal question of Fiji history at the time [1920–46]' (Gillion 1977: vii), and it had to be addressed. Roth's close ally in the development of the post-war policies which were to cause so much trouble from 1960 was a most remarkable Fijian leader, Ratu Sir Lala Sukuna (1888–1958), whose life work of preserving Fijian ways while recognising the aspirations of the Fiji Indians provided the foundation for the post-war policies of the colonial administration.

Sukuna was an aristocrat descended from Cakobau's family, a graduate in law from Wadham College, Oxford, a barrister of the Middle Temple and a decorated (*Médaille Militaire*) soldier in the French Foreign Legion (1914–16), which he had had to join as the British Army would not accept him because he was coloured. It was Sukuna who did most in holding the line for indigenous Fijian interests between the wars. His modifications of social, economic and political policies embodied in the Fijian Affairs Ordinance, the Native Lands Ordinance, the Native Lands Trust Ordinance and the Fijian Development Fund Ordinance continued for almost a century the outlines Gordon had proclaimed in the 1870s.

With Roth's retirement and Sukuna's death within a year of each in 1957–58, Gordon's dispensation could not be maintained. The winds of change were sweeping Africa, and most of the colonies there would be independent by the middle of the 1960s. What of Fiji? The sticking points, as everyone knew, were the rights of the Fiji Indians, now a substantial majority in the islands. Constitutional debate, economic reform and a sense that a climacteric of sorts was upon them persuaded the indigenous Fijian to some concessions. Under this kind of pressure, and a haste to arrive at some constitution by the end of the decade, it was little wonder that the two reports commissioned by the Colonial Government in 1959 by Professor Spate into the economic problems and prospects of the Fijian people, and the Burns report (for the Colonial Office) on the natural resources and population trends of the colony (1959), should argue that policies which protected indigenous Fijian communal ways of life were inimical to the kinds of adjustments that would have to be made after independence.

A constitution was devised which was based on communal rolls for Fijians, Indians and Europeans, the result being that sheer weight of numbers in one ethnic group could not dominate government. Despite the advantages to the Fijians, the constitution was found wanting in the Rabuka coup of 1986, which led in turn to a more democratic constitution in 1998, and the election of the Chaudry government, headed by the first Indian Prime Minister. That too would not last in face of indigenous Fijian opposition.

Conclusion

To an outsider the situation seems intractable: a large percentage of the land held by indigenous Fijians, Indians making up the majority of the population, a long history of elective apartheid for both communities and an inability to agree on an instrument for sharing political power. These are the consequences of Gordon's two policies: protection of indigenous rights and customs, and the development of an industry which would support the colony without putting great demands on the local population. It was a policy which Roth supported and for which his life's work was a long apologia, both in field research and in his public writing. It was based on the best of intentions and reflected a desire to continue the imperial values of which his father had been part. Milner's impassioned defence of him and Sukuna in 1973 and his then belief that 'the work of Sir Arthur Gordon, Ratu Sir Lala Sukuna and Kingsley Roth has stood the test of time' (Roth 1973:xxxvii) might seem in the light of the two coups and constitutional change to be somewhat optimistic, but I imagine that there would be little doubt that in 2004 few indigenous Fijians would like to exchange their places with the indigenous inhabitants of New Caledonia, New Zealand, Hawaii or Australia.

Kingsley Roth with Ratu Sukuna had preserved a social order which had voluntarily placed itself under the protection of the British crown almost a hundred years before, and had been sustained by the policies of liberal and humane governors. Milner's sense of a betrayal of these ideals by the generation of administrators, commentators and researchers who came after 1960, and his belief that sooner or later the pendulum would return to its proper position once 'the passions and the partisans have been allowed to cool' (Roth 1973:xxiii), is an eloquent testimony to the lucid prose and careful documenting of Roth's 30-year professional commitment to the Fijian people.

Works Cited

Bennett, Michael (nd) Biographical notes on George Kingsley Roth, ms in possession of Russell McDougall, School of English, Communication and Theatre, University of New England, Armidale, NSW, Australia

Burns, Alan (1960) together with Watson, TY and Peacock, AT, *Report of the Commission of Enquiry into the Natural Resources and Population Trends of the Colony of Fiji 1959*, London: Crown Agents

Croft, Julian and McDougall, Russell (2005) 'Henry Ling Roth's and George Kingsley Roth's Pacific anthropology', *Journal of Pacific History* 40(2)

de Plevitz, LRA (1987) *Restless Energy: A Biography of Adolphe de Plevitz*, Port Louis: Mahatma Gandhi Institute

Gillion, KL (1977) *The Fiji Indians: Challenge to European Dominance 1920–1946*, Canberra: ANU Press

Legge, JD (1958) *Britain in Fiji*, London: Macmillan

Macnaught, Timothy J (1982) *The Fijian Colonial Experience: A Study of Neotraditional Order under British Colonial Rule Prior to World War II*, Pacific Research Monographs Number Seven, Canberra: The Australian National University

Mayer, Adrian C (1963) *Indians in Fiji*, London: Oxford University Press

Roth, GK (1973) *Fijian Way of Life*, rev 2nd ed, Melbourne: Oxford University Press (first edition published 1953)

Roth, GK (1951) *Native Administration in Fiji During the Past 75 Years: A Successful Experiment in Indirect Rule*, London: Royal Anthropological Institute of Great Britain and Ireland
———. (ed) (1936) *Fiji: Handbook of the Colony*, Suva: Government Printer
———. (nd) *The Story of Fiji*, Melbourne: Oxford University Press
Scarr, Deryk (1980) *Ratu Sukuna: Solider, Statesman, Man of Two Worlds*, London: Macmillan Education
Snow, PA (1969) *A Bibliography of Fiji, Tonga and Rotuma*, Canberra: Australian National University Press
Spate, OHK (1959) *The Fijian People: Economic Problems and Prospects*, Suva: Government Printer

Index

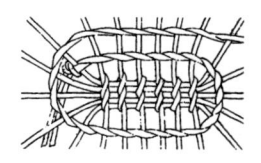

Aboriginal Indians Protection Ordinance (1902), 259–60, 262
Aboriginal Indians Protection Ordinance (1910), 256–58, 263–64
   and Walter Roth, 260–64
Aboriginal Protection Acts (British Guiana), 22, 51
Aboriginals, 16–18, 22, 50, 157–62, 176, 203
   acculturation of, 123
   attitude towards, 177–79
   children of, 49–50, 158, 183, 213, 215, 217
   conception beliefs, 117
   employment of, 18, 49, 210–11, 217
   employment regulation, 157, 159–64, 183, 188–89, 195–96, 213–15
   land claims by, 179
   legislation on, 113
   marriage practices, 201
   offenders, 213–14
   photographs of, 125–26, 193–94, 197–99, 203–04, 221, 228–30
   predicted extinction of, 162
   prisoners, 213, 214, 216
   and procreation, 201
   property of, 215
   regulation of relationships, 18, 162–65, 183, 193–96, 215
   removal of, 19, 121–23, 197–98, 215, 244
   reserves for, 50, 158–59, 189, 213, 214–15
   Roth's principles of welfare, 117–18
   Royal Commission, 19, 50
   and trade, 124–26, 128, 130–31
   treatment of, 121–22, 181, 194, 200, 210, 217, 224
   women abused, 49, 203, 204
   see also Tasmanian Aboriginals
Aboriginals Protection and Restriction of the Sale of Opium Act (1897), 18, 49, 157–60, 181, 194, 202, 217
Aborigines Act (1905), 19, 217
Aborigines Department (Aborigines Protection Board), 210–11
Aborigines Protection Act (1886)
   reforms to, 213
Aborigines Protection Board
   see Aborigines Department
Adams, William, 258–59
Africa, 73, 86, 88
   see also Benin City; Nigeria
African Studies, 73–74
Africans
   in British Guiana, 256
Aghu-Tharrnggala, 143
Akawaio, 271, 272
alcohol, 49, 262, 263–64
Amerindians, 255–57, 273
   employment of, 261
   'first nation' status, 257
   land titles, 257, 258–59, 261, 263, 264
   migration of, 271
   movement curtailed, 261
   registration of, 257–58
   removal of, 261, 263
   reservations for, 256–57, 259, 260–61, 263–64
   women abused, 274
Andaman Islands, 93, 94
Andamanese, 94, 96, 99–100

Andrews, Arthur
Australasian Tokens and Coins, 48
animism, 84
Anthropological Institute of Great Britain and Northern Ireland, 90n16
anthropology, 122–26
  and colonial administration, 88, 99, 201, 209, 217, 236
  and evolution, 117
  and language knowledge, 133–34
  and material culture, 18, 88, 124–25, 128, 130–31, 241, 280–81
  practitioners of, 209
  and the Roth family, 11–13, 15–16, 23–25, 41, 81
  and sexuality, 20
  trained and untrained observers, 68
  see also armchair anthropology; collections; cultural anthropology; descriptive anthropology; fieldwork; functionalist anthropology; photographs; physical anthropology; social anthropology; structuralist anthropology
Anti-Chinese League, 161
Arawaks, 239, 249, 257–58, 271, 272, 274
archaeology, 16–17, 126–27
Arecuna, 271
Argosy, 272
armchair anthropology, 25, 45, 65, 81, 88
artefacts, 172, 179, 270
  see also collections
Asians, 18, 157, 195
  Asian-Aboriginal families, 162–65
  employment of, 161
  exclusion of, 160–62
  'town reserves' for, 160

Association for the Advancement of Science (AAAS), 116
Atherton, 186
Australian Museum, 171–72, 178
  and Roth scandal, 188–90
  and Roth's collections, 176, 178, 187–90
Awngthim, 145
Awu Alwang, 143
axes, 124, 126, 185
Azande sorcery, 252n19

balata (gum) smuggling, 274
Balfour, Henry, 87, 108
bamboo tobacco pipes, 185
Bankfield Museum, 44, 87, 280
Banks, Sir Joseph, 98
  Guugu-Yimidhirr wordlist, 136
Barima River, 235
bark blankets, 184
bark canoe, 270
Barrington-Brown, Charles, 242–43, 251n13
Basedow, Herbert, 230
Bates, Henry, 237
Bauwiwara, 140
Bedford, Admiral Sir Frederick George Denham (Governor of Western Australia), 19, 211
  Niger River exploits, 89n5
Benin bronzes, 75, 87
Benin City, 15
  artefacts from, 74–75, 87
  expedition against, 45, 73, 74–75, 78, 79–80, 87
  press coverage of, 75, 87
  trade potential, 75
Berbice, 271
Birdsell, Joseph, 101
Biri, 140
Biskup, Peter, 210, 216–17
Blake, Barry J, and Gavan Breen
  on Roth's grammar of Pitta-Pitta, 135–36
Blanc, Louis, 37
Blathwayt, Raymond, 78–79

Bloomfield River, 183
body modification, 15, 93–95, 100–101
  classification of, 97–99
  as a racial characteristic, 95, 99
  and social value, 95
  techniques and design in, 97–99
  see also female introcision; introcision
Boehm, Wolfgang, 37
Boggy Creek Reserve, 185
Bolton, Geoffrey, 210, 216–17
Borneo, 64–67
  North Borneo, 61, 62
  Sarawak, 15, 61, 62
  see also Natives of Sarawak and British North Borneo, The (Henry Ling Roth)
Boulia and Cloncurry, 121–26, 130
  archaeological research in, 126–27
Bourne, Gilbert, 109
Brahmanism, 84, 89n13
Breen, Gavan, 135–36
Brett, Rev William, 242–43
Brisbane, 13–14
Brisbane Grammar School, 270
British Guiana, 13, 21–22, 44, 243–44, 267, 270–72
  Aboriginal Protection Ordinance, 22, 51
  Africans in, 256
  East Indians in, 256
  imported labour, 271–72
  Land of Six Peoples, 272
  Natives of, 238–39, 242–43
  Roth's expeditions into the interior, 235–36
British Museum, 188
Brown Goode, Dr G
  'The Principles of Museum Administration', 171–72
Buck, Sir Peter (Te Rangi Hiroa), 16
Burns Philp, 189
Butcher's Hill Station, 185

Cakobau (Fijian chief), 282
canoes, 184, 270
Cape Bedford, 183–84
Cape York Peninsula, 183, 184
  languages of, 141–45
Capell, A, 135
Caribs, 239, 249, 251n9, 257–58, 271, 273–74
Carpentaria, Bishop of, 199–202, 229
cattle killing, 210, 215
ceremonies, 123, 125–26
  photographs of, 123
  and stone arrangements, 129–30
Challenger expedition, 108
Chalmers, Reverend William, 65–67
Chamberlain, Basil Hall
  Aino Folk Tales, 69
Chinese, 157, 160–62
  and Aboriginal employment, 164
  in British Guiana, 272
Chirpal-ji, 141
Chitching-alla ceremony, 125
cicatrisation
  see scarification (cicatrisation)
cicatrix
  see scarification (cicatrisation)
Clifford, James, 88
Coghlan, J, 175
collections, 18, 172–77, 187–90
  from Benin City, 74–75, 87
  content of, 173–74
  of data on 'primitive societies', 122–23
  of Henry Nottridge Moseley, 108
  methods used, 123, 175, 176, 183–87
  of Pitt Rivers Museum, 109
colonial administration
  and anthropology, 11–18, 23–25, 81, 99, 201, 209, 217
  and *kanaimà*, 245–46
  and travel, 236, 237
compendia of native people, 251n11
Conan Doyle, Sir Arthur
  'The sign of four', 100
conception beliefs, 117

Conrad, Joseph
    Heart of Darkness, 75
contraception, 199, 227–28, 229
Cook, Captain James, 94, 98
    Guugu-Yimidhirr wordlist, 136, 137
    Cooktown, 185
coolamons (wooden bowls), 128
Coombes, Annie, 87, 88n2
Crevaux, Jules, 247, 253n21
Cross, Robert, 250n5
Crowley, Terry M
    Grammar of Mpakwithi, 138
Crown lands, 259, 273
Crozet, Julien Marie, 98
cultural anthropology, 25

Dappil, 140
Davidson, Basil, 73
Dawkins, Boyd, 108
de Plevitz, Adolphe, 282
De Vis, CW, 173, 175, 178
'degenerationist thesis', 87
Dell, Elizabeth
    Kachin of Burma, 90n17
Demerara, 271
Demerara River, 273
descriptive anthropology, 69
Dharumbal, 140
diacritics, 135, 140, 141
diamond rush, 274–75
    women involved in, 275
Dickens, Charles
    Hard Times, 38
Dingwall Academy, 269
dispersion, 95
Dixon, RMW
    on Roth's work on Dyirbal, 141
Drummond, Lee, 257–58
Dutch, 240
    in British Guiana, 271
Dyaks, 59–61, 64
    Land Dyak relgions, 67
    Land Dyak religions, 65
    Land Dyak women, 65
    Land Dyaks, 64–67
    photographs of, 62–64

Sea Dyak religions, 65
Sea Dyaks, 62–64
theory of sickness, 66–67
Dyirbal, 141–45

East Indians
    in British Guiana, 256, 272
    in Fiji, 284–85
    and indentured labour, 282, 283
Edo, 74
Eglinton, Willie, 129
Elkins, AP
    appraisal of Roth's *Ethnological Studies among the North-West-Central Queensland Aborigines*, 112
emancipation, 258
Enlightenment, the, 33–34, 36
Erigbe (Izhon chief), 77, 78–79
Essequibo, 235, 271
Etheridge, Robert, Jr, 171, 178, 187
    Ethnological Studies (memoir), 114
ethno-pornography, 112–13, 194, 203
eugenics, 158
    see also Aboriginals, regulation of relationships
Evans, Clifford, 276
evolution, 94, 99, 117, 201
    levels of, 100–101
    see also stadial theory

Fage, JD, 73–74
Farabee, William, 251n9
feather headdress, 185
female introcision, 221
    Roth's accounts of, 225–27
fertility control, 199, 227–28, 229
fetishism, 84, 89n6
Fewkes, J Walter, 243, 251n15
fieldwork, 16, 52–54, 88, 111–12, 235, 238–40, 249
Fiji, 23, 99, 277–84
    Deed of Cession, 281, 282
    history of, 282–84
    indentured labour in, 282, 283
    Indian population of, 283–85
    land tenure, 277, 279, 283–85

post-war planning, 279, 281, 283–84
and the Second World War, 281
First World War, 46
FitzGerald, RD, 277
Flower, WH, 96
Forres, John, 211
Forsyth, J, 189
Foster, MB, 109
Fourmile, Henrietta, 179
Foxton, Justin, 50–51
France, 14
Fraser, Eliza, 16–17
Frazer, James
on *Native Tribes of Central Australia*, 111
and totemism, 113–15
French
in British Guiana, 271
functionalist anthropology, 101
Fysh, Hudson, 224

Geertz, Clifford, 70
Gell, Alfred, 101
Georgetown Museum, 206n20, 276
Gillen, Frank, 16, 110, 123, 125, 130
dispute with Roth, 130–31
see also Spencer, Baldwin, and Frank Gillen
Gillin, John, 251n9
Gillin, Tim
cites Henry Ling Roth's *The Aborigines of Tasmania*, 101
Goa, 139
gold rush, 160–61, 274
Gordon, Sir Arthur, First Lord Stanmore, 282–83, 285
grammar
of Guugu-Yimidhirr, 136–37
of Nggerikudi, 137–38
of Pitta-Pitta, 135–36
grammatical categories, 136
Grant, Maggie, 268–69
Granville, Reginald
photographic collection, 83
Gugu-Yalanji, 142
Gulngay, 141

Gunggay, 142
Gurdjar, 144
Guugu-Yimidhirr
grammar, 136–37

Haddon, Alfred Cort, 87, 123, 184
Haigh, Nancy Harriette, 23
Hale, Kenneth L
grammar of Linngithigh, 138
'half-caste' population, 215, 217, 257–58
see also Aboriginals, regulation of relationships
Halifax, Yorkshire, 44, 87, 280
Hamilton, John, 200–201, 228–29
and Roth's photographs, 197, 198–99
Hamitic Hypothesis, 87, 90n14
Hamlyn-Harris, Ronald, 174, 178
Hare, Frederick Arthur, 213, 216
Hargreaves, JH, 189
Hartrick, VS, 212
hatchets, 126
Haviland, John, 136
Guugu-Yimidhirr wordlist, 137
Hepburn, George R, 189
Herskovits, Melville
obituary of Walter Edmund Roth, 240
Hey, Rev J Nicholas, 175
Nggerikudi grammar, 137–38
Hiatt, Les, 218
'conception and misconception', 117
Hickson, SJ, 108–09
'hierarchy of races', 24–25, 87
Hillhouse, William, 242–43
Hinduism, 90n13
Hipperholme Grammar School, 280
homoeopathy, 35–36, 42, 44
Hooker, Sir Joseph D, 250n5
Hope Vale Mission, 183
Hose, JAI, 64
Howard, Richard, 204
humanitarianism, 218
Hungarian Revolution (1848–49), 34–35, 42

Hungary, 33–35
Huxley, TH, 109

Im Thurn, Sir Everard, 242–43
    Among the Indians of Guiana, 243, 252n16
    and *kanaimà*, 243–48
    on photography, 83
Immigration Restriction Act, 195
India, 100
indigenous survival, 242
indirect rule, 259–60, 262–63
Industrial Reform Schools Act (1865), 157–58
informants, 115, 131
initiation practices, 222–25
internal colonialism, 25, 258–59
introcision, 199, 201, 203, 226–28
    as contraception, 227–28, 229
    as a preliminary to marriage, 227–28
    Roth's accounts of, 221, 224, 226–27
    see also female introcision

James, Walter, 211
Jangil, 100
Japanese, 160, 163–64
Jarawa, 100
Java, 61
Jews, 33–34
Johnsonian Club, 197
Journal of the Anthropological Institute, 59
ju-ju fetishism, 84

Kabakaburi Mission, 257–58
Kaiadilt woman, 176
Kalkadoon, 121, 129, 139
Kamakusa, 274
kanaimà, 243–48
    among the Surinam Karinya, 247
    assimilated to revenge, 244–45, 246–47
    and colonial administration, 245–46
    key accounts recycled, 246
    spirituality of, 245–46, 247
Karanya, 139
Karunbara, 140
Kayans, 59–61
Kayardilt, 139
keloid, 97
Kennedy, Alexander, 224
    destruction of Aboriginals, 127, 131
    Devoncourt, 127
Keppel Islanders
    and removal, 165–67
Keppel Islands, 185
Kingsley, Mary, 84, 280
Kinnane, Stephen, 216–17
    Shadow Lines, 215
Kirke, Henry, 239, 251n8
Koko-minni, 144
Koko-Olkulo, 144
Koko-Rarmul, 143
Koko-Wara, 142–43
Koreng-Koreng, 139–41
Kossuth, Lajos (Louis), 35, 37
Kuinmabara, 140
Kuku Mini, 142–43
Kuku-Thaypan, 143
Kundara, 144

Lake, Marilyn, 207n36
Lancet, 35
land, 99, 100–101, 257, 258–59, 263, 284–85
    claims by Aboriginals, 179
    Crown, 259, 273
    see also reservations; reserves
Lang, Andrew
    Anthropological Essays Presented to EB Tylor, 68
    Preface to *The Natives of Sarawak and British North Borneo*, 67–69
languages
    and anthropology, 133–34
    grammar of Guugu-Yimidhirr, 136–37
    grammar of Nggerikudi, 137–38

grammar of Pitta-Pitta, 135–36
multilingualism, 150n9
of Queensland, 17–18, 133–34
sound systems of, 136
spelling systems of, 135, 136, 138
wordlists in Cape York Peninsula languages, 141–45
wordlists in south-eastern Queensland languages, 139–41
wordlists of western Queensland languages, 138–39
Leitner, Gotlieb Wilhelm, 37
Lindqvist, Sven, 75
Ling, Per Henrik, 13, 36
Linngithigh, 138
Longman, Herbert, 174, 177
lost continent of Lemura, 96
Low, Hugh Brooke, 15, 66–67
   manuscript, 59–61
   in the Sarawak Government Service, 59
   and textual sources, 61

Macusi, 271
Makushi, 239, 247, 249
Malanbara, 141
Malay Peninsula, 94
Malinowski, Bronislaw
   fieldwork, 249
Manderson, Desmond, 160
Mari, 140
Markham, Sir Clements R, 250n5
Marsden, William
   The History of Sumatra, 61
Marshall, Arthur Milnes, 108
masks, 184
massi poison, 246
material culture, 18, 88, 130–31, 241
   of Fiji, 280–81
   trade in, 124–25, 128
Mathews, RH, 116
Mauritius, 282, 283
Maxwell, FRO, 62–64
May, Cathie, 160
Mayborough Grammar School, 270

Mazaruni, 274–75
McConnel, Ursula, 179
medicine men and women, 66–67
medicine string, 186
Meggers, Betty, 276
Melanesian Papuans, 93
Melanesians, 94, 98, 99
   and Aboriginal employment, 164
Meston, Archibald, 50, 194
   donations to Queensland Museum, 175–76
   ethnological collections, 175–76
   report on Queensland Aborigines, 158–59
   and Roth, 165–67
   Southern Protector of Aboriginals, 19, 49, 159, 162
Miller, Olga, 16–17
Milner, GB
   Introduction to Roth's *Fijian Way of Life*, 278–80, 285
Miorli, 139
miscegenation, 162–63, 165, 203, 204, 215, 217
mission stations, 50, 183, 211
missionaries, 136, 244, 252n18
Mitakoodi, 139
Mitchell, David Scott, 48
Mitchell Library, 48
Mitochondrial DNA, 101n1, 101n2
Miubbi, 139
modernity, 238–40
moko, 97–99
   spiral motifs, 98
Molonga (Mudlungga) ceremony, 123, 125–26
monogeny, 95, 96, 100–101
Moola Bulla Native Settlement, 214–15
Morgan, Lewis Henry, 122
Moriori, 98
Morphy, Howard
   on Gillen and Spencer, 123
Morrison, Frederic
   Aldine History of Queensland, 177
Moseley, Henry Nottridge, 108

Index

Mount Isa axes, 126
Mount Roraima, 235
Mpakwithi, 138
Mpalitjanh, 145
multilingualism, 150n9
Mulvaney, John
    'The chain of connection', 124–26
mural painting, 127
museums, 171–73, 177–79
Musgrave Native Police Camp, 186

Nana Olomu of Brohimi (Itsekiri chief)
    villages and towns destroyed, 76–78
Native Lands Commission, 277
Native Police, 158–59
Natives of British Guiana, 238–39, 242–43
Natives of Sarawak and British North Borneo, The (Henry Ling Roth)
    anthropological content of, 64–67
    difficulties with, 62–64
    origins of, 59–62
    photographs in, 62–64
    strengths and weaknesses of, 67–70
natural sciences, 199, 238
natural selection, 115
Negritos (little Negroes), 93, 94, 100
    in Borneo, 96
    dispersion of, 96–97
    migration to Tasmania, 101
New Guinea, 13–14
    influences in Cape York, 184
Ngachan-ji, 141
Ngadyan, 142
Ngaygungu, 142
Nggerikudi, 137–38
Ngikoongo-i, 141
Niger Coast Protectorate, 75, 88
    coffee plantation, 85–86
Nigeria, 14, 45, 74
    Niger River region, 73, 83
    see also Benin City
'noble savages', 99

nomadism, 160
Normanton, 184
numismatics, 44, 48, 52–54

Oba of Benin, 79, 80, 87
Obarindi, 139
ochres, 124, 126
Ogieriakhi, Emwinma
    Oba Ovonramwen, 73
opium, 49, 158, 160, 161, 163–65, 183
oral history, 16–17
orthopaedics, 35–36, 44
otherness, 31–33, 38

Pacific Islanders, 157, 161, 195
paiwarri, 262, 274
pandanus-leaf necklaces, 186
Papua-New Guinea, 94
Papuans, 94, 96
    population in New Zealand, 98
Parramatta Convent, 267
Parry-Okeden, William Edward, 49, 50–51, 159, 200
    on Aborigines, 178
Patamona, 271
Patching, Charles, Jr, 189
paternalism, 190, 259–60, 279
pathology, 66–67
Patz, Elisabeth, 142
Peace Society, 35
pearl-shell fishery, 158, 160
penile mutilation
    see introcision
Pennefather-Batavia-Embley report, 144–45
Peoples National Congress, 252n16
Perham, Venerable Archdeacon J, 65–67
Philippines, 94
phonemics, 135
phonetics, 138
photographs, 20, 83, 203, 230
    of Aboriginal ceremonies, 125–26
    of Aboriginal women, 228
    of Dyaks, 62–64
    ethnographic, 82, 83–84, 86

by Felix Norman Roth, 81–87
historical, 82, 85–86
of naked Aboriginals, 200
Niger River region, 83
scandal of Walter E Roth's, 193–94, 197–204, 221, 228–30
as science, 199–202
physical anthropology, 25
Pitt Rivers Museum, 108
ethnographic collection of, 109
Pitta-Pitta, 121, 123, 135–36, 139, 223
pituri (nicotine-based drug), 18
piwari, 262, 274
plant collecting, 237
plantation production, 258
police, 213, 216
Native Police, 158–59
polygeny, 95, 96, 100
Polynesians, 164
Pomeroon Karinya, 246
pornography, 112–13, 194, 202, 223
Portuguese
in British Guiana, 272, 273
'primitives', 93, 94–95, 201
collecting accounts of, 122–23
see also 'savages'
Pringle, Helen, 244
Prinsep, Henry, 213–14
Protector of Aborigines, 212
prisoners
in neck chains, 214, 216
prostitution, 49, 275
public health, 42, 44, 45–46
Puerto Rico, 251n15
Pulszky, Francis, 37
Punans, 64
Purcell, BH, 224

Quatrefages de Bréau, Jean Louis Armand, 96
Queensland Museum, 171–73, 177–79, 189
donors to, 175–77
and Roth's collections, 172–75, 176–77, 188
Queensland Parliamentary Papers, 200

Rabuka coup of 1986, 284
race, 95, 157–58
characteristics of, 99
hierarchy of, 24–25, 87
and segregation, 158–59, 257–58
Raffles, Stamford
The History of Java, 61
Rakiwara, 140
Rarmul, 143
Read, Charles Hercules, 87
removal, 165–67, 168n2, 194–95
of Aboriginal children, 158, 197–98, 213, 217, 244
of Aboriginal women, 197–98, 244
of Aboriginals, 19, 121–22, 210, 215
of Amerindians, 261, 263
of Andamanese, 100
and Keppel Islanders, 165–67
of 'mixed' descent people, 257–58
for Tasmanian Aboriginals, 100
reservations, 256–57, 259, 260–61
internal governance of, 263–64
and registration, 257–58
reserves, 50, 158–59, 189, 213, 214–15
for Asians, 160
white, 213
resource extraction, 160–61, 258–59, 261, 274–75
Revised Linguistic Survey of Australia, The, 133
Ridges, Malcolm, 126
Ridley, Henry, 250n5
Rigsby, Bruce, 142–44
River Navigation Regulations, 274
Robinson, Sir Hercules, 282
rock art, 127, 128
Rockhampton, 183, 185
Roth, Ada Toulmin, 181
Roth, Alfred, 280
Roth, Alfred Bernard, 23
Roth, Alfred Lawrence, 46
Roth, Anna Maria Collins, 13, 36, 42
Roth, Bernard, 13, 14, 36

Roth, Bernard Mathias, 44
  The Treatment of Lateral Curvature of the Spine, 44
Roth, David, 34, 42
Roth, Edith, 273
Roth, Edith May, 47
Roth, Emerich Emanuel, 34, 42
Roth, Eva, 267
Roth, Eva Grant, 181
Roth, Felix, 34, 42
Roth, Felix Norman, 13–15, 36, 45
  acting Vice-Consul, 75, 77–79
  diary of the invasion of Benin, 79–82
  ethnographic portraits by, 83–84
  execution of a prisoner, 78–79
  expedition against Benin City, 73, 79–80
  expedition to destroy villages, 77
  The Natives of Sarawak and British North Borneo 2 Vols., 15
  in the Niger Coast Protectorate, 73–74, 88
  photographs by, 20
  'Some experiences of an engineer doctor' (memoir), 77–78
  'Souvenir of Warri' (photograph album), 81–86
Roth, George Kingsley, 13, 23, 280–82
  District Officer in Fiji, 280
  Fiji: Handbook of the Colony, 23
  in Fijian colonial administration, 278
  and Fijian history, 283–84
  Fijian Way of Life, 23, 277, 278, 280–81
  and indigenous land rights and communal identities, 278
  interest in field anthropology, 281, 285
  publications, 280–81
  Secretary for Fijian Affairs, 281
  The Story of Fiji, 278
  trained anthropologist, 280
  writing by, 278, 285

Roth, Henry
  and *kanaimà*, 248
Roth, Henry Ling [entry subdivided into ANTHROPOLOGY; CAREER; PERSONAL LIFE; PUBLICATIONS; UNPUBLISHED WORK]
  ANTHROPOLOGY, 15–16, 24–25, 31–33, 123
    African, 86, 88
    body modification, 93–95, 97–101
    colonial administration, 99–100
    ethnographic display, 86
    evolutionary theories, 99
    'hierarchy of races', 87
    material culture, 88
    physical anthropology, 25
    working relationship with Felix Norman Roth, 88
  CAREER, 13–15, 41, 73–74
    at Bankfield Museum, 44, 280
    in British Guiana, 44
  PERSONAL LIFE, 11–13, 23, 36–37, 93, 277, 280
  PUBLICATIONS
    The Aborigines of Tasmania, 15, 44, 61–62, 96–97, 100
    Agriculture and Peasantry of Eastern Russia, 44
    Bankfield Museum Notes series, 16
    Great Benin: Its Customs, Arts and Horrors, 15, 44, 70, 84–85, 87
    The History and Settlement of Port Mackay, Queensland, 45
    in the *Journal of the Anthropological Institute*, 59, 67
    The Maori Mantle, 16
    The Natives of Sarawak and British North Borneo, 44, 96
    Notes on the Agriculture and Peasantry of Eastern Russia, 13

Oriental Silverwork, Malay and Chinese... A Handbook for Connoisseurs, Collectors, Students and Silversmiths, 15–16
on Pacific cultures, 16
Studies in Primitive Looms, 16, 45
Yorkshire Coiners 1767–1783, 44
see also *Natives of Sarawak and British North Borneo, The*
UNPUBLISHED WORK
'Souvenir of Warri' (photograph album), 81–86
Roth, Jane Violet Coats, 281
Roth, Johnny
and *kanaimà*, 248
Roth, Julia Anna
illustrations for *Aborigines of Tasmania*, 47
Roth, Mathias, 11–13, 33–34
and anti-English feelings, 36
in England, 34–35, 42
and foreign visitors, 37
Gymnastic Exercises, 42
and medicine, 34, 35–36
and public hygiene, 42
and religion, 36, 42–44
views on education, 37–38
wife and children, 36–37
Roth, Reuter Emerich, 13, 14, 36, 45–46, 267–68
Roth, Richard Cuvier, 46
Roth, Vincent, 13, 22–23, 181, 248, 267–70, 272
career, 267, 272, 275–76
difficulty enforcing trespass law, 273
illustrations, 275
Land Officer, 273–75
on Legislative Council, 275–76
and model making, 269, 276
Notes and Observations on Animal Life in British Guiana, 275

Notes and Observations on Fish Life in British Guiana, 275
radio broadcasts, 275
Roth, Walter Edmund [entry subdivided into ANTHROPOLOGY; CAREER; EDUCATION; INTERESTS; PERSONAL LIFE; PUBLICATIONS]
ANTHROPOLOGY, 11–13, 16–18, 24–25, 31–33, 41, 52–54, 114, 240
'abduction' rumour, 197–98
accounts of ritual practices, 222
and the Australian Museum, 176, 178–79, 187–90
classification scheme, 240–42
classification terminology, 114
collections, 18, 52–54, 123, 172–77, 178–79, 183–88
compendium on the folklore of 'Guiana Indians', 236, 240–42, 243–46, 249
descriptions of Aboriginals, 122–26
dispute with Spencer and Gillen, 130
evolution, 115
expeditions in British Guiana, 235
fieldwork, 16, 52–54, 111–12, 235, 238
'Games, sports and amusements of the Northern Queensland Aboriginals', 116
gaps in his work, 127–28
informants, 115, 131
and introcision, 222–27
and *kanaimà*, 243–48
linguistics, 17–18, 133–34, 183–84, 197, 223–24, 253n22
material culture, 124–25, 128, 130–31

Roth, Walter Edmund *(continued)*
    photograph scandal, 20, 193, 197–99, 200–204, 228–30
    photographs, 165–67, 199–202
    and the Queensland Museum, 172–75, 188
    reports to the Commissioner of Police, 142–45
    sign language, 112, 133
    social anthropology, 22
    and the space of 'Guiana', 248–50
    and Spencer, 107, 115–17
    stories of the Pitta-Pitta, 129
    totemism, 113–15
    on trade, 124–26, 128, 130–31
    CAREER, 110, 206n20, 267
        in Australia, 244
        in British Guiana, 21–22, 51, 235–36, 255–57, 264, 270, 272
        Chief Protector of Aboriginals, 19, 50–51, 165–67, 190, 199
        medical, 47, 48–49
        and Meston, 165–67
        Northern Protector of Aboriginals, 18–19, 49–50, 159, 162–65, 181–83, 193–94, 209
        opposition to, 20–21, 50–51, 167, 188–90, 196–97, 228
        principles of Aboriginal welfare, 117–18
        Protector of Indians, 260–64
        Royal Commissioner, 19, 50, 211–15, 218
        scientific reports, 49–50, 52, 141
        teaching, 47, 54
    EDUCATION, 199
        in England, 107
        languages, 133
    INTERESTS
        numismatics, 48, 54
        in public theatres, 47–48
    PERSONAL LIFE, 181, 252n16, 269–70
    PUBLICATIONS, 51–52
        Additional Studies of the Arts, Crafts, and Customs of the Guiana Indians, 235–36, 241
        Additional Studies of the Arts, Crafts, and Customs of the Guiana Indians, with Special Reference to those of Southern British Guiana, 21
        in the *British Medical Journal*, 47
        Bulletins, 52, 116–17, 187, 200, 201, 202
        on China and Japan, 48
        compendium on the folklore of 'Guiana Indians', 236, 240–42, 243–46, 249
        The Elements of School Hygiene, 47
        Ethnological Studies among the North-West-Central Queensland Aborigines, 16, 110–13, 121–22, 182, 193, 200, 221
        Ethnological Studies, 'Commonly-alleged Object of Introcision Discussed, The' chapter in, 201–02
        Ethnological Studies, 'Ethno-pornography' chapter, 112–13, 197–99, 203, 206n22, 222–25
        Ethnological Studies, illustrations in, 201
        Ethnological Studies, 'Mural Painting, Art, and Draughtsmanship' chapter, 127
        Ethnological Studies, Spencer's review of, 111–14
        and exclusion of Im Thurn, 243–48
        'Fires in theatres', 47
        grammar of Guugu-Yimidhirr, 136–37
        grammar of Nggerikudi, 137–38

grammar of Pitta-Pitta, 135–36
'Hygiene of the theatre', 47
An Inquiry into the Animism and Folk-Lore of the Guiana Indians, 21, 241, 243, 246, 248–49
An Introductory Study of the Arts, Crafts, and Customs of the Guiana Indians, 21
medical, 252n17
'numismatic history of Australia, A', 48
'Progressive Koko-yimider exercises', 137
Report of the Northern Protector of Aboriginals for 1899, 187
Report on Some Ethnological Notes on the Atherton Blacks, 186
reports on Aboriginal people, 176
'Scientific Report on the Natives of the Lower Tully River', 141
on sign language, 112, 146–48
'The structure of the Koko Yimidir language', 136–37
Theatre Hygiene, 47
translations, 21, 51, 236
vocabularies, 135–36, 145–46
wordlists in Cape York Peninsula languages, 141–45
wordlists in south-eastern Queensland languages, 139–41
wordlists of western Queensland languages, 138–39
Roth family, 11–13, 24–25, 31–34, 41
education of, 42
and otherness, 31–33, 38
Roth Family Conference, 277–78
Rotimi, Ola
  Ovonramwen Nogbaisi, 73
Royal Anthropological Institute, 237

Royal Commission, 19, 50
  into Aboriginal administration, 211, 216–18
  recommendations, 213–15, 217
  recommendations, objections to, 215–16
Royal Geographical Society, 237
rubber plants, 250n5
Rupununi expedition, 238, 250n2
Russia, 44
  Samara province, 13

Sakarang women, 62–63
Sale and Use of Poisons Act (1891), 158
salvage anthropology, 25, 69, 88, 242, 249, 258
Sand Creek, 238–39, 244
Sarawak, 15, 61, 62
  see also *Natives of Sarawak and British North Borneo, The* (Henry Ling Roth)
'savages', 115, 177, 239
  'noble savages', 99
scarification (cicatrisation), 94, 95, 97–99, 100
  tangi, 98
Schomburgk, Richard, 242–43
Schomburgk, Sir Robert, 242–43
science
  and photography, 230
  and pornography, 194
Sclater, WL, 108
segregation, 158–59, 257–58
  see also removal; reservations; reserves
Selwyn Range art, 127
shell chest ornaments, 185
shell head and neck band, 184
sickness, 239
  Dyak theory of, 66–67
sign language, 112, 146–48
Sinophobia, 157
skirt, 186
slavery, 100, 258
Smithsonian Institution, 276
Sobo, 83–84

social anthropology, 22, 217
social evolution, 201
Sommer, Bruce A, 142–45
sound system of language, 136
Soyinka, Wole, 74
Spanish, 240
spears, 128, 185
spelling systems, 135, 136, 138
Spencer, Baldwin, 16, 107–09, 110, 123, 130, 209, 222
   and 'facts', 111
   photographic disasters, 206n22
   Protector of Aboriginals, 117–18
   review of *Ethnological Studies among the North-West-Central Queensland Aborigines*, 111–13
   and Roth, 107, 110, 111, 115–17, 130–31
   on Roth's 'Ethno-pornography', 112–13
   on Roth's fieldwork and sign language, 111–12
   on terminology, 113, 114, 115
   and 'wild savages', 115
Spencer, Baldwin, and Frank Gillen
   Native Tribes of Central Australia, 110–11, 113, 116
   The Northern Tribes of Central Australia, 117
stadial theory, 94, 95, 99–100
Steward, Julian
   editing of *Handbook of South American Indians*, 249
Stocking, George W, 23
'stolen generation', 113, 244
   see also removal
stone arrangements, 129–30
stone knife, 124
Strathpeffer, Scotland, 268–69
structuralist anthropology, 101
subincision, 112–13
   see introcision
sugar industry, 158
Sukuna, Ratu Sir Lala, 283–84, 285
   Fijian Ordinances, 284
Sullivan, Tom, 129–30
Sumatra, 61

Summer Institute of Linguistics, 142
Surinam Karinya
   kanaimà among, 247
Sydney, 14
syphilis, 224

Tarrumburra, 140
Tarumbal, 140
Tasmanian Aboriginals, 93, 94, 96, 99–100
   and land, 99–100
   remnant of the Negritos (little Negroes), 97
   removal of, 100
   and scarification, 95
   settler violence against, 15, 101
Tasmanian stone implements, 188
tattoo, 93, 95, 97–99
   spiral motifs, 98
Taylor, Peter, 37
Thailand, 94
theatres, 47–48
Thomas, Nicholas, 99
Thomson, Donald, 179
Thorpe, WW, 188
Timehri (Guyanese journal), 248
Tindale, Norman, 179
Torres Straits, 184
totemism, 111–12, 113–15, 117
Tozer, Sir Horace, 222
trade, 124–26, 128, 130–31
Tragedy of Man, The (Hungarian play), 38
travel, 237
travel writing, 236
Tylor, EB, 99, 109, 122
   and culture, 68–69
   Introduction to Basil Hall Chamberlain's *Aino Folk Tales*, 69
   'Notes and Queries on Anthropology', 68
   Primitive Culture, 68, 69
   Researches into the Early History of Mankind and the Development of Civilization, 68
   theory of animism, 84

Ulaolinya, 138–39
Undekerebina, 121, 139
United States of America, 243
    and internal colonialism, 24–25, 258–59
Uradhi, 145
Urhobo Progress Union, 84
Urquhart, Frederick, 224

'Venezuela Balata', 274
Venezuelan land claims, 259, 260
Violet Valley Feeding Depot, 214
vocabularies, 135–36, 145–46

Waiwai, 239
Wai-Wai, 271
Walookera, 139
Walter Roth Museum, 236–37, 243–44, 250n3
Wapabara, 140
Wapishana, 238–39, 244
Wapisiana, 271
warra, 143
Warrau, 271, 272, 273
Waugh, Evelyn, 206n20
Wellesley Islands, 176
West Africa
    see Benin City; Nigeria
West Indians
    in British Guiana, 271
Western Australia, 19, 209–11
    Aboriginals in, 50
    see also Royal Commission
Western Australian Act (1905), 19, 217
White, Bishop, 229
White Australia, 158

white frontiersmen, 19
    and Aboriginal labour, 195–96
    and Aboriginal women, 195–96, 203, 204
    campaign against Roth, 196–97, 202, 228
    clashes with Aboriginals, 210
    and indigenous knowledge, 203
'white reserves', 213
Willett, Frank
    review of *Great Benin: Its Customs, Art and Horrors*, 87
Windschuttle, Keith
    cites *The Aborigines of Tasmania* (Henry Ling Roth), 101
witchcraft, 84–85
Wonkajera, 139
Woonamurra, 139
wordlists
    Cape York Peninsula, 141–45
    Pitta-Pitta, 135
    south-eastern Queensland, 139–41
    western Queensland, 138–39
Workai-a, 139
woven baskets, 185
Wragge, Clement, 175

Yaroinga, 139
Yellunga (Yulluna), 121, 129
    Dreaming stories, 131
Yettimaralla, 140
Yidiny, 142
Yinwum, 145
Yukulta, 139
Yulluna
    see Yellunga (Yulluna)
Yupngayth, 145

About the Contributors

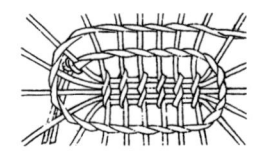

MICHAEL BENNETT is a chartered civil engineer and son-in-law of Vincent Roth. He was born in Manchester, England, and has worked in a number of countries including Guyana, and now resides in Kent, England. He is the author of *Vincent Roth – A Life in Guyana*, volumes 1 and 2.

GAVAN BREEN is a consultant linguist based at the Institute for Aboriginal Development in Alice Springs, Australia. He has done fieldwork and published on a number of the languages Roth worked on.

JUDIT BRODY, formerly with the Science Museum Library in London, is now retired and a freelance researcher in the history of science. She is the author of *The Enigma of Sunspots*.

ARIF BULKAN is a doctoral student at Osgoode Hall Law School of York University, Canada, where he is researching the land rights of Guyana's indigenous peoples. He is an attorney-at-law and a former lecturer in human rights law at the University of Guyana.

JANETTE BULKAN is a doctoral student at the Yale School of Forestry and Environmental Studies, researching forestry policies and practices in Guyana and Suriname. She was trained in anthropology and linguistics and worked at the Amerindian Research Unit of the University of Guyana and the Iwokrama Rainforest Programme in Guyana.

JULIAN CROFT, Emeritus Professor of English, University of New England, NSW, Australia first visited Fiji in 1963 and has a long interest in its history and George Kingsley Roth. He has published on the literatures of Australia, Wales and West Africa. He is also a poet and a novelist.

IAIN DAVIDSON has studied the archaeology of hunter-gatherers in Europe and Australia since the early 1970s. He has studied stone tools, animal bones and rock art, and published extensively on the archaeology of language origins, often with psychologist William Noble. He has undertaken archaeological work in North West Central Queensland since 1986. He has just retired as Professor of Archaeology and Palaeoanthropology, University of New England, NSW, Australia.

About the Contributors

REGINA GANTER is Associate Professor in Australian History at Griffith University with two prize-winning books, *Mixed Relations: Asian-Aboriginal Contact in North Australia* (2006) awarded with the Ernst Scott Prize in Australian History (2007) and the NSW Premier's History Awards (2007), and The Pearl-Shellers of Torres Strait (1994) based on the thesis that was awarded the inaugural AHA prize in Australian History (1992).

ALICE GORMAN is a consulting archaeologist and lecturer in the Department of Archaeology, Flinders University, Adelaide.

GEOFFREY GRAY is a Research Fellow at the Australian Institute of Aboriginal and Torres Strait Islander Studies, Canberra, Australia. He has published extensively on the history of Australian anthropology, particularly the relationships between anthropologists, government and indigenous (colonised) peoples. His most recent book is *A Cautious Silence: The Politics of Australian Anthropology* (2007).

ROBERT HAMPSON is Head of the Department of English at Royal Holloway, University of London, and author of *Cross-Cultural Encounters in Joseph Conrad's Malay Fiction*.

KATE KHAN is Honorary Research Fellow in the Branch of Anthropology, Australian Museum, Sydney.

RUSSELL MCDOUGALL has published widely on West African, West Indian and Australian literatures and histories. He is Associate Professor in English at the University of New England, NSW, Australia.

ANN MCGRATH is Professor of History and Director of the Australian Centre for Indigenous History at the Research School of Social Sciences at the Australian National University. She previously taught at the University of New South Wales and was a Program Director at the National Museum of Australia. She has published extensively on gender and colonialism in Australia and North America.

JOHN MULVANEY, an historian and archaeologist, was Professor of Prehistory, Arts Faculty, Australian National University, from 1971 to 1975. He was an Australian Heritage Commissioner from 1976 to 1982. With JH Calaby, he wrote a biography of Baldwin Spencer and has edited three volumes of letters to Spencer from his field informants.

HELEN PRINGLE is a Senior Lecturer in the School of Politics and International Relations at the University of New South Wales. She teaches and researches in the areas of sex and human rights, and political theory.

About the Contributors

BARRIE REYNOLDS has worked in Africa, Canada and Queensland (Australia) and written extensively on material anthropology and museums. Formerly the Foundation Professor of Material Culture, James Cook University, he is now Adjunct Professor of Museums and Collections at Macquarie University. Professor Reynolds is preparing a book on Walter Roth.

RICHARD ROBINS is a Heritage Consultant and Director of Everick Heritage Consultant. He is also an Adjunct Associate Professor at the School of Human and Environmental Studies, University of New England. Prior to this he was Senior Curator of Australian Archaeology at the Queensland Museum. His main research interest is in Aboriginal archaeology and he has undertaken extensive archaeological work in south-east Queensland, south-west Queensland and the Gulf of Carpentaria.

NEIL L WHITEHEAD is Professor of Anthropology, Latin American and Religious Studies at the University of Wisconsin–Madison and editor of the journal *Ethnohistory*. He has worked over two decades in Amazonia with Carib peoples, most recently amongst the Patamuna of Guyana, and has published widely on the literatures of travel and colonialism.